In God's Name

STUDIES ON WAR AND GENOCIDE

General Editor: Omer Bartov, Brown University

IN GOD'S NAME
Genocide and Religion in the Twentieth Century

Edited by

Omer Bartov and Phyllis Mack

Berghahn Books
New York • Oxford

Published in 2001 by

Berghahn Books

© 2001 Omer Bartov and Phyllis Mack

All rights reserved. No part of this publication may be
reproduced in any form by any means without the
written permission of Berghahn Books.

Library of Congress Cataloging-in-Publication Data

In God's name : genocide and religion in the twentieth century / edited by Omer Bartov
and Phyllis Mack.
    p. cm. -- (Studies on war and genocide ; v. 4)
    Includes bibliographical references and index.
    ISBN 1-57181-214-8 (alk. paper) -- ISBN 1-57181-302-0 (alk. paper)
    1. Genocide--Religious aspects--History--20th century. 2. Religion and
state--History--20th century. I. Bartov, Omer. II. Mack, Phyllis. III. Series.

HV6322.7 .I5 2000
291.1'7833151--dc21   99-045111

British Library Cataloguing in Publication Data

A catalogue record for this book is available
from the British Library.

Printed in the United States on acid-free paper.

CONTENTS

INTRODUCTION

Omer Bartov and Phyllis Mack

Violence and religion have been closely associated in a variety of intricate, often contradictory ways, since the earliest periods of human civilization. Institutionalized religions have practiced violence against both their adherents and their real or imagined opponents. Conversely, religions have also been known to limit social and political violence and to provide spiritual and material comfort to its victims. Religious faith can thus generate contradictory attitudes, either motivating aggression or constraining it. Individual perpetrators and victims of violence can seek in religious institutions and personal faith both a rationale for atrocity, a justification to resist violence, or a means to come to terms with the legacy of destruction by integrating it into a wider historical or theological context.

Despite the widespread trends of secularization in the twentieth century, religion has played an important role in several outbreaks of genocide since World War I. And yet, not many scholars have looked either at the religious aspects of modern genocide, or at the manner in which religion has taken a position on mass killing. This collection of essays seeks to address this hiatus by examining the intersection between religion and state-organized murder in the cases of the Armenian, Jewish, Rwandan, and Bosnian genocides. What was the importance of religion as institution, as theology, and as personal experience? Were specific theological ideas particularly important to the perpetrators of genocide, or to those who tried to come to terms with their own or other peoples' destruction? Was Christian universalism, or Jewish exclusivity, important in energizing Christian persecutors of Jewish victims? Did religion help to normalize genocide by providing myths of ultimate redemption or rationales for annihi-

Notes for this section begin on page 18.

lation? Since the Enlightenment, religion has been attacked as encouraging impulses toward fanaticism. Do modern acts of genocide bear this out? How much *religious* fanaticism do we see here?

With the exception of two chapters (by Charles de Lespinay and Gershon Greenberg), all the essays included here are reworked and expanded versions of papers presented at the conference "Genocide, Religion, and Modernity," held at the United States Holocaust Memorial Museum (USHMM) in May 1997 and co-sponsored by the Rutgers Center for Historical Analysis, the Holocaust Research Institute at the USHMM, and the Center for the Study of Jewish Life at Rutgers University. Rather than a comprehensive overview, this volume offers a series of discrete, yet closely related case-studies, that shed light on three fundamental aspects of this issue: first, the use of religion to legitimize and motivate genocide; second, the potential of religious faith to encourage physical and spiritual resistance to mass murder; third, the role of religion in coming to terms with the legacy of atrocity.

The chapters in this book concern only cases of genocide involving one or several of the three main monotheistic religions: Judaism, Christianity, and Islam. Our century has known many other cases of genocide in parts of the world where these religions do not have a significant presence, or where the main motivation of, and reactions to, genocidal policies were largely unrelated to religious belief and institutions. Hence, for instance, we have not included chapters on such instances as the murderous policies of Stalinist Russia, Maoist China, or Pol Pot's Cambodia. Nor does this book contain contributions on colonial massacres and genocides, although religion did play some role in legitimizing and inciting such actions. This has partly to do with the chronological framework of this book, and partly with limits of space. However, as will be seen from the two chapters on Rwanda, we are well aware of the impact of European imperialism on genocide in former colonies.[1]

At first glance, what strikes the reader of these essays is the apparent irrelevance or marginality of religious ideas in the history of modern genocide. Certainly, specific religious traditions and concepts had no intrinsic power to influence either genocidal behavior or the responses of rescuers and victims. Muslims were (and are) victims of Orthodox Christians in Bosnia, while in the Ottoman Empire, Muslims drowned Armenian Christian babies and forcibly converted women and children. Indeed, perpetrators of genocide define religious groups in racial and cultural terms, not in terms of ideas or beliefs of individual perpetrators or victims. People were murdered because they were Jews or Armenians or Bosnian Muslims, regardless of whether or not they (or their killers) actually believed in Jewish, Christian, or Muslim precepts.

Yet the essays presented here also reveal a consistency in the thinking of historical actors, one that seems especially paradoxical in the case of the Holocaust in Germany: the Nazi perpetrators of mass murder, at times nominally or even fervently Christian, at times strongly opposed to Christianity or to church institutions, adopted the traditional Jewish concept of the Chosen People, translating it into a doctrine of racial superiority and a collective mission to transform the world. Hitler, for instance, used Christian terminology in his speeches, and claimed to have been chosen by Providence, even as he privately spoke of the need to destroy the churches after victory in war. Conversely, Jewish victims (and those who helped rescue them) in some cases adopted and translated the traditional Christian concept of universalism: the fundamental equality of human beings before God and the injunction to love all people, especially the weak. This universalism, often combined with a highly personal and idiosyncratic mode of reflection and expression, might be characterized as an eclectic spirituality rather than a world-view that was explicitly religious.

This deployment of religious ideas was allied to the deployment of religious structures. Perpetrators, arguing that they were members of a superior people chosen for a special mission, identified that superiority and mission with their membership in religious institutions, or pseudo-religious racial or ethnic orders or castes; they imagined themselves as members of homogeneous groups, without individual responsibility for their actions. Rescuers, on the other hand, acted without institutional authority or in the interstices of official religious structures, accepting individual responsibility to mitigate destruction. Institutions operated as structures to facilitate genocide but not to counteract it.

I

As most of the contributions to Part I illustrate, the Christian churches were involved on several levels in preparing the theological, moral, political, and mythical groundwork for genocide in this century. That this was part and parcel of European political, social, and religious structures, can be seen from the rather different case of the Ottoman Empire, examined by Ronald Grigor Suny in the opening chapter. As long as collective identity in this Muslim-dominated empire was defined according to religious affiliation rather than ethnic or modern national criteria, it was possible for religious minorities to maintain a more or less tolerable existence. Thus, while Islam was the preferred religion, Christian Armenians could rise to positions of relative economic and political prominence in the Ottoman state. Indeed, it was precisely the disintegration of the old order and the rise of modern nationalism—among Turks just as much as among Armenians, Arabs, or Kurds—which made the existence of an Armenian population in Anatolia appear increasingly intolerable to the new Turkish nationalists, who perceived these lands as the heartland of their nation even though Armenians had lived there long before the arrival of the Ottomans. Consequently, just as the Armenians began defining themselves more as a people than as members of their church, the Turkish leadership began thinking of the empire in exclusionary nationalist terms. Here religious fanaticism increased precisely at a time when religion was being replaced by strident nationalism as the focus of collective identity; in the multi-ethnic Ottoman Empire it was this process that generated the genocidal policies against the Armenians.

To be sure, there were some similarities between the Ottoman case and the Habsburg Empire, which also maintained an increasingly precarious balance among a variety of religions and ethnic groups, and was finally destroyed by the forces of nationalism.[2] Yet post-World War I Europe was radically different. Thus, to cite the most obvious case, the German religious establishment strove to prove its usefulness to the Nazis by combining modern methods of biblical criticism with traditional values: religious exclusivity, conservative morality, and family values versus Jewish "urban spirituality." Taking the case of the Protestant German theologian Gerhard Kittel as his example, Robert P. Ericksen demonstrates the powerful anti-modern predilections of many Christians in Germany, and their tendency to associate the Jews with all the ills of modernity and the misfortunes of the German *Volk*. This led Kittel and a significant number of fellow Protestant theologians and clergy to lend their support to Hitler and to his antisemitic policies. The case of Kittel is especially distressing, because while he is shown by Ericksen to have also adopted the racist thinking of the Nazis, he and his like-minded students remained respectable and influential figures also in postwar Protestant German theology. Yet another aspect of this troubling episode is elaborated by Susannah Heschel, whose chapter analyzes the hitherto little known Institute for the Study and Eradication of Jewish Influence on German Religious Life. Established in 1939 by several important German theologians, this institute greatly contributed to the effort to disseminate the idea of a so-called Aryan Christianity by "proving" that Jesus was racially an Aryan who strove to destroy the Jews. Such German Christians defined themselves both as a chosen people and a victimized people. The theologian Kittel, for one, wrote to Martin Buber about the Jews' deviousness and insolence, their "raping" of German legal consciousness. Although Hitler showed little affection for this brand of racist Christianity, there is little doubt that its social, academic, and theological respectability did much to make Nazism and its genocidal policies more palatable to the Protestant population.

Clearly, many of the Protestant and Catholic clergy in Germany were less enthusiastic about Hitler's regime. And yet, as we read in Beth Griech-Polelle's chapter, even Bishop von Galen of Münster, known for his scathing 1941 attack on the "euthanasia" murder campaign against the mentally and physically handicapped, shared the strong anti-modern sentiments of the Christian supporters of Nazism and never expressed any public or recorded criticism of the persecution and eventual genocide of the Jews. While church leaders could be found among critics, just as much as among supporters, of Nazism, what most of them had in common was their more or less overt dislike of the Jewish presence in Germany (and Europe) and their association of Jews with everything they resented about modern society; hence their indifference to, if not support for, the regime's antisemitic policies. That this attitude reached down to the lower level of church leadership is shown in Doris L. Bergen's chapter, which examines the reactions of German military chaplains to the criminal policies of the regime. Unlike their senior colleagues, these men were direct witnesses of atrocity and mass murder, and yet, in the overwhelming majority of cases, the chaplains remained silent. The few instances of heroic opposition to the regime's crimes were thus overshadowed by the general tendency of chaplains to focus on providing the perpetrators with religious comfort rather than exerting their moral authority. Indeed, Bergen suggests that the chaplains, who came from more nationalist, conservative wings of the Protestant churches, wanted to portray themselves as manly so as to avoid the accusation of being soft Christians who rendered the troops "womanly, Jewish, and weak." Yet the ultimate impact of the chaplains, described by Bergen as a kind of "moral numbing," was in fact akin to traditional female roles: "In this 'spiritual relief' function, the chaplains performed a task shared by many women in the Third Reich and usually coded as feminine: providing a cozy home, domestic or spiritual, where killers could find peace, rejuvenation, and support." All of which seems to indicate that at both the top and lower echelons of the Christian hierarchy, the German churches facilitated genocide by a combination of vehement approval, silent indifference, or narrow-minded concentration on religious piety resulting in moral numbing in the face of widespread inhumanity.

The institutional Christian churches were reluctant to acknowledge their complicity in the Holocaust long after the end of the war. Thus, for instance, it took more than fifty years for the French bishops to admit that the church could have done more to help the Jews in France during the German occupation.[3] For its part, the Vatican has recently made a half-hearted apology for the conduct of some of its clergy, though without accepting any responsibility for the dubious role of the Pope and the Vatican's silence during the Holocaust.[4] In the early decades of the postwar period, both the Lutheran and the Catholic churches in Germany claimed that while Nazism had been the root of evil, they had resisted the regime and were persecuted by it; hence their self-proclaimed task was to restore the moral order in German society. In this manner, not a few of those theologians, professors of religion, and churchmen, who had welcomed Nazism in the 1930s, successfully retained their influence long after the fall of Hitler's regime.[5]

Unfortunately, this is not only a matter that concerns the genocide of the Jews. As the chapters by Timothy Longman and Charles de Lespinay amply demonstrate, the recent genocide in Rwanda can also be traced to the impact of the Catholic church on the population there dating back to the nineteenth century and, even more ominously, directly influencing the conduct of the genocide itself. Belgian and French colonialism is shown here to have originated— for its own purposes—the largely artificial categorization of the inhabitants of Burundi and Rwanda into allegedly distinct ethnic and racial groups of Tutsi and Hutu. The church, for its part, participated in this process of perpetuating and exploiting the division of the local population, and shifted its support from one group to another according to the changing balance of power between them. This eventually led to the horrifying phenomenon of parish priests taking an active part in deceiving the Tutsi population in their own congregations by calling it to find refuge in the churches, which then became sites of mass slaughter. Here we have a disturbing example of the murderous impact of the colonial legacy, one of whose most representative institutions, the church, was directly involved in creating the preconditions for genocide even as it claimed to bring the fruits of Western civilization and morality to non-European and previously non-Christian peoples. That the Vatican has denied any role in this genocide and, furthermore, that many of those clergy who were complicit in it are still active in Rwanda, is not merely another depressing indication of the manner in which religion and genocide can be intertwined, but also bodes ill for what we may expect in the future in those long-suffering African lands.

The centrality of religion for contemporary genocide can also be seen in the case of Bosnia. To be sure, we know that during World War II many hundreds of thousands of Orthodox Serbs were massacred by Catholic Croats while the Vatican looked on.[6] In the genocide of Muslims in Bosnia, it was the turn of the Serbs to turn their wrath upon those they identified with their historical enemies, the Turks. As Michael Sells shows in his chapter on Serbian religious mythology, the genocide in Bosnia was not "merely" a case of what the Serbs called "ethnic cleansing"—a euphemism for genocidal policies—but also a re-enactment of the Serbian myth of that nation's defeat by the Ottoman army six hundred years earlier. Hence the atrocities in Bosnia were seen as part of the liberation of the Serbs from a Muslim occupation that ended a century earlier and as a reassertion of Serbian nationalism, couched in religious-mythical rhetoric and imagery. Indeed, the highly placed Serbian bishops thought the Milosovic government was not militant enough in promoting religious nationalism. Along with organized crime and the secret police, they were the main basis of support for the militias. "Ethnic cleansing" was sometimes planned in local Serbian Orthodox churches, while religious rituals were held to celebrate "successful" cleansing. Serbian Christians also allied their notion of chosenness to a specific mythology of victimhood, re-enacting the stories of ancient martyrs to energize their own policy of retaliation. What makes this chapter all the more poignant is that even more recently Serbia was (and may still be) engaged in another bout of "ethnic cleansing" in Kosovo, the very site of the battle of Gazimestan in 1389, after which the Serbs came under Ottoman rule, and a region that is seen by the Serbs as the birthplace and heartland of their nation, even though the vast majority of its population are ethnic Albanians. This manner of collapsing time thus leads to a powerful, and often violent, intertwining of religion and nationalism, a confusion of history with myth, faith with vengeance, and a collective national memory densely populated with images of martyrdom and sacrifice, war and massacre.

II

The most extreme example presented by Sells of Serbian religious nationalism is the assertion that Slavic Muslims suffer from a "defective gene." In this manner, religion becomes a racial attribute, and its adherents must therefore be "cleansed" by murder or expulsion, since they cannot be transformed even by conversion. As we know, in the past conversion served as one means of avoiding persecution or massacre, although precisely for religious societies conversion evoked fears of divine punishment and social exclusion, and martyrdom was endowed with the highest moral value.[7] Modern genocide has often tended to relate religion to race, thereby preventing escape through conversion, even if individuals continued to shelter from persecution by a dissimulating their religious and "racial" identity.

Ara Sarafian's chapter, which opens Part II of the book, straddles the line between religion as a motivation for genocide and conversion as a means of physical survival. Sarafian views the forced conversion and consequent absorption of Armenian women and children into the Muslim population as a component of the Armenian genocide, since such practices led in most cases to the disappearance of Armenian identity in Turkey. And yet, this chapter also illustrates that the Armenian genocide contained elements of premodern genocide that distinguish it from later manifestations of mass murder. While the Ottoman authorities were intent on murdering all adult male Armenians, they occasionally presented women and children with the option of becoming Muslims. Thus we find that what mattered to the Turkish perpetrators was identity as defined by religious affiliation and its implication of belonging to a national group, even if the goal was indeed to terminate the Armenian presence in Anatolia. Sarafian cites some cases in which Muslim families accepted Christian Armenian children in order to save (and convert) them, while others exploited forced converts for labor and sex. There is, indeed, some similarity here between the Armenian case and the campaign of mass rape only recently unleashed by the Bosnian Serbs. And yet, one may also argue that the very fact that thousands of children were saved through conversion—albeit losing their Armenian identity—indicates that in the case of the Armenian genocide, religion both incited murder and to a limited extent also provided paths of survival, an option totally ruled out later in the century by the Nazis.

The construction of religion as a mythology of exclusivity and victimhood, allied to institutions that channeled and rationalized collective aggression, stands in contrast to the views of actual victims. Their perception and that of those who worked to mitigate the effects of genocide was at once personal and universalist. For instance, Margit Schlachta, founder and leader of the Roman Catholic Society of the Sisters of Social Service in Hungary, was the proponent of a doctrine of universalism that rejected the exclusivity of National Socialism. As asserted in the chapter by Jessica Sheetz, Schlachta's movement "narrowed the distance among faith communities" during the Nazi era; her own spirituality enabled her to overcome "the politics of difference." Schlachta believed that Christian "love obliges us to accept natural laws for our fellowmen without exception, which God gave and which cannot be taken away." She thus supplied Jews with baptismal certificates as a way to save them from the Nazis, not to convert them. Members of the official church informally acquiesced in issuing these certificates and permitted nuns to wear street clothes so as to be able to get in and out of the ghetto. They were thus willing to de-value a specific Christian sacrament and practice for the sake of universal charity. This is indeed one of the most impressive examples of assistance to Jews by believing Christians during the Holocaust, motivated by a universal humanistic interpretation of religious dogma and carried out with remarkable personal courage and devotion, as well as a talent for underground activity.

At the same time, however, we should note that the exclusively male higher echelons of the Catholic church were far less generously endowed with such qualities than Schlachta and all the other Sisters of Social Service. Thus Sheetz argues that cloistered women's experience of community life helped to generate ideas of social justice among Catholic nuns. As a lay leader and member of the Hungarian parliament, Margit Schlachta combined left-wing politics, a commitment to helping women, and communal spiritual life. Unlike more conventional orders, her community was not enclosed, though the sisters took vows of poverty, chastity, and obedience which they kept voluntarily as they moved in and out of the larger society. They considered work as social workers, nurses, and midwives as a form of prayer, and obedience as a form of confinement. This example makes one think of another remarkable case, the Protestant French village of Le Chambon, whose extraordinary feat of saving thousands of Jews was motivated by memories of their own persecution by the Catholics.[8] It seems that precisely those sectors or members of society who are themselves disadvantaged by race, gender, or faith, may show greater sympathy for other persecuted minorities than the majority population that tends more often to share and reflect the phobias and prejudices of the current regime and to distance itself from the suffering of marginalized groups. Schlachta's organization was a rare—though not unique—instance of true humanism and sacrifice emanating from religious faith at a time when carnage and inhumanity were the rule.

If religious faith motivated some of the rescuers, it was also a source of comfort for some of the victims. To be sure, while there were those who sought in belief a refuge from the torments of reality, others could not reconcile their faith with the inhumanity of the persecutors and either left the fold altogether or remained in a state of constant strife and struggle with their God.[9] There were also those who precisely at this time of upheaval and violence found their vocation, and by turning against the conventions of their society were able to bring comfort and support to many others. Regina Jonas, the first ordained female rabbi in the Jewish tradition, is one such case, examined in Katharina von Kellenbach's chapter. It was only under conditions of extreme outside pressure that the rabbinic authorities reluctantly allowed Jonas to perform the functions of an itinerant rabbi, traveling widely in Germany, serving small communities and working with the aged and the infirm. Jonas' form of spiritual resistance was a reflection of her anomalous position and activities. For while Jonas had to confront the traditions, constraints, and prejudices against women both in German civil society and in the Jewish community, she ended up as a courageous leader of her congregation during the Nazi era, accompanying it all the way from Berlin to Theresienstadt, and demonstrating the power of compassion and the moral stamina of one who had always had to fight for her place in society. But rather than celebrating the uniqueness of Jewish tradition or presenting her hard-won rabbinic status as a feminist victory, Jonas preached justice and dignity for all humanity, especially the weak.

The most innocent and helpless victims of genocide are the children; they suffer more than the adults and are often the first to die. Yet while in the Armenian genocide children were sometimes allowed to convert, during the Holocaust it was somewhat easier to hide children under false identities, often as Christians or, indeed, as converts in Christian institutions. In fact, far more children could have been saved had there been a greater willingness in gentile society to hide them, as was argued even during the war by the Polish Jewish historian Emmanuel Ringelblum.[10] For those who survived, their years in hiding and the loss of parents, childhood, and memory, often became an almost unbearable burden for the rest of their lives. One such story of a child who spent the war years in a Christian institution and found out about the Holocaust, the death of his parents, and his own Jewish identity only after the war, is told in Saul Friedländer's memoir, *When Memory Comes*. Another story of a child who survived under false identities and could no longer recapture his original, true self, is related in Louis

Begley's novel, *Wartime Lies*.[11] Here we include a brief personal account by Gabor Vermes, whose survival in Budapest during the months leading to its liberation is one more example of rescue through kindness, dissimulation, and personal courage. Raised in an assimilated Jewish family, but deeply influenced by his unconventional Orthodox grandfather, Vermes was hidden with several other children by a Lutheran pastor, while his parents went into hiding separately, sheltering from both the Germans and the fascist Hungarian militia. What Vermes remembers most distinctly from those terrifying days is his firm and very personal belief in God. And although, as he writes, he no longer maintains his faith, it was this stubborn sense of an intimate link with a divine source of good and justice that helped him survive, just as much as the self-sacrificing courage of the pastor who gave him shelter.[12]

Vermes makes a clear distinction between the specific theology of Christianity and the rituals of Judaism on the one hand, and on the other, his own experience of God as he prayed during his period of hiding. For Vermes, there was apparently no connection between his previous experience as a secular Jew and his own personal communication with a God that was neither Jewish nor Christian, as he lay in bed huddled under a winter coat. Personal prayer gave him a new sense of his own inward capacity to endure, but had no effect on his later relationship to Judaism or Christianity. From this perspective, Vermes' recollection is reminiscent of the writing of the Dutch writer Etty Hillesum, whose developing mysticism grew out of a need to speak to God directly during her incarceration at a Dutch internment camp. "To make this absolute solitude bearable she invoked God as her witness. She needed someone who would not forsake her, whom she could address in a familiar, informal tone, whom she ... could write to."[13]

III

In the aftermath of genocide, both its survivors and the societies that witnessed it have to contend with its often inextricably intertwined political, religious, and moral implications and repercussions. This process entails repression and rationalization, trauma and adaptation to normality, empathy with the suffering of others and preoccupation with one's unique pain and sorrow. Hence Part III opens with Yair Auron's analysis of the complex and changing attitudes of the Zionist movement toward the Armenian genocide both before and after the Holocaust. The similarities between the fate of these two peoples are a cause for empathy, for these are instances of religious minorities persecuted for a religious faith which simultaneously formed the focus of their national identity. Jewish fears of an approaching apocalypse at the beginning of the century were confirmed by the genocide of the Armenians, evoking a great deal of sympathy. Austrian-Jewish writer Franz Werfel's novel, *The Forty Days of Musa Dagh* (1933), about the genocide of the Armenians, completed shortly after Hitler's "seizure of power" and meant as a parable of the Jewish fight for survival over the centuries, had an immense influence on generations of youngsters in the pre-state *Yishuv* and Israel, and became a metaphor of resistance to annihilation for the fighters of the ghettoes during the Holocaust. The plight of the Armenians thus became associated with the tragedy of the Jews. And yet, the state of Israel has retained an evasive attitude toward the genocide of the Armenians, both because of its political interest in maintaining good relations with Turkey—which has never acknowledged the genocide, let alone expressed regret for it—and because of its insistence on the uniqueness of the Holocaust and its consequent reluctance to consider any other case of mass murder as comparable. Moreover, while some Israelis concede that the Armenians, too, are an ancient people and civilization, the fact that they are Christians also hampers official and individual recognition of their status as fellow victims of genocide, since for many Jews the Holocaust was directly related to Christian antisemtism.

In this sense, therefore, the debate over the Armenian genocide in Israel is ultimately about Jewish fate and Israeli identity, since it highlights both the peculiarities and the commonalties of facing persecution and surviving mass murder, the links between religious faith and national reassertion, and the contradictory pulls of identifying with other victims and insisting on the incommensurability of one's own fate. Thus Auron presents the Israeli case as a counter-example of a universalist tendency in many other discourses on genocide. This counter-example dates back to the defense of Ottoman anti-Armenian policies by the founder of modern Zionism, Theodore Herzl, who hoped to gain the Sultan's support for the Zionist project, and it continues into the present day. Yet Auron himself represents a new tendency in Israel, according to which the Shoah must be taught both as a unique event with major repercussions for Jewish fate and as one that demonstrates the value of life for all human beings.[14]

The aftermath of the Armenian and Jewish genocides is examined from a very different angle in Maud Mandel's chapter. Here the stress is on the social integration or reintegration of the survivors of catastrophe in France. The Armenian refugees of the Turkish massacre who arrived after World War I strove to become part of French society and, at the same time, to maintain their unique identity—closely linked both to religion and to geographical sites in the old homeland. Yet the French republic was devoted to the separation of state and religion and to a notion of an all-inclusive French identity. Jewish survivors of the Holocaust in France, for their part, included the remnants of French Jewry along with an increasing number of immigrants from both Eastern Europe and North Africa. This community too tried to maneuver between trends of secularization and assimilation and an urge to retain the distinctiveness of Jewish identity as expressed in religious practice, preserving traditions from the old sites of emigration, and forging links with Israel. This is thus a valuable case study of surviving national catastrophe by renegotiating the relationships between pre- and post-genocide existence, secular and religious identity, belonging to a larger national entity and adhering to a group with extra-national memories and ties, all in a country which both welcomed survivors and was often impatient with their reluctance to shed all marks of particularity and foreignness. In this sense, Mandel's essay on post-war Jewish and Armenian life is representative of other responses to genocide that produced a kind of eclectic spirituality rather than a more confined religiosity. The Jewish and Armenian communities in France are described by Mandel as disaffiliated but not alienated, providing a cultural, rather than a strictly religious connection for survivors and immigrants. On the basis of this case, we may speculate that the effect of genocide on victims and their descendants was not a process of secularization, but one in which belief and practice became more cultural and spiritual rather than specifically religious.[15]

The response of Orthodox Jews to the Holocaust is yet another facet of coming to terms with destruction and a different and more complex universalism. As Gershon Greenberg's chapter emphasizes, there was no unanimity of interpretation among the scholars and thinkers of this community. But one of the most interesting readings of the catastrophe can be found in Hayim Israel Tsimrman's book, *Tamim Pa'alo*, written in Palestine shortly after the war as part of a pastoral mission to counsel Jewish survivors. Tsimrman asserted that God's wisdom is ultimately inexplicable, because it has nothing in common with the limitations of human reason. He wished to re-embrace tradition in a pietistic frame of mind, not as an explanation for God's act in permitting genocide, but as a simple expression of God's presence, the promise of trans-historical redemption, and the transmuting of suffering into love. Just so did Abraham overcome his personalized *rahamim* (mercy) in wanting to save his son and accept God's universal *rahamim*. And yet Tsimrman is distinguished from other Orthodox inter-preters of the Holocaust by his radical position that the pious of Israel were both indirectly responsible for the catastrophe—having failed to prevent trespassing among the Jewish people—and directly responsible by having failed to restore the Land of Israel. Hence, his answer to the devastating question, "Why did God do this to this nation?" is to put the blame on the younger generation of pious Jews in the 1930s, those who, by rejecting tradition and abandon-ing the old ways, betrayed their task of carrying Judaism forward. That this abandonment of religion was accompanied by a failure to return to the Land of Israel was seen by him as an even greater tres-pass. Nevertheless, for Tsimrman the eventual suffering inflicted on the Jews also heralded their redemption, since self-sacrifice was transformed into an act of faith in God, and God's mercy was a consequence of the suffering of His people. Thus, while he views the deeper meaning of the Holocaust as trans-historical, he argues that continued faith gives meaning to suffering, and suffering con-stitutes the source of faith, whose ultimate expression is the revival and survival of Jewish life in the Land of Israel.[16]

A very different reaction to catastrophe is examined in Matthew Baigell's chapter on Jewish-American artists. For Baigell, artists working in the immediate aftermath of the Holocaust could only deal with their knowledge of mass murder by avoiding concrete images and identifiable Jewish themes in their works—not least because of an awareness of persistent antisemitism—and opted instead for abstract or mythological figures which depicted the ani-mal element in human nature. Influenced by ideas about universal-ist art, left-wing politics, as well as the desire to assimilate, artists also turned to Greek tragedy to express primitive forces and terror. Taking images from the Jewish mystical tradition of the Kabbalah—particularly that of the *tikkun*, or restoration, of God's spiritual lights—they both gave expression to and escaped from their Jewish roots in order to address a world community. Conversely, more con-temporary artists have turned to concrete images of the Holocaust imagery, suffused with Jewish references yet aiming at transcending the Jews' specific, parochial experience. Interestingly, these artists have also invoked the Kabbalistic notion of *tikkun olam* (healing the world), namely, the restitution of the original ideal order of the world which is the ultimate end of salvation. As Baigell writes, "the

Holocaust is not their subject, but rather a place from which to begin contemplation of the human condition." Thus art is conceived here as part of a healing process, a conceptualization of the artist's role which, he notes, is more fervently embraced by women artists than by men. This analysis of Holocaust representation in the United States over several decades therefore demonstrates that, while the older generation sought answers to the catastrophe but avoided direct reference to it, younger artists see their task as restorative and forgiving, yet at the same time insist on being witnesses to the specific event of the Holocaust and their personal response to it as Jews, even as they move from the parochial, ethnic dimension, to the universal.[17]

The encounter of the second generation with past atrocity is the focus of the last chapter. Michal Govrin presents us with a unique mélange of personal coming-to-terms with national catastrophe and family trauma, a biographical journey culminating in an impossible return to the fields of parental and collective memory, a literary representation of her own generation's complex maneuvers between past and present.[18] This multi-layered text shifts among a variety of perspectives and meanings as Govrin observes past events from several view-points in the present and then examines them again from an even greater chronological distance. Thus she looks now at a letter she wrote to her parents when she was living in Paris during the 1973 Yom Kippur War, having traveled through Germany and visited her mother's hometown Cracow, "obstinate, lonely, and full of contradictions," and learning about her mother singing, "I believe in Man, and in his spirit, his powerful spirit. ..." The experience

> proved to me that there is no refuge in the soothing distinctions between "then" and "now," between "there" and "here." And I also understood that there is no racial difference, imprinted at birth between "them" and "us," nor can we hide behind the fences of the Chosen People. And that, in every person, the murderer and the victim potentially exist, blended into one another, constantly demanding separation, every single day, with full awareness.

The Israel of her childhood in the 1950s, the Paris and Warsaw of her years as a student in the 1970s, and present reality, are all merged here from the perspective of a survivor's daughter, a young Israeli woman arriving in the city of lights, a Jew visiting the land of destruction, a child of a woman whose fate in the Holocaust can only be gleaned from the stories of others. Into this tale are woven the strands of religious and national identity, the torments of the mother and the daughter's emerging maturity, the unspoken yet ever-present memories of horror, and the final moment of intimacy between parent and child as Govrin reports on her travels to the sites of her mother's past. In some respects, this is the final chapter of the aftermath, the transmission of disaster from one generation to the next, the transformation of memory into vicarious experience. Yet it is also the beginning of a new chapter, the long process of imagining a no-longer-remembered event which nevertheless remains deeply etched in the consciousness of posterity. For as unmediated memory fades away with the final exit of those who had survived genocide, we witness the passage to a new identity, a new faith, a different yet no less crucial encounter with an event that both shattered belief in humanity and God, and, at the same time, made it all the more necessary to reassert faith in order to be able to look forward with a measure of hope and optimism.

Govrin's spiritual contemplation has clear affinities with that of the Dutch writer Etty Hillesum, who observed that "Nazi barbarism awakens the same barbarism in us. ... It is the only way one can live life these days, out of blind love for one's tormented fellow creatures—regardless of their nationality, race, or religion."[19] In her study of Hillesum's writings, Denise de Costa observes that as Hillesum's religion became more central to her, as she became more Jewish, she also became more Christian. "The more she turned toward the Jewish people and its body of ideas, the more receptive she became to Christian and other non-Jewish influences. ... inspired by Judeo-Christian thought on love and suffering, and under pressure from Nazi barbarism, she opted for the Jewish people and accepted their fate as hers."[20]

* * *

Why were the perpetrators of genocide attracted by the Jewish concept of the Chosen People? Why were the victims of genocide attracted by the Christian concept of universalism? As far back as the sixteenth century, Protestant theologians had defined their reformed faith as akin to Judaism, looking to Old Testament images of circumcision as a marker of exclusivity and to the city of Jerusalem as a model for a new sacred community, a "city on a hill." Conversely, ideas of Christian universalism had long held an appeal for European Jews. In her book, *Writing as Resistance*, Rachel Feldhay Brenner suggests that assimilated Jews were receptive to Christian ideals of universal brotherhood that harmonized with Enlightenment ideals of toleration and universal emancipation.[21] Ironically, while some theological legitimizers of genocide defined Christianity and Judaism as entirely separate and antagonistic cultures (even as leading Nazis rejected Christianity as a polluted and un-Aryan outgrowth of Judaism and some Christians urged the cleansing of Christianity of insidious Jewish influences), others actually perceived the event of man-made atrocity as a manifestation of the need to blur distinctions within a single Judeo-Christian religious heritage.

The concepts of religious tradition and universalism, structure and anti-structure, are also related to the issue of gender.[22] Clearly, biological womanhood had no intrinsic power to render women more or less barbaric than men. The few women who occupied high places in academic, bureaucratic, or religious institutions were enthusiastic perpetrators of genocidal policies. Thus Biljana Plavsic, member of the Bosnia-Herzegovina Academy of Arts and Sciences, was a supporter of Christoslavism and the policy of ethnic cleansing. However, the vast majority of women operated outside or on the margins of official structures. They also experienced greater fluidity of gender roles during and after periods of genocide.

Hence we can conclude that by looking at the relationship between religion and genocide in the twentieth century we learn a great deal about the manner in which humanity has both legitimized mass murder and resisted it, repressed past crimes and tried to come to terms with them, justified the perpetuation of existing social, political, and religious structures and subjected them to scrutiny and criticism. There is, of course, something almost obscene in speaking about genocide and spirituality in the same breath, for one is about savagery and cruelty, the other about love and humanness. Yet in both practice and philosophical and theological contemplation, genocide and spirituality are different aspects of the *human* spirit, the former a manifestation of its lower depths, the latter an expression of its transcendental aspirations. Both, then, are human and only human, which is why it is so difficult for us to reconcile them. But while religion has been put to genocidal use, and claims of spirituality have served to legitimize mass murder and limitless brutality, the human spirit, guided by either formal religious concepts or more rebellious and unconventional interpretations, has also manifested its greatest nobility in conditions of utter moral and material desolation. If the twentieth century is a tale of destruction and depravity, it thus also contains the scattered sparks of light that must be collected if we are to begin that mending of the world without which we cannot look into the future with any measure of hope and faith.

Notes

1. For some recent works on twentieth-century violence and genocide, see Samuel Totten et al. (eds.), *Century of Genocide: Eyewitness Accounts and Critical Views* (New York, 1997); David E. Apter (ed.), *The Legitimization of Violence* (New York, 1997); R. J. Rummel, *Death by Government* (New Brunswick, N.J., 1994); Sven Lindqvist, *"Exterminate All the Brutes"*, trans. Joan Tate (New York, 1996); Stéphane Courtois, et al., *The Black Book of Communism: Crimes, Terror, Repression*, trans. Jonathan Murphy and Mark Kramer (Cambridge, Mass., 1999).

2. See, e.g., István Deák, *Beyond Nationalism: A Social and Political History of the Habsburg Officer Corps, 1848-1918* (New York, 1990).

3. On the role of the churches in Vichy France, see W. D. Halls, *Politics, Society and Christianity in Vichy France* (Oxford, 1995); Étienne Fouilloux, *Les chrétiens français entre crise et libération, 1937-1947* (Paris, 1997).

4. Extensive extracts from the Vatican's statement, issued on March 16, 1998, were published the following day in German translation by the *Süddeutsche Zeitung* 63, p. 13. The statement expressed sorrow for the guilt of the sons and daughters of the church. See also *The New York Times*, November 1, 1997, for a statement made on October 31 by Pope John Paul II, that certain Christian teachings, based on "wrong and unjust" interpretations of the New Testament, had helped contribute to the Holocaust and the persecution of Jews in Europe over the centuries. Neither statement included a direct apology for the silence of the Vatican during the Holocaust.

5. On the impact of the return to church-oriented conservatism in the 1950s on the upheavals of the 1960s and 1970s in Germany, see Dagmar Herzog, "'Pleasure, Sex, and Politics Belong Together': Post-Holocaust Memory and the Sexual Revolution in West Germany," *Critical Inquiry* 24 (Winter 1998), pp. 393-444.

6. See Jonathan Steinberg, "Types of Genocide: Croatians, Serbs and Jews, 1941-45," in *The Final Solution: Origins and Implementation*, ed. David Cesarani (London, 1994), pp. 175-93; Walter Manoschek, *"Serbien ist judenfrei": Militärische Besatzungspolitik und Judenvernichtung in Serbien, 1941-42* (Munich, 1995), parts 3-4.

7. On the Jewish concept of martyrdom, or "kiddush hashem," see David G. Roskies (ed.), *The Literature of Destruction: Jewish Responses to Catastrophe* (Philadelphia, 1989), pp. 37-48, and his *Against the Apocalypse: Responses to Catastrophe in Modern Jewish Culture* (Cambridge, Mass., 1984), pp. 258-310.

8. Philip Hallie, *Lest Innocent Blood be Shed: The Story of the Village of Le Chambon and how Goodness Happened There*, 2d ed. (New York, 1994).

9. On Jewish religious life during the Holocaust, see Dan Michman, *The Holocaust and Holocaust Research: Conceptualization, Terminology and Basic Issue* (Tel Aviv, 1998, in Hebrew), part 6. On post-Holocaust Jewish theology, see Richard L. Rubenstein, *After Auschwitz: History, Theology, and Contemporary Judaism*, 2d ed. (Baltimore, 1992); John K. Roth and Michael Berenbaum (eds.), *Holocaust: Religious and Philosophical Implications* (New York, 1989).

10. Emmanuel Ringelblum, "Polish-Jewish Relations during the Second World War," in *Last Writings*, ed. Yisrael Gutman et al. (Jerusalem, 1994, in Hebrew), pp. 179-81, 294-95.

11. Saul Friedländer, *When Memory Comes*, trans. Helen R. Lane (New York, 1979); Louis Begley, *Wartime Lies* (New York, 1991).

12. For the historical context, see David Cesarani (ed.), *Genocide and Rescue: The Holocaust in Hungary, 1944* (Oxford, 1997).

13. Denise de Costa, *Anne Frank and Etty Hillesum: Inscribing Spirituality and Sexuality*, trans. Mischa F.C. Hoyinck and Robert E. Chesal (New Brunswick, N.J., 1998), p. 233.

14. On the changing attitudes toward the Holocaust in Israel, see Tom Segev, *The Seventh Million: The Israelis and the Holocaust*, trans. Haim Watzman (New York, 1993).

15. For some examples of the difficulty of coming to terms with past atrocity and lost identity in postwar France, see Annette Wieviorka, *Déportation et génocide: Entre la memoire et l'oublie* (Paris, 1992); Alain Finkielkraut, *The Imaginary Jew*, trans. Kevin O'Neill and David Suchoff (Lincoln, Neb., 1994); Éric Conan and Henry Rousso, *Vichy: An Ever-Present Past*, trans. Nathan Bracher (Hanover, N.H., 1998).

16. For a sociological interpretation of religion in Israel and its relationship to the Holocaust, see Menachem Friedman, "The State of Israel as a Theological Dilemma," in *The Israeli State and Society: Boundaries and Frontiers*, ed. Baruch Kimmerling (New York, 1989), pp. 165-215.

17. On Holocaust representation in commemorative art, see James E. Young, *The Texture of Memory: Holocaust Memorials and Meaning* (New Haven, 1993), and his (ed.), *The Art of Memory: Holocaust Memorials in History* (Munich, 1994).

18. For some recent analyses of Jewish confrontations with the Holocaust, see Yisrael Gutman (ed.), *Major Changes Within the Jewish People in the Wake of the Holocaust* (Jerusalem, 1996, in Hebrew), and Yechiam Weitz, *From Vision to Revision: A Hundred Years of Historiography of Zionism* (Jerusalem, 1997, in Hebrew), part 2.

19. de Costa, p. 3.

20. Ibid., pp. 208, 213.

21. Rachel Feldhay Brenner, *Writing as Resistance. Four Women Confronting the Holocaust: Edith Stein, Simone Weil, Anne Frank, Etty Hillesum* (University Park, Pa., 1997), cited in de Costa, p. 216.

22. Denise de Costa's analysis of Anne Frank and Etty Hillesum is that of a cultural feminist, stressing the differences between male and female experience, and seeking to describe and applaud behavior which she defines as feminine. For a strongly contrasting approach in feminist Holocaust studies, see the essay by Joan Ringelheim, "Women and the Holocaust: A Reconsideration of Research," in *Different Voices: Women and the Holocaust*, ed. Carol Rittner and John K. Roth (New York, 1993), pp. 373-418. Ringelheim comes close to disavowing her own previous work on women's behavior in the camps. She accuses herself of presenting an idealized portrait of feminine mutuality and compassion, a portrait which masked women's actual, more complex behavior and ultimately validated oppression by romanticizing the victim.

Part I

THE PERPETRATORS: THEOLOGY AND PRACTICE

– Chapter 1 –

RELIGION, ETHNICITY, AND NATIONALISM
Armenians, Turks, and the End of the Ottoman Empire[1]

Ronald Grigor Suny

Historians have analyzed the massive deportation and killing of hundreds of thousands of Armenians in eastern Anatolia in 1915 as the conflict of two exclusivist nationalisms, a struggle of two peoples over a single piece of territory. Carrying that view slightly further, those who would deny that a genocide took place have interpreted these events as a civil war between Turks and Armenians. In this construction, the victims are reduced to only one side in an uneven struggle that they themselves irrationally provoked, and the perpetrators are elevated to defenders of their homeland and nation.[2] The historiography of the end of the Ottoman Empire, much of it genuinely scholarly but too much of it polemical and propagandistic, has been shaped by a contemporary politics framed within the legitimizing limits of nationalist normality. What I will argue is quite different. Rather than a civil war, which indeed never took place and exists only in the imagination of professional falsifiers, the genocide occurred when state authorities decided to remove the Armenians from eastern Anatolia in order to realize a number of strategic goals—the elimination of a perceived Armenian threat in the war against Russia, punishment of the Armenians for activities which the Turkish authorities believed to be rebellious and detrimental to the survival of the Ottoman state, and realization of grandiose ambitions to create a Pan-Turkic empire that would extend from Anatolia through the Caucasus to Central Asia. Rather than resulting primarily from Turkish racial or religious hatred of the Armenians, which existed in many places and was available for exploitation, or long-term planning by militant nationalists, the genocide was a rather contingent event that was initiated at a moment of near imperial collapse when the Young Turks made a final, desperate effort at revival and expansion of the empire that they had reconceived as more Turkic and Islamic, shifting the meaning of what had been Ottoman. The year 1915, then, can be understood as a moment of imperial decline, when a fundamental reconceptualization of the nature of the state along more Islamic and Pan-Turkic lines took place, and Young Turk policies became increasingly radical in the fierce context of the First World War.

Rather than arguing that the genocide was planned long in advance and was continuous with the earlier policies of conservative restoration through massacre, I contend that the brutal policies of killing and deportation *(surgan)* that earlier regimes used to keep order or change the demographic composition of towns and borderlands must be distinguished from the massive expulsions of 1915, the very scale of which, as well as their intended effects—to rid eastern Anatolia of a whole people—made the genocide a far more radical, indeed revolutionary, transformation of the imperial setup. As in earlier and later massacres of Armenians, victims and victimizers were of different religions, but these mass killings were not primarily driven by religious distinctions or convictions. Membership in a religious community *(millet)* was an important marker of difference, and religion closely corresponded to ethnicity, even in many cases to class. But the motivations for murder were not spontaneously generated from religion or even ethnicity but were driven by a cascade of influences—decades of hostile perceptions of the "other" exacerbated by a sense of loss of status, insecurity in the face of perceived dangers, and the positive support and encouragement of state authorities for the most lawless and inhumane behavior.

Neither was the Armenian Genocide a struggle between two contending nationalisms, one of which destroyed the other. Such a scenario presupposes that two well-formed and articulated nationalisms already existed in the early years of the war. Among Armenians, divided though they were among a number of political and cultural orientations, identification with an Armenian nation had gained a broad resonance. Yet Turkish identity was not clearly focused on the "nation." Turkish nationalism was still weak, confused, and mixed in with Pan-Islamism, Pan-Turanism, and Otto-manism. The Committee of Union and Progress (CUP) elite was not so much engaged in creating a homogeneous ethnic nation as it was searching unsuccessfully, flailing around to find ways to maintain its empire. Deporting and killing Armenians was a major, deliberate effort to that end, but not in order for the Young Turks to create a "Turkey for the Turks" or a homeland for the Turkish nation, something that in the next decade would become the hallmark of the Kemalist republic. The imperial mission of the CUP still involved ruling over Kurds and Arabs, as well as Jews, Greeks, and even Armenian survivors, in what would essentially still be a multi-national Ottoman Empire. In the vision of some, like Enver Pasha, that vision was now greatly expanded to include the Turkic peoples of the Caucasus and possibly Central Asia. Even as some thinkers, notably 'Turks" from the Russian Empire, advocated an empire in the more ecumenical civic sense of the Ottomanist liberals of the nineteenth and early twentieth centuries, the policies of the Young Turks never were purely Turkish nationalist but remained Ottoman in fundamental conception. In a word, they were primarily state imperialists rather than nationalists.

Scholars have come to a general agreement over the last several decades that we need to think about nations and nationalism differently. Rather than fixed, objective, primordial categories, modern nations are the product of hard work by intellectuals and political actors, scholars and propagandists, who have applied their energies, not only to the mapping of difference and boundaries, but to the narration of a useable past. A principal trope of nationalist writers has been the recovery of what has been lost, revival of what has lain dormant, and resurrection of what appeared to be dead. But in the active imagining of communities and inventing of traditions there has also been the forced silencing of voices and the erasure of inconvenient memories.[3] In the transition from multinational empires to more homogeneous nation-states, those serving the "progressive" development of nation-making and modernization have transformed the demographic horrors of deportation, ethnic cleansing, and genocide into inevitable, unavoidable, even necessary civil conflicts. Consider the words of the eminent scholar of Islam, Bernard Lewis, which can be read as an implied rationale for the Turkish massacres of Armenians:

> For the Turks, the Armenian movement was the deadliest of all threats.
> From the conquered lands of the Serbs, Bulgars, Albanians, and Greeks,
> they could, however reluctantly, withdraw, abandoning distant
> provinces and bringing the Imperial frontier nearer home. But the

Armenians, stretching across Turkey-in-Asia from the Caucasian fron-
tier to the Mediterranean coast, lay in the very heart of the Turkish
homeland—and to renounce these lands would have meant not the
truncation, but the dissolution of the Turkish state. Turkish and Armenian villages, inextricably mixed, had for centuries lived in neighborly
association. Now a desperate struggle between them began—a struggle
between two nations for the possession of a single homeland, that
ended with the terrible holocaust of 1915, when a million and a half
Armenians perished.[4]

In what appears to be a cool and balanced understanding of
why the Ottoman rulers would have used mass violence against a
perceived Armenian danger, Lewis places the Armenians "nearer
[the Turkish] home" and "in the very heart of the Turkish homeland," employing language that already assumes the legitimacy and
actuality of a nation-state. In this transparent paragraph, Lewis
subtly rewrites the history of Anatolia , changing it from a land in
which Armenians were the earlier inhabitants into one in which
they become an obstacle to the national aspirations of the Turks,
who now can claim Anatolia, rather than Central Asia, as their
homeland. His language employs the logic of nationalism as if it
has a kind of universal relevance even in political structures that
evolved out of and still worked within a contradictory logic of
empire. In 1915 the Ottoman Empire was still an imperial state,
albeit already long existing within an international system of powerful nation-states and an increasingly hegemonic Western conviction that the nation, however defined, was the principal source of
political legitimacy. The nature of that system and its self-justifi-
cations were changing, but Lewis' reading of a notion of ethnic
homogeneity as the basis for a national republic of the Kemalist
type, which lay in the future, into the moment of Armenian annihilation is ahistorical and anachronistic. As he is well aware, in the
last years of the empire conflicting and contradictory ideas of Turkish nationalism, some deeply racist, vied with Pan-Turanism, Pan-
Islamism, and various strains of Ottomanism in an ideological
contest for new ways of reformulating the state.

Within the framework of nationalism two kinds of arguments
are made to justify a people's claim to a piece of the earth's territory: an historical argument of prior settlement, the idea of an original people; or an argument of demographic dominance, the idea
that a majority's claim has precedence over those of minorities. The
fact that Armenians after 2,500 years in eastern Anatolia had
become a minority in the overall population and that the Ottoman
Turks who through conquest and assimilation over half a millen-

nium in the region, had become the dominant population (and, along with other Islamic peoples, most importantly the Kurds, a majority), powerfully underscored Turkish claims to the territory. In the case of the Armenians, only the first claim, that they were the original settlers of the region, legitimized their claim to Anatolia as homeland. Armenian nationalists made such a claim in the late nineteenth century, and Turkish nationalists and imperial rulers responded. Yet neither of these claims, which are still to this day the basis of political as well as historiographical disputes, had any particular meaning in the older imperial paradigm, which justified rulership and possession on the grounds of conquest, raw power, and divine sanction. Both the historical and demographic claims resonate only within a concept of the nation-state in which the "people," however constituted, become the source of legitimacy.

The Imperial Paradigm and the Discourse on the Nation

The Ottoman Empire, like other great empires, can be understood as a composite state in which the metropole is distinct in some way from the periphery, which is conceived or perceived by metropolitan or peripheral actors as a relationship of justifiable or unjustifiable inequity, subordination, and/or exploitation. What might be called the "imperial paradigm" was a system in which the Turkish Sultan, by right of conquest and divine sanction, ruled over subjects of various religions and ethnicities in a structure of inequity and subordination that maintained or reinforced difference. Two kinds of distinction were institutionalized in the Ottoman Empire in its first centuries: a vertical distinction between the "ruling institution" and the ordinary subjects of the sultan; and horizontal distinctions among the various religious communities in the empire. The "ruling institution," made up of the sultan, his priests, ministers, governors, and military, those who served the state (the *askeri*), was separate and above the *reaya*, the flock (the ordinary people).[5] The former paid no taxes, while the *reaya*—the peasants, artisans, merchants, herdsmen, and others—were subject to taxation. The various religious and cultural groups, while possessing no rights that limited the power of the sultan, were, nevertheless, respected as different but subordinate to the ruling Ottoman elite. Before the sixteenth century, the *askeri* were both Muslim and non-Muslim, but thereafter they were fully Islamized, thus linking class and religious distinctions and emphasizing the inferiority of non-Muslims. Within the *askeri*, an elite of Osmanlis [Ottomans] arose, those most knowledgeable of "the Ottoman way." Occasionally non-Muslims could also rise in government service if they could demonstrate the necessary cultural competence of the Ottomans, but they always retained the stigma of difference and implied inferiority.

Thus, like other great traditional empires, the Ottoman realm was organized on the basis of strict distinctions and discriminations that were hierarchical in nature, with advantages and disadvantages ascribed to different persons and peoples according to their official position and religious belief. As a form of state, empire, then, is quite different from the ideal type of nation-state with its officially undifferentiated population of citizens who are equal under the law. Indeed, these two state forms—nation-state and empire—stood in tension one with the other in the emerging discourse of the nation in the nineteenth century, just as the Ottomans confronted the prevailing Western conceptions of the nation. A number of Turkish, Greek, and Armenian thinkers and actors were intrigued by the particularly modern form of "imagined" political community that came together in the late eighteenth and early nineteenth centuries around the notion of bounded territorial sovereignties in which the "people" provide the legitimacy of the political order.[6] But the implications of nationalism were subversive for many aspects of the imperial order. Nationalism provided a new legitimation for separation from the empire for those who could reconceive themselves as "nations." At the same time, Westernizing officials within the ruling Turkish elites were intrigued by other Western ideas, such as equality under the law, and in the reforms of the Tanzimat period (1839-1878) Ottoman bureaucrats introduced laws and practices that in their application began to undermine the legitimation formulas for the traditional distinctions and hierarchies of empire.

Though the Western discourse on the "nation" had begun as an expression of state patriotism, through the nineteenth century it increasingly became ethnicized until the "national community" was understood to be a cultural community of shared language, religion, and/or other characteristics with a durable, antique past, shared kinship, common origins, and narratives of progress through time.[7] By the twentieth century, such imagined communities were the most legitimate basis for the constitution of states, thought to be products of blood and nature, displacing dynasties and religious and class discourses and concurrently challenging alternative formulas for legitimation, like those underpinning empires. As the idea of what constituted a nation shifted toward ethnic homogeneity, the incompatibility between traditional empire and nation-state widened.

Among the most interesting questions to be explored by those who view nations as neither natural nor primordial but the result of constitutive intellectual and political efforts of elites and masses is how nations exist in particular understandings of history, what stories are told to make the nation appear as a stable subject moving continuously through time, fulfilling a project over many centuries of coming to self-awareness.[8] For the great nineteenth-century imperial elites, as well as their subordinated "peoples," this powerful rethinking of history in the idiom of the nation had the effect of homogenizing disparate events and processes into a single, progressive narrative so that other ways of understanding experience lost their authority. It was precisely in the context of the dominant discourse of the nation in the twentieth century that once-viable imperial states became increasingly vulnerable to nationalist movements that in turn gained strength from this new sense of state legitimation, namely that states ought to represent, if not coincide, with nations. At the same time the new nationalism coexisted with the spread of notions of popular sovereignty, of democratic representation of subaltern interests, and a fundamental tension arose between inequitable imperial relationships and concepts of national democracy. While empires were among the most ubiquitous and long-lived polities in premodern history, they had operated within a different legitimating paradigm—one based on rights of conquest, divinely ordained rulers, and/or mandates bestowed through dynastic continuity. The powerful combination of nationalism and democracy proved fatal to their continued existence in late modern times. Though liberal states with representative institutions, styling themselves as democracies, could be (and were) effective imperial powers in the great overseas empires of Great Britain, France, Belgium, and the Netherlands, the great contiguous empires of eastern Europe and the Middle East resisted democratization that would have undermined the right to rule of the dominant imperial elite and the very hierarchical and inequitable relationship between metropole and periphery in the empire. Yet the empire states of the late nineteenth and early twentieth centuries did not passively accept inexorable decline. Russia, Austro-Hungary, and the Ottoman Empire attempted to adjust to the new constellation of national states, to modernize their imperial structures and ideological underpinnings. These attempts, ultimately aborted by the catastrophe of World War I, were efforts at a kind of imperial refurbishing aimed at creating a political community that was multinational or multireligious rather than a single ethnic nation and a more modern state able to confront the challenges of

representation, popular mobilization, and bureaucratic efficiency
of Western nation-states.

The most effective contribution of an historicist sensibility is to
recover the past in all its particularity of time and place. Given the
hegemonic influence of the national framework in which historians
work and, indeed, in which the discipline of history itself arose, it
is essential that analysts shun the ever-present contemporary biases
and attempt to "rescue history from the nation."[9] In an insightful
article Aron Rodrigue warns against reading the whole Ottoman
experience in the light of the "modern period where the West
becomes a referent" and "when European powers became more
directly dominant and threatening."[10] He suggests that, firstly,
Islam in its historical variation must be de-essentialized and that no
easy deductions be made from the *dhimma*, the pact of toleration
of non-Muslims living under Islam, to the practices of the Ottoman
Empire throughout its entire existence. Secondly, that in the early
modern period, from the sixteenth to the eighteenth centuries, "a
society existed ... where 'difference' instead of 'sameness' was
paramount," and there was almost no desire on the part of political leaders to transform difference into sameness.[11] The Ottoman
political world was distinct from the Western Enlightenment public sphere of a value-neutral, universalistic ideal in which what is
shared is highlighted and the particular, that which is different,
becomes a problem to be resolved. Like Benjamin Braude and
Bernard Lewis in their ground-breaking collection on the non-
Muslims of Ottoman Anatolia,[12] Rodrigue emphasizes that in the
early Ottoman centuries discrimination did not necessarily mean
persecution. Difference was seen as normal and normative, something natural to be accepted. "Persecution of difference," he writes,
"was not really acceptable. Since Ottoman rulers did not like social
disorder, they attempted to fix or freeze the particular, but they did
not change it."[13]

The key difference in early Ottoman society was religion, rather
than ethnicity or language, which took on relevance only later. The
millets, the various communities headed by religious leaders that
were systematized only in the nineteenth century, were based on
religion, rather than some idea of primal origin, language, or culture. The state ruled over the *millets* indirectly and interfered little,
delegating much authority to the religious head of the *millet*. Certainly no effort was made to break down the boundaries of these
communities and homogenize the population of the empire, or even
Anatolia, around a single identity. There was no state project of
"making Ottomans" or turning "peasants into Turks" in the Otto-

man Empire, at least not before 1908, as there was to a degree in the absolute monarchies of Western Europe or the French state after the revolution of 1789. There was also no idea, until the Tanzimat reforms of the mid-nineteenth century, of equality under the law, a notion of equal citizenship for all members of Ottoman society. From the eighteenth century the term *reaya* was applied only to non-Muslims, underlining their inferior status.[14] One might restate the points made by Braude and Lewis, Rodrigue, and other Ottomanists who have written on the non-Muslim peoples in the language of empire and nation presented here: the Ottomans in the early modern period were not engaged in any kind of nation-building project but in an imperial state-building effort that sought at one and the same time to maintain the distinctions of hierarchy between rulers and ruled, Muslim and non-Muslim, without integrating a disparate society into a single, homogenous whole.[15] Unity in the empire came from the person of the sultan-caliph to whom all peoples regardless of religion or ethnicity owed allegiance.

The Imperial State and Its Armenian Subjects

Armenians in Anatolia understood that they were a subject people, that the ruling elite was Turkish and Islamic, and that even their compatriots who succeeded in society and the state had to adapt to the expectations of the ruling Ottoman elite in order to advance. The Armenian Church, itself institutionally tied into the Ottoman system of governance, usually preached acceptance of the fate befallen the Armenians and deference toward their rulers and social betters, both Muslim and Armenian. It opposed rebellion of any kind. Yet even as they legitimized the system in which their people lived, clerics remained aware of the special burdens they bore. For Armenian scribes the symbiosis of early Ottoman society was far less benign for the *giaour* (the unbeliever) than for the Muslims, and clerical writers, among them Manuel of Garahisar, noted that Armenians had to endure the oppressive rule of the Turks "because of [our] immense sins."[16] Writing in the sixteenth century, a particularly harsh period when Ottoman-Safavid wars raged through eastern Anatolia, the Armenian chronicler Hovhannes Tsaretsi wrote:

> Thus, who can write of the persecution and suffering of our times, who can write, oh my brothers, but with tears in their eyes we can tell of this only approximately. Because my sins have become so great, the Ottomans have conquered the Armenian provinces, destroying and laying low all the villages and settlements, and they rule in all places. So heavy

was their burden of taxes, that many left their property and their father's legacy. But they are unable to free themselves from this oppression, because there was no place to hide; as a consequence of this, everyone was confused and envied the dead, because the oppression of theirs was not temporary but permanent in the Armenian provinces. Their oppression spread from generation to generation, and still we find ourselves under their evil rule. As a consequence, people have left their birthplaces and scattered to all ends of the earth.[17]

Though there had been greater access to positions of power and influence for non-Muslims before the reign of Suleiman the Magnificent (1520-1566), in the following centuries religion marked a key boundary between privilege and disadvantage. Difference was not simply horizontal but vertical as well. Non-Muslims no longer were allowed to bear arms. They performed the occupations considered beneath the faithful—tanning, wine-making, money-changing, castrating slaves. It was the non-Muslim who dismounted from his horse when a Muslim approached. As I have written elsewhere,

> Armenians and Turks coexisted in an unequal relationship, one of subordination and superordination, with the Muslims on top and the non-Muslims below. The sheer power and confidence of the ruling Muslims worked for centuries to maintain in the Armenians a pattern of personal and social behavior manifested in submissiveness, passivity, deference to authority, and the need to act in calculatedly devious and disguised ways. It was this deferential behavior that earned the Armenians the title "loyal *millet*" in an age when the Greeks and Slavs of the empire were striving to emancipate themselves through revolutionary action. The Armenians in contrast worked within the Ottoman system and accepted the burdens of Muslim administration without much protest until the second half of the nineteenth century.[18]

For many Armenian writers of the last two centuries, the whole history of the Armenians is one of the emerging nation, and earlier forms of collective identity are usually understood in terms of that nation. Yet if one takes seriously what Eric J. Hobsbawm would call "protonationalism," earlier concepts of community should not be conflated with more modern notions. From the texts of the early Middle Ages it is evident that Armenians conceived of themselves as a unique Christian community, with their own church set apart from the Constantinople-centered church. Yet for over a millennium Armenia was not a single state; Armenian dynasties fought one another, allied with Arabs, Greeks, Turks, or Persians at times against other Armenian principalities. No Armenian state contained all Armenians or all of Armenia except for a very brief period. Loyalty was to particular dynasts or nobles (*nakhararner*). What linked this divided and dispersed people was a religious and linguistic affiliation rather than political ties, and the textual memory of Armenian political existence and of former glories maintained by clericals. The literary tradition, its scribes envied and emulated by Armenia's neighbors like the Georgians, became much more fragmented in the period after the Seljuk, Mongol, and Ottoman invasions and settlements, and when the last Armenian state of consequence fell in 1375, the church remained as the principal focus of identification and preservation.

In the early modern period energetic church leaders attempted sporadically to interest Western capitals in a crusade to liberate Armenians from their Islamic rulers, the Ottomans and the Persians, but with almost no results. Those sporadic church-led diplomatic missions to Rome, the courts of the German states, France, and Russia have been integrated into a narrative of a "national-liberation movement" by later writers, and in Soviet Armenian historiography the efforts by the *meliks* of Karabakh or the self-appointed liberator Israel Ori were fashioned into a "Russian orientation" that served as justification for the tsarist conquest of eastern (Persian) Armenia and the inclusion of Caucasian Armenia within the Soviet Union. Most of the "liberationist" activity came from diaspora Armenians, merchants in Persia, Europe, and India, interested in the restoration of an Armenian state. The group of merchant activists in Madras wrote political tracts that shifted the blame for the Armenian condition from their own sinful past onto the despotism of foreign rulers. The adventurer Joseph Emin, who traveled widely to interest Europeans in the Armenian cause, indicted the Armenian clergy for their message of passive acceptance of Muslim rule. But what is often not emphasized in the histories of these efforts is their fragmentary nature, the fragility or absence of connections between them, and the different motivations and ambitions of the actors who have been flattened into a single, coherent narrative of a "movement."[19]

Linked primarily by religion and the church, which nurtured a sense of a lost glorious past and ancient statehood, Armenians before the nineteenth century made up a diffuse ethnoreligious community whose people were dispersed among three contiguous empires and scattered even further abroad by their mercantile interests and the oppressive conditions in eastern Anatolia. Armenians were much more divided than united, separated by politics, distance, dialects, and class differences. Yet the clericals worked to create a collective identity for Armenians, a notion of their distinction from their neighbors of different linguistic and religious communities. Though we know very little about the identifications of ordinary Ottoman Armenians, many of whom spoke Turkish rather than Armenian, the Armenian clerical and merchant leadership in the Ottoman Empire maintained a sense of Armenian distinctiveness, marked by a particular form of Christianity, and a memory of past glory. At the same time they preached deference to the rulers that God had imposed upon them. Religious distinction was foundational to culture and identity, but local identities, a sense of place and where one came from, seem to have been extremely important to Armenians. The historiographic and literary tradition, family, place of origin, occupation, and religion, as well as recognition of the power of the state and its authorities all played parts in the construction of Armenian identity. And that identity was institutionalized in the *millets*, the official communities recognized by the sultan as the instruments of his rule over his subjects.[20] The lines of distinction among Muslims and non-Muslims drew people of one religion together with their fellow-religionists and distanced them from those of different religions. Yet *millets* did not correspond exactly to ethnolinguistic lines. The Ermeni *millet*, for instance, included not only the Armenians of the national ("apostolic") church, but also Copts, Chaldians, Ethiopians, Syrian Jacobites, and others, while Armenian Catholics and Protestants gained their own *millets* in the early nineteenth century. Even as over time Armenians borrowed the idioms of the nation, blending them with their own religious distinctions, religion remained the principal official marker of difference.

The turn from a primary identification with an ethnoreligious community to an ethnonational identity was gradual and prolonged. The genesis of Armenian nationalism occurred in the diaspora, in far-removed places like Madras, where the first Armenian newspaper was published at the end of the eighteenth century, and Venice, where the Catholic Mekhitarist fathers revived the medieval histories of the Armenians and commissioned new ones. The literary and cultural revivalists of the late eighteenth and early nineteenth century, particularly the Mekhitarist monks, saw themselves as cultivating the national spirit through promotion of the language.[21] Father Ghevond Alishan, who himself had never been to historic Armenia, wrote elegaically about the landscape in which the ruins of ancient churches were the inspiration for a revived national feeling. But even as they promoted enlightenment and borrowed the idiom of the nation from the West, the generation of religious teachers rejected the more radical and democratic aspects of Western and East European nationalism that they observed.

Though the mission of the Mekhitarists was spiritual revival, their efforts to convert Armenians to Catholicism were frustrated by state and *millet*. The sultan and the Armenian patriarch collaborated in repressing Armenian Catholics in the empire in the 1820s, and only after the devastating Ottoman defeat at Navarino (1827) and the later Ottoman rapprochement with France did the sultan agree to create a Catholic *millet*. Ironically, the Mekhitarists inspired and even trained people who later became the first secular nationalists, some of whom became bitter and outspoken opponents of clerical authority.[22] The evident possibility of being Catholic or Protestant and also being Armenian raised a critical distinction between nation and religion. Mekhitar, the founder of the order, may have claimed that " I sacrifice neither my nation to my religion nor my religion to my nation," but such a statement clearly distinguished between the two.[23] The precise connection (or disconnection) between religion and nationality became the ground upon which clerics and secular intellectuals would contest the nature of being Armenian.

The new images of community generated in Europe and by diaspora activists fit well with the new forms and institutions of Armenian life emerging in Ottoman cities, particularly Istanbul. As capitalist production and exchange penetrated the empire, different *millets* (and even segments within *millets*) benefited (and suffered) unevenly from the new economic opportunities. With the Greeks suspect as rebels (and after 1821 possessing their own independent state), the Ottomans favored the Armenians as the "loyal *millet*" (*millet-i-sadika*). In the late eighteenth and first half of the nineteenth century, urban Armenians profited enormously from their association with the Porte. The *amiras* and *sarafs*, the wealthy money-lenders and bankers who financed the tax-farming system, along with the less affluent *esnafs*, the craftsmen and artisans of the towns, accumulated wealth with which they subsidized schools, hospitals, and philanthropic organizations.[24] Though highly placed, the *amiras* were always vulnerable to the arbitrary power of the sultan, and when reforming officials progressively eliminated the tax-farming system, the wealthy *sarafs* suffered financially. When social tensions between the rich and the not-so-rich tore at the Armenian community and threatened the peace of the Ottoman capital, the sultan responded to the pleas of leading Armenians and reluctantly granted a "constitution" to regulate the Armenian *millet*. Community identity and self-sufficiency solidified, as well-to-do Armenians settled in Galata, a prosperous district of Istanbul, and other discrete sections, adopted European styles, established close ties with and even came under the formal protection of foreign states. They published the first newspapers in the empire, sent their children abroad for specialized and higher education, and drew visibly distant from the demographically and politically dominant Muslims. Armenians ran the imperial mint; an Armenian was chief architect to the sultan; and Armenians ran the Foreign Correspondence Office of the government. But for all their success and visibility, Ottoman Armenians were also the victims of unequal treatment and "other doubts and suspicions that emerged increasingly as faith in the viability of the Ottomanist synthesis of nationalities—a synthesis to which the official commitment to egalitarianism was directly linked—began to erode."[25]

The "nationalization" of Armenians occurred, not in isolation or primarily from within, but in synergy with and in response to the developing discourses on liberalism and the nation in Europe and the nationalisms of other peoples, most notably the French and the Greeks. Nationalist movements of the Ottoman peoples of the Balkans, along with the Western imperialist incursions into and defeat of the Ottoman Empire, contributed to a general sense of Ottoman decline that stimulated westernizing bureaucrats to attempt to reform the empire and Europeanized Christians to consider either separating from the empire or, in the case of the Armenians, to petition for internal reform along more liberal lines. In a vision shared both by many in power and by those they ruled, the Ottoman Empire was "backward," "sick," and was expected to collapse, for it was an unfit pre-industrial power in an age of ruthless international competition, an imperial victim of western imperialism.

Appropriately for a dispersed people faced by three imperial authorities, the nationalism of many Armenian thinkers was not primarily territorial. Neither the clergy nor the powerful conservatives in the capital, who benefited from their privileged positions within Ottoman society and close to the state, were interested in creating a territorial nation. More broadly, Armenian leaders in Turkey hoped for reform from above and spoke of their "benevolent government." Until the end of the 1870s the sense of the nation for Ottoman Armenians was still largely of an ethnoreligious community that needed to work within the context of the empire to improve its difficult position. Encouraged by the Tanzimat reformers and the theorists of Ottomanism, liberal Armenians petitioned and pressured the Porte and tried occasionally to enlist foreign support for reform.[26]

For Ottoman Armenians the great divide in the *millet* was between the community in Constantinople and the bulk of Armenians, largely peasants and petty craftsmen, living in the eastern provinces. While the wealthy Armenians of the capital both influenced the patriarch and controlled the National Assembly that dealt with certain aspects of *millet* affairs, the provinces remained radically underrepresented. A frequent complaint from the east was that Constantinople Armenians, as the leaders of the community, were not fulfilling their obligation to care for the lower orders. This alienation from the center was highlighted by the work of bishop Mkrtich Khrimian, known widely as *hairik* (Little Father), in Van, the most Armenian of the towns of eastern Anatolia. Khrimian briefly edited a journal, *Ardziv Vaspurakani* (The Eagle of Vaspurakan, the medieval Armenian name for the Van region), in 1858, exposed the suffering of his parishioners, and spoke vaguely of Armenian self-defense. In 1869-1873 he served as Patriarch of Constantinople and came into conflict with the more conservative forces among the capital's Armenians when he attempted to increase provincial representation in the National Assembly. The activist priest sent a report in 1871 to the Porte enumerating the abuses of Armenians by provincial authorities. His recommendation, in line with much of the thrust of the Tanzimat reforms, was to strengthen the role of the central authorities in the provinces, to rationalize the administration of justice, and to guarantee equality of treatment and tolerance of religious practices. Though he was supported by prominent liberal Armenians, like Grigor Otian, who earlier had been an advisor to Midhat Pasha and was president of the National Assembly, Khrimian could overcome neither the Ottoman government's unwillingness to carry out reforms in the provinces nor the conservative Armenians' indifference toward the provincial Armenians. In 1873 he resigned as Patriarch.

The horizons for Armenians changed radically with the coming to power of Abdul Hamid II (1876-1909), the Russo-Turkish War of 1877-1878, Abdul Hamid's abrogation of the Ottoman Constitution in 1877, and the turn toward a Pan-Islamic policy that involved repression of the Armenians in the 1890s. As an Armenian national discourse took shape, the more liberal and radical elements focused on the eastern provinces and the poverty and oppression suffered by the Armenian peasantry. A sense of a "fatherland" *(hairenik)* developed among Armenian writers, and a distinction was drawn between *azgasirutiun* (love of nation), which heightened the sense of a cultural nation beyond a specific territory, and *hairenasirutiun* (love of fatherland), with emphasis on the people in Armenia *(haiastantsiner)*. Men like Bishop Garegin Srvantstiants, who had long complained about the distance of Constantinople Armenians from the "fatherland," and Arsen Tokhmakhian, who later turned to revolution, celebrated the Armenians of historic Armenia who had "preserved the faith and suffered because of it."[27] Imbued with a deeply populist nationalism, centered on the peasants of eastern Anatolia, Armenian intellectuals traveled as teachers to the east in an effort characterized as *depi Haiastan* (to Armenia). The government responded by removing prominent teachers, like Mkrtich Portukalian in Van and Martiros Sareyan in Mush, from their home provinces and exiling Khrimian to Jerusalem.

Increasingly, Turkish authorities interpreted any manifestation of cultural revival or resistance, however individual or local, as an act of national rebellion. The government restricted the powers of the Armenian National Assembly, accepting only *takrirs* (petitions) dealing with churches and monasteries. The state prohibited all forms of national expression, banning the word Haiastan (Armenia in Armenian) in print and forbidding the sale and possession of pictures of the last Armenian king, Levon V, who had lost his throne five centuries earlier. Instead of seeing them as the "loyal *millet*," Turkish officials and intellectuals began to look upon Armenians as unruly, subversive, alien elements who consorted with foreign powers. The conservative Muslim clergy, long alienated by the Frenchified reformist bureaucrats among the Turks, were offended by the behavior and wealth of the most visible Armenians, those merchants who lived in the capital, particularly those in Europeanized districts of the capital, like Galata, who affected Western manners or even took foreign citizenship. A highly-placed Ottoman observer noted the resentment of religious Muslims toward the effects of the Tanzimat:

> Many among the people of Islam began complaining thus: "Today we lost our sacred national rights [*hukuk-ï mukaddese-i milliyyemizi*] which were earned with our ancestors' blood. The Muslim community [*millet-i islamiyye*], while it used to be the ruling religious community [*millet-i hâkime*], has [now] been deprived of such a sacred right. For the people of Islam, this is a day to weep and mourn."[28]

Though the overwhelming majority of Armenian leaders wished to work within the Ottoman system, on a number of discrete occasions they made overtures to the Russians and the British. In 1872 merchants in Van requested that the Russian government send a consul to their city to guarantee "the safety of trade routes and protection of religion, lives, and goods of the down-trodden Christian people of Vaspurakan."[29] Six years later, in the aftermath of the war with Russia, the Patriarch Nerses Varjabedian made contact with the Russians at San Stefano and sent Khrimian to Berlin to plead the Armenian case before the Great Powers. When the Russians were forced by Europe to retreat from their demands on Turkey, the Patriarch attempted to interpret the new role taken by Britain as the principal protector of the Ottoman state in the most positive light. These overtures to the Great Powers, along with the Western styles affected by some wealthy Armenians, conspired to create in the minds of many Turks an image of an alien population within an Islamic empire.

Not only were Armenians prominent in urban trades and crafts, finance and international commerce, but their superior economic position allowed them to buy up large landholdings in eastern Anatolia and Cilicia from the 1870s on.[30] Once the sultan permitted non-Muslims and foreigners to buy Muslim lands (1856), Armenians and Greeks began purchasing properties that Muslim debtors could no longer pay for. Armenian emigrants to America and Europe sent home their savings and on their return brought new machines and technology to their farms. At the same time Muslim refugees from the Caucasus and the Balkans, displaced by the Russian victory in the North Caucasus and the independence of the Balkan states, migrated to Anatolia, and an intense competition for land developed. Petitions to the government and the Armenian Patriarchate enumerate hundreds of cases of Muslim usurpation of Armenian lands. The state most often supported Muslim claimants, and many Armenians reluctantly moved to the towns. Only after the 1908 revolution were they able to renew efforts to return to their lands.

The self-narration by Armenian nationalists of the Armenian experience in the Ottoman Empire was of a people conquered by foreign invaders, made captive in their own ancient land, oppressed by unjust and cruel rulers, yet all the while maintaining their essential Armenian religious culture and yearning to be free. As with other nationalist constructions, Armenian writers emphasized the continuity of the national self moving through time, overcoming adversities, martyred for the faith, victimized by a government imposed upon them. As historians and novelists melded together discrete and disjointed events into a coherent story that was almost always about the nation, they argued that the empire was an illegitimate and archaic polity that prevented the full expression of the nation's aspirations. Writers translated the defense of Christianity against the Persians in the fifth century by Vartan Mamikonian into a defense of nation and fatherland, so that the story was less about religious martyrdom and salvation after death and more about national resurrection in this life. Resistance by local Armenians (sometimes in alliance with non-Armenians!) of Zeitun in Cilicia to protect tax exemptions granted more than 200 years earlier by the seventeenth-century Sultan Murad IV were scripted in a more modern idiom of rights and national oppression.[31] The local was turned into the all-national. Social bandits and brigands, like Avo near Van or Arabo and Micho near Taron, became rebels and freedom-fighters.[32] The very creation of a coherent national narrative that effaced the complexities of interethnic coexistence within the empire and stigmatized the kind of cosmopolitan adjustment to imperial life in which the Armenian merchants had flourished and Armenian Christianity had maintained its authority reinforced the sense of difference between Turks and Armenians. What had been burdensome in the past became intolerable in the present. The arbitrary rule of Islamic conquerors was now impossible to justify. In the new paradigm of liberalism and national self-determination, the Ottoman Empire was marked by social lawlessness and a predatory state that thwarted the "natural laws" of economic competition. Distance between peoples increased; borders between them hardened; and sharing in the commonalties of Ottoman culture and life became suspect on both sides. By the late nineteenth century both the nationalists in their narration of the past and present and the defenders of the Ottoman state interpreted events through the prism of the nation.

While Armenian clerics taught submission and deference and often allied with state authorities to persecute those modernizing intellectuals who attempted to bring Western enlightenment to young Armenians, Abdul Hamid II brought the reform period of the Tanzimat to an end and eliminated moderate and liberal alternatives within the system. The sultan created a system of personal, autocratic rule and centralized power within the palace. Both Christians and Turks who opposed the "bloody sultan" saw the restoration of the 1876 constitution as a principal political goal. By the 1880s a significant minority of Armenians, many of them from Russian Transcaucasia, conceived of revolution as the only means to protect and promote the Armenians. A new idea of the Armenian nation as secular, cultural, and based on language as well as shared history challenged the older clerical understanding of Armenians as an ethnoreligious community centered on faith and membership in the Armenian Apostolic Church. Faced by what they saw as the imminent danger of national disintegration, the Armenian radicals turned toward "self-defense," the formation of revolutionary political parties, and political actions that would encourage

Western or Russian intervention into Ottoman affairs. For the young nationalists revolution was the "logical conclusion" of the impossibility of significant reforms coming from the state.[33]

Small self-defense circles formed in the Armenian provincial communities in the 1880s —among them, Bashtban Hairenyats (Defense of the Fatherland) in Erzerum in 1881-1882 and Sev Khach (Black Cross) in Van in 1882. Portugalian's *Armenia*, published in Marseilles in 1885, called for Armenian independence, and its message inspired young people who formed two small parties, the Armenakans [pro-Armenians] in Van and the Hnchaks [Tocsin party], founded in Geneva. The tens, sometimes hundreds, of people in small, scattered groups were thought of as a "movement," with all the attendant connotations of coherence, coordination, and progress. But the national revolutionary intellectuals, influenced by European nationalism and Russian populism, found it extremely difficult to activate the Ottoman Armenian peasantry, their chosen constituency.[34] Abdul Hamid's alliance with Kurdish notables and the formation of the Hamidiye regiments in the eastern provinces made a bad situation worse for the Armenians. By the time a third—and eventually dominant—Armenian revolutionary party, the Hai Heghapoghakan Dashnaktsutiun, emerged in the 1890s; rather than being equal subjects in an Ottoman state, Armenians had become the double victims of state authorities and local Kurdish lords. Rather than reform, repression became the government's preferred strategy for maintaining the decaying imperial arrangement.

In 1894 Armenian refusal to pay taxes to Kurdish lords led to clashes between Kurds and Armenians in Sassun, the intervention of state troops, and the killing of hundreds of Armenians. Abdul Hamid decided to deal with the Armenian Question "not by reform but by blood."[35] This violence would later be read by Armenians as the first stage of a series of massacres that would culminate in the genocide of 1915. But unlike the genocide, these massacres in eastern Anatolia in 1894 to1896, which were largely carried out by Kurdish tribes and local lords, were part of an effort by the state to restore the old equilibrium in interethnic relations, in which the subject peoples accepted with little overt questioning the dominance of the Ottoman Muslim elite. That equilibrium, however had already been upset by the sultan's own policies of centralization and bureaucratization, as well as his strategic alliance with Muslim Kurds against Christian Armenians. This Pan-Islamic policy, which was institutionalized in the formation of irregular Hamidiye units of armed Kurds, helped to undermine the customary system of

imperial rule as much as did the emerging revisioning of nationality borrowed from the West.[36]

In his later memoirs Abdul Hamid sketched his private feelings
about the Armenians, gendering them womanly and cowardly.

> Although it is impossible to deny that the Armenians dwelling in our
> eastern provinces are a great many times well founded in their com-
> plaints, it is fitting to say also that they exaggerate. Armenians look as
> if they are crying for a pain they don't feel at all. Hiding behind the
> great powers, they are a nation [*millet*] who raise an outcry for the
> smallest of causes and are cowardly and coy like a woman. Just to the
> contrary, Kurds are strong and quarrelsome. ... In those regions
> [*buralarda*] the Kurds have always been considered the gentlemen and
> the Armenians the male servants [*suak*, also boy, youth].

In a memorandum to the British, the sultan defended his actions as
necessary for maintaining order:

> His Imperial Majesty treated the Armenians with justice and modera-
> tion, and, as long as they behaved properly, all toleration would be
> shown to them, but he had given orders that when they took to revolt
> or to brigandage the authorities were to deal with them as they dealt
> with the authorities.[37]

The Sultan's language would be repeated by other officials and
would echo in the justifications of the Young Turks and the apolo-
gist historians who would later attempt to reconceive state-initiated
massacres as "necessary," figments of Armenian imagination, or a
Muslim-Christian civil war. Yet the continuity in the rhetoric about
these events should not obscure the difference between Abdul
Hamid's essentially conservative and restorationist policy toward
unruly subjects and the Young Turks' far more revolutionary
attempt to remove surgically a major irritant.

The revolutionary nationalism of the Armenian committees and
parties was exaggerated by both the revolutionaries themselves and
by their opponents. While they struggled to convince villagers of the
"Armenian cause" and threatened businessmen who refused to contribute to their movement, the Armenian nationalists were forced to
rely on a handful of activists, many from Persia and Russia. They
engaged in a number of spectacular activities, culminating in the
seizure of the Imperial Ottoman Bank in August 1896, but this revolutionary act was followed by riots and massacres in the city that
left six thousand Armenians dead. As repression of revolutionary
demonstrations in Istanbul and of Anatolian peasants in the mid-
1890s seemed to confirm the analysis of the nationalists, their read-

ing of the Armenians' position in the empire was more broadly accepted. But the number of militants remained small and divided. The Hnchak party, Marxist in orientation, lost influence after a devastating schism in its ranks in 1896, and the Dashnaktsutiun now became the leading Armenian political party, both in the Ottoman and Romanov empires. Its program was directed, not toward separatism and independence, but in favor of autonomy within a democratic federation. In the period after 1908, the Armenians elected socialists, liberals, and nationalists to the Ottoman Parliament, where they collaborated with (and competed with) the Young Turks. Resented by the more conservative clerical and merchant leaders in Constantinople whom they displaced over time, the revolutionary nationalists became the de facto leaders of a nation that they had helped to create through their teaching, writing, and sacrifice. The leading party, the Dashnaktsutiun, made it clear in its ten-point "Platform" (December 1908) that it was in favor of "Turkish Armenia [as] an inalienable part of the empire, reorganized in accordance with the principle of decentralization."[38] Their commitment to the territorial integrity of the empire, however, did not protect the Armenians from accusations of separatism and subversion.

Social differentiation among *millets* and the resultant tensions existed throughout the nineteenth century, but the frames in which they were given meaning changed. The inferior status of Muslims in the industrial and commercial world generated resentment toward Armenians and foreigners. Ottoman westernizers recognized that the Muslims were the least prepared of the *millets* to adopt Western ways and would require the state to assist their progress. To religious Muslims the visibility of better-off Armenians in the capital and towns appeared as an intolerable reversal of the traditional Muslim-*dhimmi* hierarchy that, in turn, increased resentment toward Christians. Turkish patriots constructed Armenians as disloyal subjects suspiciously sympathetic to Europeans. Whatever resentment the poor peasant population of eastern Anatolia may have felt toward the people in towns—the places where they received low prices for their produce, where they felt their social inferiority most acutely, where they were alien to and unwanted by the better-dressed people—was easily transferred to the Armenians.[39] In a particularly toxic mix, religion, anxiety about class status, xenophobia, and general insecurity about the impersonal transformations of modern life combined to create resentment and hostility toward the Armenians.[40]

Yet ethnic differences, hostility, and even conflict need not have become genocidal. That would require a major strategic decision by elites in power. Though Abdul Hamid used violence to keep his Armenian subjects in line, he did not consider the use of mass deportation to change the demographic composition of Anatolia. He remained a traditional imperial monarch prepared to use persecution when persuasion failed to maintain the unity as well as the multiplicity and diversity of his empire. More fundamental ideological shifts took place before the images of Armenians as subversive and alien appeared absolutely incompatible with the empire as it was being reconceived.

The Young Turks and the "Modernizing" Empire

Closely attached to the discourse on the nation is a narrative of a necessary, if not inevitable, progress from "traditional" society to modern. Western-language writing on the late Ottoman period has been heavily influenced by the theories and language of modernization that have constructed a teleological tale leading to national revolution. Indeed, Kemalist Turkey has been an exemplar in social science literature of a relatively successful process of modernization, with a Western-style political system, a secularized culture, and capitalist economic development. Part of the modernization process in the Turkish case was the redefinition of the political community from a multinational one in which Islam gave authority to the rulers to one based on an ethnically homogeneous nation that would frequently be defined in terms of "race." In the words of the distinguished social scientist S. N. Eisenstadt, "The Turkish revolution completely rejected the religious basis of legitimation and attempted instead to develop a secular national one as the major ideological parameter of the new collectivity."[41]

But this shift from religion to ethnicity or race can be read more darkly than in the optimistic theories of modernization. In the second half of the nineteenth century Turkic intellectuals, both in the Ottoman and Russian empires, stimulated interest in a new conception of a Turkish nation. Responding to the works of European orientalists who discussed an original Turkic or Turanian race, men like Ismail Gasprinskii in Crimea, Mirza Fethali Akhundov in Transcaucasia, and Huseynizade Ali Bey from Baku, attempted to teach pride in being Turkish and speaking a Turkic language. Identification with a supranational community of Turks distinguished the "race" or "nation" of the Turks from the multinational Ottoman state.[42] Yet inherent in that identity with the Turkic was a confusion about the boundaries of the nation and the location and limits of the fatherland *(vatan)*. Was the homeland of the Turks Anatolia or the somewhat mystical Turan of Central Asia?

Several scholars have traced the roots of Kemalist Turkish nationalism back to the late Ottoman period, their discussion has focused exclusively on intellectuals and has revealed little about a popular response to nationalist or Pan-Turanian ideas. In a population in which multiple identifications competed, such as religion, ethnicity, empire, or subnational communities, like tribes, clans, or regions, an ambiguity about what constitutes the nation thwarts (or at least delays) the development of a strong and coherent nationalism. In the late Ottoman Empire allegiance to the "nation" of Turks was quite weak. The word "Turk," which referred to the lower classes of rural Anatolia, was in the nineteenth century contrasted to "Ottoman," a term usually reserved for the ruling elite, and Islam probably had a far more positive valence among ordinary Turks than identity with being Turkish. There were signs of change, however, in the latter part of the century, and the shift came from the top down. The Ottoman constitution of 1876 established Turkish as the official state language and required members of government and parliament to know Turkish. At the turn of the century Young Turk nationalists like Ahmed Riza began to substitute the word Turk for Ottoman.[43] Though Ottomanist views remained dominant among the first generation of Young Turk intellectuals, rival visions of the future led to tensions between the dominant Turks and the non-Turkish *millets* and reduced the commitment to Ottomanism.

The Turkish revolutionary elite at the turn of the century, including those that emerged from the Young Turk committees to lead the Kemalist movement, grew out of an intellectual milieu that exalted science, rejected religion, and borrowed freely from Western sociology. Influenced by the ideas of Charles Darwin, Claude Bernard, Ludwig Buchner, even the phrenology of Gustave Le Bon (who "proved" that intellectuals have larger craniums by doing research in Parisian millinery shops), "the Young Turk ideology was originally 'scientific,' materialist, social Darwinist, elitist, and vehemently antireligious; it did not favor representative government."[44] Neither liberals nor constitutionalists, the Young Turks were étatists who saw themselves as continuing the work of the Tanzimat reformers—Mustafa Reshid Pasha, Mustafa Fazil Pasha, Midhat Pasha—and the work of the Young Ottomans. According to Sukru Hanioglu, the historian of its early years, "The Young Turk movement was unquestionably a link in the chain of the Ottoman modernization movement as well as representing the modernist wing of the Ottoman bureaucracy."[45] Earlier, Ottoman Westernizers had hoped to secure Western technology without succumbing to Western culture, somehow to preserve Islam but make the empire technologically and militarily competitive with the West. Reform had always come from above, from Westernizing statesmen and bureaucrats, a response to a sense that the empire had to change or collapse. The Young Turks shared those values, but steadily they added new elements of nationalism to their imperial étatism.

The first generation of Turkish revolutionaries were divided in their attitudes toward working with Armenians in a common struggle. After Damad Mahmud Pasha, brother-in-law of Abdul Hamid, fled to Europe with his two sons, he made an agreement with the Dashnaks and published an open letter urging joint action. The Dashnak newspaper, *Droshak*, wrote: "Dashnaktsutiun would not accept the re-establishment of the Constitution of Midhat as a solution of the Turkish problem, but looks to a democratic federative policy as the way out." The Armenian party "would fortify the Young Turks if first it received a guarantee that the situation of the peoples would be bettered."[46] The more liberal Young Turks believed that an alliance with the Armenians would reap a favorable response in Western Europe. But the dual issue of an alliance with the Armenians and inviting European intervention to secure the end of autocracy in the empire exposed the ultimately unresolved tension among Young Turk activists between their ecumenical Ottomanist impulses and the growing influence of an exclusivist Turkish nationalism.

On February 4, 1902, the First Congress of the Ottoman Opposition opened in Paris. The nationalist minority at the Congress, led by Ahmed Riza, categorically rejected foreign intervention and special arrangements for the Armenians in the six eastern Anatolian *vilayets* (provinces), while the majority, led by Sabahaddin Bey, favored such concessions as a basis for an Armenian-Turkish alliance. When the majority came out in favor of mediation by the Great Powers to implement the treaties that the absolutist regime refused to execute, the minority essentially broke with the rest of the movement. Efforts by the majority to appease the minority failed. The Armenian delegates submitted a declaration that the Armenian committees were ready to collaborate with the Ottoman liberals to transform the present regime; that outside of common action, the committees would continue their own efforts with the understanding that their actions were directed against the present regime and not against "the unity and the organic existence of Turkey"; and that their particular actions would be directed toward implementation of Article 61 of the Treaty of Berlin and the Memorandum of May 11, 1895, and its annex.[47]

Mutual suspicions were high between the Armenians and the Turkish opposition, and the Armenian activists could conceive of collaboration only with the implementation of special reforms in the east guaranteed by Europe. For many Turks this was an outrageous demand. As Ismail Kemal, a member of the majority, put it: "I recognize you not as an independent element but as Ottomans. You have rights as Ottomans. [However,] you do not have the right to bargain with us and make offers as if you were [representatives of a] state."[48] In response to this statement, the Armenians walked out of the congress. Only later, after the Armenians sent a letter to Sabahaddin stating that they "were ready to participate in all efforts to overthrow the present regime" and that "they did not oppose the establishment of a constitutional central administration that would execute" special reforms for the six provinces, was a compromise reached between the majority and the Armenians.[49] The Young Turks even agreed that an Armenian was to sit on their central committee. Ominously for the Armenians, however, it was the minority at the Congress, not the majority, that actually represented the more powerful, even dominant, tendency in most of the Young Turk committees and newspapers.

Most analysts agree that in the first decade of the twentieth century there was a significant shift among the Young Turks from an Ottomanist orientation, in which emphasis was on equality among the *millets* within a multinational society that continued to recognize difference, to a more nationalist position in which the superiority of the ethnic Turks (already implicit in Ottomanism itself) and their privileged position within the state was more explicitly underlined.[50] In the years after the Paris Congress, a Turkish nationalism based on linguistic ties among Turkic peoples and notions of a common race spread among Turkic intellectuals, like Yusuf Akcura, outside of the Ottoman Empire and influenced those within. After the 1908 coup that brought the Young Turks to power, a number of small nationalist organizations were formed that put out occasional newspapers or *journals—Türk Dernegi, Genç Kalemler, Türk Yurdu,* and *Turk Ocagi*—in which the conception of a Turkish nation extended far beyond the Ottoman Turks or Anatolian Turks to a Pan-Turkic ideal celebrating the ties between all the Turkic peoples stretching from Anatolia through the Caucasus to Central Asia. This was expressed most vividly in Ziya Gokalp's famous poem "Turan:"

The fatherland for Turks is not Turkey, nor yet Turkestan,
The fatherland is a vast and eternal land: Turan!

Many of the Turanists argued for a purified Ottoman Turkish language, freed of Arabic and Persian words, that would serve as the
language of this Turkic nation and also serve as the official language for the non-Turkic peoples of the empire, those that made up
the Ottoman *millets*. The Young Turk government passed resolutions reaffirming Turkish as the official language of the empire,
requiring all state correspondence to be carried on in Turkish, and
establishing Turkish as the language for teaching in elementary and
higher education, with local languages to be taught in secondary
schools. Not surprisingly, the Young Turk promotion of Turkish
was seen by non-Turks as a deliberate program of Turkification.[51]
Not only Greeks and Armenians, but Arabs as well, resisted some
of the modernizing programs of the CUP that at one and the same
time attempted to universalize rules and obligations for all peoples
of the empire and threatened to undermine the traditional privi-
leges and autonomies enjoyed under the *millet* system.

Turkish nationalism, Pan-Turanism, Pan-Islamism, and Ottomanism were all part of a complex, confusing discussion among
Turkish intellectuals about the future of the Ottoman state and the
"nation." Uncomfortable with the supranational ideal of Ottomanism, the Turkish nationalists criticized the thrust of the universalism
of the Tanzimat reforms. Gokalp tried to clarify the differences:

> If the aim of Ottomanism *(Osmanlilik)* was a *state*, all the subjects
> would actually be members of this state. But if the aim was to construct
> a new *nation* whose language was the Ottoman language *(Osmanlica)*,
> the new nation would be a Turkish nation, since the Ottoman language
> was no other than Turkish.[52]

Four choices were possible for the empire after 1908: either to
remain an empire dominated by Turks, subordinating the non-Turks,
and perhaps expanding eastward to integrate other Turkic peoples
into a Turanian empire; or to transform the empire along Pan-Islamic
lines, allying Turks with Kurds and Arabs; or to adopt the program of
the Ottomanists and become an egalitarian multinational state with
the different religious and ethnonational communities within it constituting a single civil nation of Ottomans; or, finally, to cease to be an
empire altogether and become an ethnonational state of the Turks.
This last option was not yet clearly envisioned, for it would require
both the dismemberment of the empire state, the loss of the Arab territories, and the physical removal of millions of Armenians, Greeks,

and Kurds from Anatolia. Though the Ottomanist option remained part of the official rhetoric up to World War I, it was gradually abandoned by the leading theorists and activists among the Young Turks. Yet even after the coup of 1913, the triumvirate of Enver, Talaat, and Jemal Pasha never completely agreed on a clear ideological orientation and wavered among Ottomanism, the Pan-Turanian form of Turkish nationalism, and Pan-Islamism.[53] As Sir Harry Luke noted,

> [Enver] and his colleagues envisaged the three policies being pursued simultaneously and side by side, each one being emphasized in whatever place, at whatever time, it was the most appropriate policy to apply. Ottomanism continued to be the keynote of internal politics; Turkish nationalism, the keynote of relations with the Tatars of Russia, some of whom were beginning to manifest sentiments of sympathy with their cousins in Turkey in their time of trouble; Pan-Islam, that of relations with the Arabs and other non-Turkish Moslems within the Empire and of the Moslem peoples of North Africa and elsewhere outside it.[54]

The Pan-Turanian form of Turkic nationalism seemed to key leaders to offer the most effective alternative for preserving the empire and the political hegemony of the Turks. This steady shift toward Turkism and Pan-Turanism presented the Armenian political leadership with an extraordinarily difficult choice—remaining in alliance with the increasingly nationalist Young Turks or breaking decisively with the government. The Dashnaktsutiun decided to continue working with the Young Turks, while the Armenian Church leaders and the liberal Ramkavar party distanced themselves from the government party. Even when the Marxist Hnchaks denounced the Young Turks for their steady move away from Ottomanism toward Turkism and their failure to carry out agricultural and administrative reforms, the Dashnaks maintained their electoral alliance with the CUP. When war broke out in 1914, the Ottoman Dashnaks pledged to fight for the empire and to urge Ottoman Armenians to join the Ottoman army, while across the border Russian Armenians, also influenced by the Dashnaktsutiun, volunteered for the tsarist army. Armenians found themselves in armies on both sides of the Caucasian front, and high officials of both empires harbored suspicions of Armenian disloyalty. But only one government decided to act preemptively to rid itself of its Armenian "problem."[55]

From Ethnic Hostility to Genocide

The prevalence of a nationalist template among Armenian and Turkish leaders at the end of the Ottoman period reinforced and essentialized differences between the peoples of the empire. To a considerable degree, religious distinctions were transmuted by both the Armenians and the Turks into national and racial differences, far more indelible and immutable than religion. At the same time economic competition in a hard economic environment and struggles among Turks, Kurds, and Armenians over the limited resource of land intensified interethnic tensions. Stereotypes on both sides had long existed, but changes in relative status, particularly the perceived reversal of the Muslim-*dhimmi* hierarchy, created the kinds of fear and anxiety about the future than political entrepreneurs could exploit. Ultimately, however, the launching of genocidal violence in 1915 came, not from the transmutation of identities and the accompanying stereotypes, not from the accumulating tensions, but from the initiative of the state.

The Young Turk leaders' suspicions about Armenians as subversives intensified with the initial defeats of the Ottomans in the Sarikamish campaign of the winter of 1914. In the context of an imminent collapse of the empire in 1915, with the Russians threatening in the east and the Australians and British landing at Gallipoli, the Young Turk government decided to demobilize Armenian soldiers, attack the villages around Van and then the city itself, arrest Armenian intellectuals and parliamentarians in Istanbul (April 24, 1915), and order the deportations of their Armenian subjects. The state removed all legal restraints on violence toward Armenians, indeed encouraged theft and murder, punished those who protected the Armenians, and created a cycle of violence that grew from the local to the whole of eastern and central Anatolia.

Though some Armenian historians have argued that the genocide was the final stage in a long history of Turkish oppression and massacre of Armenians, [56] with the implication that mass murder was part of a widespread and popular exterminationist mentality, my own sense is that the intensifying hostility toward Armenians need not have reached the proportions of a genocide, save for the initiation and encouragement of the state in the context of war. Rather than a long-planned and carefully orchestrated program of extermination, the Armenian genocide was more a vengeful and determined act of suppression that turned into a opportunistic policy to rid Anatolia of Armenians once and for all, eliminate the wedge that they provided for foreign intervention in the region, and open the way for the fantastic dreams of a Turanian empire.

Ultimately all discussion of the historical differentiations that created a climate of hatred between Armenians and Turks provides only an understanding of the environment in which the genocide took place and why its particular brutality was possible. It provides a necessary but not sufficient cause for genocide. To understand why mass killings over vast spaces occurred, why the government initiated the arrests and deportations and allowed the murders to go on for months, requires a knowledge of the decision-making processes within the highest government circles that historians do not yet have. When the archives are fully opened, and if they have not been cleansed of incriminating documents, historians should not be surprised to find not a single decision to deport the Armenians but a series of decisions, one more radical than the other, that fed on each other until demobilization and sporadic executions and repressions turned inexorably into a massive program of physical extermination. While it is impossible as yet to be conclusive about the orders given, it is possible to recreate the political and intellectual atmosphere in which the key decisions were taken.

The Committee of Union and Progress had experienced a series of foreign policy blows in the years leading up to World War I: the loss in 1908 of Bosnia-Herzegovina to Austro-Hungary; the takeover in 1911 to 1912 of Libya and Rhodes by Italy; the independence of Albania in 1912, and the defeats in the First Balkan War (1912 to 1913) that led to the loss of much of European Turkey. In the age of nationalism, nationalism had only worked against the Ottoman Empire, and the Young Turks seemed to understand that the Turks also had to become something like a nation in order to remain a viable power in the ruthlessly competitive world of imperial Europe.[57] But the empire could not become a single ethnonation. It could be strengthened, however, by drawing together the Islamic peoples, Kurds, Arabs, and Turks; expanding to the east to include other Turkic peoples; and physically eliminating the most alien, dangerous, and disloyal of the Ottoman peoples.

The Ottoman government also needed a powerful ally as Europe moved toward war, but all of its approaches were rebuffed. Only when the Kaiser himself intervened did the German ambassador to the Porte, Hans von Wangenheim, conclude a defensive alliance with the Turks. When war broke out, the Turks declared their neutrality, despite entreaties from the Germans, and took the opportunity to take over German ships in the Black Sea, abrogate the capitulations that foreign powers had enjoyed in Turkey, and make all foreigners on Turkish soil subject to Turkish laws and courts. After the Germans paid the Young Turks two million Turkish pounds in gold, the triumvirs agreed to enter the war. A provocation against the Russians—the shelling of the Russian coast by one of the formerly German ships—led to a Russian declaration of war on Turkey on November 2, 1914.

Late in December, Enver took command of the Caucasian front and within weeks suffered a catastrophic defeat at Sarikamish. Eighty-six percent of the Ottoman Army of one hundred thousand troops was lost. A few weeks later Jemal Pasha was stopped by the British at the Suez Canal as he tried to move from Palestine into Egypt. Jemal, who had ordered all foreign Jews out of Palestine only to have to withdraw the order when the Germans and Americans protested, was driven back into Syria. Russia controlled the Black Sea, the British and French the Mediterranean, and late in February 1915 British and Imperial troops began their campaign in the Dardanelles. It was in this context of desperation and defeat that, beginning in the first months of 1915, the Ottoman authorities demobilized Armenian soldiers from the Ottoman Army, at first organizing them into work brigades and then forcing them to dig their own graves before being shot. As rumors spread of Turkish violence against Armenian villagers, Armenians in Van organized to protect themselves in April. Their activity was painted as a revolutionary uprising, and fighting broke out in the streets. The advancing Russians took the city, but those Armenians who lived behind Turkish lines now became the targets of a massive campaign to remove them from the region. To prevent any further organized resistance by the Armenians, the Ottoman government rounded up the leading Armenian intellectuals, political leaders, and even members of the Ottoman parliament in Istanbul and exiled them from the capital on April 24, the date that later would be commemorated as genocide day. Most of them perished at the hands of the authorities.

The argument often employed by Turkish leaders to German and other Western diplomats who inquired about and protested against the treatment of the Armenians was that the precarious condition of the empire and the requirements of self-defense of the state justified the repression of "rebellion." In a telling interview with the American ambassador, Henry Morgenthau, Talaat conveyed the complex of reasons that influenced the decision to eliminate Anatolian Armenians. "I have asked you to come today," began Talaat, "so that I can explain our position on the whole Armenian subject. We base our objections to the Armenians on three distinct grounds. In the first place, they have enriched themselves at the expense of the Turks. In the second place, they are determined to domineer over us and to establish a separate state. In the third place, they have openly encouraged our enemies."[58] In his own terms, the Grand Vizier spoke of the status reversal of Armenians and Turks ("they have enriched themselves at the expense of the Turks" and "are determined to domineer over us"), the government's fear of Armenian separatism and the breakup of the empire, and the collaboration of Armenians with the Russians.

In his posthumously published memoirs Talaat revealed the thinking of the state authorities at the moment of decision and how the deportations escalated into mass killing that involved ordinary civilians. Though he attempts to apologize for unintended excesses, he tells more about the motivations for mass killing than more recent apologists have.

> The Porte, acting under the same obligation, and wishing to secure the safety of its army and its citizens, took energetic measures to check these uprisings. The deportation of the Armenians was one of these preventive measures.
>
> I admit also that the deportation was not carried out lawfully everywhere. In some places unlawful acts were committed. The already existing hatred among the Armenians and Mohammedans, intensified by the barbarous activities of the former, had created many tragic consequences. Some of the officials abused their authority, and in many places people took preventive measures into their own hands and innocent people were molested. I confess it. I confess, also, that the duty of the Government was to prevent these abuses and atrocities, or at least to hunt down and punish their perpetrators severely. In many places, where the property and goods of the deported people were looted, and the Armenians molested, we did arrest those who were responsible and punished them according to the law. I confess, however, that we ought to have acted more sternly, opened up a general investigation for the purpose of finding out all the promoters and looters and punished them severely. ...
>
> The Turkish elements here referred to were shortsighted, fanatical, and yet sincere in their belief. The public encouraged them, and they had the general approval behind them. They were numerous and strong. ...
>
> Their open and immediate punishment would have aroused great discontent among the people, who favored their acts. An endeavor to arrest and to punish all those promoters would have created anarchy in Anatolia at a time when we greatly needed unity. It would have been dangerous to divide the nation into two camps, when we needed strength to fight outside enemies.[59]

The murder of Armenians was not motivated primarily by religious fanaticism, though distinctions based on religion played a role. Religion, even as it progressively mutated into an ethnic distinction, remained a principal marker of difference. While most victims of the massacres were condemned to deportation or worse because of their ethnoreligious identification, there were many cases in which people were saved from death or deportation when they converted to Islam.[60] The identity of Armenians for the Turks was not as indelibly fixed as the identity of Jews would be in the racist imagination of the Nazis. Still, the collective stereotypes of Armenians as grasping and mercenary, subversive and disloyal, turned them into a alien and unsympathetic category that then could be eliminated.

In yet another memoir of a Turkish leader, this one written after his trial and conviction for crimes committed during the massacres and just before his suicide, the Young Turk governor of Diarbekir in 1915, Resid Bey, draws a vivid picture of the chaos that accompanied the deportations.[61] As the Russians approached and order in the city disintegrated, Armenians, encouraged by the revolutionary committees, refused to be drafted. By this time, the events at Van had already occurred, and Armenians were preparing for the worst. Muslims expected vengeful attacks by Armenians. The governor sent troops into Armenian homes and discovered caches of arms. At this point, he writes, he received the "temporary law" *(Muvakkat Kanuni)* of May 27, 1915, that ordered deportation of the Armenians. He complained that there were not instructions on how to carry out the expulsions or which Armenians to deport. At first he deported only the men but then was ordered to send all Armenians into exile. With inadequate troops and no planning or provisions, the governor relied on Circassian gendarmes, decommissioned soldiers from the Balkan wars, and local recruits from the peasantry and *esnaf* class. Thousands of Armenians deported from Bitlis, Kharput, and Trabizond passed through Diarbekir province. Looters and pillagers set upon them, following the Armenians for days to pick up what they could. Like Talaat, Resid Bey claims that an orderly deportation was impossible, particularly in the face of angry and frightened Muslims. Even as he turned the homes of exiled Armenians over to Muslims, they destroyed the houses in a mad search for hidden wealth. What is most vivid in this somewhat apologetic and self-serving account is the weakness and disorganization of the state authorities and the massive participation of ordinary people in the looting and killing.

By the end of the war, 90 percent of Ottoman Armenians were gone, killed, deported to the deserts of Syria, or refugees in the Caucasus or Middle East. The number of dead is staggering—somewhere between six hundred thousand and one million killed in the more conservative estimates—and the event shocked European and American opinion. In the 1930s writers spoke of the Armenian "holocaust," and in the early 1940s when he invented the word "genocide," Raphael Lemkin applied it to two twentieth-century events—the Turkish deportation and massacres of the Armenians in 1915 and the German annihilation of Europe's Jews.

Conclusion

The Armenian genocide was a central event in the last stages of the dissolution of the Ottoman Empire. After centuries of governing the Armenians as a separate ethnoreligious community, the *Ermeni millet*, and conceiving of them as the "loyal *millet*," the Ottoman state authorities and Turkish political elites, including the Young Turks, began to see Armenians as an alien people, framed in the growing discourse of nationalism as disloyal, subversive, "separatist," and a threat to the unity of the empire. This perception was compounded more broadly by anxiety about the relative economic success of Armenian businessmen and craftsmen, the competition for limited economic resources, particularly land, among Kurds, Turks, and Armenians in eastern Anatolia, and a sense that Armenian progress was reversing the traditional imperial status hierarchy with Muslims above the *dhimmi*. Traditionally the Ottoman Empire had used its military power ruthlessly to repress those they perceived to be rebellious, e.g., the Bulgarians, Shi'ite Arabs, as well as policies of physical removal, deportation *(surgun)*. Abdul Hamid II used massacres in the 1890s to attempt to restore the traditional imperial order that his own policies of bureaucratic centralization and reduction of local power were undermining. He ended the Tanzimat reforms aimed at an Ottomanist equality among all the sultan's subjects and adopted a Pan-Islamic policy (the *Hamidiye*) of allying with the Kurds against the Armenians that further alienated the Armenians and encouraged a minority among them to turn toward revolution.

After coming to power, the Young Turks turned gradually away from Ottomanism toward Turkism, Pan-Islamism, and Pan-Turanism in an effort to find new formulas for legitimizing and stabilizing the disintegrating empire. In the first year of World War I they suffered a series of defeats in the east that convinced them of an imminent Armenian danger and decided to carry out a vicious policy of deportation and massacre to clear the region of Armenians. This policy was initiated by the state in the brutalizing context of war and became a massive campaign of murder, the first genocide of the twentieth century. Social hostilities between Armenians and Turks, Kurds and Armenians, fed the mass killings, which the state encouraged (or at least did little to discourage). More than any other instance of *surgun*, the genocide came to be seen as an opportunity to rid the empire of the Armenian problem, which had been used as a wedge by Russians and other Europeans to interfere in the Ottoman Empire. While nationalism and Pan-Turanism played a role in formulating the mood of the leaders who ordered the deportations, so did strategic notions and a perverse sense of justice and revenge against an internal threat.

The traditional imperial paradigm that had reigned in the Ottoman Empire was steadily undermined by a number of factors: the revolutionary changes in the West that rendered the Ottoman Empire a backward and vulnerable society; the attempt to modernize along western lines by the Tanzimat reformers; the differentially successful adaptations to modern life by different *millets*, with the Christians and Jews ahead of the Muslims; and the discourse of the nation that created new sources of political legitimation and undermined the traditional imperial ones. Largely marginalized in modern histories of the end of the Ottoman Empire, the events of 1915 have fallen into a "memory hole" between the Young Turk Revolution of 1908 and the Kemalist Revolution of 1919 to 1922. Nationalist readings and those by modernization theorists have, without confronting it, transformed an act of mass murder into a foundational moment of nation-building. The genocide of the Armenians took place between empire and nation-state, before the idea of an Anatolian nation-state for the Turks had developed, in the context of a last desperate attempt to save the empire in the age of nationalism. At the same time, however, the genocide provided a base for a Turkish republic in Anatolia, cleansing the now purported "homeland" of the Turks of one of their major competitors.

Notes

1. This chapter is an expanded version of an earlier essay that appeared in *The Armenian Forum*, no. 2. The author is grateful for the criticism and suggestions of Engin Deniz Akarli, Kenneth Church, Vahakn N. Dadrian, Natalie Zemon Davis, Selim Deringil, Fatma Müge Göçek, members of the Wilder House Editorial Board, and the students and faculty at Koç University in Istanbul.

2. For a discussion of the efforts to deny the Armenian genocide by constructing a theory of Armenian provocation, see Robert Melson, "A Theoretical Inquiry into the Armenian Massacres of 1894-1896," *Comparative Studies in Society and History*, XXIV, 3 (July 1982), pp. 481-509; and "Provocation or Nationalism: A Critical Inquiry into the Armenian Genocide of 1915," in Richard G. Hovannisian (ed.), *The Armenian Genocide in Perspective* (New Brunswick and Oxford: Transaction Books, 1986), pp. 61-84.

3. At two recent conferences—an SSRC workshop, "The End of Empire: Causes and Consequences," at the Harriman Institute, Columbia University, November 20-21, 1994; and a conference on "The Disintegration and Reconstitution of Empires: The USSR and Russia in Comparative Perspective," at the University of California, San Diego, January 10-12, 1996—papers by distinguished scholars Serif Mardin and Dankwart Rustow dealing with the collapse of the Ottoman Empire failed to mention the deportation and massacres of the Armenians. The papers have been published in the conference volumes: Serif Mardin, "The Ottoman Empire," in Karen Barkey and Mark von Hagen, *After Empire: Multiethnic Societies and Nation-Building: The Soviet Union and the Russian, Ottoman, and Habsburg Empires* (Boulder, CO: Westview Press, 1997), pp. 115-128; and Dankwart Rustow, "The Ottoman and Habsburg Empires," in Karen Dawisha and Bruce Parrott (eds.), *The End of Empire? The Transformation of the USSR in Comparative Perspective* (Armonk, NY: M. E. Sharpe, 1997), pp. 186-197.

4. Bernard Lewis, *The Emergence of Modern Turkey* (Oxford: Oxford University Press, 1961; 2nd edition, 1968), p. 356.

5. For the early Ottoman state, see Halil Inalcik, *The Ottoman Empire: The Classical Age 1300-1600* (New York and Washington: Praeger, 1973), especially pp. 65-118.

6. For discussion of the nation as "imagined community," see Benedict Anderson, *Imagined Communities, Reflections on the Origin and Spread of Nationalism* (London: Verso, 1983).

7. Eric J. Hobsbawm, *Nations and Nationalism Since 1780: Programme, Myth, Reality* (Cambridge: Cambridge University Press, 1990); Etienne Balibar, "The Nation Form: History and Ideology," in Etienne Balibar and Immanuel Wallerstein, *Race, Nation, Class: Ambiguous Identities* (London: Verso, 1991), pp. 86-106.

8. See, for example, Balibar, "The Nation Form" and Anderson, *Imagined Communities*.

9. The phrase is taken from the title of Prasenjit Duara's splendid study of China, *Rescuing History from the Nation: Questioning Narratives of Modern China* (Chicago: University of Chicago Press, 1995).

10. Aron Rodrigue, "Difference and Tolerance in the Ottoman Empire: Interview by Nancy Reynolds," *Stanford Humanities Review*, V, 1 (1995), p. 82.

11. Ibid.

12. Benjamin Braude and Bernard Lewis (eds.), *Christians and Jews in the Ottoman Empire: The Functioning of a Plural Society, Volume I: The Central Lands* (New York: Holmes and Meier, 1982).

13. Rodrigue, "Difference and Tolerance," p. 85.

14. Roderic Davison, "Nationalism as an Ottoman Problem and the Ottoman Response," in William W. Haddad and William Ochsenwald (eds.), *Nationalism in a Non-National State* (Columbus: Ohio State University Press, 1977), p. 36; Stepan Astourian, "Testing World-Systems Theory, Cilicia (1830s-1890s): Armenian-Turkish Polarization and the Ideology of Modern Ottoman Historiography" (Ph.D. diss., University of California at Los Angeles, 1996), p. 367.

15. While distinguishing the earlier centuries, wherein toleration and discrimination were far more common than persecution, from the nineteenth century, Rodrigue carefully treads the fine line between romanticizing Ottoman practices and reading the pre-modern experience in light of the later nationalist conceptualizations. Yet in emphasizing the element of tolerance, he, like Braude and Lewis, focuses less on the effects of discriminatory power on non-Muslims.

16. *Mair tsutsak haieren dzeragrats matendaranin Mekhitariants I Venetik*, vol. I (Venice, 1914), p. 321; cited in Gerard Libaridian, *The Ideology of Armenian Liberation. The Development of Armenian Political Movement Before the Revolutionary Movement (1639-1885)* (Ph.D. diss., University of California, Los Angeles, 1987), p. 31.

17. Quoted in M. K. Zulalian, *Armeniia v pervoi polovine XVI v.* (Moscow, 1971), p. 37.

18. "Rethinking the Unthinkable: Toward an Understanding of the Armenian Genocide," in Ronald Grigor Suny, *Looking Toward Ararat: Armenia in Modern History* (Bloomington, IN: Indiana University Press, 1993), p. 101.

19. I have explored the fragmented earlier self-images of Armenians in the introduction to *Looking Toward Ararat*, pp. 1-11.

20. "Minorities had to obey restrictions in the way they dressed and interacted in society. These restrictions prevented them from developing social ties with Muslims through marriage, inheritance, or attending the same places of worship and bathhouses. Instead, they developed social ties with other non-Muslims, who were either members of other Ottoman minorities or foreign residents of the empire, who were often connected to European embassies." (Fatma Müge Göçek, *Rise of the Bourgeoisie, Demise of Empire: Ottoman Westernization and Social Change* [New York and Oxford: Oxford University Press, 1996], p. 35.)

21. For an appreciative treatment of the Mekhitarists, see Kevork B. Bardakjian, *The Mekhitarist Contributions to Armenian Culture and Scholarship* (Cambridge, MA: Harvard College Library, 1976).

22. For an account of the development of the first secular intellectuals among Armenians, see Ronald Grigor Suny, "The Emergence of the Armenian Patriotic Intelligentsia in Russia," *Looking Toward Ararat*, pp. 52-62.

23. James Etmekjian, *The French Influence on the Western Armenian Renaissance* (New York: Twayne, 1964), p. 72.

24. Hagop Barsoumian, "Economic Role of the Armenian Amira Class in the Ottoman Empire," *The Armenian Review*, XXXI, 3-123 (March 1979), pp. 310-316.

25. Carter V. Findley, "The Acid Test of Ottomanism: The Acceptance of Non-Muslims in the Late Ottoman Bureaucracy," in Braude and Lewis (eds.), *Christians and Jews*, pp. 363-364.

26. The classic work on the Tanzimat is Roderic Davison, *Reform in the Ottoman Empire, 1856-76* (Princeton: Princeton University Press, 1963). See, also, his very useful essay, "*Millets* as Agents of Change in Nineteenth-Century Ottoman Empire," in Braude and Lewis, *Christians and Jews*, I, pp. 319-337.

27. Libaridian, *The Ideology of Armenian Liberation*, p. 191.

28. quoted in Stepan Astourian, "Testing World-Systems Theory, Cilicia (1830s-1890s)," pp. 394-395.

29. Libaridian, *The Ideology of Armenian Liberation*, pp. 145-146.

30. Astourian, "Testing World-Systems Theory, Cilicia (1830s-1890s)," pp. 552-563. See also, Donald Quataert, "The Commercialization of Agriculture in Ottoman Turkey, 1800-1914," *International Journal of Turkish Studies*, I, 2 (Autumn 1980), pp. 38-55.

31. On Zeitun, see Astourian, "Testing World-Systems Theory, Cilicia (1830s-1890s)," pp. 573-582.

32. This is the sense of much of the argumentation in Libaridian. For Armenian writers, divisions among Armenians are treated in two ways: either ignored altogether, so that the nation becomes a homogeneous whole or as an unfortunate deviance toward disunity that damaged the national cause. Libaridian, on the other hand, emphasizes class divisions among Armenians and proposes two forms of oppression on the people—by alien and incompetent Ottoman rulers and by the exploitative and self-interested Armenian upper classes, the clergy, rich merchants, and bankers. He inverts the usual treatment of the Church as the unifier and major force for preservation of Armenian culture and argues that the Church oppressed Armenians, not only through taxation and as political agents of the Porte, but through their hold on culture and education.

33. "Logical conclusion" comes from Libaridian.

34. See Ronald Grigor Suny, "Populism, Nationalism, and Marxism among Russia's Armenians," in *Looking Toward Ararat*, pp. 63-78.

35. The words are those of the sultan as conveyed by Grand Vizier Said Pasha when he fled to the British Embassy in December 1895. Quoted in Astourian, "Testing World-Systems Theory, Cilicia (1830s-1890s)," p. 606.

36. On state reform, interethnic relations, and economic developments in Abdul Hamid's reign, see Carter V. Findley, *Bureaucratic Reform in the Ottoman Empire: The Sublime Porte, 1789-1922* (Princeton: Princeton University Press, 1980); and Stephen Duguid, "The Politics of Unity: Hamidian Policy in Eastern Anatolia," *Middle Eastern Studies*, IX, 2 (May 1973), pp. 139-155; Donald Quataert, *Social Disintegration and Popular Resistance in the Ottoman Empire, 1881-1908* (New York and London: NYU Press, 1983).

37. Letter of Sir P. Currie to the Earl of Kimberley, Great Britain, Foreign Office, *Turkey, no. 1 (1895), (Part I) Correspondence Relating to the Asiatic Provinces of Turkey, Part I. Events at Sassoon, and Commission of Inquiry at Moush* (London, 1895), pp. 20-21.

38. Anahide Ter Minassian, "The Role of the Armenian Community in the Foundation and Development of the Socialist Movement in the Ottoman Empire and Turkey, 1876-1923," in Mete Tunçay and Erik J. Zürcher (eds.), *Socialism and Nationalism in the Ottoman Empire, 1876-1923* (London and New York: British Academic Press, 1994), p. 140.

39. Suny, *Looking Toward Ararat*, pp. 107, 108.

40. For a particularly telling reading of Turkish attitudes toward the *giaour* (unbeliever) and Armenians, see Stepan Astourian's analysis of Turkish proverbs in Astourian, "Testing World-Systems Theory, Cilicia (1830s-1890s)," pp. 409-431.

41. S. N. Eisenstadt, "The Kemalist Regime and Modernization: Some Compara-
     tive and Analytical Remarks," in Jacob M. Landau, *Ataturk and the Modern-
     ization of Turkey* (Boulder, CO: Westview Press, 1984), p. 9.
42. On the development of the separate nationalisms of the peoples of the
     Ottoman Empire, see Fatma Müge Göçek, "Decline of the Ottoman Empire
     and the Emergence of Greek, Armenian, Turkish and Arab Nationalisms,"
     unpublished paper.
43. M. Sukru Hanioglu, *The Young Turks in Opposition* (New York and Oxford:
     Oxford University Press, 1995), p. 216. This occurred around 1902 at the time
     of the Congress of Ottoman Oppositionists in Paris.
44. Ibid., p. 32.
45. Hanioglu, *The Young Turks in Opposition*, p. 17.
46. Ibid., p. 150.
47. Ibid., p. 193. "This text," writes Hanioglu, "reveals how antithetical the van-
     tage point of the members of the Armenian committees was to the rest of the
     movement and how they had divorced themselves from the notion of 'liberaux
     Ottomans' by emphasizing their willingness to work with them." (193) In my
     own reading, this Armenian declaration makes a clarification, which Saba-
     haddin Bey then declared had been accepted by the majority—that the clauses
     of the treaties signed by the Sublime Porte must be implemented.
48. Ibid., p. 195.
49. Ibid., p. 197.
50. See, for example, Ernest Edmondson Ramsaur, Jr., *The Young Turks: Prelude
     to the Revolution of 1908* (Princeton: Princeton University Press, 1957); and
     Feroz Ahmad, *The Young Turks: The Committee of Union and Progress in
     Turkish Politics, 1908-1914* (Oxford: Oxford University Press, 1969).
51. Hasan Kayali argues that the Young Turks "subscribed to the supranational
     ideal of Ottomanism" rather than to "a Turkish nationalist cultural or politi-
     cal program." (p. 14) "The Young Turks did not turn to Turkish nationalism
     but rather to Islamism as the ideological underpinning that would safeguard
     the unity and continuity of what was left of the empire. Islam became the pil-
     lar of the supranational ideology of Ottomanism, with religion imparting a
     new sense of homogeneity and solidarity." (p. 15) Therefore, the perception of
     Turkification on the part of non-Turks, he claims, was incorrect. My own
     understanding is that rather than primarily dedicated to a pan-Islamic policy,
     as Kayali argues, the Young Turks adopted different orientations toward dif-
     ferent constituencies and that there was no overridding consensus, let alone
     unanimity, among the Young Turks on ideology. He seems closer to the mark
     when he writes, "The Young Turks enviaged the creation of a civic-territorial,
     indeed revolutionary-democratic, Ottoman political community by promoting
     an identification with the state and country through the sultan and instituting
     representative government. Though they remained committed to the monarchy
     within the constitutional framework, they conceived of an Ottoman state and
     society akin to the French example in which religion and ethnicity would be
     supplanted by 'state-based patriotism'." (p. 9) [Hasan Kayali, *Arabs and
     Young Turks: Ottomanism, Arabism, and Islamism in the Ottoman Empire,
     1908-1918* (Berkeley, Los Angeles and London: University of California Press,
     1997).]
         The difficulty of assessing the weight of nationalism and Ottomanism among
     the Young Turks is reflected in the work of Nyazi Berkes, *The Development of
     Secularism in Turkey* (Montreal: McGill University Press, 1964). Writing about

the period just before World War I, Berkes argues, "When, later rival parties became harbingers of anti-Ottoman nationalisms, Turkish nationalism gained some influence in the Society, but never replaced Ottomanism." (p. 329) Much of his book is concerned about three competing schools of thought among the Young Turks from 1908 to 1918: the Westernist, the Islamist, and the Turkist.

52. Cited in Masami Arai, *Turkish Nationalism in the Young Turk Era* (Leiden: E. J. Brill, 1992), p. 61.

53. This position is reflected in Jemal Pasha's statement, "Speaking for myself, I am primarily an Ottoman, but I do not forget that I am a Turk, and nothing can shake my belief that the Turkish Race is the foundation stone of the Ottoman empire. ... In its origins the Ottoman empire is a Turkish creation." [Djemal Pasha, *Memories of a Turkish Statesman, 1913-1919* (London: Hutchinson, n.d. [1922]), pp. 251-252; quoted in Jacob Landau, *Pan-Turkism in Turkey: A Study of Irredentism* (London: C. Hurst and Co., 1981), p. 50]

54. Harry Luke, *The Making of Modern Turkey: From Byzantium to Angora* (London: Macmillan, 1936), p. 157.

55. On shifting Russian attitudes toward Armenians, see Ronald Grigor Suny, "Images of the Armenians in the Russian Empire," in his *Looking Toward Ararat*, pp. 31-51.

56. Prominent among them is Vahakn N. Dadrian, whose *The History of the Armenian Genocide: Ethnic Conflict from the Balkans to Anatolia to the Caucasus* (Providence and Oxford: Berghahn Books, 1995) makes the argument that the Hamidian massacres, the events in Adana in 1909, the genocide of 1915, as well as the campaigns of nationalist Turks in 1918 into Transcaucasia should be seen as part of a consistently genocidal Turkish policy.

57. David Fromkin writes, "Talaat, Enver, and their colleagues were nationalists without a nation." (*A Peace to End All Peace: Creating the Modern Middle East, 1914-1922* [New York: Henry Holt and Co., 1989], p. 48.) He quotes Mark Sykes, "How many people realize, when they speak of Turkey and the Turks, that there is no such place and no such people." (*The Caliph's Last Heritage: A Short History of the Turkish Empire* [London: Macmillan, 1915], p. 2.)

58. Henry Morgenthau, *Ambassador Morgenthau's Story* (Garden City, NY: Doubleday Page, 1918), pp. 336-337.

59. Talaat Pasha, "Posthumous Memoirs of Talaat Pasha," *Current History*, XV, 1 (October 1921), p. 295.

60. See, Ara Sarafian, "Conversion of Armenian Women and Children," paper delivered at the international conference on "Genocide, Religion, and Modernity," at the United States Holocaust Memorial Museum, May 11-13, 1997.

61. Ahmet Mehmetefendioglu (ed.), *Dr. Resid Bey'in Hatiralari, "Sürgünden Intihara"* (Istanbul: Arba, 1992), esp. pp. 43-76. My thanks to Fatma Müge Göçek for translating the relevant passages.

Chapter 2

GENOCIDE, RELIGION, AND GERHARD KITTEL
Protestant Theologians Face The Third Reich

Robert P. Ericksen

This chapter will consider the relationship between Christian teachings and genocide in twentieth-century Germany. Everyone knows that German people, of a generation still partially with us, perpetrated the Holocaust, the most purposeful and carefully developed genocide ever undertaken. The world has grappled with that brutal and virtually incomprehensible fact for more than half a century. How could it happen? How could they do it? Our most comfortable answers place the perpetrators on the far side of some vast gulf, completely "other." Our best historical answers, however, tend to reduce that gulf, as indicated, for example, in Christopher Browning's choice of a title for his book, *Ordinary Men*.[1] The more ordinary the perpetrators, the less comfortable we feel.

This chapter will describe significant, representative, twentieth-century Christian leaders in Germany who supported the antisemitic policies which led to mass murder. That fact highlights at least two jarring aspects of the Holocaust. First, it is a representative part of our twentieth-century world, one of many pieces of evidence to suggest that mass murder is a particularly modern behavior. As much as we might like to consider genocidal murder primitive and savage, in order to place it on the other side of a chronological divide and render it foreign to ourselves, people and regimes in the twentieth cen-

---

Notes for this section begin on page 76.

tury have made this the premier century of death.[2] For all that we might appreciate other modern phenomena—the spread of democracy and education, progress against slavery and racial apartheid, a more widespread acceptance of gender equality, the convenience of the Internet and other wonders of modern technology—this century has an extraordinary amount of blood on its hands.

The second jarring note comes from focusing on religion. We might be inclined to think that religion, at least our own, would nurture humane behavior. Is it more likely to produce violence and murder? If we think so, it is perhaps the religion of the "other" that we would blame, not our own: a different religion, a fundamentalist religion, a superstitious religion of some past era. Religion in Germany, of course, fits firmly within the history of Western Christianity, with the entire Protestant Reformation deeply rooted in German soil and with centuries of powerful Roman Catholic influence in southern and western Germany. The actual gulf between Christians in Nazi Germany and those in the Western democracies is uncomfortably narrow.

A standard response to this disconcerting fact has been to label the Nazi regime anti-Christian and to assume that self-professed Christians in Germany comprise another set of victims, not as persecuted as Jews, perhaps, but victims none the less. That is simply not a satisfactory explanation. Some Christians did indeed suffer under Nazi persecution, with Dietrich Bonhoeffer and Martin Niemöller two of the best known. However, research into the actual attitudes and behavior of Christians in Germany increasingly illustrates widespread support for and acceptance of the Nazi regime among self-professed Christians.[3]

Gerhard Kittel was such a Christian, a famous professor of New Testament theology who prayed and read his Bible regularly, who preached frequently, who held daily devotions with his family. He also supported Adolf Hitler enthusiastically, as did a large percentage of his colleagues, and he devoted much of his research and writing activity after 1933 to explaining why Jews did not belong in and were a danger for Germany. If Gerhard Kittel had not taken this particular stance at that particular time, he would not seem especially "other." I believe his intelligence, his scholarship, his academic success, his personal manner, and his piety would have seemed impressive and/or attractive to many. Why did he take this stance in enthusiastic support of Hitler? How and why did he become a supporter, implicitly if not also explicitly, of genocide?

First, the modern aspect of this story plays a role. Kittel did not like modernity. He and many of his Christian contemporaries believed that the modern, secularizing world threatened to destroy the traditional, Christian, German culture they loved. This opposition to modernity drew them to National Socialism, an ideology which seemed equally opposed to modern trends.

Please note that the definition of anti-modern assumed in this chapter involves primarily a rejection of the political and cultural content of the Enlightenment. Gerhard Kittel and his romantic, nationalistic, and conservative fellows rejected the ideals of Western democracy which grew out of the Enlightenment and the French Revolution. They did not affirm equality or tolerance as valuable in themselves, nor did they endorse progress as a political ideal. On the contrary, they looked back to the supposed good old days when respect for the church and for one's social superiors and for the established political authorities could be expected. They saw in tolerance and equality and other ideals of the Enlightenment the seeds of secularism, social disorder, and moral degeneration. Neither did they approve of the modern economy. Industrialization led to the transfer of God-fearing, village-dwelling peasant farmers into rapidly growing cities where they came up against urban temptations in a setting of modern anonymity. This created a new proletariat, feared for its attraction to Marxism and its potential violence and representing a force antagonistic to traditional church teachings and middle class values.

Gerhard Kittel shared with many of his fellow German Protestants a dislike for these offspring of the French and the Industrial Revolutions, an anti-modern stance which made them politically vulnerable. Following World War I they could manage little or no respect for the Weimar Republic (an heir to the French Revolution), and they eventually gave their support to the anti-modern rhetoric of National Socialism. In one respect, however, Kittel's assessment of modernity gets more complicated. He was trained in an academic tradition which viewed Enlightenment rationalism as the accepted mode for Christian theology. His tradition did not turn to fundamentalism nor a rigid insistence on inerrant scripture. None the less, Kittel and his colleagues wanted to celebrate *Geist* and faith and feeling as well as dry rationalism. Tension between these two options never entirely disappeared.

A similar complexity can be found in the relationship of National Socialism to the modern world, as the "modernity debate" has shown. Although Nazi rhetoric opposed modernity—as seen in its call for a return to the soil, its rejection of Weimar democracy, and its denunciation of progressive and "soft" Western values— National Socialist reality accepted the use of modern ideas and practices. For example, social and human sciences such as genetics and Social Darwinism were appropriated in order to provide a cool and amoral foundation for racist theories and practices. In the realm of industrial and military matters, no "return to the soil" could effect the sort of power Hitler required for his plans. Thus, a full acceptance of modern industrialization, science and engineering proved necessary.[4]

These complexities add nuance to our understanding of the reality of National Socialism. This chapter will assume, however, that Gerhard Kittel can best be understood as an anti-modern individual attracted to what he perceived to be an anti-modern political movement. This is true to his own assessment of the issues and consistent with the stance taken by many of his fellow Protestants. Kittel consciously opposed the Enlightenment's main political and cultural ideals, and in that he was anti-modern. He also saw in National Socialist rhetoric an opposition to modern values and practices, and this attracted him to the party. It is on these terms that Kittel's relationship to genocide and religion in the twentieth century will be examined.

*   *   *

The story of Gerhard Kittel to be considered here did not take place in a vacuum, but in the midst of a political, religious, and academic environment of which he was a product and a representative. Elsewhere I have argued that significant Protestant theologians of Kittel's generation, such as Paul Althaus and Emanuel Hirsch, developed an anti-modern stance which helped determine their acceptance of the National Socialist worldview and their enthusiastic support of Adolf Hitler's rise to power.

Emanuel Hirsch, professor of systematic theology at Göttingen University and one of the brightest theologians of his generation, discovered and emphasized Sören Kierkegaard's warning about the "all-encompassing debate about everything." Hirsch believed that open-ended debate, based upon the freedom to question all inherited beliefs and values, characterized and debilitated both Enlightenment rationalism and modern democracy. German society, in Hirsch's view, would disintegrate into moral chaos unless Germans consciously chose to avoid this "all-encompassing debate." They should accept the parameters of their *Volk*, the traditional values of their *Volk*, and obedience to a *völkisch* leader as the necessary antidote to openness and freedom.[5] Hirsch said of modern science and rational thought as it developed in the nineteenth century:

It appears on the one hand as growing always richer in objective knowledge, and on the other hand as growing always poorer in the ultimate,
inner, binding, living power of truth.[6]

He believed that inner, binding truth and the solution to his
nation's cultural crisis could be found in Germanness. To those,
such as the Swiss theologian Karl Barth, who criticized his view,
Hirsch responded,

> Whoever is not in the position with us to bring tremblingly before God
> the fate of Germany and to stake his own and his children's existence on
> that fate, whoever is not called through his very existence to stand with
> us in our inner self-determination, that person also cannot stand in
> judgment on whether our will is bound on God or not.[7]

Paul Althaus, professor of systematic theology at Erlangen
University and president of the Luther Society for thirty years, also
disliked modernity and loved his *Volk*. When Hitler came to
power, Althaus exulted, "Our Protestant churches have greeted the
turning point of 1933 as a gift and miracle of God."[8] He also identified a list of problems of modernity which he believed would now
be resolved:

> The dissolution of criminal law into social therapy and pedagogy, which
> was already far along in development, has reached an end: punishment
> shall again be taken seriously as retribution. ... It [the new state] has
> destroyed the terrible irresponsibility of the parliament and allows us
> again to see what responsibility means. It sweeps away the filth of cor-
> ruption. It restrains the powers of decomposition in literature and the
> theater. It calls and educates our *Volk* to a strong new will for commu-
> nity, to a "socialism of the deed," which means the strong carry the bur-
> dens of the weak.[9]

Both Althaus and Hirsch placed their faith in the mystical, irrational concept of the German *Volk*, and they viewed with regret
modern, urban, democratic society, using terms like "corruption,"
"decomposition," and "moral decadence" to describe it. Thus they
represent romantic, conservative, *völkisch* nationalism and they
accepted Hitler's claim that he and the Nazi Party embodied their
point of view. Both theologians also believed that this viewpoint
allowed them—or even required them—to accept antisemitism. As
Althaus wrote as early as 1928,

> It does not have to do with Jewish hatred—one can reach an agreement
> directly with serious Jews on this point—it does not have to do with
> blood or with the religious beliefs of Judaism. But it does involve the

threat of a quite specific disintegrated and demoralizing urban spirituality, whose representative now is primarily the Jewish *Volk*.[10]

This statement suggests that Althaus in 1928 did not accept the *racist* presuppositions of National Socialism. He refused to condemn Jews by race or religion, but that did not prevent him from condemning Jews on other grounds. They represented for him the vanguard of modernity, the advocates and beneficiaries of a tolerant, pluralist society rather than a traditional, authoritarian, Christian one.

Gerhard Kittel parallels Althaus and Hirsch as a major theologian who held a similar anti-modern attitude and who developed a similar enthusiasm for Hitler's rise to power. Ominously, Kittel also held the conviction that he was the best-suited person to become National Socialism's theological expert on the "Jewish question." Thus he provides us with an especially useful angle on the relation of genocide to religion in the modern world.

Son of a famous theologian, Rudolf Kittel, Gerhard ended up with the New Testament chair in the prestigious theological faculty at Tübingen. He then became the founding editor of a major, still-widely-used reference work, *The Theological Dictionary of the New Testament*, and the "doctor father" to a number of twentieth-century theologians.

Kittel exhibited his anti-modern stance in a speech he delivered in 1921. Invited to lecture in Sweden, he used the occasion to describe his view of "The Religious and Church Situation in Germany." In that aftermath of war and leftwing revolution, Kittel described a sick Germany, a nation which he believed would require as much as a century to return to its accustomed vitality and greatness. Why? Not because of war damage or the Versailles Treaty, but because Germany had sold out to the Enlightenment. He listed rising levels of prostitution, venereal disease, divorce, and crime, as well as decadence in movies and theater as examples of the moral breakdown of German life. He cited materialism, rational secularism, and "socialistic religion" as causes of this cultural disintegration. He rested his hopes on a church renewal, especially as led by the Christian student movement, and also on a turning away from rationalism. "Our entire intellectual life, from philosophy to poetry, stands under the sign of a return from rationalism,"[11] he proclaimed with obvious approval.

Kittel maintained this anti-Enlightenment stance for the next twenty-five years. It led to his decision to join the Nazi Party in 1933. In 1943 and 1944, despite the excesses of *Kristallnacht*, the removal of Jews from Germany, and Kittel's admitted knowledge of the annihilation of Jews in the East,[12] he gave lectures in Vienna expressing his continued hostility to the Enlightenment and his support of Adolf Hitler. Christianity had known how to deal with the Jewish threat, he argued: place it behind ghetto walls. The Enlightenment, however, and its political counterpart, the French Revolution, opened the door to democracy, tolerance, pluralism and the assimilation of Jews into European society. Christianity and National Socialism were lauded by Kittel as the twin bulwarks against this Jewish menace.[13]

Despite the nature of these sentiments expressed in 1944, Kittel had shown no particular inclination toward "eliminationist anti-semitism" in the 1920s. On the contrary, many considered him a friend of Jews. His father Rudolf, an Old Testament scholar, had produced a widely-admired translation of the Jewish Bible. Gerhard, though he chose to study the New Testament, made use of his father's interest in Judaism by focusing on the Jewish religious environment in which Jesus developed his teachings. In 1914 the younger Kittel published *Jesus und die Rabbiner*, a book which argues that there is great similarity between rabbinical teachings in the Talmud and Jesus' teachings in the New Testament. By 1926 Kittel wrote that every ethical teaching attributed to Jesus can find its counterpart in the Jewish tradition.[14] In the same publication he added,

> One need only make these connections clear to know how absurd and historically false it is, without any exception, to attempt to separate Jesus and Christianity from the Old Testament and from the spiritual history of its people ... The ethic of Jesus did not arrive unassisted, it did not grow *ex nihilo*. ... It is nothing less than the most concentrated development of that powerful movement of Israelitic-Jewish religious history which finds its condensation in the literary complex that we call the Old Testament.[15]

After 1933, however, Kittel proved no friend to the Jews. He signaled the change not only by joining the Nazi Party in May of that year,[16] but also by giving a public lecture on "The Jewish Question" one month later. Here Kittel called for the removal of Jews from all the important areas of German life. In terms of method, he casually dismissed both annihilation and Zionism as unworkable solutions, and he condemned assimilation as a worsening of the problem (that is, hidden Jews would just be more dangerous). Thus he settled upon "guest status" so that discriminatory new laws could be written and applied to Jews alone.[17] Kittel admitted that some of these Jews might be perfectly upstanding individuals and many might have considered themselves German for generations. So he warned Christians against feeling sympathy: "God does not require that we be sentimental, but that we see the facts and give them their due."[18] He also prepared himself for criticism:

> We must not allow ourselves to be crippled because the whole world screams at us of barbarism and a reversion to the past. ... How the German *Volk* regulates its own cultural affairs does not concern anyone else in the world.[19]

Kittel's Jewish readers turned away with the publication of this diatribe. Herbert Loewe, who taught rabbinics at Cambridge University, wrote in a letter to Kittel in August, 1933:

> It gives me great pain to find that so great an authority and leader of thought should give expression to such views. I have read your previous books with pleasure and profit, and I have learned much from them. ... Your present pronouncement is quite incompatible with your previous teaching, and it is as unjust to Christianity as it is to Judaism. ... It is a grievous disillusionment to find that one's idol has feet of clay.[20]

Martin Buber also responded, in his case with an open letter to Kittel. He acknowledged that the ideas expressed by Kittel were the "ruling ideas," but, he added, "What I did not know is that you shared them."[21]

Kittel gave no ground to his critics. In a letter to Loewe he refused to recant any portion of *Die Judenfrage* and he denied writing it under any sort of political pressure, as Loewe had suggested.[22] Kittel responded to Martin Buber in a fifteen-page open letter printed in the second and third editions of his booklet. He first noted bitterly, "I thought we ... could have a discussion, and ... I see that this is ... hardly the case."[23] Kittel went on to argue that he had not defamed Jews. Was it defamation to bar Jews from legal practice, he asked,

> if we first establish that in recent years Jewish judges and Jewish lawyers have attempted to distort German law and rape German legal consciousness, and, secondly, if we believe "justice" is not an abstraction, but something which grows out of the blood and soil and history of a *Volk*?[24]

It is clear from this statement that already in 1933 Kittel accepted the stereotypes common to National Socialist antisemitism, and he seemed surprised to find that Martin Buber or other Jews would find that point of view objectionable.

Soon Kittel stepped deeper into the rising tide of Nazi antisemitism. In 1936 the young historian Walter Frank created the

Institute for the History of the New Germany in hopes that it would attract reputable scholars in support of the Nazi *Weltanschauung*. He also edited *Forschungen zur Judenfrage*, the journal in whose pages he intended to concentrate the best of German scholarship on the so-called "Jewish Question." Gerhard Kittel signed on as a charter member of this Nazi institute, and he became the single most prolific contributor to the eight volumes of *Forschungen zur Judenfrage* published between 1936 and 1943.

Kittel was hardly alone. The work in this journal disappeared from the academic landscape after 1945; so far as I can tell, no one who contributed to its pages ever mentioned the accomplishment in his postwar *vita*. However, the opening ceremonies of Frank's institute attracted seven professors among the nine lecturers, and these academics represented the Universities of Berlin, Tübingen, Göttingen, Munich, Freiburg, Würzburg and Hamburg. "Professor doctors" penned thirty-two of the fifty-four contributions to *Forschungen zur Judenfrage*, and all but three contributors held the doctorate. Gerhard Kittel happily added his reputation to this anti-Jewish venture.

Kittel's main goal in his work for Walter Frank was to try to show how the admirable Israelites of the Old Testament experienced a racial and moral breakdown which turned them into the decadent Jews of the modern day. He blamed the diaspora, he blamed the transition from rural to urban occupations, he blamed the "mongrelization" of Jewish blood through intermarriage. He also claimed that the decomposition of Jews as a racial group coincided with their perversion of the "chosen people" theme into a desire for world conquest. Kittel and the "racial scientist" Eugen Fischer (who assisted the career of Joseph Mengele) took over the entire volume seven of *Forschungen zur Judenfrage*. Fischer analyzed Egyptian burial portraits in order to identify which individuals were Jewish and then to read in their faces typical Jewish character traits such as deviousness and insolence, proving, in his mind, that Jews were already decadent by the second and third century. Kittel then contributed his perception and argument that the Jewish plot to take over the world was fully in place those many centuries ago:

> There is always one goal: power over the world ... always, at all times, whether in the first or the twentieth century, the dream of world Jewry is sole domination of the world, now and in the future.[25]

Clearly, Kittel's writings in the period from 1933 to 1944 represent a strange turn for a Christian theologian. He no longer spent his energies primarily on an explication of the New Testament and of Christian teachings; instead, he attempted to show the degeneration and danger of Jews. In 1943, Kittel wrote an article on the subject of Jewish morality for a Joseph Goebbels publication. He asserted that in the Talmud

> a deep-seated hatred against the non-Jew comes to expression, out of which all consequences are drawn, right up to the full freedom to murder; for example, when it can read: You may kill even the best among the gentiles, just as you should smash the brains of even the best snake.[26]

By 1943, when this article appeared, Jews had almost entirely disappeared from the streets of Germany and murder had become German policy in the East. Why would Kittel have written such a diatribe, if not to justify German murder of Jews as a necessary preemptive strike? He admitted that the Talmud has mild passages which emphasize love and justice, and he acknowledged that Jewish spokespersons did not openly interpret this right to murder as he did. However, he said, that was only a cover while Jews were too vulnerable and too thinly dispersed. None the less, Jews continued to want world rule, and this moral right to murder was a weapon held ready.[27]

When French troops arrived in Tübingen in 1945, they arrested Kittel and charged him with aiding and abetting the Nazi crimes against Jews. He lost his professor's chair as well as his editorship of the *Theological Dictionary of the New Testament*, and he spent about one-and-one-half years in prison before his premature death at the age of fifty-nine in 1948.[28] The one thing he did not entirely lose was his reputation. Although many knew of his connection with the Nazi regime, his *Theological Dictionary* remained a staple reference work and it is widely used to this day. Kittel also continued to be remembered in the theological faculty at Tübingen as one of the giants in its rich tradition,[29] and, of course, his students continued to teach and write as they filled chairs at various universities.

Today we find Kittel's name as posthumous editor of rabbinical texts published by Kohlhammer Press of Stuttgart. Prior to 1933 Kittel had inspired a project which resulted in a series of translations and commentaries upon Jewish texts from the second century. He edited fifteen volumes which appeared between 1933 and 1937. His student, Karl Heinrich Rengstorf, picked up the project after Kittel's death and the series resumed publication in 1952. A 1960 volume, for example, is dedicated to Kittel's memory and praises him for his contribution to Jewish studies "at a time in which the Hitlerian political goals set themselves against all things Jewish."[30] In another volume Rengstorf blames the 1937 collapse of the pro-

ject on "the political development in Germany, which brought
National Socialism to power in 1933 [and made] Jewish studies of
this sort anything but popular."[31] From our perspective, of course,
these words ring hollow. It seems quite clear that by 1937 Kittel
had begun to expend his energies in Walter Frank's anti-Jewish
institute, rather than on Jewish textual study. It is surely ironic that
Kittel's name should posthumously grace library shelves in the guise
of promoting rabbinical texts. A further irony finds his antisemitic
students benefiting after 1945 from their knowledge of Hebrew
and of Jewish sources. One example, Karl Georg Kuhn, who produced a major translation in this series in 1959, found himself by
that year a professor at Heidelberg. Earlier, as a protege of Kittel,
he had published antisemitic articles in the first three volumes of
Walter Frank's *Forschungen zur Judenfrage*.[32] He also pursued an
antisemitic agenda working for Walter Grundmann's Institute for
Research on and the Elimination of Jewish Influence on German
Church Life,[33] but neither activity stifled his postwar career as a
scholar of Jewish texts.

* * *

How does this story of Gerhard Kittel fit into the larger picture of
genocide and religion in the twentieth century? First there is the fact
of his support for the National Socialist state, a genocidal regime. I
believe that he, Althaus, and Hirsch were broadly representative of
Christians in Germany in their support for Hitler. Christians who
resisted the Nazi regime, men such as Martin Niemöller and Dietrich Bonhoeffer and women who risked their lives sheltering Jews,
never spoke for the majority. After 1945 it was tempting for church
historians to highlight these heroes, and it is tempting for us today
to regard them as inspiring examples of the human and the Christian spirit.[34] However, active dissenters were few in number and
they were often dismissed by other Christians as troublemakers.[35]
Furthermore, alongside the limited evidence of Christian resistance,
there is extensive evidence of support and complicity. Even Martin
Niemöller welcomed the Nazi regime at first, and many of those we
designate "heroes" expressed open and honest enthusiasm for the
regime, despite bravely criticizing it on specific ecclesiastical or
moral grounds.[36]

   If we look for the reason for Christian enthusiasm for Hitler, I
believe that the anti-modernist stance of Althaus, Hirsch, and Kittel is a good starting point. Most Christians had been loyal to the
Kaiser and were offended by the Versailles Treaty. Their patriotism
was tinctured with conservative opposition to communism, social-

ism, democracy, the Weimar Republic, and the social and moral changes associated with industrialization, urbanization and secularization.[37] They welcomed the aggressive anti-communism of the Nazi Party. They accepted at face value Hitler's apparent endorsement of family values when he opposed pornography, prostitution, abortion, and the "obscenity" of modern art. When he said a woman's place is in the home and when he offered bronze, silver, and gold medals to women with large families, they applauded.[38] As Ian Kershaw has shown, confidence in the Führer and belief in the "Hitler Myth" remained strong, even when "Little Hitlers" in the party violated the hopes and expectations of middle-class Christians.[39] Carl Amery has described what he calls "milieu Catholics" who also found Hitler's emphasis on the bourgeois values of discipline, cleanliness, and godliness irresistable.[40]

These attitudes seem clearly "anti-modern" in the sense that they represent opposition to the rationalism, secularism, pluralism, and democratic values which developed after the Enlightenment. They also implicitly represent opposition to the socio-economic impact of industrialization and urbanization. Kittel and most of his fellows did not like the openness protected by the Weimar Republic. They identified within that open culture a tolerance which they defined as moral decadence. They did not want to see new rights and opportunities for women, nor for socialists, nor for Jews. In all of these significant ways they were anti-modern.

Beyond pluralism and democracy, there is the question of Enlightened rationalism. Is it necessarily an implacable enemy of religion? There can be no doubt that secularism has increased in the last two centuries, perhaps especially so in Europe. Individuals in the modern world feel increasingly free to modify their religion, switch religions, or abandon religion altogether. It is certainly possible that religious people, including theologians, are tempted to view rationalists or "free thinkers" as the enemies of faith. To that extent, the irrational side of National Socialist ideology may have seemed attractive and it may be that religion anywhere will feel tempted by anti-modernity in this anti-rational sense.

It is hard to know how best to understand Kittel and other German Protestant theologians in this regard. A professor at Greifswald in 1921, when he gave his anti-modern lecture in Sweden, Kittel was five years away from his promotion to Tübingen and hardly ready to give up the tools of rational scholarship. The German theological tradition accepted *intellectual* modernity. Schleiermacher and his heirs cultivated the enlightened, rational skills of historical-critical analysis in an attempt to bring Christian theology into a respectable place in the modern world. This was not a fundamentalist tradition, nor did it ask for a rejection of rational inquiry. One heir to this tradition, Dietrich Bonhoeffer, wrote letters from a Nazi prison advocating theology for a "world come of age." His concept inspired postwar theologians to embrace rather than oppose modernity, accommodating secularism in their thoughts about religion even to the point of proclaiming the "death of God" in some cases.

Kittel, however, just like Hirsch, Althaus, and other romantic nationalists, had learned to value *Geist* and the mystery of *Volksgemeinschaft* as special German virtues and as the appropriate counterpoints to "sterile" rationalism. This window of irrational opportunity allowed these men, trained in a modern intellectual tradition, to gratify their distinctly hostile response to the social, economic, and cultural implications of the modern world. After 1933, Kittel's willingness to bend the tools of rational scholarship to an irrational and evil purpose marked the dark, Nazi side of this otherwise respectable theologian's career.

Most importantly, the mystery of *Volksgemeinschaft* accepted by Kittel led him very close to an open endorsement of genocide. Wolfgang Gerlach has shown that even within the Confessing Church there was precious little Christian sympathy for Jews.[41] For Kittel and his fellows, their sense of excitement over the national renewal of the *Volk* under Hitler encouraged them to accept the basic Nazi stance on the "Jewish question." They easily convinced themselves that German national weakness could be blamed on the Jews, a weakness predicated on national disunity exacerbated by democratic pluralism. In the good old days, Jews had known their place and Christianity had commanded respect, but modern trends had turned that world upside down. Furthermore, the long and virulent history of Christian antisemitism could be called upon to justify hostility toward Jews.

The story of this prominent theologian—son of a great theologian and representative of a very significant tradition of Christian theology—suggests that the extent of Christian culpability for the Holocaust has not been adequately appreciated.[42] It also suggests that in twentieth-century Germany, religion and genocide fit together more comfortably than we would like to think. Gerhard Kittel, a successful and respected Christian theologian, opposed the basic trends of modernity, he gave enthusiastic support to the rise of Hitler, and he accepted the Nazi idea that the removal of Jews from Germany was an appropriate and necessary step to bring back the good old days.

Kittel did not come to this conclusion on his own or solely through his religious convictions. His open hostility toward Jews and outspoken attacks against Jewry appeared only in 1933 and thereafter, so the rhetoric and political impact of the Third Reich must be considered an influential factor. Kittel's more benign pre-1933 attitude had included a foundation of prejudice, but it seems to have been tempered with some admiration for Jews and restrained by Christian and bourgeois values. Admiration for Jews and bourgeois restraint disappeared after 1933. Althaus and Hirsch also increased their antipathy toward Jews and their willingness to accept racial terminology and concepts after 1933.[43] "Racial science" permeated the German university and German life under National Socialism. In the strange atmosphere of the Third Reich, the national discourse changed. Kittel even managed to convince himself that the work he did for Walter Frank's anti-Jewish institute constituted real, interdisciplinary scholarship. By then, his anti-semitism was both unrestrained and eliminationist.

Despite these unacceptable excesses, I do not believe Gerhard Kittel was sufficiently "other" to make us feel entirely comfortable. No huge gulf separated his religious beliefs or academic career from our own world, which helps explain why Anglo-American students flocked to Tübingen to study with him in the 1930s.[44] Is it over-reaching, then, to suggest that he represents a nexus between religion and genocide?

Kittel never openly and directly advocated the murder of Jews. However, he endorsed the removal of Jews from German society. Knowing that this would seem brutal, he encouraged Christians in particular not to be sentimental or soft in the face of harsh measures. He also accepted and disseminated the Nazi view of Jews as a "problem." He was willing to use racist concepts like "mongrelization" and to argue that Jews, a tiny minority group, represented a threat to destroy Germany and/or take over the world. By accepting the Nazi justification for its anti-Jewish policies so completely, Gerhard Kittel must be seen as a facilitator of genocide.

It is difficult to trace the path of Kittel's ideas—from the printed page and the lecture room, into the notebooks of future pastors, and then into sermons and teachings. But there is no reason to think this path did not exist. He was a well-known Christian leader who devoted a major portion of his life to an anti-Jewish diatribe consistent with the Nazi worldview. When "ordinary men" pulled their triggers and ordinary bureaucrats sent their memoranda, Gerhard Kittel's enthusiastic support for National Socialism and his harsh teachings about Jews may well have filtered through to some as a justification for what they did. His was not quite an explicit plea for genocide. Kittel fell short of that. But he provided an explicit call for harsh measures to solve the "problem" of the Jew, and he did so while accepting the stereotyped assumptions of Nazi antisemitism and while speaking to Christian Germany as a significant Christian voice.

Notes

1. Christopher R. Browning, *Ordinary Men: Reserve Police Battalion 101 and the Final Solution in Poland* (New York, 1992).
2. See, for example, Richard L. Rubenstein, *The Cunning of History: The Holocaust and the American Future* (New York, 1975).
3. With regard to the so-called "Jewish question," consider Robert P. Ericksen and Susannah Heschel, eds., *Betrayal: German Churches and the Holocaust* (Minneapolis, 1999). See also Ericksen and Heschel, "The German Churches Face Hitler: An Assessment of the Historiography," *Tel Aviver Jahrbuch für deutsche Geschichte 1994* (Tel Aviv, 1994), pp. 433-459.
4. Jeffrey Herf provides a useful summary of these issues in *Reactionary Modernism: Technology, Culture, and Politics in Weimar and the Third Reich* (Cambridge, 1984), pp. 1-17.
5. See Robert P. Ericksen, *Theologians under Hitler: Gerhard Kittel, Paul Althaus and Emanuel Hirsch* (New Haven, 1985), pp. 124 ff.; and also Emanuel Hirsch, *Die gegenwärtige geistige Lage im Spiegel philosophischer und theologischer Besinnung* (Göttingen, 1934).
6. Hirsch, p. 16.
7. Quoted in Jens Holger Schjorring, *Theologische Gewissensethik und politische Wirklichkeit: Das Beispiel Eduard Geismars und Emanuel Hirschs* (Göttingen, 1979), p. 173.
8. Paul Althaus, *Die deutsche Stunde der Kirche*, 3rd ed. (Göttingen, 1934), p. 5.
9. Ibid., p. 7.
10 Paul Althaus, *Kirche und Volkstum. Der völkische Wille im Lichte des Evangeliums* (Gütersloh, 1928), p. 34.
11. Gerhard Kittel, *Die religiöse und die kirchliche Lage in Deutschland* (Leipzig, 1921), pp. 4-7, 16-17.
12. See Gerhard Kittel, "Meine Verteidigung," p. 27, where Kittel admits that early in 1943 he learned about the murder of Jews from his son on leave from the Eastern front. (This document is a defense statement written in June 1945 as Kittel faced a French tribunal. I am indebted to Dr. Herman Preus, an American friend of Kittel, from whom I received a copy. A revised and expanded defense statement written in November/December 1946 can be found in the Tübingen University Archive).
13. I found the typescript of these two lectures by Kittel, "Die Entstehung des Judentums" (1943) and "Das Rassenproblem der Spätantike und das Frühchris-

tentums" (1944), in the Tübingen University Theological Library. He delivered both lectures in Vienna, where he had held a visiting professorship from 1939 to 1943.

14. Gerhard Kittel, *Die Probleme des palästinischen Spätjudentums und das Urchristentum* (Stuttgart, 1926), p. 96.

15. Ibid., p. 125, n. 3.

16. Kittel had membership card number 3,243,036 (Berlin Document Center).

17. See Gerhard Kittel, *Die Judenfrage* (Stuttgart, 1933), and also Ericksen, pp. 54-61.

18. *Die Judenfrage*, p. 9.

19. Ibid., p. 39.

20. Herbert Loewe to Gerhard Kittel, 11 August 1933, in the Kittel personality file, Wiener Library, London.

21. Martin Buber, "Offener Brief an Gerhard Kittel," first published in *Theologische Blätter* , vol. 12, no. 8 (August 1933), pp. 148-150, and reprinted in Robert Raphael Geis and Hans-Joachim Kraus, eds., *Versuche des Verstehens. Dokumente jüdisch-christlicher Begegnung aus der Jahren 1918-1933* (Munich, 1966), pp. 166-170.

22. Gerhard Kittel to Herbert Loewe, 10 September 1933, in the Kittel personality file, Wiener Library.

23. Gerhard Kittel, *Die Judenfrage*, 2nd ed. (Stuttgart, 1933), p. 87.

24. Ibid., p. 90.

25. Eugen Fischer and Gerhard Kittel, "Das antike Weltjudentum. Tatsachen, Texte, Bilder," *Forschungen zur Judenfrage*, VII (Hamburg, 1943), pp. 10-11.

26. Gerhard Kittel, "Die Behandlung des Nichtjuden nach dem Talmud," *Archiv für Judenfragen*, vol. 1, Group A1 (Berlin, 1943), p. 7.

27. Ibid., pp. 15-16. Psychological projection may be another explanation for Kittel's ascribing to Jews behaviors then typical of Germans.

28. See Ericksen, p. 28.

29. Klaus Scholder, church historian at Tübingen in the 1960s and 1970s, wrote a massive study of the church struggle, *The Churches and the Third Reich*, vols. 1 and 2 (London, 1987, 1988), without once mentioning Gerhard Kittel, though Kittel was a major theological figure and was active as a participant, correspondent and commentator on the fray.

30. Walter Windfuhr, "Vorwort," in *Die Tosefta. Seder VI: Toharot* (Stuttgart, 1960), p. ix.

31. Karl Heinrich Rengstorf, "Geleitwort des Herausgebers," in Karl Georg Kuhn, tr., *Der tannaitische Midrasch Sifre zu Numeri* (Stuttgart, 1959), p. v.

32. Ibid. See also Karl Georg Kuhn, "Ursprung und Wesen der talmudischen Einstellung zum Nichtjuden," *Forschungen zur Judenfrage*, vol. 3 (Hamburg, 1938), pp. 199 ff., as an example of Kuhn's work for Walter Frank.

33. For more on Grundmann's Institute see the chapter by Susannah Heschel in this volume.

34. See Ericksen and Heschel, "The German Churches Face Hitler."

35. Such statements, for example, can be found in the *Landeskirchlichesarchiv* in Hanover, file S1 HII 133a, with reference to the "radical Niemöller wing" of the Confessing Church.

36. See, Ian Kershaw, *Popular Opinion and Political Dissent in the Third Reich: Bavaria 1933-1945* (Oxford, 1983), for a sense of the complexity of this issue. For a somewhat more positive view of the role of the lower clergy in relation to anti-Jewish policies, see pp. 246-257.

37. See, for example, Shelley Baranowski, *The Confessing Church, Conservative Elites, and the Nazi State* (New York, 1986).

38. See Doris Bergen, *Twisted Cross: The German Christian Movement in the Third Reich* (Chapel Hill, 1996), which considers the question of gender. See also, Claudia Koonz, *Mothers in the Fatherland: Women, the Family and Nazi Politics* (New York, 1987).

39. See Ian Kershaw, *The Hitler Myth: Image and Reality in the Third Reich* (Oxford, 1987), especially pp. 83-120.

40. Carl Amery, *Die Kapitulation oder Der real existierende Katholizismus* (Munich, 1963, 1988).

41. Wolfgang Gerlach, *Als die Zeugen schwiegen: Bekennende Kirche und die Juden* (Berlin, 1987). See also Ericksen and Heschel, *Betrayal*.

42. For example, the impact of religious training is one factor to be considered in attempting to understand Christopher Browning's "ordinary men" (see n. 1, above) and Daniel Goldhagen's "willing executioners" (*Hitler's Willing Executioners: Ordinary Germans and the Holocaust* [New York, 1996]).

43. This statement holds true for all three, but it should be noted that Althaus never accepted as much of the anti-Jewish rhetoric as his two colleagues, and he backed away from his enthusiasm for National Socialism after *Kristallnacht*. See Ericksen, pp. 83-98.

44. This includes Hermann Preuss, of Luther Seminary in St. Paul, mentioned in note 12 above, and also Richard Gutteridge, who later wrote an important book on this topic, *The German Evangelical Church and the Jews, 1879-1958* (London, 1976).

– Chapter 3 –

WHEN JESUS WAS AN ARYAN
The Protestant Church
and Antisemitic Propaganda*

Susannah Heschel

The combination in Germany of racial theory with religion, beginning in the nineteenth century and blossoming during the early decades of the twentieth, led to the creation of Aryan Christianity, a phenomenon Saul Friedländer has called "redemptive antisemitism."[1] Born, he writes, "from the fear of racial degeneration and the religious belief in redemption," it advocated Germany's liberation from the Jews and from the Jewish. An authentic Germany would be free of all Jewish accretions, those that had entered via modernity and those that had entered via Christianity. If the contemporary savior was Hitler, his mission was that of Christ. The redemption of Christianity itself was at stake, and could only be accomplished by purging Jesus of all Jewish associations and reconstructing him as he allegedly really was, an Aryan.

The implementation of Aryan Christianity within the institutional Protestant church was the goal of the pro-Nazi German Christian Movement, described by Doris Bergen. The Movement reached its zenith in 1939 with the establishment of an antisemitic research institute, known as the Institut zur Erforschung und Beseitigung des jüdischen Einflusses auf das deutsche kirchliche Leben, (Institute for the Study and Eradication of Jewish Influence on German Church Life). Several of the major figures within the Institute

---

Notes for this section begin on page 101.

had met as students of Gerhard Kittel's, and had worked under
him at the University of Tübingen during the early 1930s on the
Theological Dictionary of the New Testament. Based on church
archives, it is possible to reconstruct the establishment, activities,
membership, funding, and theology of the Institute, which was
located in central Germany, in the town of Eisenach (Thuringia),
and to trace the postwar careers of its leaders within the church and
the theological faculties. Until now, the very existence of the Institute, from 1939 to 1945, was barely known, as a result of postwar
efforts to hide all of the church's pro-Nazi activities.

The significance of the Institute lies in its efforts to identify
Christianity with National Socialist antisemitism by arguing that
Jesus was an Aryan who sought the destruction of Judaism. Its
members proclaimed, "We know that the Jews want the annihilation [Vernichtung] of Germany."[2] "Jesus had taken up a fight
against Judaism in all sharpness and had fallen as victim to [his
fight]."[3] Once aware of the deportations and murders, they continued to justify this treatment of the Jews, on Christian grounds. In
1942, Walter Grundmann, professor of New Testament at the University of Jena, and academic director of the Institute, declared:

> ... a healthy Volk must and will reject Judaism in every form. This fact
> is justified for and through history. Should someone be upset about Ger-
> many's attitude toward Judaism, Germany has the historical justification
> and historical authorization for the fight against Judaism on its side! [4]

Of the several research institutes in Nazi Germany, this one had
the largest membership of academics and was the most productive
in terms of publications. That it was run by theologians is highly
significant; the site of academic expertise on Judaism lay within
Protestant theological faculties, particularly among New Testament
scholars, who had some training in post-biblical Hebrew and Greek
Jewish sources. It is worth noting that precisely those scholars who
trained in early Judaism during the 1920s became active members
in the Institute: Paul Fiebig, Hugo Odeberg, Georg Bertram, and
Georg Beer, among others.

The efforts of these theologians to synthesize Christianity with
National Socialism should be seen as motivated by political opportunism, to be sure, but also by an internal crisis within liberal Protestant theology that welcomed Nazi racial theory as its solution. The
crisis arose in the late nineteenth century, as liberal Protestant New
Testament scholars sought to define the historical figure of Jesus
and identify Christianity with the faith *of* Jesus, not the faith *about*
Jesus. The discovery that the historical Jesus was a Jew whose

teachings were identical to those of other rabbis of his day led to the problem of determining the uniqueness of Jesus and the boundary between liberal Protestantism and liberal Judaism, as Uriel Tal has delineated.[5] That problem motivated the embrace by Protestant theologians of racial theory: while the content of Jesus' message may have been identical to Judaism, his difference could be assured on racial grounds. Thus, serious theological debates about whether Jesus was a Jew or an Aryan began long before Hitler came to power. What was innovative about the Institute was its goal of revising radically Christian doctrine and liturgy as practiced in churches throughout the Reich, and bringing them into accord with racial antisemitism.

The theologians' embrace of National Socialism was an unrequited affection. Hitler showed little interest in church affairs after 1934, and the hopes of theologians for positions of power and influence within the regime met with disappointment. When Reich Bishop Ludwig Müller delivered the eulogy in Eisenach at the funeral of Thuringian Bishop Sasse on 31 August 1942, he voiced the situation: "When Bishop Sasse was consecrated as bishop eight years ago in this church, it was absolutely obvious that the higher representatives of the Party and the State would take part. Today there is hardly a brown-shirt to be seen in the church."[6] The historiography presents the Protestant church as the persecuted victim of the Nazi regime, as argued by Kurt Meier and John Conway, among others, or as theologically intact, thanks to the rigors of the German theological method, as argued by Trutz Rendtorff.[7] Such claims have to be radically revised in light of the control attained by members of the German Christian movement within most of the regional churches in Germany and within the university theological faculties. If persecution was experienced by the church, it reflects primarily the lack of interest by the regime in church affairs. For example, unpublished archival documents show that in 1935 the official representative of the theological faculties submitted several formal petitions requesting membership in the SS for theology students and pastors; the petition was rejected by Himmler.[8] Other evidence reveals that in 1936, when Nazi Party officials ordered the swastika removed from church altars and the mastheads of church newspapers, numerous church officials protested, claiming that the swastika on the altar was a source of profound inspiration to churchgoers.[9] During those years, church leaders would have defined persecution very differently from the way the term is used by some church historians today.

Origins of the Institute

In order to enhance the role of the church within National Socialism, the League for German Christianity (Bund für deutsches Christentum) met on 26 January 1938, organized by Berlin church superintendent Herbert Propp, to plan a massive show of church support for the regime.[10] The renewed centrality of government anti-Jewish measures that began in late 1937 provided a focus. The group decided that a thorough dejudaization of the church would be part of Hitler's "world struggle against world Jewry" (Weltkampf gegen das Weltjudentum). Hugo Pich, a church superintendent in Thuringia, prepared the report during the summer of 1938: "The Führer of our Volk has now been called to lead an international fight against world Jewry. ... In order to lead the National Socialist German struggle against world Jewry, the quick and thorough implementation of the de-Judaization of the Christian church is of high and essential significance. Only when the de-Judaization of the Christian church is completed can the German people join in carrying out the fight of the Führer within its Christian membership and within its religious beliefs, and can the divine commission of the German Volk assist in its fulfillment."[11] Pich proposed that the work be carried out by a special office within the church that would supervise the de-Judaization process.

Shortly after the *Kristallnacht* pogrom in November 1938, church headquarters in Berlin circulated Pich's proposal to the regional churches, and received favorable responses. To give the plan a broad backing of support, the Godesberg Declaration was formulated in the spring of 1939, signed by leaders of most regional churches, and adopted as official church policy. It stated that National Socialism carried forward the work of Martin Luther and would lead the German people to a true understanding of Christian faith.[12] The centerpiece of the Declaration was the statement: "What is the relation between Judaism and Christianity? Is Christianity derived from Judaism and is it its continuation and completion, or does Christianity stand in opposition to Judaism? We answer this question: Christianity is the unbridgeable religious opposition to Judaism." The Declaration, signed by representatives of eleven regional churches, was printed in the official *Gesetzblatt* of the German Protestant Church with an addendum stating the church's intention to implement the Declaration by establishing an Institute for the Study and Eradication of Jewish Influence on the Church Life of the German Volk.[13]

Bishop Martin Sasse of Thuringia, an early member of the Nazi Party (he joined in January 1930), supported the proposal energetically and called for the establishment of a research institute at the University of Jena, in Thuringia, whose theological faculty was dominated by members of the German Christian movement. The rector of the university, however, was Karl Astel, professor of medicine and an ardent Nazi, who opposed any expansion of the theological faculty, so no formal linkage was made. Eventually, the Institute was housed in the church's training seminary in Eisenach, independent of the university, but run by members of its faculty as well as local ministers, who were leaders within the German Christian movement. Grand opening ceremonies took place on Saturday afternoon, 6 May 1939, in the old, historic Wartburg castle in which Martin Luther had once taken refuge. Quartets by Mozart and Schubert, telegrams of congratulations, and learned speeches filled the program. Julius Streicher had hoped to attend, but was prevented by recent surgery; his telegram declared: "Verspreche mir von Ihrer Arbeit viel Gutes für unser Feld."[14] The audience was welcomed by the Institute's nominal director, Siegfried Leffler, one of the original founders of the German Christian movement, now serving in the Thuringian Ministry of Education. The president of the German Protestant Church, Friedrich Werner, also attended and welcomed the Institute with the hope that it would distance itself from theological special-interest groups and bring honor to German theological scholarship.[15] Grundmann, the academic director of the Institute, had served since 1936 as professor of New Testament and Volkish Theology at the University of Jena. His address at the Institute's opening, "The Dejudaization of the Religious Life as the Task of German Theology and Church," set forth his aspirations: "The elimination of Jewish influence on German life is the urgent and fundamental question of the present German religious situation." Theological scholarship had made apparent the "deformation of New Testament ideas into Old Testament preconceptions, so that now angry recognition of the Jewishness in the Old Testament and in parts of the New Testament has arisen, obstructing access to the Bible for innumerable German people."[16] Grundmann's lecture was printed in six thousand copies and distributed through the German Christian movement's publishing house, run by Heinz Dungs, an Institute member.[17]

Membership in the Institute was open and became large, even larger than published records indicate. More than fifty professors of theology at universities throughout the Reich joined, including many distinguished figures, as well as dozens of instructors and graduate students.[18] The Institute also listed about one hundred pastors and bishops as members. Most members were young, hav-

ing studied theology in the late 1920s and 1930s, too young to
have fought during WWI, and had shown their Nazi sympathies
through early membership in the NSDAP, the German Christian
Movement, or the SA. Many were trained in the field of New Testament and assumed they were experts in what they called "late
Judaism"—a term used by scholars to designate Judaism during the
centuries just before the advent of Christianity. Numerous pastors, religion teachers, and lay people also joined. The Institute
established at least one branch, in Rumania in 1942, and built an
alliance with faculty and students in Scandinavia, led by Hugo
Odeberg, a distinguished scholar of Judaica at the University of
Lund. In 1941 Grundmann and Meyer-Erlach formed a working
group, *Germanentum und Christentum*, which brought Scandinavian theologians and writers to participate in two annual conferences in Germany.[19] Odeberg took the initiative among the
Scandinavians, inviting thirty academics, students, and writers
from Sweden, Norway, and Denmark to lecture at the conferences,
which were held in Weissenfels and in Eisenach. Impressed by the
high quality of scholarship practiced by Institute members, Odeberg sent seven Scandinavian students to Jena to write doctoral dissertations under Grundmann.

Because its publications generated income and because its
members were employed by churches and universities, the financial
needs of the Institute were minimal. Indeed, in 1943, the only year
for which its accounts are extant, the Institute had a surplus
income.[20] The Institute did not pay expenses for participants in its
conferences; pastors who attended were reimbursed for travel
expenses by their regional churches, since the conferences were
considered to be work-related.[21] Still, the Institute received financial support from funds collected from the regional churches by
national church headquarters in Berlin.

Work of the Institute

Of all the so-called research institutes that flourished during the
Nazi era, the Eisenach Dejudaization Institute (Entjudungsinstitut),
as it was informally called during its heyday, proved the most prolific and had the largest membership. Its members were divided into
working groups, rapidly producing publications. The Institute's de-
Judaized version of the New Testament, *Die Botschaft Gottes*, first
appeared in 1940, eventually selling around 250,000 copies, including a small, abridged version.

A de-Judaized hymnal, *Grosser Gott Wir Loben Dich*, also appeared in 1940, to great commercial success, and a catechism, *Deutsche mit Gott: Ein deutsches Glaubensbuch*, was published in 1941 to summarize the Institute's theological principles. All were sold to churches throughout the Reich, in small towns and villages as well as cities. Each eliminated Hebrew words, references to the Old Testament, and any links between Jesus and Judaism. For example, the hymnal expunged words such as "amen," "hallelujah," "Hosanna," and "Zebaoth," while the New Testament eliminated Jesus' descent from David, and the catechism proclaimed: "Jesus of Nazareth in the Galilee demonstrates in his message and behavior a spirit which is opposed in every way to that of Judaism. The fight between him and the Jews became so bitter that it led to his crucifixion. So Jesus cannot have been a Jew. Until today the Jews persecute Jesus and all who follow him with irreconcilable hatred. By contrast, Aryans in particular can find answers in him to their ultimate questions. So he became the savior of the Germans."[22]

The Institute's publications were not the first efforts to produce de-Judaized Christian liturgical materials. For example, Bishop Weidemann of Bremen issued a de-Judaized New Testament, composed with the assistance of the noted theologian Emanuel Hirsch.[23] Reich Bishop Ludwig Müller issued a "germanized" version of the Sermon on the Mount in 1936 to eliminate what he considered inappropriate Jewish moral teachings.[24] Yet those publications were generally limited to local church usage, whereas the Institute's publications were in far more widespread use; 100,000 copies of both the *Die Botschaft Gottes and Grosser Gott Wir Loben Dich* were printed in the first edition to meet the demands of pre-publication orders from parish churches throughout the Reich.[25]

In addition to its liturgical materials, the Institute sponsored conferences and published books and articles delineating its view of Christian theology and history. The conferences were held in town halls and universities throughout the Reich, opening and closing with hymns, prayers, and the Nazi salute, and attracting anywhere from thirty to six hundred participants. Most of its publications emphasized the degeneration of Judaism after the eighth century B.C.E., which supposedly reached its nadir during the Second Temple period; Judaism's final and utter destruction was the mission of Jesus. The degeneracy of Judaism served to explain why God sent Jesus and why the Jews failed to recognize him as divine; it also served to highlight the extraordinary nature of Jesus' own religious personality, compared to the Jews.

At one of the Institute's first conferences, held in July 1939, Heinz Eisenhuth, professor of systematic theology at the University of Jena, explained "The Meaning of the Bible for Faith." He argued that Luther's translation of the Bible had transmitted the meaning of the gospel for the German people, but new historical-critical scholarship would refine Luther's understanding. The tie of Christians in Germany to the Bible was not legalistic, but ethical: "*Völkish* ethics also need an inner religious foundation." The Old Testament, however, was the expression of a racially foreign soul and a non-Christian religion.[26] Jewish influence had infiltrated Germany not only through the Old Testament, but also through secularization processes. Spinoza was one example of such a nefarious Jewish influence, explained Martin Redeker, professor of systematic theology at the University of Kiel. He argued, "Just as the Jew does not know and see the living God and his will, but only the Torah, the law and its development in the Talmud, so for Spinoza nature is not a living reality. Rather, he sees only rigid natural laws and seeks to explain them. Natural law takes the place of divine law for him. Jews lack the awe before nature that Germans have, and the sense of being bound up with nature; [the Jew] stands cold in relation to nature. The German experiences God as being in the background of all events and affecting all events; for the Jew there isn't this view of faith behind the superficiality of life and history, for him there is only the visible, material world."[27]

Exposing the dangers of the Jews for German society continued to be a major theme at Institute-sponsored conferences. At a meeting held in July 1941, the writer Wilhelm Kotzde-Kottenrodt argued that Jews had eliminated God from the world ("Juda hat die Welt entgottet"); they are unable to understand the higher thoughts of Nordics, that the world is filled with God. The Old Testament itself is an unreliable document, since Jews have used and distorted it to their own purposes through the centuries.[28]

The Institute's publications tried to prove that the Jews had always been aggressive and threatening. The Maccabees were cited as an example, as were the Hasmoneans generally, and the Zealots. Judaism continued to be violent and dangerous; Jesus' goal was clear: to save the world and fight against Judaism.[29] Subtle perversions of society characterize Judaism; Bertram argued that from Philo to the present day, Jewish assimilation had the goal of decomposing a society and then taking control over it.[30]

In their discussions of how to de-Judaize Christianity, Institute members debated how to define Judaism. Eisenhuth argued that the entire Old Testament, including the prophetic literature, should be eliminated, while the New Testament should be purged of all texts except the four gospels—Paul being considered a Jewish theologian. Heinz Hunger, a pastor who served as business director of the Institute, argued that de-Judaization consisted of removing the "Gestalt" of the Jew ("Entjudung heisse nur Ausmerzung der Gestalt des Juden"). Friedrich Wienecke, one of the German Christian leaders in Berlin, identified Jewishness with Pharisaism, in which depravity is religiously embellished; that is, the stock market is transformed into religion—the Jewish Trick. Wienecke was supported by Redeker and Grundmann. Redeker emphasized the materialist influence of the Jews on German society, even on some major theological figures, such as Karl Barth.[31]

The purging of everything Jewish from Christianity that was proposed by Institute members was perceived by many as radical and illegitimate. Grundmann defended his proposals by arguing that "Just as people couldn't imagine Christianity without the Pope during the time of Luther, so, too, they can't imagine salvation without the Old Testament."[32] De-Judaizing Christianity was simply a continuation of the Reformation.

The problem of removing "Judaism" from Christianity was theologically complex. According to Grundmann, the very concept of God is radically different in Judaism and Christianity: "The Jewish concept of God is fundamentally determined through the *Vergeltungsgedanken*: God is the Judge who rewards and punishes. But Jesus sees God as One who forgives, in order to generate community."[33] The distinction is not an accident; Jesus undertook a fight against Yahweh as a tribal God and against Judaism.[34] In the Sermon on the Mount, he argues, Jesus expresses a sense of community between God and human beings, and elsewhere Jesus addresses God in intimate terms, as "Abba," father, rather than the Hebrew term, "Yahweh." Grundmann devoted a book to discussing the ethical implications of that relationship.[35] He concluded that Jesus introduced a new understanding of God and of divine expectations for human beings that entailed a situational ethic that overrode commandments such as the prohibition against murder. Jesus' authority was rooted in himself, rather than in the Bible, and it was insignificant that Jesus cited the prophets and psalms of the Old Testament, because "so much more that is in the Old Testament was not cited by Jesus."[36] Rather than being bound by the Old Testament's laws and commandments, which represent a Jewish outlook, Christians are to follow Jesus' example and make moral decisions by listening to the religiosity of their own hearts, which transcends commandments, even those prohibiting murder.

He wrote: "With the proclamation of the kingdom of God as present, a new experience of God and a new understanding of God were linked. Internally, it had nothing to do with Judaism, but meant the dissolution of the Jewish religious world; that should be recognizable from the fact alone that the Jews brought Jesus Christ to the cross."[37]

Jesus as Aryan

The German Christians liked to claim that their mission was not to create a new Christianity, but to provide a Christianity appropriate to the German people. Christian missionaries in other parts of the world had not hesitated to synthesize elements intrinsic to the native culture with Christian beliefs and liturgies, and native Germanic expressions should be similarly included in a German Christianity, they argued. What is striking, however, is how they defined those native Germanic expressions: "German" was equated with the elimination of everything "Jewish." While purging Hebrew words from the liturgy or Scriptures was a fairly easy task, the greater problem was what to do with gospels accounts describing Jesus as Jew. What role could there be for a Jewish savior in a religion of German Christianity?

For Grundmann, who served as academic director of the Institute, that assumption was false; Jesus was not a Jew at all, but the great enemy of the Jews. That Jesus was an Aryan was not a new idea; it had already been proposed during the nineteenth century by some German philosophers and scholars. Fichte, in his *Addresses to the German Nation,* suggested that Jesus may not have been of Jewish origin, based on the omission of his genealogy in the Gospel of John.[38] The rise of racial theory in the nineteenth century provided a new vocabulary, allowing scholars such as Ernest Renan to distinguish between a Semitic Old Testament and an Aryan New Testament.[39] Renan sought to prove that Christianity was not Semitic in origin because Jesus came from northern Galilee, rather than Judea;[40] Jesus' Galilean origin was not an uncommon motif in the 1860s and 1870s in German lives of Jesus.[41] Friedrich Delitzsch added the further suggestion that the Galilee had been resettled after the Assyrian conquest with Babylonians of mixed Aryan descent.[42]

Paul de Lagarde, one of Germany's great Semitic scholars, rejected Christianity's understanding of Jesus as an "intolerable distortion."[43] Jesus was no Jew, but a rebel against Judaism who deliberately called himself a Son of Man to escape any association with the Jews. In another kind of approach, Edmon Picard argued in 1899 that Jesus must have been an Aryan because of his antipathy to capitalism, the tool of the Jews.[44] Houston Stewart Chamberlain gave widespread popularity to the idea that Jesus was racially Aryan, and German professors of Protestant theology in the 1910s and 1920s found themselves debating the issue, granting the claim even greater legitimacy.[45] Ernst Lohmeyer developed the theory of a two-site origin of early Christianity: Galilee, where a universalistic, son-of-man eschatology prevailed, and Jerusalem, dominated by nationalistic, Jewish eschatology.[46] Rudolf Otto had made a similar claim, based on his phenomenological observations of Jewish and Christian religiosity.[47]

In his 1940 study of Jesus, *Jesus der Galilaeer und das Judentum*, Grundmann concluded that because Jesus rejected the Jewish title of "messiah" in favor of the title "son of man," he must have been of Galilean origin, and was therefore, "with the greatest probability," not a Jew, but a member of one of the foreign peoples living in northern Palestine since the Assyrian conquest in the 8th century B.C.E., most likely an Aryan. Although Grundmann declared Jesus to have been an Aryan, the troubling problem remained to account for Jewish concepts and texts within the very body of the New Testament, attributed to Jesus. But the explanation was simple: the image and message of Jesus had been falsified by the early Jewish Christians, who presented Jesus as "the fulfiller of the law and the new teacher of law, sent only to the house of Israel."[48] Furthermore, the Jews expected a messiah who would be their ruler, whereas Jesus' message was to be a server of God and the community.[49] Johannes Hempel, professor of Old Testament at the University of Berlin and one of the early organizers of the Institute, argued that Jesus' monotheism broke with the Old Testament's henotheism, and that he similarly universalized the promise of salvation.[50] Opening his address to the Institute's conference in March 1941, Grundmann declared, "Our Volk, which stands above all else in a struggle against the satanic powers of world Jewry for the order and life of this world, dismisses Jesus, because it cannot struggle against the Jews and open its heart to the king of the Jews."[51]

The Institute took the argument a step further, seeking its recognition within the institutional church. Grundmann argued that Jewish motifs in the New Testament represent falsifications of the original text, introduced by early Jewish Christians to distort the tradition, in order "to make Christianity serve the purposes of Judaism."[52] German New Testament scholars were considered the finest in the world, and so could emend the biblical text to remove

Jewish elements. As students trained by Gerhard Kittel, Grundmann, Bertram, and other leaders of the Institute were considered experts on Judaism, though their work shows limited awareness of the Hebrew sources, and a very narrow reading of Greek Jewish sources.

The eradication of Jewish influences from Christianity was viewed, in other words, as a restoration of the original message of Jesus and a recovery of his historical personage. Not the Aryan Jesus, but the Jewish Jesus was the falsification, and the sophistication of modern theology's historical-critical methods finally enabled that recognition and the reformation of church life it engendered. Far from being a threat to religious faith, National Socialism was viewed as a great opportunity for the revival of true Christianity.[53]

The Theological Faculty at the University of Jena

Most of the theological faculties at German universities had professors who were supporters of the German Christian movement, or even members of the Institute, and they inevitably brought their anti-Jewish viewpoints to their scholarship and teaching. In some cases, such professors dominated and controlled the kind of theological education provided. The situation at the University of Jena, located just a short distance from the Institute's headquarters in Eisenach, was highly politicized, and the theologians were no exception. The theological faculty at Jena strove to create, in the words of one of its professors, Wolf Meyer-Erlach, "a stronghold of National Socialism."[54] To that end, only Nazi supporters were appointed professors, student dissertations had to comply with Nazi racial theory, and "Jewish" topics such as the Hebrew language were eliminated. Several other theological faculties had also abolished the study of Hebrew or made Old Testament studies optional. In 1938 Grundmann urged eliminating the study of Hebrew from the curriculum at the University of Jena because, he argued, the early Christians had read the Greek Bible and because the Greek text of the Old Testament is older than the extant Hebrew manuscripts. The decision to make Hebrew study optional was announced by the Dean, Eisenhuth, on 1 April 1939.[55]

Both Grundmann and Eisenhuth were appointed to the faculty in 1936. According to the recommendation written by Meyer-Erlach, who was then serving as rector of the university, Eisenhuth was "unquestionably a reliable Party member, who, out of deepest convictions, stands true to the Führer and to the movement and with greatest earnestness works to bring a decisive recognition of

National Socialism to his discipline."[56] Similarly, Meyer-Erlach recommended Grundmann as a long-time member of the NSDAP who expressed his loyalty to National Socialism in his theological scholarship, which "will be path-breaking for a National Socialist perspective in the field of theology."[57] On 17 December 1937, Eisenhuth was appointed tenured professor, on orders signed by Hitler. Identical orders making Grundmann a tenured professor were signed by Hitler on 5 October 1938.

During the Nazi era, approximately thirty-six students submitted doctoral dissertations in theology at Jena; ten were rejected, always on grounds that they had not paid sufficient attention to issues of race. Several of the students as well as faculty were active members of the Institute and used the Jena faculty to promote their antisemitism. The students' dissertations frequently treated topics concerning Christianity's relationship to National Socialism; the faculty evaluated their work on political grounds.

Of the thirty-six doctoral dissertations submitted to the theological faculty during the years 1933-1945, twelve were written under Grundmann's direction, and several students were Institute members. For example, although one student was an active member of the NSDAP since 1931, his dissertation, "Notwendiger Christ," claimed that Jesus' ideas must be understood within an Old Testament context. It was rejected. Meyer-Erlach explained, "The theologian lacks the understanding of National Socialism, that the racial question is the fundamental question for everything." On the other hand, the 1941 dissertation by another student, on "Präexistenz und Unsterblichkeit," received a mixed review from Grundmann: "The author observes correctly that Judaism took over its ideas about the preexistence and immortality of the human soul from other perspectives and religions. This, however, did not lead him to the fundamental observation of the spiritual unproductivity of Judaism. ... Judaism represents a level of human spirituality that has been left behind ... and which has degenerate effects on higher perspectives."[58] A third student, although himself a member of the Institute as well as of the NSDAP, had to make revisions in his 1942 dissertation, "Die Wandlung der katholischen Kirche in ihrer Stellung zur Judenfrage seit der franzosischen Revolution," because he gave too much credit to the Roman Catholics for developing antisemitism, thereby unfairly denying adequate credit to the Protestants.

The situation at Jena was not exceptional, although the small size of the theological faculty and the dominance of leading figures from the Institute made it particularly problematic, and it can be said to have fulfilled Meyer-Erlach's goal of creating a "stronghold of National Socialism." Through their academic work, Institute members were able to transform their antisemitism into "respectable" teachings of Christian theology. Through theological faculties the antisemitic Christian theology of the Nazi era was transmitted to the next generation of ministers and theologians.

The Final Years

The distinguished church historian Kurt Meier has argued that the Institute was established as a defense of Christianity against Nazism.[59] There is, however, no evidence that the churches were in any danger of being dissolved by the regime, nor does Meier's claim explain the enormous enthusiasm with which Institute members set about their tasks of de-Judaizing Christianity. On the contrary, Institute members seem to have been sincerely committed to the work they were undertaking. An exchange of letters between Grundmann and Institute member H. J. Thilo, written in November 1942, makes clear Grundmann's commitment to an Aryan Christianity: "I cannot go back to the old church ... thus there remains nothing else but to go humbly into the corner and take up other work as a German literature scholar or historian."[60] Disappointed over the failure of the German Christian movement to achieve its hoped-for recognition by the regime, Grundmann had confidence that the Institute at least had broad popular support among German soldiers, as he wrote to another Institute member, Gerhard Delling, who was serving in 1942 as a military chaplain.[61] Grundmann articulated in that correspondence his awareness that his Christian support for National Socialism was an unrequited affection.

In the fall of 1943, Grundmann was drafted into military service and replaced as director of the Institute by Georg Bertram. Even as growing numbers of Germans came to believe that they would not win the war, and as Goebbels's total war propaganda lost any credibility, Carl Schneider, a member of the institute and professor at the University of Königsberg, called for an even more radical de-Judaization of Christian theology, redefining early Christianity as itself an antisemitic movement. Bertram sent a report to Institute members in March 1944, in which he described his goals: "'This war is the fight of the Jews against Europe.' This sentence contains a truth, which is over and over again confirmed by the research work of the Institute. However this work serves not only as a head-on attack, but also as a strengthening of the inner front to attack and defend against all clandestine Judaism and Jewish essence which has seeped into occidental culture during the course of the centuries."[62]

In the summer of 1944, Church Superintendent Hugo Pich, whose 1938 report had served as the basis for establishing the Institute, sent a proposal to church officials for a more thorough de-Judaization of the Scriptures, entitled "The Jew Saul and his Proclamation of Christ." Pich called for a thorough overhaul of the Pauline epistles, arguing that they were infected with Jewish notions that had contaminated Christianity. By this time, both church and Institute officials were unsympathetic, given the war conditions.[63] Moreover, one German Christian church official argued, Pich's proposal regarding the Pauline epistles would imply that for so many centuries the church had been held hostage by a Jew: "I consider Pich's statements totally misguided and moreover an insult to our Volk, whom one indirectly insults by saying that in its miserable narrowness and lack of instinct for 1500 years it was duped into servility by some stinking Jew."[64]

It is noteworthy that even at the end of the war, Institute members did not give up their efforts. In May of 1945, as Thuringia fell under Allied occupation, Bertram petitioned the Thuringian church, now run by former members of the Confessing Church, to retain the Institute, on the grounds that its work was "neither politically determined, nor expressed politically." Rather, its goal was to demonstrate scientifically that "Jesus had taken up a fight against Judaism in all sharpness and had fallen as victim to [his fight]."[65] The Church Council of Thuringia met with Bertram on May 24, 1945, to decide whether the Institute should be retained as a research center. According to the minutes of the meeting, Pastor von Nitzsch thanked Bertram for his work but stated that such a worldwide project could not be supported by the small church of Thuringia. Church Consul Büchner stated the importance of retaining the Institute, especially since the theological library at the University of Jena had been damaged during bombings. Moritz Mitzenheim, soon to become bishop of Thuringia, urged dissolution of the Institute, but retention of its property. Church Consul Phieler wanted the Institute retained, but with its goals changed to a historical study of the Luther Bible and its effects on German culture and the Protestant people. On May 31, 1945, Phieler wrote to Bertram with the decision that the Institute would not be reopened. Bertram was thanked for his service, but rejected for future work within the Thuringian church.[66] He returned to Giessen.[67]

In the fall of 1945, Grundmann returned from a Russian prisoner-of-war camp and appealed to church officials to maintain the

Institute, arguing that since non-German scholars had arrived at the same conclusions, the work of the Institute could not be seen as merely reflecting "tendencies of the era" *(Zeittendenzen),* but was the result of serious scholarship that should be continued.[68] He explained that the Institute's research had concluded that Jesus was independent of the Old Testament and stood in opposition to the Judaism of his day. Moreover, he wrote, the Institute's goal had been a defense of Christianity against National Socialism; "The National Socialist system led the fight against Christianity with all legal means at its disposal." In the eyes of the Nazis, he continued, "Christianity is of Jewish origin, is Judaism for Aryans and must therefore be rooted out. As spiritual Judaism it poisons the German soul." The Institute, Grundmann concluded, was a defense of the church.

But Grundmann's argument produced no effect and his proposal to maintain the Institute was rejected in January of 1946. One church official, who shortly thereafter was appointed to the professorship in practical theology at the University of Jena once held by Meyer-Erlach, wrote that he regretted the curtailment of Grundmann's scholarship, which he respected, but that the church could not retain the Institute.[69] The Institute was closed, its extensive library was incorporated into the Thuringian ministerial training seminar (Predigerseminar), and the liturgical materials it had published were no longer used. Readings from the Old Testament were reintroduced into church services after the war. No official condemnation of the Institute's antisemitism was ever issued by the Thuringian church.

Most institute members continued their careers unhampered after the war. Grundmann, Meyer-Erlach, and Eisenhuth lost their professorships at the University of Jena because of their early membership in the NSDAP, but all were given positions of distinction within the postwar church. Jena replaced them with other institute members, Herbert Preisker and Rudolf Meyer. Other Institute professors and instructors retained their academic positions. Georg Bertram moved from Giessen to Frankfurt, Gerhard Delling left Leipzig for Greifswald, Rudi Paret left Heidelberg for Bonn and then Tübingen. Martin Redeker remained at Kiel, Johannes Leipoldt at Leipzig, Wilhelm Koepp at Greifswald, Fritz Wilke and Gustav Entz at Vienna. Karl Georg Kuhn, one of the most notorious figures, lost his position at Tübingen, but moved on to Mainz and then Heidelberg. Other members who retained their professorships include Hempel, Bertram, Hartmut Schmoekel, and Carl Schneider, among others. Grundmann, who had joined the NSDAP in December 1930, protested the loss of his professorship in a letter to the new rector, claiming that he had not been a perpetrator, but rather the victim of a struggle by the Nazi party against his work and his person.[70]

Grundmann's return to the church came as a result of support from state officials. In January 1946, state officials in Thuringia had refused Grundmann's request for support in securing a church position.[71] Less than a year later, however, they reversed their position. In the fall of 1946, the state urged Grundmann's retention by the church on the grounds that he had waged a "manly struggle" *against* National Socialist ideology. Testimony came from Grundmann's erstwhile colleagues, Eisenhuth and Meyer-Erlach, who declared that Grundmann had been persecuted by anti-Christian Nazi officials. His early membership in the NSDAP was dismissed as the error of an "unworldly" theologian who realized his error soon after 1933. His value as an internationally recognized scholar was cited by pointing to his membership in the distinguished Society of New Testament Studies, which had offered him membership in 1938. Like so many other leaders of the German Christians, Grundmann emerged from the de-Nazification process relatively unscrutinized. Yet Grundmann's Nazi-era activities were known to East German officials. As late as 1990 an East German secret police (Stasi) document lists his name among other Nazi supporters and war criminals who had eluded responsibility by receiving a church position.[72] Gerhard Besier suggests that the information was used by the Stasi to control Grundmann.[73]

Few members of the Institute expressed any public repentance for their Nazi-era activities. In the later years of their lives, both Meyer-Erlach and Grundmann continued to present themselves as persecuted victims of the Nazi regime. Meyer-Erlach claimed that "despite threats and temptations" he had never abandoned the church and that he had "fought the Party" in his writings. Further, he had been mocked by regime officials because his name, Meyer, sounded Jewish and because he had once attended a synagogue service in Würzburg in 1929, which had led Nazi officials to mock him as "der Synagoge-Meyer."[74] He was no antisemite, he further stated, since he retained his Jewish family physician until November 1933, and once permitted a Jewish doctor to operate on two of his children. By contrast, Grundmann's postwar defenses do not even mention antisemitism, and in his 1969 unpublished autobiography he barely acknowledges that he erred during the Third Reich: "We attempted to pose the questions raised by the period and not to avoid them. I admit that in so doing we made [big—this word is crossed out in the manuscript] mistakes." While most of the materials pertaining to Grundmann's denazification remain closed, he

writes in his autobiography that he had stood in real danger of
Nazi retribution as the result of his writings criticizing Rosenberg.[75]
Their claims were effective; in January 1962 Meyer-Erlach, now
living in Hessen, received the Federal Republic of Germany's Ver-
dienstkreuz, First Class.[76] In meetings with church officials of
Thuringia in late 1945, to clear himself of any Nazi suspicions,
Grundmann insisted that his fundamental commitment to Christ
had never wavered during the Nazi years. Church leaders asked
him to express an acceptance of the Barmen Declaration as a sign
that he accepted the ultimate sovereignty of Christ, rather than of
political leadership; Grundmann agreed.

In the postwar years, Grundmann was appointed rector of the
seminary in Thuringia that trained religion teachers and church
organists. He also taught at the ministerial seminary in Leipzig,
and served as advisor to the Protestant publishing house of the German Democratic Republic, a powerful position. He continued to
publish extensively, and his commentaries on the synoptic gospels
became highly-regarded reference works in the post-war theological communities of East and West Germany. Shortly before his
death in 1976 he was appointed Kirchenrat of Thuringia, an honorary position that indicates the esteem with which he was
regarded by the post-war church in East Germany.

Church Opposition to the Institute

The Institute was not without its critics within the church. The so-
called "church struggle" refers to the ongoing clash for control of
the church that developed between two Protestant factions, the
German Christian movement and the Confessing Church. Members of the Confessing Church came from a more conservative theological tradition that objected to alterations in the biblical text,
liturgy, and catechism, although many were sympathetic to the
Hitler regime. Their opposition to the Institute and its theology
was rooted in its radical changes of traditional Christian teachings,
and was not directed primarily against its antisemitism. Indeed,
Wolfgang Gerlach has documented the failure of the Confessing
Church to take a stand in support of Jews, other than those who
had already converted to Christianity, and he has also exposed the
theological anti-Judaism in the writings of many Confessing
Church theologians.[77] For example, the Godesberg Declaration of
April 1939, which created the Institute, evoked Confessing Church
hostility and resulted in a counter-declaration, issued on 31 May

1939, and signed by leading Confessing Church bishops, including Theophil Wurm (Württemberg), Hans Meiser (Bavaria), and August Marahrens (Hannover): "In the realm of faith there exists the sharp opposition between the message of Jesus Christ and his apostles and the Jewish religion of legalism and political messianic hope, which is already emphatically fought against in the Old Testament. In the realm of the volkish life an earnest and responsible racial politics is required for the preservation of the purity of our people."[78] In the argument of this statement, elimination of the Old Testament is unnecessary because it is not a Jewish book, but an anti-Jewish book. Racial policies are acceptable and necessary, according to the statement, and Christianity stands in opposition to Judaism, as the Godesberg Declaration had also formulated.

Opposition to the Institute's publications also came from some of Grundmann's colleagues in the field of New Testament studies who sided with the Confessing Church. For example, Grundmann's 1940 study of Jesus' racial background, *Jesus der Galiläer*, which argued that Jesus could not have been a Jew, was reviewed negatively by Hans von Soden, professor of New Testament and Church History at the University of Marburg and an active member of the Confessing Church.[79] Yet von Soden simply argued that the racial question was theologically irrelevant, and criticized Grundmann for his sloppy scholarship; he did not fault Grundmann's negative presentation of Judaism.[80]

Most striking in the Confessing Church opposition to German Christian measures is the negative attitude toward Judaism shared by both sides. For example, in a pamphlet issued by the Confessing Church in 1939 to repudiate the Institute, von Soden distinguishes between the historical phenomenon of Judaism, which formed the basis of early Christianity, and a spiritual "Jewishness," which fails to understand religion because it "confuses outward and inward." This "Jewishness," he writes, "shudders before every Hebrew word in the liturgy or hymnal, but has itself fallen victim to the Jewish-anti-Christian spirit."[81] The German Christian movement is infected with this "Jewishness," according to von Soden, as illustrated by the de-Judaization efforts called for in the Godesberg Declaration. Trying to de-Judaize Christianity by banning the Old Testament and re-writing the hymnal and New Testament actually "threatens a spiritual Judaization" of the church, according to von Soden. While von Soden, along with the majority of Confessing Church members, vigorously opposed German Christian measures, they agreed with the basic assumption that Judaization represents a real threat to Christianity. The difference between the two groups lay in their definition of what constitutes Judaization. For von Soden, the threat comes not from the Old Testament, Hebrew words, and other elements within traditional Christian theology, but from what he saw as an antispiritual, materialistic theology promoted by Grundmann and his German Christian colleagues.

The response of the Confessing Church represents a tradition that does not repudiate antisemitism, but redefines it. Judaism is a recognizable religion that can be debated, opposed, or accepted. Jewishness, however, was seen as an evil that potentially can afflict all people, even Christians, and must therefore be opposed with the strongest means available. Just as German antisemitism toward the end of the nineteenth century considered the greatest danger to be assimilated Jews, because they could inflict a nefarious influence before they were ever recognized as Jews, Jewishness could infiltrate Christian theology and poison it. The great danger of modern Christian anti-Judaism was not its opposition to the religion of Judaism, nor to Jews—Jews and Judaism were not the problem, and were even at times viewed with respect and concern during the Nazi era—but rather the imaginary danger associated with the loosely-defined but far more threatening concept of "Jewishness."

Historiographical Observations

The history of the Institute calls into question aspects of the historiography concerning developments within the Protestant church during the Third Reich. The relatively few studies of the German Christians have not examined its effective exploitation of antisemitism after 1938 to gain adherents and win support from the Nazi regime. Through the Institute the German Christians achieved an effective structure for disseminating its theology and avoiding disintegration after the onset of the war. Moreover, the German Christians cannot be considered an insignificant movement within the church, considering the support the Institute won from professors of theology at prominent German universities and the large number of orders placed for its liturgical materials by churches throughout the Reich. Its effectiveness is also shown by the individuals who at first kept themselves at a distance from the German Christians, such as Werner, but who eventually became supporters of the Institute.

How should the Institute's relation to the Nazi regime be evaluated? Viewing the Institute primarily as a creation of Nazi antisemitic ideology would sever its links to pre-1933 theological tendencies and would not explain why church members found its theology respectable. On the other hand, without the Third Reich and its intensification of anti-Jewish policies after 1938, German Christian leaders might well have developed a different ideology; they clearly realized antisemitism would be politically advantageous. The Institute made effective use of traditional Christian anti-Judaism to support Nazi policy, offering theologians for the service of the regime. Institute membership included not only a few well-known theologians, but a large number, in all fields of theology, at universities throughout the Reich. Finally, it is significant that Institute associates continued to work within the churches and university theological faculties after 1945. Records of the churches' de-Nazification proceedings remain closed to scholars, in many cases, but they would be important for establishing the degree to which the Institute's theology was viewed as acceptable even after the Third Reich collapsed.

The conventional treatment of the German Christians as a marginal phenomenon within the German churches is called into question by the accomplishments of the Institute. The popular and academic publications, the extent of their distribution to churches throughout the Reich, and the representation of its membership from the ranks of university faculties and church hierachies, all indicate a higher level of influence attained by the German Christians than has been recognized. Finally, the Institute's theology should be analyzed as a phenomenon parallel to Nazism itself; that is, one with roots within the history of German antisemitism and Christian theological anti-Judaism, taken to radical extremes out of both genuine conviction and quest for political power. The Institute undertook within Christianity the goals of National Socialism: as the Nazi regime was creating an Aryan Germany, the Institute was creating a Aryan Christianity.

Conclusion

Scholars in several fields have articulated their conviction that the Holocaust calls into question the basic frame of reference of their fields. Edith Wyschogrod writes that "the meaning of self, time, and language are all affected by mass death. ... We are in the grip of immense experiential changes which both create and reflect new philosophical perspectives."[82] No other field has been challenged as severely by the Holocaust as that of Christian theology. Held responsible as the major source for antisemitism, its moral legiti-

macy is called into question. Not only its specific teachings about
Jews and Judaism, beginning in the New Testament, but one or
another of its modes of thinking—apocalyptic, gnostic, redemptive—are interrogated as the modes by which Nazism structured its
ideology. Only among some church historians studying the Nazi
period do we find a tendency to hold the church exempt from
responsibility for the Holocaust, as persecuted victims of National
Socialism along with the Jews, as Kurt Meier argues, or as independent wellsprings of theological purity, as Trutz Rendtorff argues.[83]
Such conclusions are possible only when disconfirming data is
ignored by avoiding the holdings of certain archives, a problem
that has plagued the field of church history until recently, particularly in Germany. Few church historians, for example, have investigated the holdings of the Berlin Document Center, which contains
membership information for the NSDAP and related organizations.
As a result, no conclusions can be drawn regarding the membership
of ministers and theologians in the Nazi Party in relation to other
professional groups.

The theological problem is whether the German Christian
movement is a product of Christianity, or of Christianity gone awry.
What the experience of the churches in Nazi Germany makes clear
is that no mechanism exists within Christian theology that was
capable of excluding Nazi excesses as un-Christian. The story of the
Institute calls into question whether German Protestant theology
has an intrinsic moral commitment and self-judgment, as it is clear
that Grundmann's efforts would have been praised had the Nazis
won; the sympathetic judgment of several contemporary church historians makes that clear. I would argue that Christian inhibitions
against violent atrocities were eroded once four conditions were
met: the institutional church gave its approval; the actions and
beliefs were routinized by citing older, well-known theological anti-
Judaism; the Jews were presented as a moral danger to Christians;
and a theological appeal to so-called higher authority, values, or
spirituality was formulated. That the German Christian movement
emerged out of liberal Protestantism is crucial; it presented itself as
a modern, scientific theological movement, not as a religious faith
rooted in the supernatural; it was a religion that affirmed society, its
political structures, and its intellectual discourse.

In his critique of Emil Durkheim's claim that "man is a moral
being only because he lives in society," Zygmunt Bauman has
argued for the social production of immoral behavior. Morality,
Bauman writes, "may manifest itself in insubordination towards
socially upheld principles, and in an action openly defying social

solidarity and consensus."[84] Morality is not the product of society, but is pre-social, Bauman argues, and it is something that society manipulates and exploits. If responsibility, as Levinas argues, is the essential structure of subjectivity, morality is the primary structure of intersubjective relation, and its creation is pre-social, Bauman argues. Morality is not a product of society, but is something that society manipulates and exploits. So, too, with theology. While it claims to be the creator and upholder of morality, morality is both prior to and independent of theology. The Institute functioned as the religious justification for the social production of Nazi antisemitism. What the German Christian movement created was a theology able to manipulate and exploit morality.[85]

Notes

* Note: a version of this article, entitled, "Redemptive Antisemitism: The De-Judaization of the New Testament in the Third Reich," has appeared in: Robert P. Ericksen and Susannah Heschel, eds. *Betrayal: German Churches and the Holocaust* (Minneapolis: Augsburg-Fortress Press, 1999).

Abbreviations:

BDC	Berlin Document Center
EZA	Evangelisches Zentral Archiv, Berlin
LKA Thüringen	Landeskirchenarchiv Thüringen
THW	Thüringisches Hauptstaatsarchiv, Weimar
TMV	Thüringen Minister für Volksbildung
UJ	Universitätsarchiv, Jena

1. Saul Friedländer, *Nazi Germany and the Jews* (New York, 1997), p. 87.
2. Walter Grundmann, "Das Heil Kommt von den Juden: Eine Schicksalsfrage an die Christen deutscher Nation," *Deutsche Frömmigkeit* 9 (September 1938), p. 1.
3. Georg Bertram, *Denkschrift* betr. Aufgaben eines theologischen Forschungs-Instituts zu Thüringen 6 May 1945, 1. LKA Thüringen, p. A921.
4. Walter Grundmann and Karl Friedrich Euler, *Das religiöse Gesicht des Judentums: Entstehung und Art* (Leipzig, 1942), Vorwort.
5. Uriel Tal, *Christians and Jews in Germany*, Trans. Noah Jacobs (Ithaca, 1975).
6. BDC, Sasse materials.
7. Kurt Meier, *Kreuz und Hakenkreuz, Die evangelische Kirche im Dritten Reich* (Munich, 1992); John S. Conway, *The Nazi Persecution of the Churches, 1933-1945* (New York, 1968); Trutz Rendtorff, "Das Wissenschaftsverständnis der protestantischen Universitätstheologie im Dritten Reich," in *Theologis-*

che Fakultäten im Nationalsozialismus, ed. Leonore Siegele-Wenschkewitz and Carsten Nicolaisen (Göttingen, 1993), pp. 19-44.

8.   The exchange, between Hans Schmidt, president of the Fakultätentages der evangelisch-theologischen Fakultäten Deutschlands, the umbrella organization representing the seventeen Protestant theological faculties in Germany, and Heinrich Himmler, head of the SS, can be found in the UJ Bestand J, Nr. 292, and in Universitätsarchiv Heidelberg H 1/055, and in Universitätsarchiv Giessen, B6, Band 1.

9.   Berlin Document Center: Schumacher Collection on Church Affairs, T580, R. 42; also in Bundesarchiv, Koblenz BA R43II/150 Fiche #3.

10.   LKA Thüringen, DC III 2 f., Letters to Grundmann from Hempel; Letter to Grundmann from Propp, dated 5 February 1938.

11.   Hugo Pich, Superintendent in Schneidemühl, "Entjudung von Kirche und Christentum: Die praktische Durchführung." LKA Thüringen, A921.

12.   EZA, fols. 7/4166 and 7/4167. The Godesberg Declaration was printed in the *Gesetzblatt der deutschen evangelischen Kirche*, 5 (6 April 1939), p. 1.

13.   Other provisions of the addendeum, including founding a central office in the church to fight against the misuse of religion for political goals, were not carried through.

14.   Nordelbisches Kirchenarchiv, Kiel. Repertorium des Archivs der Bekennenden Kirche Schleswig-Holstein, Signatur 51; Neue Nummer 292.

15.   EZA, fol. 7/4166. Werner joined the NSDAP on 1 January 1931; membership 411184. BDC, Werner materials.

16.   Walter Grundmann, *Die Entjudung des religiösen Lebens als Aufgabe deutscher Theologie und Kirche* (Weimar, 1939), pp. 9-10.

17.   EZA, fol. 7/4166.

18.   Letter 19 Mai 1942 from Brauer to Finanzabteilung bei der Deutschen evangelischen Kirche; EZA 1/C3/174.

19.   Archiv des Auswärtiges Amt Inland I-D 3/4, Signatur R98796: Überwachung von Arbeitstagungen der Arbeitsgemeinschaft 'Germanentum und Christentum' und ihrer Leiter Professor Wolf Meyer-Erlach und Professor Grundmann, Verweigerung von Reisesichtvermerken, 1942-1944.

20.   LKA Thüringen, DC III 2 a.

21.   In some cases the church of Thuringia reimbursed, e.g., for five pastors from Austria. LKA Thüringen, DC III 2 a.

22.   Walter Grundmann, Wilhelm Büchner, Paul Gimpel, Hans Pribnow, Kurt Thieme, Max Adolf Wagenführer, Heinrich Weinmann, Hermann Werdermann, eds., *Deutsche mit Gott: Ein deutsches Glaubensbuch* (Weimar, 1941), p. 46.

23.   Reijo E. Heinonen, *Anpassung und Identität: Theologie und Kirchenpolitik der Bremer Deutschen Christen 1933-1945* (Göttingen, 1978).

24.   Ludwig Müller, *Deutsche Gotteswort* (Weimar, 1936). See also Müller's defense of the project, "Warum ich die Bergpredigt 'verdeutschte,'" *Briefe an Deutsche Christen*, 5:8 (15 April 1936), p. 82.

25.   LKA Thüringen, C VI, 2.

26.   Report of Tagung held 6-7 July 1939 in Thüringen; EZA 1/C3/174.

27.   EZA 1/C3/174.

28.   Wilhelm Kotzde-Kottenrodt, "Eine Deutsche Gottes- und Lebenskunde," lecture delivered at Institute-sponsored conference on the Wartburg, 19 July 1941. Text in LKA Thüringen.

29. Walter Grundmann, *Gestalt und Sinn der Bergrede Jesu.* Schriften zur Nationalkirche Nr. 10. (Weimar, 1939).

30. Georg Bertram, "Philo und die jüdische Propaganda in der antiken Welt," In: *Christentum und Judentum; Studien zur Erforschung ihres gegenseitigen Verhältnisses.* Sitzungsberichte der ersten Arbeitstagung des Institutes zur Erforschung des jüdischen Einflusses auf das deutsche kirchliche Leben vom 1. bis 3. März 1940 in Wittenberg, hrsg. Walter Grundmann (Leipzig, 1940), pp. 79-106.

31. Report by Wieneke, dated July 12, 1939, on Tagung in Thüringen July 6-7; EKA Akten betreffend Institut zur Erforschung und Beseitigung des jüdischen Einflusses auf das kirchliche Leben. Bestand: 7/4166 vom April 1939 bis März 1941 and 7/4167 vom April 1941 bis Dezember 1959.

32. Walter Grundmann, *Die Entjudung des religiösen Lebens als Aufgabe deutscher Theologie und Kirche* (Weimar, 1939), p. 17.

33. Walter Grundmann, *Die Bergrede Jesu.* Schriften zur Nationalkirche Nr. 10 (Weimar, 1939), p. 16.

34. Walter Grundmann, *Der Gott Jesu Christi* (Weimar, n. d.). Delivered at conference in 1936.

35. Walter Grundmann, *Die Gotteskindschaft in der Geschichte Jesu und ihre religionsgeschichtlichen Voraussetzungen* (Weimar, 1938).

36. Grundmann, *Jesus der Galiläer,* p. 143.

37. Walter Grundmann, *Die Gotteskindschaft in der Geschichte Jesu und ihre religionsgeschichtlichen Voraussetzungen* (Weimar, 1938), p. 162.

38. "Es bleibt auch bei diesem Evangelisten immer zweifelhaft, ob Jesus aus jüdischem Stamme sei, oder, falls er es doch etwa wäre, wie es mit seiner Abstammung sich eigentlich verhalte." Fritz Medicus, ed., *J. G. Fichte Werke,* Vol. IV (Leipzig, 1910-12), p. 105; see also *Addresses to the German Nation,* trans. by R. F. Jones and G. H. Turnbull (Chicago, 1922), pp. 68-69.

39. Ernest Renan, *Essai psychologique sur Jesus Christ* (Paris, 1921), pp. 55-57.

40. Ernest Renan, *La Vie de Jesus* (Paris, 1863).

41. See, for example, Theodor Keim, *Geschichte Jesu von Nazara* (Zurich, 1867).

42. Friedrich Delitzsch, *Die grosse Täusching: Kritische Betrachtungen zu den alttestamentlichen Berichten über Israels Eindringen in Kanaan, die Gottesoffenbarun vom Sinai und die Wirksamkeit der Propheten* (Stuttgart, 1920).

43. Fritz Stern, *The Politics of Cultural Despair,* (Berkeley, Calif., 1961), p. 41. See also Paul de Lagarde, *Deutsche Schriften,* "Die Religion der Zukunft," vol. 1 (Munich, 1934), p. 262; cited by Alan T. Davies, "The Aryan Christ: A Motif in Christian Anti-Semitism," *Journal of Ecumenical Studies* 12 (fall, 1975), pp. 569-79.

44. Edmond Picard, *L'Aryano-Semitisme* (Brussels, 1899).

45. Houston Stewart Chamberlain, *Die Grundlagen des neunzehnten Jahrhunderts* (Munich, 1902).

46. Ernst Lohmeyer, *Galiläa und Jerusalem* (Göttingen, 1936).

47. Rudolf Otto, *Reich Gottes und Menschensohn: ein Religionsgeschichtlicher Versuch* (München, 1933).

48. Walter Grundmann, "Das Problem des hellistischen Christentums innerhalb der Jerusalemer Urgemeinde," *Zeitschrift für neutestamentliche Wissenschaft* 38 (1939), p. 26.

49. Walter Grundmann, *Jesus der Galiläer und das Judentum* (Leipzig, 1940), pp. 57-58.

50. Johannes Hempel, "Der synoptische Jesus und das Alte Testament," *Zeitschrift für alttestamentliche Wissenschaft* 56 (1938), pp. 1-34.

51. Walter Grundmann, "Das Messiasproblem," in *Germanentum, Christentum und Judentum: Studien zur Erforschung ihres gegenseitigen Verhältnisses.* Sitzungsberichte der zweiten Arbeitstagung des Instituts zur Erforschung des jüdischen Einflusses auf das deutsche kirchliche Leben vom 3. bis 5. März 1941 in Eisenach, hrsg. Walter Grundmann (Leipzig, 1942), p. 381.

52. See Friedrich Schenke, *Das Christentum im ersten Jahrhundert völkisch gesehen* (Weimar, 1940).

53. Walter Grundmann, *Der Gott Jesu Christi* (Weimar, 1936), p. 7 and passim.

54. Meyer-Erlach to TMV 6 March 1937 re. Eisenhuth's appointment. Universitätsarchiv Jena D, No 603.

55. LKA Thüringen, DC: Hochschulangelegenheiten, 1937-1940. Memorandum dated May, 1938 to Reichsministerium für die kirchliche Angelegenheiten.

56. UJ Meyer-Erlach to TMV 6 March, 1937.

57. UJ Meyer-Erlach to TMV 23 October 1937.

58. Promotionsakten der Theologischen Fakultät, 1939-1941, Bestand J No. 90.

59. Kurt Meier, *Kreuz und Hakenkreuz,* p. 164.

60. LKA Thüringen, Nachlass Grundmann, NG 44, vol. 2; *Briefe* August 1942-April 1943, 18 November 1942.

61. LKA Thüringen, NG 44, vol. 2, 5 November 1942.

62. Report on March 1944 Tagung, held in Predigerseminar in Thüringen. Report signed by Georg Bertram. LKA Thüringen, Akten des Landeskirchenrats der Evangelisch-Lutherischen Kirche in Thüringen über Entjudung der Kirche, 1939-47; fol. A, no. 921.

63. Sievers to Pich, 15 August 1944, re. "The Path to the Dejudaized German National Church among the Discipleship of Jesus": "... after the total war has set in its sharpest form, we are allowed only one thought, how we can serve and assist our fatherland in this fateful war. I must, both personally and as chairman of the union of Protestant church leaders, and as acting director of the Institute for Research ... refuse to deal with the restructuring of the church and I would urgently recommend that you also let this issue rest now."

64. Bishop Walther Schultz to President Rönck , 2 August 1944 re. Pich's Denkschrift, *Der Jude Schaul.* LKA Thüringen, Personalia: Leffler, Grundmann: Institut 1938-1944.

65. Georg Bertram, *Denkschrift* betr. Aufgaben eines theologischen Forschungs-Instituts zu Eisenach 6 May 1945, 1. LKA Thüringen, Bestand A921: Akten des Landeskirchenrats der Evangelisch-Lutherischen Kirche in Thüringen über Entjudung der Kirche, 1939-47.

66. LKA Thüringen, A 921.

67. The University of Giessen was closed by American military forces in 1945 because of its Nazi sympathies. In 1955 Bertram was reinstated as instructor in Old Testament. He was also given an instructorship in Hebrew at the University of Frankfurt. Bertram died in 1979.

68. 12 December 1945. LKA Thüringen, DC III 2 a.

69. Hertzsch to Grundmann 14 January 1946, LKA Thüringen, DC III 2 a.

70. Letter from Thüringen Landesamt für Volksbildung, 13 September 1945, signed Wolf, Landesdirektor: "We are therefore dismissing you immediately from public service, on grounds of #2 of the decree concerning the cleansing of the public administration of Nazi elements." LKA Thüringen, DC III 2 a.

71. THW, Personalakte Walter Grundmann.

72. Gerhard Besier and Stephan Wolf, eds., *Pfarrer, Christen und Katholiken: Das Ministerium für Staatssicherheit der ehemaligen DDR und die Kirchen*, 2d ed. (Neukirchen-Vluyn, 1992): Document 133, p. 653.

73. Ibid.

74. Wolf Meyer-Erlach "Verfolgung durch die Partei," 12 June 1945. UJ Bestand J, No. 92: Promotionsakten, 1941-47. Regarding his name: Gaudozenten-bundsführer to Reichsamtsleitung des NSD-Dozentenbundes Dr. Redenz, Munich, 8 August 1938. UJ D, 2031: Wolf Meyer-Erlach Akten. An unsigned report to the Gestapo describes Meyer-Erlach's attendance at the synagogue and refers to him as "der Synagoge-Meyer." "Meyer-Erlach: Notorious for his speech at the inauguration of the synagogue of the Jewish community of Heidingsfeld near Würzburg in 1929, leading mind behind the German Christians. Faker and actor by nature with a strong element of the hysterical. Very strong need for admiration."

75. LKA Thüringen. Grundmann, "Erkenntnis und Wahrheit," pp. 44f.

76. Bundespräsidialamt Bonn, Ordenskanzlei. Personal correspondence, Az: OK 123-032-05 (H 89/61). The commendation mentions his establishment of a home in 1952 for East European refugee girls, and his organization since 1956 of 5,000 Christmas and Easter packages for shipment to Germans living in the Soviet zone.

77. Wolfgang Gerlach, *Als die Zeugen Schwiegen: Bekennende Kirche und die Juden* (Berlin, 1987).

78. EZA, 1/A4/170.

79. Together with his colleague Rudolf Bultmann, von Soden was active in formulating the "Marburg Report" of September 1933, which opposed application of the Aryan Paragraph in the realm of the Church. See E. Dinkler and E. Dinkler von Schubert, eds., *Theologie und Kirche im Wirken Hans von Sodens. Briefe und Dokumente aus der Zeit des Kirchenkampfes 1933-1945*, vol. 2 (Göttingen, 1984).

80. Hans von Soden, review of *Jesus der Galiläer und das Judentum. Deutsches Pfarrerblatt: Bundesblatt der deutschevangelischen Pfarrervereine und des Bundes der preussischen Pfarrervereine*, vol. 46, no. 13/14 (5 April 1942), p. 49.

81. Hans Freiherr von Soden, "Die Godesberger Erklärung," n.d., [private archive], University of Marburg.

82. Edith Wyschogrod, *Spirit in Ashes: Hegel, Heidegger, and Man-Made Mass Death* (New Haven, 1985), p. ix.

83. Trutz Rendtorff, "Das Wissenschaftsverständnis der protestantischen Universitätstheologie im Dritten Reich," in *Theologische Fakultäten im Nationalsozialismus*, ed. Leonore Siegele-Wenschkewitz and Carsten Nicolaisen (Göttingen, 1993), pp. 19-44.

84. Zygmunt Bauman, *Modernity and the Holocaust* (Ithaca, 1989), p. 177.

85. The author would like to thank the archivist of the Landeskirchenarchiv Thüringen, Pfarrer Heinz Koch, as well as Bill and Jill Shapiro and Jacob Aronson.

Chapter 4

A PURE CONSCIENCE IS GOOD ENOUGH
Bishop Von Galen and Resistance to Nazism

Beth Griech-Polelle

"Servants, be subject to your masters in all fear, not only to the good and moderate, but also to the severe." I Peter 2:18

In 1937 several German Catholic cardinals and bishops, including Bishop Clemens August Graf von Galen, travelled to Rome to ask Pope Pius XI to issue a public statement referring to the perils faced by Catholics in Nazi Germany. The German clergymen drafted what later came to be known as the papal encyclical, *Mit brennender Sorge*. The encyclical, focusing primarily on the ideological errors of National Socialism, contains no outright condemnation of antisemitism nor does it endorse Catholic participation in an open rebellion against the government. The advice given to Catholics is to shun unjust laws; advice essentially recommending passive disobedience in particular cases.

When the German bishops and cardinals met at Fulda following the publication of *Mit brennender Sorge*, two factions emerged. Bishop von Galen favored public protests against some aspects of Nazi ideology while Cardinal Bertram led a faction that feared any direct confrontation with the government. Bertram, as leader of the Fulda Conference, claimed that direct opposition would result in another *Kulturkampf* and asked that the clergymen agree to present a united front to the public. As a result, the men agreed not to reveal any discord in public and they "adopted a position that would be least offensive to them all."[1]

Von Galen has been portrayed as a staunch anti-Nazi resister, primarily because of three powerful sermons he delivered in the summer of 1941. However, upon closer examination, von Galen's "resistance" emerges as selective opposition to particular issues such as euthanasia and attacks on the Catholic clergy. Why did von Galen choose to object to certain policies and not to others? How does von Galen differ from the other church leaders of the Nazi era and where do their views coincide? How can we place his choices in the broader context of church-state relations in the 1930s and 1940s? I want to argue that von Galen serves as a useful example of a German Catholic bishop who never truly went beyond the limits of the prevalent theologically based notion of resistance. I maintain that the combination of the memory of the *Kulturkampf* in contemporary theological writings and von Galen's sense of nationalist citizenship all contributed to limiting the possibilities of responses to Nazism. If one defines resistance as being able to go beyond the enabling resources of one's area of expertise at a particular historical moment (i.e., Catholic moral reasoning in von Galen's case), then the bishop, like so many others in the Catholic hierarchy of the time, was simply unwilling to practice open, active resistance.

Historiographical Background

In the aftermath of World War II, the Catholic Church made no declaration of guilt concerning its position on the National Socialist regime. When von Galen was raised to the purple in February 1946,[2] this action drew attention to so-called resistance by Catholic clergy during the Third Reich. Books covering the opposition of the church began to appear which portrayed the church as a great opponent of the ideology of National Socialism.[3] Ecclesiastical historians such as Bishop Johannes Neuhäusler and Nathaniel Micklem used evidence concerning Hitler's anti-church policy to integrate church figures into the pantheon of German resisters.[4] Later historians examining the church's role under National Socialism began to write about a perceived lack of resistance on the part of the Catholic hierarchy. Authors such as J. S. Conway, G. Lewy, H. Müller, and G. Zahn wrote of a failure on the part of the church leaders to exert any moral or political leadership which might have inspired others to

work to lessen the impact of National Socialism.[5] Pathbreaking
works such as Kurt Nowak's 1978 study of the relationship between
the churches and euthanasia seriously question whether there was in
fact any resistance at all in the churches of Germany.[6] E.C. Helmreich[7] and Donald Dietrich, going beyond the euthanasia question,
suggest that the church hierarchy, in order to present a united front
to the public, mixed protests against certain Nazi policies with continuous assertions of loyalty and obedience to the state, which
resulted in confusion among their Catholic followers. Most of the
bishops and Cardinals in Germany decided to combine circum-
scribed opposition with assurances of patriotism, rationalizing their
inaction by stating that they could criticize the specific government in
authority while still supporting the German state. Their failure to act
decisively—coupled with their seeming inability to perceive the
impact of Hitler's racial policy on the state—deprived the church of
the moral prestige it would have enjoyed had it worked to mobilize
the limited pockets of resistance that initially existed in Germany.
This argument, put forward most strongly by Dietrich, leads one to
question why the bishops did not condemn Nazi policies more forcefully (or at all) and thereby mobilize resistance. Conversely, one wonders whether German Catholics would have supported the bishops
had they attacked what was seen by many as a legitimate regime?[8]
More specifically, I would like to show that von Galen, although portrayed as a staunch resister by his hagiographers,[9] merely mixed limited opposition with patriotic reassurances in his public speaking. I
would argue that this type of rhetorical resistance, rather than challenging the Catholics of Münster to resist the regime, served only to
confuse and restrict them to limited instances of disobedience.

In order to answer this question, let us begin by examining the
three moral questions raised by Dietrich which Catholics might
have asked themselves under the National Socialist regime:

1) How were they to fulfill their duties as citizens in the
   totalitarian Third Reich?
2) Was Hitler's war legitimate and if so, how were Catholics
   to fulfill their patriotic obligations and simultaneously
   secure their faith in the increasingly oppressive Reich?
3) How were Catholics to respond to the vitriolic racism of
   Nazi Germany and to the implementation of Hitler's
   eugenic policies?[10]

For many Catholics in Germany, the memory of the *Kulturkampf*, the desire to prove that Catholics could be loyal (rather

than the *Reichsfeinde* that Bismarck had branded them) combined with a longing to be accepted and no longer considered to be a minority in Germany, led many church leaders to emphasize that Catholics should be law-abiding citizens. Most did not question whether Hitler's war was a "just" one; rather they embraced nationalism, urging Catholics to prove that they too were German to the core. As for the racist policies of Nazism, the bishops tended to call for a lessening of persecution of converted Jews. It was not until much later in the war that some clergymen protested the mistreatment of Jews and by then it was too late to effectively stop the process of the Final Solution. There were, obviously, Catholic individuals such as Pastor Bernhard Lichtenberg, or Father Alfred Delp, who recognized the evil inherent in Nazism. But, as an entity, Church leadership chose to focus on maintaining institutional structures on German soil while losing sight of the moral and existential issues involved. Narrowing their protests to strictly "religious questions," they implied that governments rose and fell, but the church was eternal. "Religious" came to mean not supporting the human values of brotherly love and equality, but rather, keeping confessional schools, organizations, and associations alive. For the rare individual who did consider opposing Germany's government, it is necessary to examine what type of theological support existed, i.e., what theological resources could be called upon within the Catholic tradition to support ideas about active resistance?

Theological Writings on the Question of Resistance

Mother Mary Alice Gallin, in her excellent study of German resistance, examines the four "types" of disobedience which appeared in theological writings of the time. The four possibilities that emerged are:

1) passive disobedience
2) use of legal means to have the laws changed
3) armed self-defense against force used by the government to compel obedience
4) a rebellion in which the people take the offensive against the authority from which the law emanated.[11]

In Catholic theology, Gallin emphasizes that the first three possibilities of resistance are permissible while the fourth is not.[12] Why was active, open rebellion against the state authority not permitted by theologians?

Catholic theology in Germany by the late 1800's was dominated by a neo-scholastic movement which had embraced the
teaching of St. Thomas Aquinas. In *Summa theologica*, Aquinas
considers the possibilities of civil disobedience and discusses the differences between a leader who has seized power legitimately and
one who has come to power through illegal or illegitimate means.
In the case of a legitimate ruler, Aquinas condemned the idea of disobedience, or at the very extreme, tyrannicide. By the end of the
19th century, condemnation of tyrannicide had become accepted
doctrine in Catholic teaching. It was reinforced when the pope
issued the encyclical, *Syllabus of Errors* in 1864. The *Syllabus* not
only condemned tyrannicide, it also forbade revolution. "For revolution, even against a government which practices injustice and
exemplifies a tyranny is not permitted."[13] Similar themes were
expressed in Leo XIII's encyclical, *Immortale Dei*, which prohibited
revolution against the established government: "To cast aside obedience and by popular violence to incite revolt, is therefore treason,
not against man only, but against God."[14] Other encyclicals appearing at this time that examined the suffering of Catholics in Mexico,
Spain, and Russia gave encouragement to citizens who refused to
violate their consciences, "but never encouraged the citizens to
open revolt."[15] These teachings were reinforced in would-be professors and future bishops such as von Galen because the neo-
scholastic philosophy was vigorously taught by faculties in Mainz,
Münster, and Fribourg, Switzerland.[16] As von Galen attended
schools in both Münster and Fribourg, we can assume that he was
exposed to this tradition.

The Catholic Church in Germany desperately wanted to prove
that it was German and, within the constraints of such a role, active
political revolutionary resistance was practically non-existent.
Most of the Catholic bishops chose to tolerate, accommodate, and
collaborate with Nazis, tending to make it easier for Catholics
swept up in the enthusiasm of National Socialism to still remain
within the church.[17] In March 1933, a common bishops' statement
was issued:

> For Catholic Christians, to whom the voice of the Church is sacred, it
> is not necessary at the present moment, to make special admonition to
> be loyal to the lawful government and to fulfill conscientiously the
> duties of citizenship, rejecting on principle all illegal or subversive
> behavior.[18]

A statement such as this one only served to confuse Catholics and
reconfirm in their minds that it would somehow be possible to rec-

oncile the two conflicting value systems of National Socialism and Catholicism. Catholics were being told that they could be both members of Nazism and Catholicism simultaneously. An example of the mixed message sent by the Catholic hierarchy has to do with von Galen's appointment as Bishop of Münster.

Von Galen was the first clergyman to be appointed bishop after the signing of the Concordat. According to the treaty, von Galen had to appear before Prussian Minister Hermann Göring and swear an oath of loyalty to the state. Appearing before Göring in Berlin, von Galen made a point of producing his own crucifix and a copy of the New Testament stating that he thought Göring might not have these items on hand (which Göring did not).[19] Although von Galen drew attention to Göring's lack of religiousity, he still attended the meal hosted by the Prussian Minister following the ceremony. He also left his card with Hitler and visited with President Hindenburg, observing all of the niceties and formalities of the situation.

Upon returning to Münster, Cardinal Schulte, Archbishop of Cologne and the Bishops of Osnabrück and Trier officiated at von Galen's consecration.[20] The cathedral was the scene of columns of SA and SS men marching in processon with swastika flags flying. The SA lined the roads leading to the cathedral and in the evening they participated in a torchlit procession in front of the bishop's palace.[21] As part of the ceremony, Nazi party office holders, from the Gauleiter to the lowest-ranking SA member filed past von Galen, giving him the Nazi salute.

Eyewitness interpretations of the event vary widely. The Bishop's would-be hagiographers, H.Portmann and R.L.Sedgwick, emphasize Catholic Münster's support for their new bishop: "Ordinary folk ... had limitless confidence in the new Bishop; a sound instinct led them in the confusion of the time to look for safety and rescue from the aggressive Catholicism of one of the race of von Galen."[22] In contrast, Catholic scholar and philosopher, Josef Pieper, who was a resident of Münster, observed, "... it is just not true that, in the summer of 1933, when the name 'Galen' was announced as the new Bishop, the whole diocese broke out in rejoicing. ... Nor is it the case that Galen was immediately recognized as being a great opponent of the despotic regime. On the contrary, the pugnacious pastor of St. Lambert's was regarded, to put it bluntly, as a Nazi. ..."[23]

Despite the varying opinions of eyewitnesses concerning the reaction of Catholic Münsterlanders, one thing emerges from both accounts. Men in SA and SS uniforms marched alongside the bishop and the bishop gave the appearance of at least accepting National Socialism as legitimate. Von Galen, although he had placed Göring in a slightly embarrassing situation at the swearing in, did not attempt to stress the differences which existed between the two ideologies. Appearing alongside the Nazis at the consecration day ceremonies, von Galen made it easier for Catholics to think that they could be both Catholic and Nazi.

In the summer of 1934, von Galen once again allowed a similarly confusing message to be sent to Catholics. Celebrating the commemoration of Bishop Johann B. Brinkmann's return from *Kulturkampf* exile, von Galen spoke quite strongly to the participants, reminding them of the dark days of *Kulturkampf* persecution.[24] Processions, pilgrimages, and outdoor masses were typically used by German Catholics in the Second Reich to demonstrate their continued existence despite Bismarck's oppressive anti-Catholic legislation. If von Galen meant to convey a strong statement that the Nazis were similar to anti-Catholics persecutors of the 1870s, his message would have been much more forceful had he refrained from appearing with Nazis in uniform as they marched alongside of him.

If processions were going to be used as vehicles for expressing dissatisfaction with the current regime, most of the impact of the ceremony's message was lost on the audience when it confronted the strong visual symbol of Nazis participating in the event. As a member of the audience, one could walk away asking: are Nazis persecuting Catholics or are they Catholics themselves?

The power of *Kulturkampf* memories was repeatedly diminished when bishops, such as von Galen, chose to attack the Nazi state's actions indirectly without offering a clear indictment of anti-Catholic actions. Most of the church authorities, von Galen included, had matured during the *Kulturkampf* era and chose to get along with the legally established authorities despite their reservations and misgivings. "To preserve as much as possible and to prevent even worse things, the church authorities often cooperated with the state. ..."[25] By cooperating, church authorities allowed Catholics to think that "... they could cooperate in the stirring events of the day without qualms and shout with all the rest, 'Heil Hitler.'"[26] Thus, the memory of the *Kulturkampf* actually was imagined in such a way as to limit the possibilities of resistance.

To more fully understand von Galen's attitude toward the Nazi regime, it is helpful to explore his conception of the ideal German state, the ideal German citizen, and the church's relationship to both state and citizen.

Notions of State and Citizenship

One of the major influences in von Galen's life concerning the role of morals in politics was his father, Ferdinand Heribert. Ferdinand, in turn, had been deeply influenced by his uncle, Wilhelm Emmanuel von Ketteler, the "working bishop" of Mainz. Ketteler (1811-77), with whom Ferdinand had lived for a time, became one of the most influential Catholic authors on questions of German national identity. As bishop of Mainz, Ketteler used his position to address the dominant social questions of the day.

He promoted the freedom and rights of Catholics in particular and a "program for all believing Christians ... in Germany."[27] Ketteler, like Johann Fichte and Friedrich Jahn, believed that the newly-unified German state should be grounded in Christian principles. His conception of the ideal state harkened back to medieval times when Germany ruled the Holy Roman Empire (when no Protestants existed in Germany).[28] In a pamphlet in 1866, Ketteler reiterated his idea that freedom of conscience came only through a society organized into feudal estates.[29] He favored a paternalistic, quasi-medieval universalism, but he argued that in order for Catholics to attain more power in Germany they had to embrace the national and military objectives of Wilhelmine society.[30] He acknowledged that German society was dominated by Protestants and believed that behaving in an intolerant fashion towards them would only impede Catholic integration into the national community. He expressed the sentiment that Catholics could be just as loyal as Protestants, "We too are German in word and deed, we are true to Kaiser and Reich, we think and feel German ... we do not have to betray our religion in order to be patriots."[31] Underlying this notion that Catholics and Protestants were equals in German citizenship was the idea that others, such as Jews and liberals, were not equal in status. "The German Catholic vision of a Christian state could be conceived as marginalizing Jews or Social Democrats but not Württenberg Pietists or Silesian Lutherans."[32] In Ketteler's conception of the state, Christians would rule together against the forces of liberalism, socialism, capitalism, and behind these forces of modernism, the Jews.

Ketteler's program of "social Catholicism" was embraced by von Galen's father, Ferdinand. The elder von Galen attempted to translate the sociopolitical ideas of Ketteler into practical legislation. He passed on his ideas of the "Christian social" program to his son, Clemens August. Part of this ideological inheritance included the belief that Germany must be a Christian state.

So how did Clemens August envision his society? The best example would be his 1932 pamphlet, *Die Pest des Laizismus und ihre Erscheinungsformen*. Based on many of the ideas contained in Pope Pius XI's 1925 encyclical, *Königtum Christi*, von Galen denounced the secularization of a society which had divorced itself from God and the Commandments. He lamented the unraveling of religion and life and, like Ketteler, recalled medieval times when religion and life were intertwined. In von Galen's opinion, the modern world was fighting an epidemic in which public life was being corrupted by original sin and a love of materialism.

Von Galen feared the loss of Catholic-Christian values in an increasingly modern world. He was against liberalism, individualism, socialism, and democracy. He thought that these "isms" were destroying belief in the Christian God. He wanted hierarchy, ritual, and a foundation firmly rooted in Christianity.[33] Unfortunately, the Nazis offered a pseudo-version of this. Von Galen relied on the teachings of his father's uncle, his father, and the education he received at various Catholic institutions, all of which reinforced the notion that Catholics could survive best if they were obedient to the state. Reinforcing this reliance on obedience was the belief that "every human authority is a reflection of divine rule and is a participation in the eternal authority of God."[34] Thus the religious *Führerprinzip* coincided with the Nazi's secular *Führerprinzip*.

Despite increasing governmental violations of church rights, von Galen continued to preach obedience and duty to the state. In a sermon delivered in September 1936, he used the story of the martyrdom of St. Victor as the jumping off point to encourage obedience to the state. "My dear listeners! I do not need to tell you, Christianity demands obedience, obedience to God, but also obedience to men. Already common sense tells us that only through obedience can order be maintained in the community."[35] Throughout the sermon, von Galen invoked numerous biblical citations which stress obedience to earthly authority. He ended by telling the congregation that it is better to die than to sin.[36] Unfortunately, it is left up to the individual and his/her own conscience to decide which laws are just and which laws are unjust. He certainly never endorsed anything more than passive disobedience in his sermon.

Even the texts of von Galen's world-famous 1941 sermons—the sermons which bestowed the title of "resister" on him—continued the established pattern of protests watered down by conservative German patriotism. In each of the three sermons, he protested the evictions of religious orders, the scandalous immorality and currency trials, the closing of various Catholic organizations and, finally, the euthanasia project. In powerful language, he starkly pointed out that the mentally ill were being murdered systematically. He charged the murderers with violating the Fifth Commandment, "Thou shalt not kill." However, in each one of the three sermons, von Galen still attempted to stress themes of duty and obedience. In his sermon of 20 July 1941, he stated:

> We Christians, of course, are not aiming at revolution. We shall continue loyally to do our duty in obedience to God and in love of our people and fatherland. Our soldiers will fight and die for Germany. ... We shall continue to fight against the external enemy; but against the enemy within, who strikes us and torments us, we cannot fight with arms. Against him we have one weapon: endurance—strong, tough, hard endurance.[37]

In the three sermons of 1941, von Galen generated a great deal of publicity, reinforced an already mobilized public opinion about euthanasia, and more importantly, gave the church a seeming renewed credibility that was sorely lacking. However, it is critical to keep in mind that he only attacked portions of the National Socialist ideology and continued to urge loyalty to the fatherland.[38]

Clearly, von Galen was advocating a popular opinion in German Catholic theological writings. Passive disobedience to laws that violate the church's teachings is permitted, but there is never an endorsement of active revolution or, at the extreme, tyrannicide. In this way, we see the limit of the resources of a theologically- based notion of resistance. To the bishop, it was more important that Catholics maintain the institutional structures of the church.

Von Galen's thinking was representative of the thoughts of the Catholic hierarchy in general. They tended to focus on ecclesiastical-cultural goals: "... Catholics were to make decisions on their political conduct within the state with an emphasis on religion, the church, and schools as the building blocks of good political order."[39] Von Galen, much like the rest of the Catholic hierarchy, placed his faith in the hope that the church would be able to outlast any secular government as long as it kept its structures intact. One way of keeping those structures intact was with the signing of the Concordat.

The Concordat and Resistance

Von Galen, in his sermons, revealed that he believed that the Concordat would assist the church hierarchy by protecting various

Catholic organizations and structures from a Nazi seizure. The German bishops, underestimating the regime's opposition to the existence of Catholicism in Germany, reinforced the legitimacy of Hitler's government by signing the Concordat. Once the treaty was signed, the German bishops faced the question of how to criticize the National Socialists and still be considered "good Germans." They met at Fulda in August 1933 to discuss just that question.

Essentially the German bishops and cardinals decided to take up a defensive posture by protesting violations of the Concordat through written petitions, remonstrances, and formal sermons. To von Galen, the Concordat was a way for the state and church, working together, to avoid another *Kulturkampf*.[40]

If the Concordat did bring some strength to German Catholics, it also brought weakness in that the church, because of the restrictions of the Concordat, limited its focus to strictly church-related problems, thereby failing to address the higher question of religious values.[41]

The Church Hierarchy and the "Jewish Question"

At the August 1933 Fulda Bishops' Conference, the clergy present agreed to ask the Pope to add some words in the Concordat which would protect Christians who had converted from Judaism and who were suffering under recent "non-Aryan" legislation. The Pope declined the request as he would not interfere in Germany's internal affairs.[42]

Persecution of non-converted Jews aroused little interest on the part of the Catholic leadership. What we find is virtually no protests by the papacy or members of the German hierarchy against the antisemitism of the regime. Following the April 1, 1933, boycott of Jewish-owned and -operated stores, Cardinal Secretary of State Eugenio Pacelli (former papal nuncio in Munich and Berlin and Pope Pius XII as of 1939) received a letter from Cardinal Faulhaber explaining why the church would not intervene to protect Jews. "This is not possible at this time because the struggle against the Jews would at the same time become a struggle against Catholics, and because the Jews can help themselves, as the sudden end of the boycott shows. ..."[43]

The church would concern itself with converts, but unconverted Jews could fend for themselves. Neither the Pope in Rome nor the Catholic leaders in Germany pursued an aggressive policy of fighting to protect persecuted Jews for fear that they would bring down greater troubles on their Catholic followers.[44] The same policy of non-intervention was followed with the passage of the 1935 Nuremburg Laws. Churchmen sought to be impartial and neutral, falling back on the Concordat and legalistic procedures.

As for von Galen, he often stressed in his sermons that he was violently opposed to the racism of the Nazis, but he rarely addressed the topic of antisemitism specifically. In 1934 he sponsored Professor Wilhelm Neuss's work which attacked the teachings of Alfred Rosenberg's *Myth of the Twentieth Century*.[45] He sponsored Neuss not because of the violent antisemitism of Rosenberg's book, but rather because Rosenberg sought to exalt one race over all others.

Perhaps more revealing concerning von Galen's position on the "Jewish Question" is his behavior surrounding the events of *Kristallnacht*. The bishop was out in some of Münster's outlying regions performing confirmations when *Kristallnacht* occurred. Upon his return, von Galen issued no public pronouncement condemning the violence. The events of *Kristallnacht* had presented a unique opportunity for the church leadership to regain some moral high ground as the majority of the German population seems to have disapproved of the vicious pogrom. What is even more intriguing is that, after the war, Rabbi Steinthal, who had been the leader of the Jewish community in Münster, claimed that the bishop had sent a priest to his home to see if the rabbi needed assistance in getting out of the local jail. The priest, who also survived the war, claimed that the rabbi was mistaken. He asserted that he was never sent by von Galen and that he, upon witnessing the damage to the Jewish community in Münster, went of his own volition to the Steinthal home.[46] Even though Rabbi Steinthal believed that von Galen cared about the fate of Jews in his community, the priest's account contradicts this. It seems like a typical case where a lower level clergyman performed an individual act of courage without receiving official support from the upper echelons of the church hierarchy.

The occurrence of Catholic antisemitism or, at the very least, indifference to the fate of the Jews, should not be surprising in light of Catholics' desire to be integrated fully into the German nation and culture.[47] With the rise of Germany as a modern, industrialized liberal state, most Catholics felt that they could either oppose the new German state or attempt to be politically integrated by working within the system. Once the Catholic Center Party was created, most Catholics opted for inclusion in the Second Reich. When Bismarck attacked Catholics as *Reichsfeinde*, many responded by seeking to align themselves with Protestant conservatives. Both denominations shared common ground in their opposition to liberalism and socialism. They often shared antisemitic sentiments also. The real enemy to many Christians was not the heathen or pagan but the Jew. In von Galen's pastoral of January 1934, he told Catholics that Jesus's blood redeems all people. What he implied though is that those who have rejected Jesus as the Messiah cannot be saved.[48] It appears that both bishops and theologians could be classified as intellectual antisemites.[49]

Von Galen, although in the abstract often critical of racist literature and remarks, was quite quick to point out to listeners that his blood was just as German as the next person's, if not more so due to his family's lineage. In a 1937 sermon at Vreden, he declared that he was descended from centuries of Westphalian Catholic nobility and, "If anyone stands up and asserts that German blood speaks in him, I stand up here and assert the same myself ..."[50] In his effort to assert that Catholics were just as German as Protestants, he co-opted language similar to what the Nazis used when asserting that blood could establish one's "credentials." The fears of blood purity were expressed by many Catholic theologians and bishops.

Bishop Ketteler in the 1860s attacked what he considered to be the corrupting influence of Jews on the German national economy, the family, and public morality. In the 1870s he claimed that "liberal Jewish dominance had reached a point where even 'German character' was being warped."[51] By the early 1900s Protestant racists were seeking alliances with the Catholic Center Party because they believed that the party was "safe from Jewish infiltration."[52] Theologians writing between 1918 and 1933 tended to offer Catholics a mixture of nationalism and "normal" antisemitism. Scholars developed what Werner Jeanrond terms "*Volkstheologie*" or "*Reichstheologie*." Karl Adam, one of the foremost theologians of the time, stressed that *Volk* and *Kirche* should work to support one another. He believed that it was the state's responsibility to maintain the purity of the *Volk*'s blood.[53] He also condemned what he called the "Jewish mentality" which had pervaded German life. Many theologians argued for the equality of all the redeemed. Those who had not been "redeemed" through Christianity were to be excluded from society.[54]

Many theologians who rejected antisemitism on the social level, still supported the theological underpinnings of religious antisemitism, thereby aiding the Nazis by making "anti-Jewishness" more acceptable.[55] Repeatedly, Catholics were told by various theologians and clergymen that only those who had accepted Jesus as the Messiah could be saved.

By 1934, theologians had generally ceased to comment on the "Jewish question." They retreated into abstract moral treatises which "certainly went unread by the average Catholic layman. ... Early adaptation and later opposition could only confuse those who looked to the Church for guidance. ..."[56] Theologians failed to subject the National Socialist *Weltanschauung* to rigorous critiques and failed to promote the basic premise that all individuals are created by God and as such have an inherent right to live unharmed. In the attempt to remain "good" Germans and "good" Catholics, theologians worked to reduce the conflict between Christian virtues and Nazi values. In doing so, subtle distinctions were so embedded in theological verbiage that they were lost on the faithful. The theologians contributed to the impression that "the Church was supporting the basic policies of the regime and only differing over minor issues."[57]

The German bishops and the Pope had decided that, in order to fulfill the church's mission, it had to be a viable institution with proper relations between church and state. Few theological writings existed for guiding opposition to the regime. The "resistance" offered was that of civil disobedience to specific laws but the "right to overthrow the government by force was not clearly delimited in the theology of the churches."[58] Von Galen thought that preserving Catholic institutions and organizations on German soil would keep Catholic values alive; not a very ambitious or creative goal. By declaring the purity of von Galen family blood, refusing to offer outright, public condemnation of antisemitic policies, and recognizing Hitler's regime as a legitimate authority, von Galen contributed to the general impression that "despite superficial faults, National Socialism could not really be as evil as some had earlier suggested."[59]

Locked into following a policy which promised security and blind to suggestions of open rebellion, the German Catholic hierarchy, von Galen included, failed to convey to the faithful that National Socialism and Catholicism were irreconcilable philosophies. In their desperate attempts to preserve Catholic organizations and associations while still maintaining their loyalty to the German state, the bishops failed to defend the rights of all human beings.

Notes

1. Donald J. Dietrich, *Catholic Citizens in the Third Reich: Psycho-Social Principles and Moral Reasoning* (New Brunswick, 1988), p. 158. The term *Kulturkampf* refers to the campaign against political Catholicism launched by German Chancellor Otto von Bismarck and his Minister of Education and Cultural Affairs, Adalbert Falk. Beginning in July 1871, the Catholic division of the Ministry of Culture was dissolved and placed under a Protestant administration. Between 1871 and 1872 a series of laws were enacted that sought to limit the influence of the clergy over political and cultural life. Priests were forbidden to participate in political activities, confessional schools were placed under state control, and Jesuits were expelled from Prussian soil. By 1875 most religious orders had been disbanded or exiled, their institutions seized, remaining members of orders imprisoned, and the state had taken over the appointment of bishops. Politically active Catholics were labeled *Reichsfeinde*, meaning enemies of the state or internal enemies. For a concise chronological summary and a detailed bibliography, see Rudolf Lill, "Der Kulturkampf in Preussen und im Deutschen Reich (bis 1878)," in *Handbuch der Kirchengeschichte*, ed. Hubert Jedin (Freiburg, 1973), vol. 6, no. 2, pp. 28-47. See also Jonathan Sperber, *Popular Catholicism in Nineteenth-Century Germany* (Carbondale, IL, 1984).

2. Von Galen was elevated to the rank of Cardinal along with two other "anti-Nazi" bishops, Archbishop Joseph Frings of Cologne and Bishop Konrad, Count von Preysing of Berlin.

3. See works such as Wilhelm Corsten, ed., *Kölner Aktenstücke zur Lage der katholischen Kirche in Deutschland, 1933-1945* (Cologne, 1949); Walter Mariaux, ed., *The Persecution of the Catholic Church in Germany: Facts and Documents translated from the German* (London, 1942); Nathaniel Micklem, *National Socialism and the Roman Catholic Church* (London, 1939); Johann Neuhäusler, *Kreuz und Hakenkreuz. Der Kampf des Nationalsozialismus gegen die katholische Kirche und der kirchliche Widerstand* (Munich, 1946); Hans Rothfels, *Die deutsche Opposition gegen Hitler. Eine Würdigung* (Frankfurt am Main, 1960). This volume originally appeared in 1948 under the title, *The German Opposition to Hitler* (Hinsdale, IL, 1948).

4. Neuhäusler collected Nazi anti-Church information until he was arrested and imprisoned for the remainder of the war. His evidence was incorporated into Micklem's work, *National Socialism and the Roman Catholic Church* (London, 1939). In 1946, Neuhäusler published *Kreuz und Hakenkreuz* (Munich, 1946).

5. John S. Conway, *The Nazi Persecution of the Churches, 1933-45* (New York, 1968); Günter Lewy, *The Catholic Church and the Third Reich* (New York, 1964); Hans Müller, *Katholische Kirche und Nationalsozialismus. Dokumente 1930-1935* (Munich, 1963); and Gordon Zahn, *German Catholics and Hitler's Wars. A Study in Social Control* (New York, 1962).

6. See Kurt Nowak, *"Euthanasie" und Sterilisierung im "Dritten Reich." Die Konfrontation der Evangelischen und Katholischen Kirche mit dem "Gesetz zur Verhütung erbkranken Nachwuchses" und der "Euthanasie"-Aktion* (Göttingen, 1978). For other more recent works which address the euthanasia project, see: Michael Burleigh, *Death and Deliverance. 'Euthanasia' in Germany c.1900-1945* (London, 1994); Ernst Klee, *"Euthanasia" im NS-Staat* (Frankfurt, 1983); Robert Proctor, *Racial Hygiene: Medicine under the Nazis* (Cambridge, Mass., 1988).

7. Ernst Christian Helmreich, *The German Churches under Hitler: Background, Struggle, and Epilogue* (Detroit, 1979).

8. D.Dietrich, p. 285.

9. Here I am referring to the most prolific and earliest biographers of von Galen, among other works see: Max Bierbaum, *Kardinal von Galen, Bischof von Münster* (Münster, 1947), *Nicht lob, nicht furcht: das Leben des Kardinals von Galen, nach unveröffentlichen Briefen und Dokumenten* (Münster, 4th ed., 1960); Heinrich Portmann, *Der Bischof von Münster* (Münster, 1946); *Bischof von Galen Spricht! Ein apostolischer Kampf und sein Widerhall* (Freiburg/ Breisgau, 1946); *Der Bischof von Münster: Das Echo eines Kampfes für Gottesrecht und Menschenrecht* (Münster, 1947); *Kardinal von Galen* (Münster, 1953).

10. Ibid., p. 294.

11. Mother Mary Alice Gallin, *German Resistance to Hitler: Ethical and Religious Factors* (Washington, D.C., 1961), p. 28.

12. Ibid., p. 28.

13. Helmreich, p. 366.

14. Gallin, p. 32.

15. Ibid., p. 32.

16. Thomas Franklin O'Meara, O.P., *Church and Culture: German Catholic Theology, 1860-1914* (Notre Dame, 1991), pp. 34-43.

17. Helmreich, p. 239.

18. Helmreich, p. 239.

19. Heinrich Portmann, *Kardinal von Galen. Ein Gottesmann seiner Zeit. Mit einem Anhang: "Die drei weltberühmten Predigten"* (Münster, 1981), p. 82.

20. Heinrich Portmann, *Cardinal von Galen*, trans. R.L. Sedgwick (London, 1957), p. 60.

21. Ibid., p. 60.

22. Ibid., p. 59.

23. Josef Pieper, *No One Could Have Known: An Autobiography. The Early Years, 1904-45*, trans. Graham Harrison (San Francisco, 1987), p. 93.

24. Peter Löffler, ed., Nr. 54, "Erlass v. Galens," 101-103 in *Bischof Clemens August Graf von Galen. Akten, Briefe und Predigten 1933-46* (Mainz, 1988).

25. Helmreich, p. 296.

26. Ibid., p. 240.

27. Maria Anna Zumholz, "'Die Tradition meines Hauses.'" Zur Prägung Clemens August Graf von Galen in Schule und Universität," ed. Joachim Kuropka, *Clemens August Graf von Galen: Neue Forschungen zum Leben und Wirken des Bischofs von Münster* (Münster, 1992), p. 14.

28. Ibid., 63.

29. Helmut Walser Smith, *German Nationalism and Religious Conflict: Culture, Ideology, Politics, 1870-1914* (Princeton, 1995), p. 62.

30. Ibid., p. 174.

31. Ibid., p. 63.

32. Ibid., 75.

33. Portmann, *Bischof Graf von Galen spricht*, p. 20.

34. Dietrich, p. 153.

35. Predigt v. Galens, 6 September 1936, Nr. 189 in Peter Löffler, ed., *Bischof Clemens August Graf von Galen: Akten, Briefe und Predigten 1933-1946*, vols. I-II (Mainz, 1988), p. 439.

36. Ibid., pp. 439-447.

37. Quoted in *Clemens August Kardinal von Galen: Predigten in dunkler Zeit* (Münster, 1994), p. 27. The currency trials mentioned above revolved around Nazi efforts to "prove" that Catholic priests and nuns were engaged in treasonous activity, smuggling foreign currency across Germany's borders. They were quite frequently paired with other charges of alleged scandalous behavior on the part of the clergy.

38. Dietrich, pp. 227-228.

39. Dietrich, p. 84.

40. "Vorwort v. Galens zum Hirtenbrief der deutschen Bischöfe," 25 August 1935, Nr. 127 in Löffler, p. 287.

41. Helmreich, p. 256.

42. Ibid., pp. 253-254.

43. Ibid., p. 276.

44. Ibid., p. 277.

45. Wilhelm Neuss, *Kampf gegen den* Mythos des 20. Jhts. *Ein Gedenkblatt an Clemens August Kardinal Graf von Galen* (Cologne, 1947).

46. Heinz Mussinghoff, *Rassenwahn in Münster. Der Judenpogrom 1938 und Bischof Clemens August Graf von Galen* (Münster, 1989).

47. Ibid., p. 216.

48. Portmann, *Cardinal von Galen*, p. 63.

49. Dietrich, p. 242.

50. Portmann, *Bischof Graf von Galen spricht*, p. 41.

51. Dietrich, p. 14.

52. H.W.Smith, p. 155.

53. Dietrich, p. 185.

54. Dietrich, p. 71.

55. Ibid., p. 193.

56. Dietrich, p. 207.

57. Ibid., p. 209.

58. Gallin, p. 37.

59. Ibid., p. 187.

– Chapter 5 –

BETWEEN GOD AND HITLER
German Military Chaplains
and the Crimes of the Third Reich

Doris L. Bergen

Scholarship over the past decades has exploded the long cherished myth that the German military had little to do with the crimes of the Third Reich.[1] But what about the Wehrmacht chaplains? What roles did they play? Precise answers to that question are difficult to find. Chaplains' records and memoirs provide glimpses,[2] but for the most part the existing literature avoids the issue.[3] Some historians of the churches in the Third Reich claim that German military chaplains remained "above politics" and simply tried to do an impossible job under terrible conditions.[4] Some studies highlight Nazi authorities' open hostility toward the chaplaincy.[5] Indeed, a regulation known as the "Uriah law"—a reference to the husband of Bathsheba whom King David in the Bible disposed of by dispatching to the most dangerous area of battle—even required chaplains at the front to situate themselves in areas of heaviest fighting.[6] In this way chaplains too felt the ruthlessness of National Socialist rule.

But the so-called Uriah law had unforeseen consequences. Intended both to maximize the chaplains' morale-boosting function and to increase their rate of mortality, it also forced them to observe the brutal reality of German warfare, including the destruction of the Jews, at close range. About a thousand men served the German military as chaplains throughout the war.[7] Some of them echoed Hitler with their own crusades against Jews, Communists, and other purported enemies of the Reich. A few courageous individuals protested atrocities. Most kept a low profile. But whether proponents or opponents of genocide, German military chaplains were its witnesses.

From Poland to France, from the sites of mass executions in Yugoslavia to the killing fields of Ukraine and Byelorussia, Christian chaplains, Protestant and Catholic, accompanied the German armies. They provided spiritual relief to the men in their care; they preached, administered the sacraments, soothed the sick and wounded, and buried the dead. In the geography of genocide, murder and piety existed side by side. The moral prestige of the chaplains' office, together with their ties to the historic legacy of the Christian churches, meant they could not be neutral bystanders. Instead their presence helped legitimize the Nazi war of annihilation and propagate among its warriors the comforting illusion that despite the blood on their hands, they remained decent people, part of a venerable religious tradition.

One Case: Chaplains and the Holocaust in Belaya Tserkov

A specific, unusually well-documented case illustrates the two key themes of this paper: first, that German military chaplains were eyewitnesses to genocide, and secondly, that their presence helped create an illusion of normalcy and morality for the killers. In mid-August 1941, German authorities in the Ukrainian town of Belaya Tserkov, more than two hundred miles east of Lwow, ordered local Jews to report for registration. Over the next few days, SS and German soldiers scoured the area for Jews, slaughtering hundreds of men and women. That massacre was far from unique; similar killings occurred all over eastern Europe. But in the case of Belaya Tserkov, eyewitnesses recorded the presence and activities of German chaplains.[8]

The murderers of the Jews of Belaya Tserkov did not initially kill all the children. Instead they dumped those captured at the "registration" in a nearby school. Young children of parents murdered during the following days were pushed into the same building. German soldiers in a field hospital nearby heard babies crying in the night. Disturbed but uncertain how to respond, they put the matter in the hands of their spiritual leaders: the chaplains. The two clergymen, one a Protestant pastor named Wilczek, the other Ernst Tewes, a thirty-one-year-old Catholic priest, went to see for themselves. Years later, with the help of the diary he had kept at the time, Tewes recalled the scene:

> We found about ninety young Jewish children, among them some tiny babies, in a desperate situation: packed together, moaning, crying, hungry and thirsty in the midday heat. Some of their parents had been shot; some of the mothers were locked in an adjoining room, from which they had to watch the misery of their children through a window, without being able to help them.[9]

According to Tewes, the two clergymen decided to defy orders and get involved. They realized that the children and their mothers, "like others before them," were to be shot by an SS Special Unit. The chaplains appealed for mercy to the local commander, an elderly Austrian. That effort failed, Tewes reported, because the man "turned out to be a convinced antisemite."[10] They then approached colleagues in the area, the Protestant and Catholic chaplains of the 295th Infantry Division. Tewes and Wilczek showed their fellow clergy "the repulsive misery" in the school building. In their written report, the chaplains were careful to avoid insult to fellow Germans. The men guarding the school, they emphasized, were "Ukrainians," whom they suspected of acting "on their own initiative."[11]

Together the chaplains convinced staff officer Lieutenant-Colonel Groscurth to take up the cause. When Groscurth asked an SS man what the fate of the children was to be, he was told that the families of the children had been shot and the children "should also be eliminated." Urged on by the chaplains, Groscurth tried to delay murder of the children by asking his superiors to confirm the decision. Army High Command approved one postponement, but Security Service representatives and military officers on the spot prevailed, pointing to instructions from General Field Marshall Walter von Reichenau himself, the commander of Army Group South. On 21 August 1941, the children were taken from the school and killed. It is unclear whether it was members of the Waffen SS or Ukrainian "volunteers" who did the job.[12] When he described the event years later, Tewes refused to assume a heroic stance. "All those we wanted to save," he said, "were shot. Because of our initiative it just happened a few days later than planned."[13]

The story of the chaplains and the murder of the Jewish children of Belaya Tserkov is unusual in a number of ways. In no other case do we have such a detailed account, based on records kept at the time, of a chaplain's effort to intervene in the Holocaust. Moreover, external sources corroborate Tewes's version of events. In 1968, Tewes and his Protestant counterpart Wilczek testified in the German trial of the surviving members of the Belaya Tserkov murder commando, and a number of related documents came to light then. The case attracted considerable attention, and in February 1968, the *Neue Zürcher Zeitung* lauded the "two former German military chaplains who tried to obstruct the machinery of destruction, albeit it without success."[14]

But it is above all the chaplains' role as resistors that makes the Belaya Tserkov events atypical and perhaps unique. During the war chaplains would have had little incentive to record events that seemed so natural they took them for granted, such as supporting the war effort and saying nothing about German crimes. But they might, like Tewes, confide the extraordinary to their diaries.[15] After the war, former chaplains would be even less likely to reveal incidents of cooperation with Nazi authorities, especially when such collaboration furthered the cause of genocide. But the incentive to publicize resistance activity would be enormous. In other words, if many other chaplains had stories like Tewes's to tell, we might safely assume that we would have heard at least some of them. Viewed this way, the chaplains of Belaya Tserkov provide a clear example of how, in the case of German chaplains and the Holocaust, an exceptional act of resistance proves the general rule of acquiescence.

Tewes's account allows us to venture some additional generalizations. First of all, it is evident that chaplains witnessed German atrocities against civilians, including the slaughter of eastern European Jews. Tewes and his three colleagues were appalled by the situation of the Jewish children at Belaya Tserkov, but they expressed no surprise at the fact that Special Task Units *(Einsatzgruppen)* and their accomplices in the regular military had murdered hundreds of Jewish adults. They knew about the annihilation of the Jews and assumed that colleagues in the chaplaincy and fellow nationals in the military shared that knowledge.

Tewes's account also indicates that some German soldiers at least looked to their chaplains for moral leadership. The men in the hospital who approached their chaplains regarding the Jewish children were not unthinking "eliminationist antisemites,"[16] nor were they brainwashed automatons who had swallowed uncritically Nazi propaganda describing Jews as subhuman vermin; they still felt some human compassion for the children whose cries they heard. They took their concerns to the chaplains, men whose job it was to promote their spiritual well-being. Even in Hitler's army, it appears, chaplains retained a substantial measure of moral authority.

Also significant in the Belaya Tserkov case is the chaplains' willingness to challenge military authorities. The four clergymen were neither silenced by fear nor paralyzed by threats of punishment.

And indeed, they had a degree of immunity: nothing happened to them when they spoke out. A week after the murder of the children, Tewes was transferred to an armored division in Russia. Partisan attacks made his new assignment more dangerous, but nothing suggests that he considered the transfer a punishment.[17]

Tewes and his counterparts dared to speak out, but even they confined their protest to a specific incident. Perhaps limiting their protest this way was a tactical consideration. Even so, it highlights with terrible irony the way in which, in the context of a genocidal war, gestures of resistance could be transformed into new forms of legitimation. No doubt the German soldiers who appealed to the chaplains to do something for the Jewish children in the school experienced a sense of relief at having "dealt with" the "problem" and assuaged their consciences at the same time. The chaplains themselves may have felt they had done their part when they risked their personal security by protesting. Failure to stop the killings only reinforced a sense of powerlessness and made them less likely to repeat such defiance unless they had some reason to expect they might do so more successfully.

The account by the Catholic chaplain Tewes suggests precisely this depressing dynamic. His new placement in Russia was the scene of brutality equal to or even beyond what he had witnessed in Ukraine. But he developed ways to explain German atrocities that reduced them to part of normal warfare. "There were partisans," he observed in describing his new post. "German soldiers and officers were shot in partisan attacks. Then there were the terrible reprisals, shootings of hostages, to which Jews and others fell victim. The furies of war had been unleashed."[18] In the mind even of Chaplain Tewes, the targets of Nazi genocide had changed from innocent children to dangerous bandits. Instead of shock and outrage, he mustered only the truism that war was hell for everyone concerned.

Military Chaplains and Nazi Ideology

The incident at Belaya Tserkov provides insight into how particular chaplains responded to German atrocities, but like any single anecdote it cannot capture the full range of chaplains' actions. A broader perspective reveals considerable variation, from eager endorsement of Nazi ideology to protest against genocide and brutality. At the same time, a more general analysis confirms that chaplains witnessed German atrocities and brought spiritual relief to those who perpetrated them.

Both antisemitism and anti-Communism, mainstays of Nazi teaching, were ideas that many Protestant and Catholic clergy felt comfortable preaching in the 1930s and 1940s.[19] It is no surprise that chaplains, who tended to come from the more nationalist, conservative wings of the churches, shared those hostilities. One of the most prominent wartime chaplains, the Catholic Military Bishop of the Wehrmacht, Franz-Justus Rarkowski, was a particularly vociferous proponent of Nazi ideas.[20] Rarkowski's 1940 Christmas message, sent to all Catholic soldiers, blamed Jews for the war and for all of Germany's misfortunes:

> The German people ... has a good conscience and knows which people it is that before God and history bears the responsibility for this presently raging, gigantic struggle. The German people knows who lightheartedly unleashed the dogs of war. ... Our opponents ... believed in the power of their money bags and the repressive force of that shameful and un-Christian Treaty of Versailles. ...[21]

It is difficult to assess how typical Rarkowski's views were because few chaplains had similar opportunities to publish their sermons. In diaries and memoirs chaplains tend to be silent about their participation in Nazi ideology. But often those vague memories about their own roles coexist with precise recollections of colleagues who shared the regime's prejudices. For example, the diary of Josef Perau, a Catholic chaplain, betrays little about his response to Nazi ideas. But its description of Protestant colleagues affirms that at least some chaplains openly endorsed Nazi goals. Chaplain Perau's entry of 27 July 1941, from Tomaszow-Lubelski, identified his Protestant counterpart as a "German Christian," a member of an explicitly pro-Nazi group within the church.[22] That pastor, Perau wrote, announced to the entire officers' mess that he had made sure all of the "asocials" in his congregation were sterilized. According to Perau, the Protestant chaplain also favored moving all Poles out of Poland and replacing them "with farmers of the Germanic race."[23]

Another Catholic priest at the front contrasted his (silent) opposition to the Holocaust with the enthusiasm of his co-religionists. He recalled his shock at hearing Hitler in a radio speech proclaim that "Jewry must be destroyed, and not only in Germany. The hour of reckoning has come." The priest himself witnessed a forced transport of Jews from a marketplace piled high with bodies; he saw train cars jammed with people he knew were to be killed. But what surprised him most was the discovery that "various people welcomed the destruction of the Jews." Even a fellow priest told him at the time, "There is a curse on this people ever since the crucifixion of Jesus when they cried: 'Let his blood be on our heads and the heads of our children.'"[24]

Some chaplains were more subtle. Instead of trumpeting Nazi ideology, they tried to deflect criticism by downplaying or denying Christianity's Jewish roots. At a 1936 meeting in Stuttgart, Protestant base chaplain Bernhard Bauerle urged colleagues to avoid the "language of Canaan" in preaching to soldiers.[25] Years later on the eastern front, Bauerle, now in charge of chaplains with the Sixteenth Army, warned his clergy that one neopagan who took offense at some aspect of the Christian message counted for more than the ninety-nine soldiers who accepted it gladly.[26] Propaganda blaming Jews for the war and linking Germany's enemies in a global Jewish conspiracy inundated the Wehrmacht, and chaplains found themselves bombarded with questions from the men, especially concerning the "well-known issues about the Old Testament and Judaism."[27] In that climate, chaplains found it easier to preach a "de-Judaized" form of Christianity. Many abandoned the Old Testament so as not to anger antisemitic soldiers with that "Jewish book"; they also distributed hymnbooks from which Hebraisms such as "Hallelujah" and references to the Hebrew Bible had been purged. Such hymnals included publications sponsored by the Eisenach Institute for Study and Eradication of Jewish Influences in German Church Life.[28] Although not necessarily motivated by antisemitism, doing so perpetuated the notion that Christianity and Judaism could and must be separated. At the same time, it destroyed one brake to genocide that might have operated in Christian Europe: an awareness of and loyalty to Jews as the precursors and originators of Christianity.

Chaplains, Almost-Chaplains, and Resistance

What about chaplains who resisted National Socialism? Were Tewes and his colleagues really so exceptional when they protested the torture of the Belaya Tserkov children? The answer is a qualified yes. Research on German military chaplains does uncover examples of courageous behavior against Nazi atrocities. Some individuals tried in various ways to obstruct the crimes of the regime, to spread knowledge of its crimes, and to aid its victims. But even combing archives and published sources uncovers a minuscule number of such heroes—fewer than ten—against a group of one thousand military chaplains. And on close examination, all of the clear-cut cases of resistance involve people who do not in fact qualify as military chaplains. Nevertheless their stories are instructive. They help delineate the range of possibilities; they indicate what it was possible to know and what forms defiance could take. The following four accounts present stories of resistance, not of military chaplains but men close to them, "almost-chaplains," whose actions in turn highlight the inaction of those within the chaplaincy.

In November 1951, the Harvard *Crimson* ran a story under the headline, "War Plaque Lists German Chaplain." At issue was the inclusion of Adolf Sannwald among the names of World War II dead on the wall in Memorial Church. Sannwald, a visiting fellow at the Harvard Divinity School in the 1920s, became pastor of a Lutheran church in Stuttgart. Drafted into the German army in 1942, he was killed on the Russian front in 1943.

Sannwald, it turns out, was anything but a Nazi. In 1934 he published a pamphlet that repudiated National Socialist notions of race. Banished to an obscure village, in the late 1930s Sannwald and his family sheltered fugitive Jews. But this Christian rescuer never became a military chaplain. In fact, Sannwald had only one opportunity to preach to his fellow soldiers, at an Easter service in 1943. He chose as his topic "the Resurrection and collective guilt."[29] No existing records suggest that any "real" chaplain dared preach on such a provocative theme.

Other clergymen too tried to rescue Nazism's targets. A Protestant chaplain named Harald Poelchau used his post to aid the Communist and Jewish underground in Germany. But this courageous man had no military appointment; he was a prison chaplain.[30] Wilhelm Grosskortenhaus, a German soldier and member of the Catholic order of "White Fathers," met another Christian rescuer. While on duty in Italy, Grosskortenhaus visited a brother from France. The Frenchman invited him to the house, where to Grosskortenhaus's astonishment, Jews were hiding.[31] Comparable stories of German military chaplains engaged in rescue have yet to surface.

The fourth case comes closest to the military chaplaincy itself. It involves two Catholic priests with ties to the military, although neither served as a chaplain at the front. In 1942 Herbert Simoleit was a priest in Stettin whose responsibilities included providing pastoral care to the local military base. Friedrich Lorenz, a priest and veteran of World War I, was also active in Stettin. In 1939, Lorenz had done a stint as divisional chaplain for the Pomeranian reserves. There he had learned about the German slaughter of Polish Catholic priests during the first months of the war. Released from the military in 1942, Lorenz, together with Simoleit, made contact with a third priest, Carl Lampert, who had spent the previous two years in the concentration camps of Dachau and Sachsenhausen. By the summer of 1942, the three men had started a "Wednesday Circle" of Catholic soldiers from the base who gathered for discussion of political and military affairs.

A Gestapo informer joined the group and denounced all three priests. In 1944, a military court charged them with sedition. Simoleit, host of the Wednesday meetings, had been most outspoken in condemning the slaughter of Jews. The official charge against him recorded his outrage at the actions of German murder squads: "The accused ... sharply criticized measures of the SS, and in this regard, said the following: 'On one single day, SS men in Estonia shot 3,500 Jews in mass graves.' He spoke of the cruelty of the brutish SS murders and said in closing it was clear that the God of love would not reward such atrocities with victory." Herbert Simoleit and Friedrich Lorenz were beheaded on 13 November 1944. Carl Lampert was executed less than a week later.[32]

As "lights in the darkness," these cases of resistance do more to reveal the enabling inaction of the chaplaincy as a whole than to indicate any trend of disobedience. Simoleit did not witness the front like the priests and pastors in the military chaplaincy did, yet he managed to obtain precise information about the murder of Estonian Jews. His location within Germany and his cooperation with known enemies of the Reich meant he was much more vulnerable to Nazi assault than were most military chaplains. Nevertheless he was able to sustain his discussion group and promote awareness of German crimes for two years before his arrest. What might military chaplains have accomplished if they had shared his courage?

It is tempting to assume that chaplains were simply afraid to speak out. When one sees how some clergy in weaker positions acted, however, that argument loses some of its force. Moreover, many chaplains did dare to protest issues other than genocide. For example, the staunchly pro-Nazi naval chaplain Friedrich Ronneberger complained to military authorities about the "paganization" of Christmas celebrations in the German armed forces. Protestant military bishop Franz Dohrmann criticized the lack of religious literature for distribution to soldiers and grumbled about reductions in chaplains' numbers.[33] Some high-ranking military men took issue with German atrocities in Poland in 1939, and by 1944, openly conspired against Hitler. Fear was certainly a factor but it alone does not account for chaplains' silence.

There is an additional possibility: that chaplains did protest German atrocities but their criticisms went unrecorded. Given the fact that Nazi authorities were looking for ways to discredit the chaplaincy, however, it seems unlikely that a chaplain who offered open opposition would have left no trace. And as the Simoleit/ Lorenz case suggests, even private conversations were frequently denounced to authorities. Nevertheless the possibility of new sources always remains. Eyewitness accounts suggest, however, that the chance of uncovering evidence of widespread resistance from chaplains is extremely small. In moving and sometimes disarmingly frank passages, chaplains and those close to them describe both the opportunities presented for resistance and their failure to seize those moments. It seems important to note that accounts of even these would-be gestures of defiance come overwhelmingly from Catholic, not Protestant, clergy.[34]

Catholic military chaplain Josef Perau, for example, made a telling admission of his own lack of courage. In early 1944, Perau witnessed a round-up of local civilians in Byelorussia. Some were to be transported to Germany as slave laborers, the others driven out, plundered, and killed. Perau described the scene. An enormous space had been enclosed in barbed wire. The prisoners' belongings were strewn everywhere. Someone dragged the corpse of an old man across the field "like a piece of beef." An old woman lay dead on the path, a fresh gunshot in her forehead. A military policeman showed Perau two piles in the muck: they were dead children whose mothers had abandoned them in an effort to escape. Perau appealed to a medic, but he responded, "Father, leave this to us. I already shot a couple of helpless children myself, out of pity. Once we have won the war, Germany will soon be a people of culture again." Even the church service Perau had scheduled for the German soldiers had to be cancelled because the troops were needed to "evacuate" civilians.

Perau confided to his diary his failure to oppose the carnage. In the distance, he wrote, he had seen a general crossing the "field of agony." For a moment he had an urge to approach him, "and in the name of God, demand justice." But "the spirit did not call him to prophecy," and he managed only modest forms of protest. "In all of my conversations," Perau said, "I openly expressed my disgust. I also prevented some of my comrades from enriching themselves in a terrible way on the possessions of those poor people."[35]

What explains the weakness of resistance among the military chaplaincy? One factor may have been the insecurity of the chaplains themselves. Most were acutely aware of the precariousness of their situation as representatives of the church in the Nazi cause. Afraid of confirming anti-Christian views that they were traitors who softened up the troops and rendered them womanly, Jewish, and weak, they insisted instead on their manliness, anti-Judaism, and ability to stiffen the backbone of the men. In the process, they replicated in their own work the very Nazi ideas that threatened Christianity. They took the side of the perpetrators rather than risk being accused of fighting a war with what Hitler had derided as "Salvation Army tactics."

The procedures by which military chaplains were selected also helps explain their overall acquiescence. Potential chaplains needed approval from military authorities, church officials, and the Gestapo. All three agencies did their best to block perceived troublemakers from the service. Clergyman with even a hint of pro-Jewish sentiment or activism in their records stood no chance of appointment. It is remarkable how sensitive the Gestapo agents were to this issue; people were excluded on the basis of very small indications of positive feelings for Jews or even "insufficient" anti-semitism. Such "high standards" could be insisted upon, presumably, because they in fact did not disqualify many people. I have found only a handful of cases where prospective chaplains were disqualified for statements they had made or actions they had taken on behalf of Jews or in protest of German treatment of Jews, Gypsies, or people deemed handicapped.[36] Such cases were notable exceptions. Agreement with Nazi policies on issues of "race" seems simply to have been taken for granted.

Silent Witnesses and Spiritual Relief

Contemporary evidence allows us to situate many specific chaplains in locations where it was impossible not to witness the mass murder of civilians.[37] The overwhelming response of chaplains to the sights and events of the Holocaust was silence, both at the time and in their subsequent accounts. That silence was not neutral, but served to legitimize atrocities, by failing to offer a moral challenge to genocide and by implying acquiescence.

One incident suggests the moral power chaplains might have wielded. In 1940, a priest named Heinrich Pachowiak was the assistant to the German military chaplain stationed in Chartres. Through that contact he heard the following story. One evening General von Stülpnagel invited the senior Catholic chaplain to dine with him. When the two were alone, the general asked the priest,

"What do you think of the practice of shooting hostages?" The priest answered evasively. "Sir, you are under orders. What can you do?" But the general would have none of it. "Not like that, Father! I want your opinion as a Catholic priest!" And the chaplain answered, "If you ask me that way, then I have to tell you that you cannot justify it." "My opinion exactly," said the general, and handed in his resignation. Von Stülpnagel was transferred to a distant post and later became involved in the 20 July 1944 plot against Hitler.[38] But what of the chaplain? Any subsequent opposition activity on his part has left no trace.

The unnamed chaplain in France used his moral authority, albeit reluctantly, as a check on wartime atrocities. Far more of his counterparts weighed in on the side of the perpetrators, condoning and blessing their crimes through words, actions, and silence. One of the most obvious manifestations of this function was the provision of group absolution for soldiers.[39] The chaplains' presence provided a kind of spiritual relief, a moral numbing for the men in their care, a haven of normalcy that harked back to the religious practices of childhood. In this "spiritual relief" function, the chaplains performed a task shared by many women in the Third Reich and usually coded as feminine: providing a cozy home, domestic or spiritual, where killers could find peace, rejuvenation, and support.[40] Perhaps that spiritual numbing was the chaplains' major contribution to the crimes of the Third Reich.

Notes

I am grateful to my colleagues at the University of Notre Dame—Patricia Blanchette, Laura Crago, the late John H. Yoder—and the members of the writing group who worked through this project with me—Kathy Biddick, Julia Douthwaite, Sandra Gustafson, Barbara Green, and Glenn Hendler—for their helpful comments on earlier drafts of this paper. Thanks as well to Beate Ruhm von Oppen, Michael Phayer, Pawel Zietara, and the organizers and participants of the 1997 conference on Religion and Genocide for insightful feedback.

1. For examples, see Omer Bartov, *The Eastern Front, 1941-1945: German Troops and the Barbarisation of Warfare* (London, 1985); Helmut Krausnick and Hans-Heinrich Wilhelm, *Die Truppe des Weltanschauungskriegs* (Stuttgart, 1981); and Hamburger Institut für Sozialforschung, catalogue to the exhibit, *Vernichtungskrieg. Verbrechen der Wehrmacht 1941 bis 1944* (Hamburg, 1995). The issue of military participation in the atrocities of the Third Reich continues to spark intensely emotional responses within Germany, as indicated by the recent publicity surrounding the "Vernichtungskrieg" exhibit in Munich. For an account of the exhibit and the controversy, see Rudolf Augstein, "Anschlag auf die 'Ehre' des deutschen Soldaten?," *Der Spiegel*, no. 11 (10 March 1997), pp. 92-99.

2. One important set of sources is the activity reports of German chaplains to their military superiors at the divisional and army levels. See National Archives, Washington, D.C., Microfilmed Records, Captured German Documents: T-315, Records of German Field Commands: Divisions; and T-312, Records of German Field Commands: Armies. These reports tend to be terse and impersonal.

3. For examples, see: Wilhelm Schabel, *Herr, in Deine Hände: Seelsorge im Krieg* (Bern, 1963); Albrecht Schübel, *300 Jahre Evangelische Soldatenseelsorge* (Munich, 1964); Dietrich Baedeker, *Das Volk das im Finsternis wandelt: Stationen eines Militärpfarrers, 1933-1946* (Hanover, 1987). None of these firsthand accounts address the Holocaust. Hans Leonhard provides some glimpses in *Wieviel Leid erträgt ein Mensch? Aufzeichnungen eines Kriegspfarrers über die Jahre 1939 bis 1945* (Amberg, 1994).

4. This impression is conveyed in Eberhard Müller, "Feldbischof unter Hitler," in Hermann Kunst, ed., *Gott läßt sich nicht spotten. Franz Dohrmann, Feldbischof unter Hitler* (Hanover, 1983); see also works by Wilhelm Niemöller.

5. On Nazi measures against the Wehrmacht chaplains, see Manfred Messerschmidt, "Aspekte der Militärseelsorgepolitik in nationalsozialistischer Zeit," *Militärgeschichtliche Mitteilungen* 1/1968, and Messerschmidt, "Zur Militärseelsorgepolitik im Zweiten Weltkrieg," *Militärgeschichtliche Mitteilungen* 1/1969.

6. On specific National Socialist measures against the military chaplaincy, see Messerschmidt, 1968 and 1969; also postwar manuscript by Schubring, "Die Arbeit der Feldseelsorge im Kriege," in Bundesarchiv-Militärarchiv, Freiburg/Br. (hereafter BA-MA Freiburg), N282/v.4; and Protestant Military Bishop Franz Dohrmann's files in BA-MA Freiburg, N282, e.g.: "Bestimmungen für besondere Dienstverhältnisse der Kriegspfarrer beim Feldheer," 18 June 1941, BA-MA Freiburg, N282,/v.3; and 1942 OKH order 23 Dec.1933, BA-MA Freiburg, N282/v.3.

7. Estimated numbers of chaplains vary. The estimation of one thousand total is based on a figure of 480 Protestants who served throughout the war, and an assumption that about equal numbers of Catholics held positions in the chaplaincy. See "Zusammenstellung der eingesetzten Pfarrer," [1941] BA-MA Freiburg, RH 15/281, p. 35; "Kriegsdienst der evang. Geistlichen Deutschlands, nach den statistischen Angaben der Deutsch-Evangelischen Kirchenkanzlei Berlin, Stand 1.10.1941," in Landeskirchenarchiv Nürnberg (LKA Nuremberg), Kreisdekan Nürnberg/121; and "Aufstellung der Soll- und Iststärke an Evangelischen Kriegspfarrern nach dem Stande vom 25.11.1944," BA-MA Freiburg, N282/8.

8. See the reminiscences of former Catholic chaplain Ernst Tewes, "Seelsorger bei den Soldaten 1940-1945. Aufzeichnungen und Erinnerungen," pp. 244-287 in *Das Erzbistum München und Freising in der Zeit der nationalsozialistischen Herrschaft*, ed. Georg Schwaiger, vol. 2 (Munich, 1984); also Bernd Boll and Hans Safrian, "Auf dem Weg nach Stalingrad: Die 6. Armee 1941/42," in Hannes Heer and Klaus Naumann, eds., *Vernichtungskrieg. Verbrechen der Wehrmacht, 1941-1944* (Hamburg, 1995), pp. 260-296, especially pp. 275-77.

9. Tewes, p. 251. This and all other translations from the German are mine unless otherwise specified.

10. Ibid.

11. "Meldung des katholischen Kriegspfarrers Tewes und des evangelischen Kriegspfarrers Wilczek an die 295. Infanterie-Division vom 22.8.1941," quoted in Tewes, p. 252.

12. Boll and Safrian, p. 277.

13. Tewes, p. 252.

14. *Neue Zürcher Zeitung*, 11 Feb. 1968, quoted in Tewes, p. 252.

15. *"In the last two days,"* Tewes wrote on 22 August 1941, "I have experienced things that really got under my skin. I felt it was my duty to get involved. I don't know what will happen. ... Let come what may." Tewes' diary, quoted in Tewes, p. 251.

16. Here my understanding of the motivations of the killers differs from that of Daniel Jonah Goldhagen in *Hitler's Willing Executioners: Ordinary Germans and the Holocaust* (New York, 1996). I accept Goldhagen's emphasis on antisemitism as an important corrective to many interpretations, including Christopher R. Browning's excellent *Ordinary Men: Reserve Police Battalion 101 and the Final Solution in Poland* (New York, 1992). Nevertheless, the need to rationalize and in many cases deny their actions, to numb their sensibilities with alcohol, and to attempt to reduce their victims to something as far removed as possible from normal human conditions indicates that the killers still had to overcome some natural compunctions in order to carry out their murderous tasks.

17. Tewes indicated it was only at the 1968 trial that he realized how angry von Reichenau had been at the chaplains and how seriously the Field Marshall had contemplated punitive measures. Tewes, p. 252.

18. Tewes, p. 253.

19. For more detail, see Doris L. Bergen, "Catholics, Protestants, and Anti-Jewish Christianity in Nazi Germany," *Central European History*, vol. 27, no. 3 (1994).

20. On Rarkowski, see Erwin Gatz, ed., *Die Bischöfe der deutschsprächigen Länder 1785/1803 bis 1945: Ein biographisches Lexikon* (Berlin, 1983), p. 595.

21. Rarkowski, "Hirtenschreiben an der Wende des ersten Kriegsjahres," in *Verordnungsblatt*, no. 7 (1. Sept. 1940), p. 29. See also passages quoted in Gordon C. Zahn, *German Catholics and Hitler's Wars: A Study in Social Control* (New York, 1962), p. 154.

22. On the influence of the *Deutschen Christen* (German Christians) in the Wehrmacht chaplaincy, see Doris L. Bergen, "'Germany Is Our Mission—Christ Is Our Strength': The Wehrmacht Chaplaincy and the 'German Christian' Movement," in *Church History*, vol. 66, no. 3 (Sept. 1997).

23. Josef Perau, *Priester im Heere Hitlers: Erinnerungen 1940-1945* (Essen, 1963), pp. 29 and 33.

24. Gordian Landwehr OP, "So sah ich sie sterben," in Hans Jürgen Brandt, ed., *Priester in Uniform: Seelsorger, Ordensleute und Theologen als Soldaten im Zweiten Weltkrieg* (Augsburg, 1994), pp. 349-50.

25. Schieber, "Bericht über die Versammlung der evangelischen Standortpfarrer des Wehrkreises V in Stuttgart am 22. Juni 1936," 7 July 1936, p. 5, BA-MA Freiburg, RH 53-5/73, p. 8. Although others have used the phrase "Die Sprache Kanaans" to refer more generally to pious jargon, Protestants in the Third Reich commonly employed the label to point to terms associated with Judaism and the Hebrew Bible.

26. Unlabeled page of circular from Bauerle to chaplains in the Sixteenth Army, in "Rundschreiben Armeepfarrer 16," Nachlaß Bauerle, Landeskirchliches Museum, Ludwigsburg (LKM Ludwigsburg). Many thanks to Eberhard Gutekunst and Andrea Kittel for permission to examine this collection.

27. For an example of antisemitic literature distributed to the troops, see the *Feldzeitung* in Nachlaß Bauerle, LKM Ludwigsburg. For chaplains' complaints about challenges from nazified soldiers, see Willy Horneff to Bishop Ludwig Diehl, 31 Jan. 1940, Zentralarchiv der Evangelischen Kirche der Pfalz, Nachlaß Diehl, 150.15/1 (G-L); and Doerne, "Lazarettseelsorge: Referat bei der Standort- und Lazarettpfarrerkonferenz im Wehrkreis IV Dresden, 7.7.1943," in *Mitteilungsblatt des Evangelischen Feldbischofs*, no. 3 (15 October 1943):5, BA-MA Freiburg, RW 12 I/13:6.

28. On the issuance of New Testaments only and the "dejudaized" songbooks, see Bergen, "'Germany Is Our Mission'."

29. Joyce Palmer Ralph, "Vita: Adolf Sannwald," in *Harvard Magazine*, July-August 1995, pp. 44-45.

30. *Junge Kirche* 1980: vol. 5, pp. 214-220, "Eine Jüdin im antifaschistischen Widerstand: Gespräch mit Lotte Holzer," interview by Andreas Schmutz, Mitarbeiter des Hendrik-Kraemer-Hauses, Berlin, pp. 215-217.

31. Wilhelm Großkortenhaus WV, "Rein und durch!" in Hans Brandt, ed., p. 81.

32. Bernward Dörner, "'Der Krieg ist verloren!' 'Wehrkraftzersetzung' und Denunziation in der Truppe," in Norbert Haase and Gerhard Paul, eds., *Die anderen Soldaten. Wehrkraftzersetzung, Gehorsamsverweigerung und Fahnenflucht im Zweiten Weltkrieg* (Frankfurt/M, 1995), pp. 105-122.

33. See, for example, Dohrmann's notes, BA-MA Freiburg, N282/v. 1, p. 163.

34. One explanation for this discrepancy might be the different relationship Catholic and Protestant clergy had to the Wehrmacht in general. Catholic clergy did not serve as regular combat soldiers; those conscripted who were not chaplains worked as medics or in other noncombatant roles. Protestant clergy, in contrast, could be and were drafted into all positions in the armed forces. When it came to selecting military chaplains, Protestant clergymen with combat experience were given preference.

35. Perau, pp. 159-61.

36. For examples of the approval procedure at work, see Ministry of Church Affairs to Supreme Command (OKW), 22 May 1944, BA-MA Freiburg, RH 15/272, pp. 216-17; Church Affairs to OKW, BA-MA Freiburg, RH 15/272, p. 116; same file, Bunke, "Bericht der Wehrmachtkommandantur Berlin," 18 Dec. 1943; OKW (Gruppe S) memo to military bishops, 21 March 1944, p. 113; report of Gestapo Hanover on Pastor Friedrich Voges, in Deputy Chief Command, District XI, to OKH, 17 Nov. 1944, BA-MA Freiburg, RH 15/270, p. 25; and church ministry files re: chaplains, BA Potsdam, 51.01/23846 and 23847.

37. For examples, see activity report for early 1942 of the Catholic chaplain with the 1st Mountain Division in Russia, T-315/48/1312-1316; or activity reports for 1942 of the Protestant chaplain with the 1st Mountain Division, T-315/48/1317-1322; or for June 1942 to July 1942, Protestant chaplain with the 5th Jäger Division, stationed around Smolensk and then near Starya Russa, T-315/248/906-908.

38. Heinrich Pachowiak, "Auf den Hinterhöfen des Krieges," in Brandt, pp. 27-28.

39. *Verordnungsblätter des katholischen Feldbischof der Wehrmacht*, no. 6 (12 Aug. 1944), p. 30, "Generalabsolution," signed Rarkowski.

40. For additional discussion of women's roles in Nazi warfare, see Claudia Koonz, *Mothers in the Fatherland: Women, the Family and Nazi Politics* (London, 1987); Gaby Zipfel, "Wie führen Frauen Krieg?" in Heer and Naumann, pp. 460-474; and Gitta Sereny, *Into that Darkness: An Examination of Conscience* (New York, 1983), especially pp. 355-62.

– *Chapter 6* –

CHRISTIAN CHURCHES
AND GENOCIDE IN RWANDA

Timothy Longman

In 1994, the small East African state of Rwanda was torn by one of the century's most brutal waves of ethnic and political violence. In a three-month period from April to June, the Rwandan Armed Forces (FAR), working with trained civilian militia, systematically massacred as many as one million of the country's 7.7 million people. The primary targets of the violence were members of the minority Tutsi ethnic group, who were chased from their homes, gathered in churches and other public buildings, ostensibly for their protection, then methodically murdered, first with grenades and guns, then with machetes and other traditional weapons. In the weeks that followed, death squads carefully hunted down and killed survivors of the large-scale massacres. While the exact portion of the Tutsi population killed in the genocide cannot be accurately determined, it seems fair to estimate that at least 80 percent of the Tutsi living in the country lost their lives.[1]

In the aftermath of this horrific bloodbath, Rwanda's Christian churches have faced extensive criticism. Many journalists, scholars, human rights activists, politicians, and even some church personnel have accused the churches not simply of failing effectively to oppose the genocide but of active complicity in the violence.[2] According to a report by a World Council of Churches team that visited Rwanda in August 1994, "In every conversation we had

with the government and church people alike, the point was brought
home to us that the church itself stands tainted, not by passive indifference, but by errors of commission as well."[3] My own research in
Rwanda from 1992 to 1993 and from 1995 to 1996 confirms these
conclusions. According to my findings, church personnel and institutions were actively involved in the program of resistance to popular
pressures for political reform that culminated in the 1994 genocide,
and numerous priests, pastors, nuns, brothers, catechists, and Catholic and Protestant lay leaders supported, participated in, or helped
to organize the killings.[4]

As the contents of this volume indicate, that religious insti-
tutions should be implicated in a genocide is not exceptional. In
Rwanda, however, unlike the genocides of Armenians in Turkey,
Jews in Europe in World War II, and Muslims in Bosnia, and in
contrast to the genocidal violence between Hindus, Muslims, and
Sikhs in India, and Christians and various Muslim groups in
Lebanon, religion did not serve as an ascriptive identifier to demar-
cate a social group as an essential "other."[5] Both Catholic and
Protestant churches in Rwanda are multi-ethnic, and the genocide
in Rwanda occurred *within* religious groups. In most communities
members of a church parish killed their fellow parishioners and
even, in a number of cases, their own pastor or priest.

Although religious identities did not separate perpetrators from
victims in Rwanda, my research indicates that religion was nevertheless an essential element in the Rwandan genocide. Contrary to
the claims of some church authorities,[6] the involvement of the
churches went beyond a simple failure to act in the face of atrocities or the individual transgressions of church members. As I will
attempt to demonstrate in this paper, the culpability of the churches
lies not only in their historic role in teaching obedience to state
authority and in constructing ethnic identities but also in their
modern role as centers of social, political, and economic power,
allied with the state, actively practicing ethnic discrimination, and
working to preserve the status quo.

Christianity and the Colonial Project

Christianity and Respect for Authority

The first mission stations in Rwanda were established in 1900 by
the Society of Our Lady of Africa, commonly known as the White
Fathers. Monseigneur Lavigerie, the founder of the order, promoted the idea that to implant Christianity successfully in a society,

missionaries should focus their efforts at conversion first and fore-most on political authorities. If chiefs and kings could be convinced to adopt Christianity, Lavigerie argued, their subjects would natu-rally follow.[7] The principle that evangelization should focus on chiefs profoundly affected the nature of the Catholic missionary project in Rwanda and has had far reaching consequences both for the Catholic Church in Rwanda and for Rwandan society generally.

As Ian Linden demonstrates in his thorough study of church-state relations in colonial Rwanda, the leaders of the order of White Fathers consistently pushed their priests to focus their attention on converting the leaders of Rwandan society—local chiefs, people attached to the royal court, and other important individuals. As in other countries, mission stations in Rwanda first attracted socially marginalized individuals who saw conversion as an opportunity for advancement. Some missionaries in the early decades of the cen-tury believed that the church should take up the cause of the mar-ginalized against the powerful, arguing that setting the church up as an alternative to indigenous institutions would be an easier route to converting the population, but the leaders of the order reiterated the instruction to target prominent personalities. In the first several decades, the number of conversions remained small, but ultimately the strategy proved successful. By the 1920s, a number of nobles had converted to Christianity, and after 1931, when the missionar-ies were instrumental in the deposition of one king and the selection of his successor, the number of chiefs and courtiers who became Christian soared. In subsequent decades, much of the Rwandan population did in fact follow the example of their leaders and con-verted to Catholicism.[8]

While the strategy of focusing missionary efforts on political leaders succeeded in making Rwanda one of the most Catholic soci-eties in Africa, it imparted a distinct character to the Catholic Church in the country. From their arrival in Rwanda, the Catholic mis-sionaries sought to appease political authorities and avoid conflict. In practice, church-state relations were not always smooth, since Yuhi V Musinga, who served as king from 1896 to 1931, resented the power of the missionaries and frequently opposed the church, but the missionaries nevertheless sought his approval. At the same time, they cultivated supporters within the royal court, using their influence to advance pro-Catholic elements in the struggles for power within the court, and they maintained excellent relations with colonial authorities. Once they had developed a sufficient backing within the court, the missionaries actively interceded with the Bel-gian administration to remove Musinga from power and replace him with his most pro-Catholic son. The missionaries maintained excellent relations with Mutara III Rudahigwa, who served as king until his death in 1959, and under his reign the church flourished.[9] The idea that gaining the support of state leaders assures the smooth functioning of the church thus became accepted doctrine for Catholic leaders in Rwanda.

Linked to the desire to solicit the support of state leaders, the missionaries taught their followers to demonstrate obedience to public authorities. As in other colonies, missionaries in Rwanda played an important role in pacifying the population. As early as 1913, the German colonial administrator Dr. Kandt wrote to the vicar of Kivu, Monseigneur Hirth, the head of the White Fathers for Ruanda-Urundi, thanking him for the work of the church and requesting that mission stations be opened in another region that had yet to be fully brought under colonial control:

> Sir,
>
>   The missions that you have founded in the north of Rwanda contribute a good deal to the pacification of that district. They facilitate substantially the task of government. The influence of your missionaries has saved us the necessity of undertaking military expeditions. ...[10]

In the system of indirect rule employed by the Germans and Belgians, the king remained the chief political authority in the land. Even though the missionaries themselves quietly challenged the authority of the king, they nevertheless taught their converts to respect his orders provided they rested within the bounds of Christian moral teachings. Even this final caveat was eliminated once Musinga was replaced by the Christian Rudahigwa. While the missionaries certainly did not introduce the idea of respecting authority to Rwanda, their advocacy of obedience as a Christian value helped to guarantee a compliant population even at a time when the system was becoming increasingly centralized and autocratic and was providing fewer material benefits to subjects.[11]

During the colonial period, Protestant missions were less significant, both in terms of political influence and number of converts, but their general conduct did not differ substantially from that of the Catholic missionaries. The first Protestant mission stations were established in 1907, but Protestant evangelism was seriously disrupted by the First World War, and new large-scale Protestant missionary efforts did not begin again until the 1930s. Like their Catholic counterparts, the Anglican, Reformed, and Adventist missionaries who established missions in Rwanda sought the favor of the state, both in its European and Rwandan embodiments. They also taught obedience to authority as an important Christian value. To some extent, once the Catholics established close ties with the state, the Protestant missions attracted socially marginalized or discontented individuals who saw these missions as an alternative to the status quo. Hence, Protestant churches were a location of greater rebelliousness. In the 1930s, a movement known as *abarokore* arrived in the Anglican Church from Uganda and challenged the authority of the missionaries, but the missionaries moved quickly to suppress the movement, which disappeared within a few years (only to re-emerge fifty years later in a new form). Despite their position as relative outsiders, however, the Protestants did not base their appeal on a rhetoric of rebellion. Rather, Protestant leaders envied the Catholics their privileged position and sought as much as possible to follow their lead in seeking support and cooperation from the state.[12] Given this fact, it is rather surprising that Rwanda did not experience the emergence of independent African Christian churches or other alternative religious movements like those that emerged in neighboring Kenya and Zaire.

In the 1950s, the close alliance between the Catholic Church and the Rwandan court broke down. In the post-war period, a number of the missionaries who came to Rwanda were influenced by social-democratic philosophies and became concerned by the plight of the Hutu people who, despite constituting more than 80 percent of the population, were entirely excluded from political office and other opportunities for advancement. As Linden points out, while the majority of Catholic missionaries continued to sympathize with the Tutsi minority who dominated the society, the new progressive priests cultivated a Hutu counter-elite, providing opportunities for education and employment to select Hutu. The progressive priests and their Hutu protégés helped raise the consciousness among the Hutu masses of their exploitation, and in the late 1950s, ethnic tensions increased sharply. In November 1959, Hutu mobs attacked Tutsi chiefs and officials in several locations, causing thousands of Tutsi to flee the country. The Belgian administration, influenced by the missionaries, abruptly switched its allegiance from the Tutsi to the Hutu and rapidly replaced Tutsi chiefs and officials with Hutu. Rwanda achieved independence in 1962 with an almost entirely Hutu government.[13]

While Catholic support for the Hutu masses during the late 1950s would seem to represent a sharp break with Lavigerie's principle of accommodating the elite, it was in fact only a momentary change of focus. The Hutu named to replace the exiled Tutsi authorities were drawn from the Hutu counter-elite cultivated by the Catholic Church, and they owed their positions substantially to the church. Grégoire Kayibanda, the first president, had served as editor of the Catholic newspaper *Kinyamateka* and later became head of a Catholic consumers' cooperative. Catholic missionaries sent him to Europe for training and provided him other forms of support that helped him emerge as a leader. Other Hutu officials and politicians at independence were church employees or were recruited out of Catholic seminaries. Minor conflicts between church and state arose in the 1960s as the new political class sought to demonstrate its independence from the church, but in general the alliance of church and state was even stronger after independence than during most of the colonial period.[14] A cynical reading of the Catholic Church's "support for revolution" in the 1950s as a calculated strategy to guarantee the church would be politically well situated after independence is not entirely unreasonable.

Christianity and the Construction of Ethnicity

In the introductory essay to his edited volume on the construction of ethnicity in Southern Africa, Leroy Vail argues that European Christian missionaries played a crucial role in the development of ethnic ideologies in Africa. According to Vail,

> In addition to creating written languages, missionaries were instrumental in creating cultural identities through their specification of "custom" and "tradition" and by writing "tribal" histories. ... Once these elements of culture were in place and available to be used as the cultural base of a distinct new, ascriptive ethnic identity, it could replace older organizing principles that depended upon voluntary clientage and loyalty and which, as such, showed great plasticity. Thus firm, non-porous and relatively inelastic ethnic boundaries, many of which were highly arbitrary, came to be constructed and were then strengthened by the growth of stereotypes of "the other". ...[15]

Vail argues that missionaries "incorporated into the curricula of their mission schools the lesson that the pupils had clear ethnic identities," and claims that they "educated local Africans who then themselves served as the most important force in shaping the new ethnic ideologies."[16] Combined with the policies of colonial administrators and the popular acceptance of ethnic ideas as a means of coping with the disruptions of modernity, the actions of missionaries helped to create the deep social divisions that are at the root of ethnic conflict in many African countries.

The role of missionaries in the construction of ethnicity in Rwanda offers an excellent example of the process that Vail describes. In Rwanda, missionaries played a primary role in creating ethnic myths and interpreting Rwandan social organization—not only for colonial administrators, but ultimately for the Rwandan population itself. The concepts of ethnicity developed by the missionaries served as a basis for the German and Belgian colonial policies of indirect rule which helped to transform relatively flexible pre-colonial social categories into clearly defined ethnic groups. Following independence, leaders who were trained in church schools relied extensively on ethnic ideologies to gain support, thus helping to intensify and solidify ethnic divisions.

The exact meaning of the categories of Hutu, Tutsi, and Twa in pre-colonial Rwanda, Burundi, and Zaire is a subject of considerable debate among scholars. Nearly all scholars, however, agree that the three were not clearly distinct and rigidly separated ethnic groups. The three groups shared a common language and common religious practices, and they lived in the same communities throughout the region. The groups were distinguished primarily by their position within the political and economic system, which assigned members of each group specific economic activities and social roles. The Tutsi, who are generally thought to have constituted about 14 percent of the population, dominated most political offices and made their living predominantly from raising cattle, while the Hutu, who made up around 85 percent of the population, worked primarily as farmers. The Twa lived as hunters and gatherers and fulfilled certain social functions such as making pottery. Intermarriage between Hutu and Tutsi was relatively common, and those Hutu who acquired cattle, the traditional sign of wealth and source of power in the *ubuhake* patron-client system, could eventually be considered Tutsi, a process known as *icyihuture*. While the Tutsi clearly gained the greatest benefits from this system, each group had certain economic opportunities reserved for it, and a complex political system of overlapping chieftaincies helped to prevent the concentration of power.[17]

When colonial administrators and Catholic missionaries arrived in Rwanda, they were enchanted by the Tutsi rulers they encountered. To the missionaries, the Tutsi seemed tall and elegant, with refined features and light skin, in some ways closer in appearance to Europeans than to their short, stocky, dark Hutu compatriots. As elsewhere in Africa, in order to convert the population in Rwanda, the missionaries considered it important to understand the indigenous culture and social structures, and the interpretations that came from their study of the culture greatly influenced both the colonial administration and, subsequently, Rwandan self-perceptions. Influenced by contemporary European notions of race which

held that the world could be divided into clearly defined and hier-
archically ranked racial and national groups, the missionaries,
ignoring important divisions within each of the groups, viewed
Hutu, Tutsi, and Twa as three distinct peoples representing three
separate waves of immigration. They viewed the Twa as the
autochthonous population, the original inhabitants of the region,
who many centuries earlier were subdued by Bantu migrants from
the west who became the Hutu. According to the missionary
account, the Tutsi arrived from the northeast sometime later,
around 1600, and because of their clear superiority, conquered the
Hutu, whom they had ruled ever since. Doubting that Africans
could have designed so complex and efficient a political system, the
missionaries hypothesized that the Tutsi were not really African
but a Hamitic or Semitic group from the Middle East, perhaps a
lost tribe of Israel.[18]

The Tutsi, not surprisingly, failed to challenge the missionaries'
assertions of their superiority and instead participated in the development of a mythico-history that portrayed them as natural rulers
with superior intelligence and morals. When the Catholic Church
began to recruit native Rwandan clergy early in the century (the
first native-born priest was ordained in 1917), they selected exclusively Tutsi, and these priests, nuns, and brothers played an important role in interpreting Rwandan history and culture. A group of
Tutsi intellectuals emerged within the church—most importantly
historian Alexis Kagame and Bishop Aloys Bigirumwami—whose
anthropological and historical texts, based largely on oral histories,
reinforced many of the ideas of strict ethnic separation and Tutsi
political dominance. As Alison DesForges writes, "In a great and
unsung collaborative enterprise over a period of decades, Europeans and Rwandan intellectuals created a history of Rwanda that
fit European assumptions and accorded with Tutsi interests."[19]
This history became widely accepted by Rwandans of all ethnicities, and following the transfer of power from Tutsi to Hutu after
the 1959 revolution, Hutu leaders used the historical account of
centuries of ethnically based exploitation to inspire support among
the Hutu masses.

The policy of indirect rule implemented by both the Germans
and Belgians (after they took control of the colony during World
War I) left the Rwandan monarchy in place, using the existing
political structures to administer colonial policies. The system lost
much of its complexity, as power became increasingly centralized.
Since indirect rule required identifying indigenous authorities, the
Belgian administration registered all of the population in the 1930s

and issued identity cards that designated each person's ethnicity. This and other policies effectively eliminated the flexibility in Rwanda's ethnic structure, making it "almost impossible for Hutu to become Tutsi just at a time when being Tutsi brought all the advantages."[20] Educational, employment, and economic opportunities were reserved for Tutsi, producing a huge gap between the ethnic groups which was at the root of the Hutu anger and resentment that inspired the 1959 insurrection.

The shift in missionary support from Tutsi to Hutu in the 1950s did not substantially alter either the nature of the Rwandan ethnic system or the role of the churches in defining ethnicity in Rwanda. While myths of Tutsi superiority and a long history of dominance over the Hutu served to justify continued Tutsi control of Rwanda in the early colonial period, the same inaccurate history became justification for revolution in the era following World War II. The new "progressive" missionaries who championed the cause of the Hutu in the 1950s promoted an ideology of exploitation that identified the Tutsi as the culprits in Rwandan history while ignoring exploitation by the German and Belgian colonial rulers. Hence, when the Hutu uprising occurred in 1959, attacks were directed against the Tutsi rather than the Belgian administrators.[21] The inaccurate idea promulgated by the missionaries that Tutsi had grossly exploited the Hutu for centuries continues to shape Hutu understandings of Rwandan history and eventually became a primary ideological justification for genocide.

The Churches in Post-Colonial Rwanda

The roots of Christian church complicity in the Rwandan genocide, thus, lie to a substantial degree in the role of missions as part of the colonial project, helping both to subdue the Rwandan population and to shape ethnic self-identity. The mission churches developed a close alliance with the state during the colonial period, an alliance that continued after independence when a Hutu elite that owed its rise to power to the Catholic Church took over the reigns of government. After the disruptions of the 1959 uprising, the churches returned to teaching a theology of obedience, which they justified now not with conservative notions of the destiny of superior social groups to rule, but with populist ideas of the Hutu as the exploited masses now coming into their own. The military coup in 1973 that drove the regime of Grégoire Kayibanda from power, after a decade of economic stagnation and disruptive ethnic violence, did not substantially upset the close alliance of church and state, as the new military president, Juvénal Habyarimana, identified himself as a devout Catholic. Although Habyarimana did not owe his position to the churches, he recognized their influence within Rwanda and actively courted their support. The churches, in turn, welcomed his rise to power and offered their support to his new regime.

In addition to the legacy of close church-state ties that continued after independence, the role of Christian churches in shaping ethnic relations in colonial Rwanda has continued to have a profound impact on post-colonial ethnic politics. The missionaries and their Rwandan protégés played an essential role in eliminating the flexibility in Rwanda's ethnic structure, creating a rigidly defined system in which the Tutsi monopolized power and benefits. The national history they constructed presented this new structure as an historical artifact and became a basis for pride among the Tutsi and, later, resentment among the Hutu. Just as the churches had previously been the champions of the "noble Watusi," at independence they became champions of the humble Hutu, and having played a vital role in the ethnic transfer of power, the churches remained largely silent as ethnic violence occurred repeatedly in the early 1960s and again in 1973. The ties of the churches to state power were increased in the 1960s even as the state was espousing Hutu ethno-nationalist rhetoric that fostered a climate of fear and violence.

To fully explain the active involvement of church leaders and institutions in the Rwandan genocide, however, requires exploring not only the colonial legacy, but also the position of churches within post-colonial Rwandan society. In a society where a single-party state dominated most aspects of public life, the churches were the largest non-state organizations. The Mouvement Révolutionnaire National pour le Développement (MRND) established by President Habyarimana in 1975 as Rwanda's only political party served not simply as a tool for organizing public support for the regime but as a means of monitoring and regulating the population. Women's organizations, youth groups, labor unions, and farmer's cooperatives were subsumed under the party umbrella, and all citizens were required to be MRND members and to pay party dues. Churches were among the only organizations that remained outside formal party control as ostensibly autonomous organizations. They were nevertheless integrated into the system of power through a variety of means. The archbishop of the Catholic Church held a seat on the central committee of the MRND for a decade, while the leaders of the Presbyterian and Anglican churches also held important MRND positions.

To view the churches, however, as weak institutions, unable to challenge the state as some apologists have suggested in the aftermath of the genocide,[22] is to grossly misconstrue the relationship between church and state in Rwanda and to ignore the substantial independent power that the churches enjoyed. In the 1991 census, 89.8 percent of the population claimed membership in a Christian Church—62.6 percent claimed to be Catholic, 18.8 percent Protestant, and 8.4 percent Seventh Day Adventist.[23] The churches, thus, had a very large constituency that they could potentially mobilize, and through their parishes, they had excellent access to people at all levels of society. The resources the churches could draw from their members were augmented substantially by contributions from international church bodies. Each church ran offices of education, health, and development, which oversaw significant expenditures throughout the country. In my field research, I found that churches represented a massive presence within Rwandan society and economy. Particularly in rural areas, where the state's presence was more limited, the population turned to churches not only for spiritual needs, but as their primary social center, for healthcare, for education, for assistance in developing economic alternatives, and for charity. With few natural resources and a very low level of industrialization, churches were the largest off-farm employers in many rural areas.

The significant financial and human resources controlled by the churches made them important centers of power within Rwanda. People holding church offices, such as pastors, priests, and school directors, generally lived in brick houses, often with running water or electricity, they had access to vehicles, and their children could attend secondary school. In a society with high levels of malnutrition, periodic famine, and other vestiges of severe poverty, these advantages set them apart from other people in their communities. Church employment also presented opportunities for personal enrichment and a chance to assist family and friends. As a result, patrimonial networks developed within Rwanda churches like the patrimonial networks that state officers used to organize their support. In the Presbyterian Church, for example, members of the church president's family and people from his home community in Kibuye prefecture dominated prominent positions throughout the country, from the director of development to the secretaries in the national church office.

In theory, churches in Rwanda could have used their independent bases of power to challenge state power. There was potential for church-state conflict, since the imperatives of the state and the churches were not identical, and in fact conflict did arise over various issues, such as a conflict over birth control policy in the 1980s. In general, however, the churches and the state cooperated closely. Both institutions, building on the history of cooperation established during the colonial era, found that they could function more effectively by working together on education, health care, and development. The interests of church employees at all levels were closer to the parallel state elite, with whom they may have attended school and who lived a similar privileged lifestyle, than to the rest of society. In the local communities I studied, I found that strong reciprocal relationships existed between church, state, and business elites. They often socialized together, and they frequently cooperated on business ventures. These links were true at the national level as well. President Habyarimana and the Catholic archbishop were known to be close friends, and they frequently appeared together at public events. Leaders of the churches, like leaders of the state, had a vested interest in preserving the status quo that had allowed them to gain significant privilege and power.

Given the links between church and state, it should not be surprising, then, that when demands for democratic reform began to emerge in Rwanda in the early 1990s, the churches generally offered little support.[24] The Habyarimana regime had enjoyed strong popular favor during its first decade, since it had attracted extensive international development investment and had effectively managed the volatile ethnic situation. By the mid-1980s, however, the population was becoming increasingly discontent with the regime, resenting high levels of official corruption and the opulent lifestyles of state officials. A collapse in the price of coffee, Rwanda's primary export, seriously affected both small farmers and the middle class. As governments internationally came under pressure to allow greater democracy and increased personal freedom, the continuing repression of the Habyarimana regime stood out, and people in Rwanda began to object increasingly to required MRND membership, communal labor, and loyalty rituals. Hutu from the south of the country and Tutsi objected to the monopoly of political positions held by Hutu from Habyarimana's home region in the north.

In 1989, an explosion of new publications appeared in Rwanda after the oldest paper in the country, the Catholic biweekly *Kinyamateka*, began to ignore censorship rules and published open accounts about corruption and the country's economic problems. Various groups that had begun to emerge in the 1980s outside the auspices of the MRND, such as women's groups, youth associations, and informal associations of intellectuals, became increasingly politicized and began to demand that Habyarimana implement democratic reforms. The democracy movement in Rwanda gained momentum after the national conferences in Benin and Congo in February 1990 replaced authoritarian rulers in those countries. Feeling increasingly pressured, Habyarimana announced in July 1990 that he would allow a free debate on the country's future and would begin to implement reforms. Believing that Habyarimana was sufficiently vulnerable that he could easily be driven from power, a rebel army based in Uganda, the Rwandan Patriotic Front (RPF), composed primarily of Tutsi refugees from the ethnic violence of the 1960s and 1970s, invaded Rwanda in October 1990, adding further pressures on the regime but also providing Habyarimana with a justification for cracking down on his critics.

Some church personnel and institutions, like *Kinyamateka*, supported the democracy movement, and the Catholic hierarchy even published pastoral letters in February and May that in vague terms denounced corruption and called for expanded respect for human rights. In general, however, the churches offered little support to those groups and individuals seeking to force the state to accept reforms. After the October RPF invasion, Habyarimana's government arrested thousands of Tutsi and southern Hutu. Church leaders refused to support human rights groups that formed to object to the arrests, and the Catholic hierarchy, in a pastoral letter released shortly after the outbreak of the war, expressed strong support for the government and entirely ignored the issue of detention, ignoring even the detention of several Tutsi priests. When a new constitution was adopted in June 1991 and opposition parties were legalized, the national leaders of each of the major churches, as well as many regional and local church leaders, remained public supporters of the MRND.

As both the demands for democratic reform and the war continued to expand over the next several years, Habyarimana and his allies turned increasingly to ethnic arguments to bolster their support. Even as he publicly accepted political reforms that legalized opposition parties, Habyarimana sought to undermine the new parties by portraying them as traitors to the interests of the Hutu. Rhetoric on state radio and in MRND newspapers incited the population with claims that the RPF was fighting to re-establish the monarchy and once again exploit the Hutu. Ethnic tensions were heightened by a series of massacres of Tutsi that occurred in various parts of the country, beginning just after the start of the war. While the government portrayed these massacres as spontaneous expressions of public anger over the war, investigations by local and inter-

national human rights groups revealed that in each case government or MRND party officials were involved in organizing and
carrying out the violence.[25]

The Christian churches met the massacres of Tutsi that took
place from 1990-1993 with resounding silence, even when on several occasions church property and personnel were targeted. This
silence confirmed for most Rwandans the widely held assumption
that church leaders were themselves biased against Tutsi. Ethnic
issues within the Christian churches in independent Rwanda were
quite complex. Because of limitations in other spheres of employment (Tutsi were almost entirely excluded from government jobs
under both Kayibanda and Habyarimana), Tutsi were actually dis-
proportionately represented among both Catholic and Protestant
clergy. Leadership positions, however, were reserved for Hutu. The
churches themselves practiced ethnic discrimination, as in a much
discussed incident in 1988 in which a Tutsi who was appointed
bishop in the Catholic Church withdrew "for personal reasons"
just before his installation; rumors spread that he withdrew under
pressure from Habyarimana and the archbishop, who did not want
another Tutsi bishop. (Of the eight bishops serving at the time, one,
who was named before independence, was Tutsi). In the Protestant
churches, Hutu held the prominent offices, while Tutsi were relegated to obscure parishes and less influential positions. During the
period of democratic reform and renewed ethnic conflict in the
early 1990s, church leaders completely failed to condemn ethnic
violence and to support political reforms, but instead lent their support to the government that was organizing the violence.

The Genocide and the Churches

Although the Western media portrayed the 1994 genocide as a
product of "centuries old" intractable divisions between Hutu and
Tutsi "tribes," in fact genocide in Rwanda was never inevitable.
Genocide was the final product of a strategy used by close supporters of President Habyarimana to preserve their power by
appealing to ethnic arguments. Since Hutu and Tutsi continued to
intermarry regularly and lived together in relative peace in most
communities, the strategy required going well beyond reminding
the Hutu of Tutsi dominance during the colonial period to create an
atmosphere of fear and misunderstanding. The president's allies
launched a concerted propaganda effort, using the print media,
public meetings, and—most importantly—the radio, to character-

ize the Tutsi as an "essential other." The propaganda built on the mythic "history" of Hamitic conquerors to claim that the Tutsi were foreigners who had come to Rwanda to exploit the rightful occupants, the Hutu, and should be "sent back down the Nile."[26] With the largely Tutsi RPF attacking the borders of the country, claims that the Tutsi still sought to subdue the Hutu gained credence, and Tutsi within Rwanda could be scapegoated as RPF agents, effectively diverting public attention from the government corruption and repression that had inspired the democracy movement. By identifying the opponents of the president as traitors to the Hutu, supporters of Habyarimana were able to discredit and divide the opposition parties, and by accepting a role in a coalition government installed in 1992, the opposition parties relinquished their position as a clear alternative to the Habyarimana regime and lost much of their popular appeal.[27]

The groundwork for genocide was laid over a period of several years. The small-scale massacres that began in 1990 helped condition the population for larger massacres later. In 1992 a group of hardline Hutu created a new extreme political party, the Coalition for the Defense of the Republic (CDR), that appealed to supporters with virulently anti-Tutsi rhetoric. While publicly more extreme in its positions than the MRND, the CDR in fact cooperated closely with the ruling party, allowing MRND leaders to resist compromise with the RPF and the internal opposition by pressuring the MRND from the far right. As one source told me, "The CDR says what MRND leaders think but cannot say." Meanwhile, the MRND transformed its youth wing, the *Interahamwe,* into a militia, and the armed forces provided para-military training to both the *Interahamwe* and a new CDR militia. After the government and RPF signed a peace accord in August 1993 that would have brought the RPF into the government and integrated them into the Rwandan armed forces, the president's supporters sought to ensure that the accords would never be implemented. They intensified their propaganda efforts, creating a new radio station, Radio-Télévision Libre des Milles Collines (RTLM) to broadcast propaganda against Tutsi and moderate Hutu.[28] The armed forces expanded militia training and began distributing arms to civilians. At some point in late 1993 or early 1994, a group of officials close to the president drew up a plan to guarantee their power through a massive campaign of violence that would eliminate all of their opponents, including Tutsi and prominent moderate Hutu.

The genocide ultimately had much more to do with the contemporary political concerns of an authoritarian regime under attack than with "ancient tribal hatreds," and as such it could have been averted. The military support offered to the Habyarimana regime by France and other countries helped the regime rebuild its strength at a moment when domestic opposition had seriously weakened its position. The vast expansion of the military that foreign support made possible—from about five thousand troops at the beginning of the war to more than fifty thousand in 1992—allowed the government to place soldiers throughout the country, where they harassed and subdued the population and eventually oversaw the implementation of genocide.[29] Even with the military expansion, genocide could have been prevented if efforts had been made to counter the ideological and logistical preparations. Although they could not have single-handedly stopped the genocide, the Christian churches were nevertheless the organizations best situated within Rwanda to challenge the progress toward genocide, because they remained the largest non-state actors even with the explosion of civil-society associations in the preceding decade.

Some individuals and agencies within the churches did, in fact, contest the scapegoating of Tutsi. A number of progressive pastors and priests supported the work of human rights groups, helping, among other things, to provide information about massacres. The Catholic newspaper, *Kinyamateka*, continued to speak out in favor of reform and denounced the rising ethnic tension as diversionary. *IWACU*, a national center for cooperatives with close ties to both Catholic and Protestant Churches, organized civic education projects. The Catholic bishop of Kabgayi issued several letters in 1992 and 1993 demanding political reform and criticizing his church for its inaction; and in late 1993, the Catholic bishop of Nyundo, the diocese in Habyarimana's northern home region, published a letter denouncing the training of civilian militia and the distribution of arms to civilians. In my own research, I encountered church personnel in several of the communities where I studied who, at some personal risk, called for ethnic unity and denounced government abuses.

On the whole, however, the churches did little to halt the build up to genocide. Many church leaders had profited substantially from the status quo and had a vested interest in preserving the existing configurations of power. With several bishops refusing to sign onto more forceful statements—the Catholic archbishop was a close friend of the president, and another bishop was from the president's family—the Catholic episcopacy during the period leading up to the genocide published only vague and non-specific pastoral letters, calling for ethnic peace without referring to any actual instances of ethnic violence. Protestant leaders, many of whom also had close associations with the regime, were similarly circumspect. As tensions in the country mounted in late 1993, particularly after the first Hutu president of Burundi was killed in an attempted coup in October, Catholic and Protestant hierarchies fell entirely silent. My research found that local and regional church leaders were as reticent to criticize the government as their national counterparts. In one Catholic parish in the north of the country where the communal mayor had overseen a massacre of several hundred Tutsi in 1991, the sister in charge of the parish told me in 1992 that polygamy was the major problem in her community. In several of the parishes where I conducted research, church employees and prominent lay leaders took leadership roles in the CDR and Interahamwe. I have no evidence that any church personnel were among the small cadre of people who ultimately drew up the plans for genocide, but church leaders certainly made no concerted effort to hinder the expansion of ethnic ideologies and hatreds, to condemn the scapegoating of Tutsi, and to oppose the growing militarization of society that made the genocide possible.

When the genocide finally occurred, church personnel and institutions were, not surprisingly, intimately involved. Just hours after President Habyarimana's death in a mysterious plane crash on April 6, 1994 (probably the work of his own presidential guard), elite troops spread out into Kigali with lists of people to kill—opposition politicians, leaders of the civil society, and prominent Tutsi. Over the next few weeks, the violence expanded throughout the country, as the Rwandan Armed Forces (FAR) and the Interahamwe militia targeted the entire Tutsi population: men, women, and children. Orders traveled through a pre-established network, and a pattern of attack occurred with frightening consistency from one community to the next: The local militia attacked Tutsi families, burning their homes, killing some Tutsi, and driving out the rest. Local politicians then encouraged Tutsi to gather in a central location, usually a church, ostensibly for their security. Once the Tutsi population of the community was assembled, the militia moved in, often with the support of troops, and systematically massacred the gathered Tutsi. In many communities, a handful of moderate Hutu were killed early in the violence as a warning to other Hutu. After the large scale massacre was complete, the entire male population of the community was organized into security patrols that acted as death squads, searching homes where sympathetic Hutu had hidden their Tutsi friends and family and setting up barricades where Tutsi trying to flee could be stopped; anyone wanting to pass the barricade had to show an identity card that indicated their ethnicity.

The church was implicated in the genocide in numerous ways. People who sought sanctuary in church buildings were instead slaughtered there. According to some estimates, more people were killed in church buildings than anywhere else.[30] At one parish I studied, the communal mayor reported that 17 thousand bodies were unearthed from one set of latrines alongside the church. Numerous Tutsi priests, pastors, brothers, and nuns were killed, often by their own parishioners, sometimes by their fellow clergy. While the failure of the population to respect the principle of sanctuary cannot be blamed on the churches, the failure of the church leadership to condemn massacres on church property and attacks on church personnel in the years preceding the genocide clearly undermined the principle of sanctuary in Rwanda.

In some parishes Hutu clergy attempted to protect those gathered within their church, but in many others, clergy assisted the killers. One Tutsi woman who was a teacher at the Catholic grade school in Kaduha in Gikongoro prefecture told me:

> The priest, Nyandwe, came to my house. My husband [who is Hutu] was not there. Nyandwe asked my children, "Where is she?" They said that I was sick. He came into the house, entering even into my bedroom. He said, "Come! I will hide you, because there is an attack." ... He said "I'll take you to the CND [police]." He grabbed me by the arm and took me by force. He dragged me out into the street and we started to go by foot toward the church. But arriving on the path, I saw a huge crowd. There were many people, wearing banana leaves, carrying machetes. I broke free from him and ran. I went to hide in the home of a friend. He wanted to turn me over to the crowd that was preparing to attack the church. It was he who prevented people from leaving the church.[31]

In a number of communities where I conducted research, people testified that pastors and priests and other church employees participated in the violence that occurred. Church personnel were apparently involved in meetings held in mid-April in which the organizers of the genocide told mayors in the southern prefectures of Butare, Gikongoro, and Gitarama, many of whom had resisted the genocide and protected their Tutsi citizens, that they would be removed if they did not support the genocide. It was immediately after these meetings that the massacres began in these areas. There are numerous examples of clergy who turned people over to be killed. In one incident in May, the Catholic archbishop himself turned over to a death squad a number of nuns and priests gathered at the cathedral at Kabgayi.[32] In several cases I investigated, clergy participated in death squads. In some cases, clergy helped to locate parishioners who were in hiding.[33]

In response to the massacres, the church hierarchies remained mostly silent. Catholic and Protestant leaders signed a joint letter in May that called for an end to massacres yet failed to condemn them or to characterize the violence as genocide.[34] Church leaders otherwise refused to speak out, portraying the genocide as a justified defensive action within the context of a civil war. When the government collapsed in advance of an RPF victory, most church leaders fled with the government into exile in Zaire. Even today, many of these former church officials now in exile deny that a genocide occurred.

The result of the participation by clergy and the silence of the official church is clear. Many Christians clearly believed that in participating in the massacre of Tutsi, they were doing the will of the church. In a number of cases, people apparently paused in the process of carrying out massacres to pray at the church altar. In Ngoma parish, a Tutsi priest who was hidden during the war in the sanctuary by his fellow Hutu priests told me, "People came and demanded that my fellow priest reopen the church and hold mass. People came to mass each day to pray, then they went out to kill."[35]

Conclusions

Given the facts that I have presented, it should be clear that the failings of the Rwandan churches during the genocide were not the result of a few corrupt individuals but rather were deeply rooted in the very nature of Christianity in Rwanda. The manner in which Christianity was implanted in Rwanda and the policies and ideas promoted by missionaries began a transformation of Rwandan society that ultimately made genocide possible. After independence, the churches stood as important centers of social, economic, and political power, but rather than using their power to support the rights of the population, the churches were integrated into wider structures of power that allowed wealth and privilege to become concentrated in the hands of a select few. The churches as institutions worked with the state to preserve existing configurations of power, which, in the face of increased public pressure for reform, culminated in the strategy of genocide. While never publicly endorsing genocide, the churches nevertheless are complicit because they helped to create and maintain the authoritarian and divided society that made genocide possible and because the entanglement of the churches with the state made the churches partners in state policy. People could thus kill their fellow Christians on church property and believe that their actions were consistent with church teachings. The complicity of the churches in the genocide is not merely a failing of Christianity in Rwanda, but of world Christianity as it has established itself in Africa, and it should lead people of faith throughout the world to question the nature of religious institutions and the ways in which they exercise their power.

Notes

1. The exact ethnic composition of Rwanda is difficult to determine, in part because of the relatively flexible nature of ethnic identity. The generally accepted figure for ethnic distribution—85 per cent Hutu, 14 per cent Tutsi, 1 per cent Twa—is based on official colonial estimates that do not take into account the flight of thousands of Tutsi from the country during the first period of ethnic violence from 1959 and 1973. The 1991 census estimated the Tutsi population at just under 10 per cent, but these figures are again suspect given the politically charged nature of ethnicity in the country and the large numbers of Tutsi who had sought to mask their identity and pass as Hutu. The actual number of Tutsi in Rwanda at the time of the genocide probably lies somewhere between the estimates of 770,000 and 1,078,000. The estimated numbers of dead include thousands of Hutu killed during the genocide and in its immediate aftermath; some authors have suggested that as many as 300,000 Hutu were killed.

2. African Rights, *Death, Despair, and Defiance* (London, 1995); "Archbishop Carey's Visit to Rwanda: Rwandan church voice 'silent' during massacres, Carey says," Ecumenical News International, May 16, 1995; Julian Bedford, "Rwanda's churches bloodied by role in genocide," Reuters, October 18, 1994; Raymond Bonner, "Clergy in Rwanda is Accused of Abetting Atrocities: French Church Gives Refuge to One Priest," *The New York Times*, July 7, 1995, p. A3; "Churches in the Thick of Rwandan violence," *The Christian Century*, November 8, 1995, pp. 1041-1042; Joshua Hammer, "Blood on the Altar: Rwanda: What did you do in the war Father?," *Newsweek*, September 4, 1995, p. 36; Gary Haugen, "Rwanda's Carnage: Survivors describe how churches provided little protection in the face of genocide," *Christianity Today*, February 6, 1995, p. 52; Donatella Lorch, "The Rock that Crumbled: The Church in Rwanda," *The New York Times*, October 17, 1994, p. A4; Thomas O'Hara, "Rwandan bishops faltered in face of crisis," *National Catholic Reporter*, September 29, 1995; Wolfgang Schonecke, "The Role of the Church in Rwanda," *America*, June 17, 1995; Dominique Sigaud, "Genocide: le dossier noir de l'Eglise rwandaise," *Le Nouvel Observateur*, February 1-7, 1996, pp. 50-51; "Sin and Confession in Rwanda," *The Economist*, January 14, 1995, p. 39; Henri Tincq, "Le fardeau rwandais de Jean Paul II, *Le monde*, May 23, 1996; Alan Zarembo, "The church's shameful acts: Many Rwandans refuse to return to sanctuaries where blood was spilled," *Houston Chronicle*, January 29, 1995.

3. "Rwandan churches culpable, says WCC," *The Christian Century*, August 24-31, 1994, p. 778.

4. My initial field research in 1992-93 served as a basis for my PhD dissertation and was funded in part by the Graduate School of the University of Wisconsin and the Board of Higher Education of the Christian Church (Disciples of Christ). My second period of research in 1995-96 was conducted under the auspices of Human Rights Watch/Africa and the Fédération International des Ligues des Droits de l'Homme (FIDH).

5. See Henri Zukier's informative description of the Christian identification of Jews as an essential "other" in European history. Henri Zukier, "The Essential 'Other' and the Jew: From Antisemitism to Genocide," *Social Research* vol. 63, no. 4, winter 1996, pp. 1110-1154.

6. C.f., "Pope says Church is not to Blame in Rwanda," *New York Times*, March 21, 1996, A3; Ian Linden, "The Churches and Genocide: Lessons from the Rwandan Tragedy," *Month,* July 1995, 28:256-263.

7. Ian Linden, *Church and Revolution in Rwanda*, New York: Africana Publishing Company, 1977; Justin Kalibwami, *Le catholicisme et la société rwandaise, 1900-1962*, Paris: Presence Africaine, 1991.

8. Linden, *Church and Revolution in Rwanda*. See also, Alison Liebhafsky Des-Forges, *Defeat is the Only Bad News: Rwanda Under Musinga, 1896-1931* (Ph.D. dissertation, Yale University, 1972); Ferdinand Nahimana, *Le blanc est arrivé, le roi est parti,* Kigali: Printer Set, 1987.

9. DesForges, *Defeat is the Only Bad News*; Kalibwami, *Le catholicisme et la société rwandaise*; Linden, *Church and Revolution in Rwanda*; Nahimana, *Le blanc est arrivé, le roi est parti.*

10. Quoted in Kalibwami, *Le catholicisme et la société rwandaise*, p. 169.

11. For a masterful discussion of the process of political centralization and the growth of inequality, see Catharine Newbury, *The Cohesion of Oppression: Clientship and Ethnicity in Rwanda, 1869-1960*, New York: Columbia University Press, 1988.

12. Tharcisse Gatwa and André Karamaga, *La présence protestante: Les autres Chrétiens rwandais*, Kigali: Editions URWEGO, 1990; Michel Twagirayesu and Jan van Butselaar, *Ce don que nous avons reçu: Histoire de l'Eglise Presbytérienne au Rwanda*, Kigali: EPR, 1982; Linden, *Church and revolution in Rwanda.*

13. Linden, *Church and Revolution in Rwanda*; René Lemarchand, *Rwanda and Burundi*, New York: Praeger Publishers, 1970.

14. Lemarchand, *Rwanda and Burundi*; Linden, *Church and Revolution.*

15. Leroy Vail, "Introduction: Ethnicity in Southern African History," in *The Creation of Tribalism in Southern Africa*, edited by Leroy Vail, Berkeley and Los Angeles: University of California Press, 1989, pp. 1-19. Citation from p. 12.

16. Ibid.

17. Newbury, *The Cohesion of Oppression*; Gérard Prunier, *The Rwanda Crisis: History of a Genocide*, New York: Columbia University Press, 1995; Alison DesForges, *Genocide in Rwanda*, New York: Human Rights Watch, 1998.

18. DesForges, *Genocide in Rwanda*; Prunier, *The Rwanda Crisis*, pp. 5-23. The idea first developed by John Hanning Speke, *Journal of the Discovery of the Source of the Nile* (London, 1863) that the cattle-raising people of the region were descendants of a conquering tribe from Ethiopia shaped missionary notions of the Tutsi as a separate people. Speculations about the Semitic or Hamitic origins of the Tutsi appeared in the earliest missionary reports and writ-

ings, but received their most famous articulation in André Pagès, *Un royaume Hamite au centre de l'Afrique* Brussels: Institut royal du Congo Belge, 1933.

19. Kalibwami, *Le catholicisme et la société rwandaise*, pp. 236-253; Linden, *Church and Revolution*. Quotation from Alison DesForges, "The Ideology of Genocide," *Crisis: A Journal of Opinion*, 23, 2, 1995, p. 45.

20. Human Rights Watch, *Playing the "Communal Card:" Communal Violence and Human Rights*, New York: Human Rights Watch, 1995, p. 2.

21. Linden, *Church and Revolution*.

22. Saskia Van Hoyweghen, "The Disintegration of the Catholic Church of Rwanda: A Study of the Fragmentation of Political and Religious Authority," *African Affairs*, July 1996, 95, no. 380, 379-402; Alan Cowell, "In Rwanda, Catholics in the Crossfire: Killings Provoke a Sense of Failure," *The New York Times*, June 12, 1994, p. 9; "Churches agonize over Rwanda horror," *The Christian Century*, May 4, 1994, p. 464; Linden, "The Churches and Genocide."

23. Government of Rwanda, *Recensement General de la Population et de l'Habitat au 15 Août 1991: Analyse des Resultats Definitifs*, Kigali: April 1994, pp. 126-128.

24. I discuss the tepid support churches offered to the democracy movement in "Christianity and Democratisation in Rwanda: Assessing Church Responses to Political Crisis in the 1990s," in Paul Gifford, ed., *The Christian Churches and the Democratisation of Africa*, Leiden: EJ Brill, 1995, pp. 188-204.

25. FIDH, Human Rights Watch, et al., "Rapport de la Commission Internationale d'Enquête sur les Violations des Droits de l'Homme au Rwanda depuis le 1er Octobre 1990 (7-21 janvier 1993)" Paris: FIDH, March 1993; Association Rwandaise Pour la Defense des Droits de la Personne et des Libertés Publiques (ADL), *Rapport sur les Droits de l'Homme au Rwanda* Kigali: ADL, December 1992.

26. Leon Mugesera, later one of the chief architects of the genocide, was the first to demand that the Tutsi be sent back down the Nile in a speech to MRND party members in 1992.

27. Prunier, *The Rwanda Crisis*, offers the most comprehensive discussion of the build up to genocide in Rwanda, focusing in particular on the effect of the RPF invasion on domestic politics.

28. Article 19, *Broadcasting Genocide: Censorship, Propaganda and State-Sponsored Violence in Rwanda 1990-1994* (London: Article 19, 1996) and Jean-Pierre Chrétien, with Jean-François Dupaquier, Marcel Kabanda, and Joseph Ngarambe, *Rwanda: les medias de la haine* (Paris: Karthala, 1995) both provide excellent discussions of the role radio and print media played in distributing propaganda and promoting the genocide.

29. Africa Watch, "Arming Rwanda: The Arms Trade and Human Rights Abuses in the Rwandan War," (New York: Africa Watch, January 1994).

30. This assertion by Africa Rights in *Death, Despair and Defiance* (London: 1995) is borne out by my own research.

31. From interview conducted in Kaduha by the author on June 12, 1996, in French and Kinyarwanda.

32. This according to Alison DesForges.

33. Bedford, "Rwanda's churches bloodied."

34. Bedford, "Rwanda's churches bloodied."

35. Interview conducted by the author March 26, 1996, in Ngoma in French.

Chapter 7

THE CHURCHES AND THE GENOCIDE IN THE EAST AFRICAN GREAT LAKES REGION

Charles de Lespinay[1]

"In God's Name?" No way. The 1994 Rwanda genocide, the crimes against humanity, and other genocidal acts that have occurred in the Great Lakes region for over thirty years were not committed "in God's Name." Nonetheless, during the entire Rwanda genocide, the propaganda of the criminal perpetrators had emphasized the idea that God was on the people's side.[2] Was it for this reason that the murderers felt themselves allowed to use as human slaughterhouses the very churches where persecuted and excluded Tutsi took refuge?

Ever since Rwanda and Burundi became independent, there have been, albeit for different reasons, recurrent massacres of civilians, including women, children, and babies. These violent acts have caused countless persons to flee. Massacres have principally affected the Tutsi, a category of citizens regarded as a foreign ethnic body. They have often been accompanied, in Burundi, by bloody repression against the Hutu, another group of citizens, this one considered indigenous. (There are other categories of victims that everybody has forgotten about.) Only one of the massacres, which aimed in 1994 at totally eradicating the Tutsi population of Rwanda, was classified as genocide by the United Nations. This was probably because of its extensive death toll—nearly one million people. The other mass killings can be classified as crimes against humanity, but some of them, directed at the Hutu educated class (particularly in Burundi), have been acts of genocide. For the most part, these massacres and their authors go unpunished, and this neglect has almost sanctioned these acts as legitimate.

Because up to 90 percent of the populations of Rwanda and Burundi are supposed to be Christian, many questions have been raised about the role of the churches in the propagation of exclusionary ideologies and the genocidal explosion across the Great Lakes region of East Africa. One should not overlook the courageous deeds of both clergymen (many of whom were killed) and parishioners during and after the massacres. Research by various specialists (notably the French scholars J. P. Chretien, D. Franche, and C. Vidal), however, has highlighted the church missionaries' *principal* contribution to the official recognition and teaching of biblically based racial myths. This institutionalized practice began in the early colonial era and has persisted after independence, quite apart from the more direct involvement of some priests in genocidal acts.

While it may not be fair to hold religious institutions equally responsible as political authorities in mass killings and genocide, it still appears, at first blush, that religious officials, backed by their respective churches, were directly involved, either through complicity or incompetence, in the promotion of criminal ideologies. A clear-cut, overt condemnation of all the massacres, regardless of their classification, and without the usual confusion between assassins and victims, is still awaited from the Christian churches, especially the Catholic Church.

Recently, the publication of numerous books and articles by concerned Christians has induced a new focus on the role of the clergy in the disasters. Still to be considered is the eventual penal *responsibility* of many of them, *perhaps as propagators, albeit sometimes unwittingly, of false information tending to maintain a climate of fear, suspicion, and hatred.* Further, the clergy's *denial of a genocidal reality inadvertently encourages new onslaughts of killing.* As a first step, it is necessary to examine briefly the missionaries' historical contribution to the present situation.

I. The Missionary Background of "Annihilated" Countries

Since their early contacts at the end of the 19th century, European missionaries in the Great Lakes region have adopted as their own the biblical interpretations of local populations' origins advanced by European explorers such as J.H. Speke in 1863. In order to establish effective conversion policies, missionaries had first to determine who the various groups of people were and then identify their respective leaders. Making converts of the chiefs would necessarily force their subjects to follow suit. To facilitate this task, they developed a standard schema inspired by both the Bible and the history of early western Europe.[3]

Selecting Supposed Chiefs in Order to Convert their Subjects

According to missionaries, the Tutsi, a population group of whom a minority hold most of the power in central Rwanda (but not in Burundi), were "Hamites,"[4] a group of Nilotic herdsmen with "light" skin. As Hamites, these people were thought to have "arrived" in the region sometime during the 15th century. They were seen as "aristocratic," superior beings and were believed to be relatives of the Jews and cousins of white men. They were also supposed to be easily recognizable by their exceptional height. Joseph-Arthur de Gobineau, in his *Essai sur l'Inegalité des Races humaines* (1853-1855), a book that inspired Hitler, refers to the migration of the "Chamites" (Hamites). Descended from Ham, son of Noah, the Hamites were white peoples who came supposedly from north central Asia via Arabia to East Africa. All of the pastoral peoples of Africa fitting their description were deemed to be the "Africanized" descendants of these Hamites.

There were other peoples to be accounted for. The Twa group was seen to be composed of artisans and indigenous pygmy hunter-gatherers, who were considered "small" in size despite their average anthropometric height of 1.59 meters. Another group, the Hutu, a subgroup of the population labeled "Bantu" who are deemed to have arrived in East Africa some 2,000 years ago, supposedly inherited the land legitimately from the Twa. The Hutu, the most numerous population, were regarded solely as farmers of "average" height and "dark" skin, thus true Africans. Fabricated from A to Z, these piecemeal myths are still awaiting scientific confirmation. Missionaries (for the most part, French and Belgian) were convinced of the truth of this theory of successive migrations because it seemed to parallel that of the Gauls and Franks in Franco-Belgian history. Once these myths were adopted, the missionaries could envisage no alternative history for the region, in which the Hamite Tutsi were considered the civilizing cornerstone.

Like the German colonizers who preceded them and had been insufficient in number and means, the Belgian colonizing forces[5] that came to the region after World War I bestowed upon the more numerous missionaries the responsibility of education and health services. Progressively, almost total responsibility was left in the hands of the Catholic missions' administrators (Msgrs. Hirth, Classe, and Gorju). They were responsible for converting and training what they called "elites," largely the so-called Tutsi aristocracy. Their teachings insisted on identifying distinct categories of the population in racial terms.[6] They added a feudal discourse concerning socio-political phenomena: All Tutsi, on the bottom as well as on the top of the social spectrum, were seen as "feudal lords," while all Hutu, including the chiefs and the descendants of former kings, were viewed as "serfs" destined to be dominated.

This schema would be one of the initial causes for the ensuing "class" struggle fought over securing the reins of power. Yet the analysis, uniquely European in the way it viewed the Rwanda and Burundi kingdoms as feudal constructions, is anachronistic and not transferable to Africa. Moreover, it is completely illegitimate, as the term "feudal" implies a weak and divided central authority, which was not the case. However, it enabled the religious teaching staff to emphasize the relative "backwardness" of local populations when compared with Europeans. The discourse viewed the "civilizing" mission as inherent in both colonization and conversion.

Not all missionaries, however, were take in. Some "White Fathers" who were keen observers became aware of the existence of ruling "Hutu" kings on the periphery of central Rwanda in the first years of the 20th century. Several "Hutu" principalities and a non-Tutsi monarchy were also found to exist in Burundi. Some of these missionaries challenged the harsh levies imposed by certain chieftains and princes of the royal court, who furthermore continued to challenge the new religion. Although the new data induced some of the "White Fathers" to contest both the myth of the Hamite Tutsi civilizing influence and the alliance with the Tutsi chiefs, none dared to undermine the premise of racial differences, thus condoning the arbitrary classification of the population into two "ethnic" groups that avowed a growing reciprocal hatred.

Burundi's categories and professional activities at the beginning of the 20th century

category		farming	cattle breeding	hunting	fishing	pottery	smithy	power
Twa	M	*	–	**	*	–	*	–
	F	***	(*)	–	–	*	–	–
Hutu	M	*	*	*	*	*	*	religion,
	F	***	–	–	–	–	–	politics
non-	M	*	*	**	**	*	*	religion,
Tutsi	F	***	–	–	–	–	–	politics
Tutsi	M	*	***	*	–	(*)	(?)	prestige
	F	***	–	–	–	–	–	politics
Ganwa	M	manage-ment	manage-ment	**	–	–	(?)	politics
	F			–	–	–	–	ritual

(M= male, F= female)   (in: Mageza & Lespinay, 1990)

Stars indicate the prevalence of activity:
*   = only by small groups
**   = widespread
***   = the most common
(*)   = rare
–   = no known instance
(?)   = unknown today but tradition mentions
          it in the past, though without evidence

The Erosion of Indigenous Religion and of the Sacred Royal Power

The *bami* (kings) of Rwanda and Burundi realized the threat that the diffusion of Christianity represented to their sacred authority, which was at the very basis of the elaborate socio-political and institutionalized property arrangements and guaranteed the perpetuation of the social and political equilibrium. They were thus suspicious of the missionaries' growing power and influence. Moreover, the expanding mission program paid no heed either to the admonitions of local leaders or to the people's religious practices, often building their missions without permission close to or even on royal or sacred sites. In addition, the local *Kubandwa* religion was deemed nothing more than a superstitious practice unworthy of respect and therefore to be prohibited.

In 1931, the "White Fathers" began a massive program of conversion in Rwanda. It was a true religious conquest. As conqueror, the Catholic Church did not tolerate local religious practices nor the proselytizing efforts of other Christian denominations. The Church went so far as to encourage tale-telling on lapsed converts through public posters and the public burning of religious objects used in the rites of the *Kubandwa* cult. (Public exposure of lapsed converts was still practiced in 1980 in Mpinga, Nkoma province, Burundi.)

In Rwanda, the "White Fathers" converted Rudahigwa, the son of king (or *mwami*, which is singular of *bami*[7]) Musinga, and then, upon the recommendation of Msgr. Classe, succeeded in having the colonial administration depose Musinga in favor of his son and *replace legitimate Hutu chiefs with members of the Tutsi aristocracy*. Having been made *mwami*, Rudahigwa took the name Mutara III and, following lengthy religious training, was solemnly baptized in 1943. In 1946, Rwanda was dedicated to "Christ the King," but this new Christian monarchy no longer held the religious legitimacy of the former regime. Musinga was forced into exile. Furthermore, on the suggestion of the missionaries, who continued a pattern started during the German colonial period, the leadership, chosen systematically from the Tutsi aristocracy, imposed exactions that created a rift between them and the rest of the population. As a consequence, the ancient value system that had ensured a balanced harmony between different layers and segments of the population was destroyed.

The clergy also continued its training of the new "elite" (today they are still called "intellectuals"), chosen from among the Tutsi, who were taught they belonged to a *superior race that excluded the Hutu*. Nonetheless, individual Hutu were able to gain access to the world of the white man by entering seminaries, where they were exposed to the same ideological indoctrination, with some subsequent resentment.

An identical situation was created in Burundi, where Catholic missions obtained from colonial authorities the suppression of the national religious festival, *Muganuro*, and the dismissal of the Hutu religious aristocracy. Such measures weakened the royal power of the (non-Tutsi) *Ganwa* to the benefit of the leading Hutu and Tutsi princely families, who were placed in important supervisory positions previously held by many common Hutu.[8] As in Rwanda, the "elites" (globally seen as Tutsi, even when they were not) were taught the same ideologically tainted doctrine that the "inferior" Hutu (i.e., all non-Tutsi[9]) were learning in seminaries. The administrative reform of 1925 to 1933, the objectives of which were highlighted in a 1929 inquiry, decreed that "belonging to or leaning toward the Roman Catholic faith is a sufficient criterion to remain a chief. ... Correspondingly, many pagan chiefs turned toward the Christian religion."[10] The conversion process was identical to that adopted in Rwanda, and the ensuing brutal turnaround of missionary and colonial politics that took place during the 1950s was alike in both countries.

The Break With "the Dominant Tutsi Race"

The first Rwandese bishop, Monsignor Bigirumwami, was consecrated in 1952. In 1956, he anointed himself Monsignor Perraudin, took up opposition to the Catholic Church's pro-Tutsi stance, and came out in favor of the Hutu cause. Soon after, he became Rwanda's archbishop and head of the country's Roman Catholic Church. As King Mutara began to withdraw the support he had given the colonial authorities, Msgr. Perraudin broke off the Church's privileged ties with the Tutsi aristocracy. The colonial administration followed suit. The Tutsi, both the upper caste and the predominantly popular base, were suddenly considered enemies. Since then, the Catholic Church, which retained its monopoly on formal schooling, has encouraged the formation of a Hutu counter-elite, of which Gregoire Kayibanda, the future first president of independent Rwanda, was the leading figure.

Apparently assisted by the "White Fathers,"[11] along with other "evolué" (advanced) Hutu, Kayibanda drew up in March 1957 the *Manifeste des Bahutu* (Bahutu Manifesto), which demanded that the Tutsi authorities surrender part of their power, which they refused to do. The manifesto, treating the social problem in strictly racial terms, also demanded a new system of racial quotas in educational institutions, a system to be facilitated by the "ethnic" identity passbooks issued by the colonial authorities.

The 11 February 1959 pastoral letter, written by Msgr. Perraudin, contributed to the onset of the revolution which followed. The letter, although moderate in tone, reflects clearly what was to come (as can be seen from the case of Overdulve, cited below):

> We do not think to overstate our case when we say there is not enough charity in our dear Rwanda, even between Christians. ... In our cherished Rwanda, as in many other countries across the globe, there is a number of disparate social groups. What distinguishes these groups arises from racial differences, but also from other factors such as wealth levels. Among the Africans, there are the Batutsi, the Bahutu, and the Batwa; there are rich and poor; there are herdsmen and farmers, there are trades people and artisans ...; there are those who govern and those who are governed.

The parallel drawn between the Batutsi (Tutsi) as rich, cattle raisers, entrepreneurs, and leaders holding positions in government, and the Bahutu (Hutu) as poor, cultivators, artisans, and devoid of political prominence was anything but fortuitous. This viewpoint is still widely held today by many priests and clergymen after thirty-four years of hegemonic "Hutu" rule in Rwanda. It is also the common understanding in Burundi, which has remained in the hands of a few people who descended from the Tutsi "minority" group.

The pastoral letter went on:

> Let us observe first, that in fact there are several races with clearly distinct characteristics in Rwanda. ... All races are equally respectable and well considered by God. Each race has its own qualities and faults. ... In our Rwanda, social differences and inequalities are for the most part a result of racial differences. ... But clearly this situation in no way fits the norms of a healthy social organization in Rwanda, thus posing delicate and inevitable problems for those who run public affairs. ... The Church is opposed to any kind of struggle between classes, regardless of whether the origin of these classes lies in race or wealth ... but the Church allows a class to fight for its legitimate interests by honest means.

The letter preaches unity and condemns hatred, and even though he seems to overlook the sixty years of manipulation by the Catholic missions that created the current inequality, Msgr. Perraudin's style seems to be conciliatory. Nevertheless, he legitimizes the need to fight against the obvious social inequalities on the premise of race! In 1959, shortly after a unanimous condemnation of Nazi war crimes, the men of the church do not seem to be aware of the racist connotations of their speech. This is because they were imbued with a biblical concept of race, seen as a genealogical fact. Herein lies the basis for the equivocations underlying the stance adopted and still held by the Christian churches with regard to the means of achieving reconciliation, as will be shown further on.

The *mwami* Mutara III died in 1959, and his successor, Kigeri V, was proclaimed king without the approval of the Belgian governor, Harroy. Open conflicts broke out between the Tutsi leadership and some Hutu opponents. Colonel Logiest, sent to reestablish order, ousted Tutsi chiefs and sub-chiefs with Msgr. Perraudin's approval, and replaced them with Hutu leaders. A new Hutu power structure was appointed, *from which all Tutsi were excluded*. This marked the beginning of serious clashes between government forces and opponents in exile, followed by genocidal massacres of Tutsi that have plagued the new republic for its entire life. The new leaders had adopted the dogma of three distinct races taught them by the missionaries. During the presidencies of Kayibanda and Habyarimana, the Rwandese leaders of the Catholic Church, the most significant local economic force, unfailingly backed "Hutu" power until its final demise in 1994.

In Burundi, the position of the Catholic Church was not different, except for the fact that the Hutu seminary-educated cadres never had the opportunity to take power at the time of the country's independence. In the 1960s, certain Tutsi factions, concerned with the growing carnage in Rwanda and the subsequent streams of refugees, took the initiative, dissolved the monarchy and took power, hoping to avoid their own extermination. However, the leaders of Burundi were not able to stave off extremist provocations and subsequent Tutsi massacres. Instead, they were often dragged into an intractable spiral of senseless and bloody repression.

Burundi President Bagaza (1976-1987) broke with the churches. He saw them as too powerful and much too solicitous of the people, particularly the Hutu. Even though the political and social history of the country differs from Rwanda's, Catholic and Protestant churches spread even today the same racial myths with the same ideological manipulation aimed at the seizure of power by the "majority Hutu people." Today the two camps, both artificially created, suffer the same mutual fear.[12] But the exacerbation of past and present rivalries is entirely the fault of the missionary-educated intellectual "elites."

II. A "Christian" Teaching of Hatred

A significant part of the literature published after the Rwanda genocide by both Catholic and Protestant clergy and concerning Rwanda, Burundi, and the eastern regions of the former Zaire shows clearly that men of the church have been continuously involved in manipulating consciences before, during, and after the genocide. They are apparently unable to assess objectively their own failures, the part played in the massacres by their ideological teachings, their errors, their role in the violation of their churches as sanctuaries during the apex of the killings, and their own contributions to the inauguration of the climate of terror. Some still go so far as to stir open conflicts between the rigorously entrenched parties.

It is in this sense that the churches seem to have shown how badly they have failed in their calling, how dangerous they remain (until proven otherwise) for populations which, to this day, are culturally alien to them. Indeed, without a heartfelt self-examination, they seem unable to stop proceeding along a very dangerous path.

The Responsibility Rests With the Devil Not the Hutu

The 1995 account of the Vendée-born French priest R.P. Gabriel Maindron,[13] who was a student in a Rwandan seminary at the moment of Rwanda's independence, confirms the many parallels that Europeans are inclined to draw between their own history and the history of the Great Lakes. They are inclined to see local events in terms of France's Merovingian past, the feudal system, the French Revolution, class struggle, religious wars, etc.

Father Maindron exemplifies Church complicity with the genocidal regime. He explains the violence in Rwanda as the reciprocal responsibility of racists and democrats, Tutsi and Hutu, who are represented as having distinct physical characteristics. Distraught over events, he reveals his own uncertainties and equivocations. For example, in the midst of the genocidal campaign, large numbers of Hutu women attended mass in his church, while their husbands hunted down the persecuted Tutsi, who where hiding outside in close proximity to the church. In another instance, he expects people mortally wounded and others who had barely escaped death to offer a wholesale pardon to their would-be murderers, before those murderers return to carry out their unfinished killing. (During the French Revolution, Catholic priests often entreated those about to be slaughtered to pardon their assassins.) At the peak of the genocide, Father Maindron still trusts the police force of a regime that had condemned to death scores of Tutsi, and he goes so far as to turn over to the police 200 refugees he had hidden. In his eyes, as in those of other priests, responsibility for the hellish massacres lies in the hands of the devil, not in those of the Rwandese authorities.[14]

The Failure of the Churches?

Several lesser known texts have brought to our attention the current failure of the churches in Rwanda and Burundi, where massacres continue to "trickle down" (to paraphrase the United Nations rapporteur P.S. Pinheiro about the Burundese Hutu). Numerous first-hand accounts from priests and pastors paint the concrete horror of the genocide in Rwanda committed against Tutsi and Hutu in the opposition, as well as the massacres committed in Burundi against some members of both groups. The participation in the genocide by Father Wenceslas Munyeshyaka, now in France in his own church of the Holy Family, offers a sad case in point. He was seen separating Tutsi from Hutu and, day after day, turning the former over to death squads. The isolation of many religious institutions in eastern Zaire is also brought to light, as they face incessant waves of refugees with far less material support than the non-governmental organizations delivering aid in the region.

According to H. McCullum, the Rwandese ecclesiastical hierarchy received support and more than ample financial assistance from the party in power; it often remained silent in the face of widespread injustice, reluctant to make use of its authority to fill the moral vacuum experienced by Rwandese society in the closing Habyarimana years. [15] In any event, on the international level the churches have not been able or have not been willing to provide what they had been extending to South Africa's apartheid victims in the way of assistance for twenty-five years: solidarity and unconditional support. The systematic profanation committed inside the churches when they were used as human slaughterhouses should also be noted as indicators of a severe moral decline in the society at large. A number of Protestant and Catholic authorities still refuse to condemn those responsible for the massacres and to classify the killings as genocide.

Many other texts defend the thesis of a double genocide, undoubtedly aiming at reconciling opponents and enabling them to talk to one another. The "Groupe Jeremie," a Christian human rights group in Zaire, offers a case in point. In 1996, under the direction of "White Father" Philippe de Dorlodot, Groupe Jeremie edited a collection of letters, tracts, and statements issued by Hutu organizations, personalities, and certain sympathizers in Europe and Zaire. In this collection, the Groupe transmogrifies a crime against humanity committed in Rwanda into a "humanitarian crisis" of one million Hutu refugees driven to flee with the sponsors and organizers of the 1994 massacres. These Christian writers sidestep completely the creation of over six hundred thousand Tutsi refugees by the Rwandese "Hutu" regime. Some of these refugees tried to return in 1990, armed and organized as the Rwanda Patriotic Front (FPR). To the Groupe Jeremie writers, this Tutsi invasion army was responsible for all the region's ills, and their previous exile was justified because they were monarchists, would-be exploiters of the masses.[16]

The Groupe Jeremie texts begin with a biography of one of its contributors, Msgr. Munzihirwa, of whom it is said, "He knows Rwanda from the inside, and he has witnessed the humiliations endured by the Hutu. ...," forgetting that for the past thirty years the Hutu were no longer humiliated, unlike the Tutsi. The purpose of the Tutsis' demonization quickly becomes evident. From the very introductory page, all the arrests in Rwanda of Hutu participants in massacre are presented as arbitrary and their prisons are depicted as "houses of death," "showing the extent of generated ethnic purification by FPR" against the Hutu. The Burundi and Rwanda Hutu refugees in Zaire are described as "in a large majority, the victims of political exclusion," a statement that this peculiar kind of

Christian morality sees as carrying more weight than the genocide of hundreds of thousands of Tutsi. The manipulative use of refugees by genocidal government forces is seen here as pure fabrication (although it was shown to be otherwise in 1997). Subsequently (p. 39), Father de Dorlodot himself affirms that the killings are due to both races (Tutsi and Hutu): "... the differences between them are very deep. For the centuries of royal Tutsi overlordship, the Hutu were treated as serfs and slaves. They were scorned." In addition, he justifies the use of quotas, and refers to the organized killings of defenseless populations, including women, children, and the elderly, in terms of a "civil war" and the "resistance of the Rwandese army" before hesitantly accepting the term "genocide."

Another text written by Father de Dorlodot (p. 88) summarizes the concern of the Groupe to find a new social balance:

> Two genocides have taken place in Rwanda, now in ruins because of extremists from both camps. There has been the genocide ... perpetrated against the Tutsi. ... And also the genocide—the one never spoken of—perpetrated by the FPR in the zones it occupied. It is widely known that massive killings took place, as now long-awaited witness accounts are becoming available. As many as 400,000 to 500,000 displaced persons are still unaccounted for. ... Furthermore, at least two refugee camps, peopled by Hutu, have disappeared. ... More than one million of the refugees streamed into Goma [in Zaire] and its surrounding area because they were thrown into a panic by the FPR. ... This is genocide!

The FPR is presented as having provoked the departure of the Hutu refugees. While the acts of revenge carried out on those presumably guilty of slaughtering people are certainly reprehensible, they are described as "selective genocide" of the Hutu. The Tutsi genocide is minimized, and the people killed in 1994 are presented as being primarily Hutu as proof of a real genocide practiced against them. These texts that represent a denial of the 1994 Tutsi genocide are identical to those produced by the planners of the genocide both before and after it took place. The fact that their authors were educated in the same Christian missionary schools cannot be dismissed as fortuitous.

To be sure, it is easy to understand that many priests, in both Rwanda and Burundi, speak in more measured tones to avoid the possibility that the Tutsi massacres might overshadow other mass killings of innocent Hutu in Burundi for 30 years and in both countries more recently. As one Burundi Christian remonstrates, "the 'Tutsi genocide' has become a fixed obsession that is politically lucrative, but it obscures the regular killing of thousands of Hutu

by the army and the Tutsi militia" in Burundi.[17] The Burundi massacres of Hutu leaders and intellectuals in 1972 stand out as particularly objectionable, even as they have remained unpunished to
this day. But that is no reason for allowing the killings of Hutu to
take precedence over the Tutsi genocide, while it is still in progress.

That "Guilty" Victims Should Ask to be Forgiven By Their "Innocent" Assassins

The most extreme position to come from a man of the church is
held by the Dutch pastor C.M. Overdulve, who has lived in
Rwanda for many years. He has adopted the genocidal propaganda's anti-Tutsi hatred in his book, *Rwanda: A People with a
History*.[18] Thinking that in order to reconcile the Rwandese people,
a true history, illustrating Tutsi responsibility must first be written,
Overdulve adopts a scandalous reasoning that justifies the crimes
against the Tutsi in terms of a false interpretation of the biblical
"eye for an eye."

According to Overdulve, the present situation results from the
domination exerted by the Tutsi between the invaders' "arrival" in
the 14th century[19] and 1959, perpetuated since then by means of
raids launched from outside by Tutsi "royalists," members of the
FPR. These people are the ones truly guilty of the massacres because
they provoked them, while the real victims are the Hutu. Overdulve
makes no distinction between the dead and their assassins. His
accusation is clumsy, exaggerated, and unlikely to create a climate
of reconciliation. It illustrates the damage that mindless reading of
the Bible and scholarly articles on the Great Lake region can cause
in the minds of incompetent persons. How can children and babies
provoke their own deaths?

Overdulve intended to write a "history of poverty and struggle
for survival." But in order to do so, he borrows once against the
myth of "the conflict over many centuries between the victors
[Tutsi] and the vanquished [Hutu]." All Tutsi, without exception,
reputedly formed a warrior caste that excluded all Hutu (which is
a false assertion). According to Overdulve, the Tutsi were the
"lords" who elaborated land-tenure arrangements designed to
dominate the Hutu. The corvée *(uburetwa)* was supposedly created
at the end of the 19th century by King Kigeri Rwabugiri in order to
reduce the Hutu to the status of slaves working for the wealthy and
poor Tutsi alike. "Compared to the Hutu men, the poor Tutsi man
[notice the singular form] was far from destitute." Colonization
had no bearing whatsoever on the drastic opposition between a
Hutu "majority" and a Tutsi "minority," even though it did aggra-

vate Hutu poverty. According to Overdulve, it was the quota system, which obligated many unemployed Tutsi to engage in commercial ventures (an activity alien to the traditional local culture),
that enabled the Tutsi to become wealthy. Then, Overdulve criti-
cizes the Tutsi for having surreptitiously violated the quota system's rule of exclusion, which makes them even more despicable.

Overdulve assures his readers that it is difficult "to know who
were the guilty and who were the victims" during the 1994 "civil
war," to which he devotes a mere six lines. He then purports to
uncover the hidden intentions of the Tutsi FPR, whose aristocratic
agenda was to reinstate the monarchy. Besides relying on the traditional distinction between the notions of the Tutsi and of the "people" or "population" signifying Hutu, he writes:

> One of the hidden but identifiable aspirations of the FPR was to
> destroy the basic rights established by the Republic so as to retaliate
> against the 1959-1961 Revolution by the people [Hutu]. The country's
> Tutsi, who would be supposed to welcome a FPR regime with open
> arms, were for the most part assassinated. ... Should those guilty of
> genocide be brought before justice? Without a doubt! However, they
> exist in both camps.

The massacres perpetrated by the FPR upon the Hutu "show identical genocidal patterns." As early as 1990, these activities supposedly caused "carnage" among the civilian population. Further,
Overdulve writes, "The Tutsi genocide in the country was provoked
by the Tutsi forces of the FPR-*Inkotanyi*, who knew what they were
doing. If they had not invaded Rwanda, there would never have
been a genocide of Tutsi" (page 73). This "shows the complexity of
the Rwanda drama." Overdulve's discourse duplicates Rwanda's
genocidal propaganda and the texts of those who today deny the
genocide by invoking the argument of legitimate defense in time of
war, even when it involves the preemptive killing of babies.

This clergyman professes to be particularly interested in reconciliation and justice, important tasks that require the churches'
involvement. He reminds us that according to the Bible and the
Torah, reconciliation is possible only with God. But there is a prerequisite which consists in "repairing the bonds between human
beings," meaning "the liberation of oppressed people." The Biblical Prophets did not call for national reconciliation, but "criticized
the injustices done to the poor" by the rich who exploit them. "In
these relations, the issue is justice and equity. In reality, reconciliation is evoked so as to set up an alibi allowing injustice and
oppression to continue." Overdulve affirms more than once, in

contradiction to available evidence, that "it was not against Juvenal Habyarimana's regime as such but against the people [Hutu] that the FPR unleashed its war in October 1990."

Overdulve mentions "the deep repugnance that was felt toward the Tutsi regime, toward any Tutsi regime that stands as a reminder of the one overthrown in 1961." But there should not be any hostility against the Hutu regime that led Rwanda to genocide, because Habyarimana was forced by the Tutsi to act as he did. "The FPR kills silently, quickly hides the bodies of the dead, and erases all its traces or else forbids observers to enter the suspected killing zones." Indeed, this seems to have been the pattern followed by Kabila's Tutsi troops in eastern Zaire in areas where Hutu refugees remained behind. No investigations have taken place concerning the violence and killings carried out by the FPR at the time it entered Rwanda. The accusation, if proven, involves the killing of about five hundred thousand Hutu, but it does not absolve the Hutu perpetrators of genocide. Yet, for Overdulve, the Tutsi seem to be a "criminal" ethnic group.

For him, in order for justice to prevail, it must be remembered "that the massacre of Tutsi was decided after and because of the invasion carried out by the FPR, and after it was known that the mass killings of northern Hutu had been committed by the Inkotanyi. ... Without the invasion of the FPR, the genocide would never have occurred as there would never have been a need to resort to such action." But the genocide had begun well beforehand, though to be sure, very slowly. For Overdulve, even though his preceding observations illustrate the contrary, nothing of importance took place before 1990 that could have provoked the Tutsi genocide. He concludes that "the churches should stop being heretic and take up ... the defense of the expelled and oppressed population [Hutu]," forgetting that a Hutu government ruled from 1959 to 1994.

Overdulve is regarded as an honorable man in Rwanda and Europe for, among other things, his study of the Kinyarwanda language. But it would be worth weighing the legal responsibility of this pastor whose writings are far from preaching reconciliation. His statements that reconciliation with God cannot take place until the oppressed Hutu people have been freed, or until justice has been granted the poor and humiliated Hutu, clearly imply that the "guilty" Tutsi victims should ask forgiveness from their murderers for having been obliged to kill them. His case, along with many others, should be closely examined by church officials and a competent legal tribunal so as to ascertain whether it is appropriate to propose *reconciliation through the promotion of a false version of history and ideologies of hatred*, while denying genocide.[20]

Conclusion

The information presented here clearly illustrates the blindness of several clergymen, since what lies behind their conciliatory words is far from the church's commandments. Christian doctrine advocates peace, charity, and love and promotes understanding between human beings. Many clergymen excuse the murders carried out by numerous Hutu, arguing that they were committed in the name of revolution, or in the name of what the Hutu's ancestors were supposed to have suffered under Tutsi rule before the Hutu revolution. They make the Tutsi responsible for their own deaths along with extremists from every side. That such viewpoints—originating in the educational environment of the early mission schools for generations—have persisted until 1998 is indicative of what most of the population of the Great Lakes area continue to think, and it does not bode well for the future of the region.

Another concern emerges. According to a number of priests from Rwanda and Burundi, among the prayers taught in the seminaries of their youth, one in particular stands out in the minds of many: "My God, deliver us from the Jews." It would appear to be a poor translation of the Christian prayer "My God, let us pray that the Jews convert," which far from seeking to exclude the Jews, calls for union under the banner of Christianity. In the racist ideology spread by the missionaries, the Hamite Tutsi are considered to be cousins of the Jews and other whites, meaning that they were a sort of African Jews. This notion had positive connotations until 1950, but increasingly negative ones thereafter. Is Father de Dorlodot's book, *The Rwandese Refugees at Bukavu in Zaire: The New Palestinians?*, in which he describes Hutu refugees in the former Zaire as "the new Palestinians" facing the Tutsi FPR, an innocent text?[21] For de Dorlodot, the Tutsi, just like the Jews of Israel, are attempting to create their own state on the ruins of the Hutu state, thereby condemning the Hutu "people" to live in refugee camps far from their homeland. In choosing this particular phraseology, it would almost seem that Father de Dorlodot has combined the negation of the Tutsi genocide and the exclusion of that accursed population with what can only be seen as an astonishing reference, in the context of contemporary Christianity, to the aberrant survival of that other "cursed people," namely, the Jews of Israel.

Notes

1. Many thanks to Alice Depret and Remi Clignet for a translation which was difficult to achieve because of the matter's strangeness and seriousness, and perhaps also because of the author's complex French style. Thanks to J.P.B. and C. Ross for the English corrections.

   A Warning to the reader – The author of any text that presents the distinction between races in the Great Lakes region as being of mythological origin may be looked upon as a defender of the Tutsi, a supporter of the injustices committed against the Hutu, or as a denier of the past (recent) domination of the Hutu by the Tutsi (although partially true, but not a generalization to be made of all Tutsi), therefore a person harboring criminal intent. This is not the chapter's objective. The reason for its writing has not been to settle accounts or even political scores in lieu of the parties involved. Its only aim is to demonstrate how certain ideologies, promoted by the missionaries, played an important part in the recent massacres.

2. In particular, the broadcasts calling for murder issued by the infamous national radio station, "Radio of the Thousand Hills" (RTLM, Radio des Mille Collines)

3. J.H. Speke, *Journal of the Discovery of the Source of the Nile* (Edinburgh, 1863). See works by a man of peace, Father Augustin Mvuyekure of Burundi, particularly: "Idéologie missionnaire et classification ethnique en Afrique Centrale," in *Les Ethnies ont une histoire*, ed. J.P. Chrétien and G. Prunier (Paris, 1989), pp. 314-324. "Search for the Peoples" is the theory of *Volksmission* as presented by Lutheran missionary societies described by Gustav Warneck circa 1880. The same recommendation was made by French Cardinal Lavigerie to the Missionary Society of Africa, (nicknamed "White Fathers"), with the objective of converting the chiefs of each of the "races" or "tribes," classified as such in order to create Christian kingdoms. Mvuyekure writes, "The mission to convert the entire population will be given to this race or that tribe through the intermediary of its king or chiefs. For the 'Merovingian' African, a black 'Clovis' must be found."

4. Quotation marks are used here to designate terms carrying a dubious meaning.

5. Joseph Gahama sums up perfectly the racial myth and its usage in Burundi in "Le jeu ethnique de la Politique Coloniale au Burundi," in *Les Ethnies*, pp. 303-313.

6. See the texts by those priests fascinated with the Hamite Tutsi theory, i.e., Msgr. Classe; Father Pagès with regard to Rwanda in his *Un royaume Hamite au Centre de l'Afrique*; Msgr. J. Gorju for Burundi in *En Zigzags à Travers l'Urundi* (Brussels, 1926) and *Face au Royaume Hamite du Ruanda: Le Royaume Frère de l'Urundi* (Brussels, 1938). Msgr. Gorju's 1926 text listed the princely Baganwa lineages in Burundi as Hutu. According to A. Mvuyekure, their classification was changed in 1938 to Tutsi as in Rwanda, because of the Church's demand for a homogeneous regional classification. Mvuyekure, "Idéologie missionnaire," p. 320

7. A Bantu word contains a prefix or class (for example *mu-* for the singular of human, and *ba-* for the plural), and a fixed radical or root. In kirundi (the language of Burundi, with the prefix *ki-* and root *-rundi*) and kinyarwanda (the language of Rwanda, which is close to kirundi), the inhabitants of Burundi are called *Barundi* (plural) or *Murundi* (singular), *Hutu* is *Muhutu* (singular) or *Bahutu* (plural); *Tutsi* is *Mututsi* (singular) or *Batutsi* (plural), king is *Mwami* (singular, for *mu-ami*) or *Bami* (plural, for *ba-ami*).

8. Ganwa is the name of the Burundi royal lineage. It is not a lineage of Tutsi origin. Its origin is either Hutu or Ha (from Buha in Tanzania). It is difficult here to offer any counter argument to Joseph Gahama's probing and thoughtful published thesis on the subject, *Le Burundi sous l'administration belge* (Paris, 1983). See also Jean Rumiya's thesis, *Le Rwanda sous le régime du mandat belge: 1916-1931* (Paris, 1992) .

9. During field research by the author in 1986 within the border provinces of Burundi conquered during the 19th century expansion of the Burundi Kingdom, the local people did not claim to be Hutu. They refused to have anything to do with a label they viewed as a late import from north-central Rwanda and Burundi. Today however, they have been classified as Hutu. The same problem is beginning to be apparent in the neighboring Tanzanian province of Buha. Here for decades, scientific studies have classified many royal lineages as Tutsi, while the rest of the population has been deduced as Hutu. See Bonaventure Mageza, Charles de Lespinay, "Les droits de L'homme et L'ethnologie: l'exemple du Burundi," in *Droit et Cultures* (No. 19, 1990), pp. 192-214.

10. Mvuyekure, "Idéologie missionnaire," p. 319.

11. Dominique Franche, Rwanda, *Généalogie d'un génocide* (Paris, 1997). Recommended for its brevity and clarity, this is one of the best works on the origins of events in Rwanda. It has been a source of inspiration for the present text which hopefully is faithful to its line of thought.

12. D. Franche speaks of "communities of fear," a devastating but true description of these fabricated ethnic groups. Ibid., pp. 57-61. The communities of fear are the only reality in the Great Lakes region today.

13. The Vendée region of France was the site in 1793-94 of a systematic massacre because of its opposition to the new government that came to power during the French Revolution very much in contradiction to the ideas behind the 1789 *Declaration of the Rights of Man and of the Citizen*. The republican leaders painted the slain as traitors in league with agitators abroad, as aristocrats following the dictates of the Catholic Church and supporting the prohibited monarchy, and as such, a race to be put to death. At the present time, the descendants of these Vendean victims are still considered by French intellectuals holding a distorted view of republican principals, as heirs of traitors, "revisionists," denying revolutionary beneficence.

    Like this priest, every cultivated individual from the Vendée is imbued, 200 years later, with similar value judgments, partisan to one side or the other. The Vendée massacres are still considered (and justified) as having been necessary to secure the nation as well as a founding act of the modern French Republic. In order to promote reconciliation, the Protestant and Catholic Churches have placed the blame on both parties, the victims as well as the assassins. The same deductions can be read into the situation in Rwanda and Burundi where the Tutsi and their Hutu "accomplices" are viewed as aristocratic defenders of the abolished monarchy, traitors used by interested parties in Uganda, detractors of the national revolution and the Republican project. And today the churches do not differentiate between killers and victims.

14. Nicolas Poincaré, *Rwanda. Gabriel Maindron. Un Prêtre dans la Tragédie* (Paris, 1995).

15. Hugh McCullum, *The Angels Have Left Us: The Rwanda Tragedy and the Churches*, (Geneva, 1995).

16. Père Philippe de Dorlodot, *Les Réfugiés Rwandais à Bukavu au Zaïre: De Nouveaux Palestiniens?* (Paris, 1996).

17. P. Bwarikindi "Des Prêtres théoriciens de la domination Tutsi," in *Dialogue* no. 194 (Nov.-Dec. 1996), pp. 91-92. This Christian review offers a forum for an exchange of different points of view in Burundi and Rwanda. The tenor of its texts reflects the opinions of young Christian intellectuals in the Great Lakes region torn between angry resentment and a desire for justice and reconciliation.

18. C.M. Overdulve, *Rwanda. Un Peuple avec une Histoire* (Paris, 1997).

19. While Overdulve speaks of Tutsi "arriving" in the 14th century, many other historians refer to the 15th century without, however, any historical evidence for either date. In fact, we do not know when the Tutsi arrived in Rwanda, if indeed they came from elsewhere in the first place.

20. Charles de Lespinay, "Génocide et Idéologies d'Exclusion Importées en Afrique des Grands Lacs," in *Parler de camps, penser les génocides*, ed. Catherine Coquio (Paris, 1999), pp. 310-321.

21. De Dorlodot, *Les Réfugiés Rwandais.*

Chapter 8

KOSOVO MYTHOLOGY AND THE BOSNIAN GENOCIDE

Michael Sells

Passion plays collapse time. In major passion plays, such as those commemorating the death of Jesus or the death of the Shi'ite martyr Imam Husayn, the play occurs after at least a month of intense meditation on the sufferings, in graphic detail, of the martyred hero. During the actual play, actors representing those who do the evil deed are instructed to carry out their role with dispatch, lest the audience rush the stage to stop them; and they are instructed to exit the stage immediately after, lest the audience rush the stage and attack them physically. At this moment of rushing the stage, the boundaries between actor and audience are broken down, as are the boundaries between the mythic time of the primordial event and the present moment. The audience no longer views itself as an audience watching a re-enactment of a past event, but as participants in an event that takes place in a kind of eternally present moment.

On June 28, 1989, Serbian President Slobodan Milosevic mounted the platform set up on the battle plain of Gazimestan in Kosovo. The occasion was the 600th anniversary of the death of the Serbian Prince Lazar in 1389 at the hands of the Ottoman army led by Sultan Murad. Every annual celebration of Lazar's death (the day known as St. Vitus Day or Vidovdan), in which Lazar is portrayed as a Christ-figure and his death as the "Serbian Golgo-

Notes for this section begin on page 198.

tha," is a major event. A centennial anniversary of of enormous national significance.

The Vidovdan celebration of 1989 had been preceded by preparations of acute ritual and civic intensity. Behind Milosevic was a large set of symbols commemorating the Kosovo legend. In front of him was a crowd estimated at between one and two million people, fully one tenth of the population of Serbia. Milosevic spoke of battles in the past and battles to come, and praised Serbia as the defender of Christian Europe against Islam, while members of the crowd waved pictures of Lazar and Milosevic.

The group psychology of fear and hatred generated by the Vidovdan celebration was based upon a symbolic matrix that included mythic time (1389, the foundational event of Serbian national consciousness), sacred space (Kosovo, known as the Serb Jerusalem), historical memory (the memory of Serbs killed in World War II), and a highly developed ideology that presented Slavic Muslims as Christ-killers and race traitors. As other peoples in Yugoslavia observed the mood at the Vidovdan celebration and Milosevic's use of it to seize absolute power in Serbia, they began to wonder if they could remain safely in a Yugoslavia ruled by Milosevic. In 1992, the rage manipulated through the use of Kosovo ritual and symbolism was to be transformed into a program of genocide in Bosnia-Herzegovina.[1] In 1999 the violence circled back upon its symbolic epicenter in Kosovo. At the time of this writing, outside observers have been blocked from entering Kosovo by the Belgrade authorities. The true nature and extent of the atrocities against Kosovar Albanians may take years to be uncovered and years more to be fully grasped.[2]

Mythic Time: The Serbian Golgotha

Although historians have considered the battle of Kosovo (in which both the Serb Prince Lazar and the Sultan Murad were killed) as incon-clusive, in Serbian consciousness it became the symbol for the eventual defeat of Serbia and its 500-year absorption into the Ottoman Empire.[3] In the 19th century, certain strands of Kosovo legend were reconfigured and made more explicit. In the art, poetry, drama, and other literature of the period, Lazar was portrayed at a "last supper" surrounded by knight-disciples, one of whom, Vuk Brankovi, was a traitor who was to give the battle plans to the Turks. The Turks were thus Christ-killers and Milos Obili, the Serbian knight who assas-sinated Sultan Murad in revenge for the death of the Christ-Prince

Lazar, became the object of intense veneration. The most famous Serbian Bishop of the twentieth century, Nikolaj Velimirovic wrote that Serbian religious nationalism was built upon the "altar of Obilic."[4]

The implications of the presentation of Lazar as a Christ-figure reached their most lethal form in the acknowledged literary masterwork of Serbian religious nationalism, *The Mountain Wreath* by Bishop Petar Petrovic II, better known by his pen name of Njegos.[5] *The Mountain Wreath,* composed in 1857, begins with the Serbian bishops and knights of Montenegro complaining that even the mountains "stink of non-Christians" and that it is time to "cleanse" the nation. The Slavic Muslims of Montenegro are invited to one last-chance meeting and are told they can convert by water or convert by blood; if they do not convert it will be a war of extermination between the two sides.

The Slavic Muslims suggest a "godfather" *(kum)* ceremony, the ritual by which blood feuds in Montenegrin tribal society were healed.[6] The Serbian leaders reply that in a godfather ceremony, the two children, one from each of the warring groups, must be baptized. The Muslims argue that Orthodox and Muslim Slavs are all one people and suggest an interreligious godfather ceremony, with the Christian child to be baptized and the Muslim child to have a ritual tonsure. The overture is rejected and the Muslims are sent away as the "brood of the accursed Muhammad."

The last part of *The Mountain Wreath* consists of the celebration and glorification of the Christmas day extermination of all the Slavic Muslims of Montenegro—men, women, and children—and the burning of their settlements, mosques, and towers. After the extermination, which is described in powerful and graphic terms, the Serbian warriors return and are given holy communion without prior confession. In South Slavic Christian societies, whether Catholic or Orthodox, to go to communion after a killing, without going to confession would be a sacrilege, a desecration of the most sacred moment of life. By making a point of offering communion without confession, the Serbian Orthodox priests and bishops make the clear proposition that the act of exterminating the Slavic Muslims, whom they called "Turkifiers," was inherently sanctifying and purificatory, and thus prepared the souls of those who participated in it for the sacrament of the eucharist.

To this day Croat and Serb nationalists refer to Slavic Muslims as "Turks," even though they speak the same language, trace their descent from the same Slavic tribes, and share the same cultural and physical traits as their Catholic and Orthodox neighbors. The notion of "Turkification" at the heart of *The Mountain Wreath* is based upon the ideology of Christoslavism. Slavs are held to be Christian by nature. Any conversion then is not only a betrayal of the Slavic people or race, but an actual ethnic or racial transformation. To convert to Islam is to become a Turk. It is for this reason that when the Slavic Muslims argue that Muslim and Orthodox Slavs are one people and suggest an interreligious *kum* ceremony, the suggestion is rejected. They cannot be part of "the people" because, by converting, their ancestors transformed themselves into another people, the Turks.

The religio-mythic implications of "Turkification" are particularly dangerous. By transforming themselves into Turks, the Slavic Muslims transform themselves into Christ-killers, the people held responsible for the Serbian Golgotha and the death of the Christ-Prince Lazar. *The Mountain Wreath's* portrayal of Slavic Muslims as Turkifiers that must be "cleansed" before the Serbian people can be resurrected was taken up by the Nobel Prize winning author Ivo Andric, who wrote that Njegos' view of Slavic Muslims was the timeless and eternal view of "the people" (which again, of course, implied that Slavic Muslims were forever alien), and who tied that view of "Turkification" more explicitly to a twentieth-century preoccupation with race and racial and linguistic purity.[7]

Andric, who was born a Catholic but ultimately embraced a Serb identity, was particularly influential in popularizing Njego's view of Bosnian Muslims among a new generation of Serbs, as well as among Croats and ultimately an international readership. Andric was also a key figure in popularizing the image of the depraved and "blood draining" Ottomans through his treatment of the Ottoman *devshirme* system of forced conscription into the Janissary corps.[8] By the time of the 1989 Vidovdan commemoration, this ideology that the Ottomans, and by extension, the Slavic Muslims, were parasites who lived on the blood drained from the Serbian people, had been fully revived for ten years and intensified through manipulation of the passion play.

Sacred Space: The Serb Jerusalem

Kosovo is known as the Serb Jerusalem. Not only is it the site of the foundational event in modern Serbian national consciousness, but it is also home to many of the Serbian monasteries, churches, and artistic treasures, the masterworks that make up the heritage of Serbia.[9] In the decade of the 1980s, after the death of Yugoslav President Marshall Tito, tensions began to grow in Kosovo between the majority Albanian population (nominally, at least, Muslim and Catholic) and the minority Serbian and nominally Orthodox population. There were riots by Albanians and repression by Yugoslav authorities. Both Albanians and Kosovo Serbs suffered.

In 1986 the Serbian Orthodox Church published an official claim that Serbs were being subjected to "genocide" in Kosovo province and that there was a plot to "ethnically cleanse" Serbs from Kosovo.[10] Human rights groups and even Serbian police reports disputed the claims of mass-murder, organized rape, and systematic annihilation of the Serbian cultural heritage,[11] but those claims were taken up by a wide group of Serbian intellectuals and academics and became the basis for the *Serbian Memorandum* of 1986, the document that in the view of many marked the beginning of the end of Yugoslavia.[12] The *Serbian Memorandum* made repeated and heated claims that Serbs were subjected to persecution by Yugoslavian authorities and to genocide in Kosovo and demanded radical steps to change the situation, including the abolition of the autonomous status of Kosovo province and its incorporation into Serbia. In 1987, a Communist official, Slobodan Miloevic, seized upon the tensions in Kosovo to transform himself into the spokesperson for the militant religious nationalism in Serbia. In 1988-89, the relics of Prince Lazar were translated, that is, ritually transported, from site to site through areas claimed as Greater Serbia and throughout Kosovo Province, finally arriving at the Gracanica monastery in Kosovo in time for the 600th Vidovdan anniversary. The translation of the relics engendered ritual celebrations that were politicized and used by religious nationalism to stir up calls for revenge against the eternal persecutors of Lazar and of Serbs. While the sacred time of 1389 was being collapsed into the present of 1989, the sacred space of a Greater Serbia and Kosovo was being ritually demarcated in a procession moving toward the epicenter at the site of the ancient battle and the nearby Gracanica monastery which would hold Lazar's relics.

Historical Memory, Fear, and Generic Blame

Concurrent with the rituals marking the procession of the relics of Lazar were another set of ritual acts: the formal disinterring of the remains of Serbian victims of atrocities at the hands of the World War II fascists known as the Ustashe. [13] During the era of Marshall Tito, discussion of World War II atrocities was suppressed, on the grounds that the wounds were so raw and deep that to allow debate would be to risk renewed interethnic war. During the Second World War, the Ustashe-led "Independent State of Croatia," a puppet of Nazi Germany led by the fascist Ante Pavelic, carried out genocide against Jews, Gypsies, Serbs, and dissidents throughout the areas under its control. A Serbian army known as the Chetniks fought for restoration of the Serbian King, collaborated at times with the Nazi forces, and committed mass-atrocities against non-Serbs, particularly in Bosnia. The communist Partisans, led by Marshall Tito, were a multiethnic group that ultimately triumphed and that carried out its own mass reprisals against Ustashe and Chetnik soldiers and "class enemies." Tragically, however, those most guilty, Ustashe leaders, escaped, some with the help of the Vatican.[14]

When the remains of Serbian victims of World War II were disinterred, then, there was a most tangible and palpable return of repressed memories, that came back all the more strongly because of their prior repression. These ceremonies were also taken over by religious nationalists, who proclaimed the Croatian people to be genocidal by nature, and who branded all Muslims, generically, as collaborators with the Ustashe (despite the fact that many Muslims and Croats fought against the Ustashe in the partisan army and most contemporary Muslims and Croats had not yet been born during the terrible years of World War II). The accusation that Croats and Muslims were a genocidal people and were plotting a new genocide was repeated throughout Serbian Orthodox Church publications, intensified when militants took over the disinterment of Serb victims of World War II, and combined with the inflammatory allegation that Serbs were already undergoing genocide at the hands of Albanians in Kosovo province.[15]

When Slobodan Miloevic mounted the stage then, the mythic time of 1389 had been collapsed into the present moment, combined with the actual historical memory of atrocities of World War II, and with the alleged genocide supposedly occurring at that moment in Kosovo province, all welded together into the sacred space of the Kosovo, the sacral heart of the Serbian nation. This matrix of symbolism, reinforced by the passion plays, created an intense mass psychology that was to be harnessed and used to motivate and justify genocide in Bosnia, often against those who were former neighbors, friends, in-laws, colleagues, and lovers.

Instrumentalizing The Mythology

The religious mythology was necessary for motivating and justifying genocide, but it was not sufficient. To be effective, it needed to be combined with three years of systematic manipulation of the army, secret police, religious-nationalist militias, and the media.

At this point (1989-1992), the government of Serbian president Slobodan Milosevic, the Serbian academics and intellectuals who had signed the *Serbian Memorandum,* and the hierarchy of the Serbian Orthodox Church were largely united, although some bishops complained that the Miloevic government was not militant enough in pursuit of the goals of religious nationalism. The Yugoslav army, which had been a multi-ethnic institution, was put through several purges, from the top down. When Slovenia and Croatia seceded from Yugoslavia in 1991, the army withdrew quickly from Slovenia, after some brief skirmishes. Serbia had little claim on Slovenia, which contained few Serbs, and Milosevic was willing to let it go. But when Croatia, with a large Serbian minority population declared independence, a savage war broke out between Croat and Serb militants, both of whom targeted civilians. During this period, there were massive desertions from the Yugoslav army by both non-Serb and Serb soldiers, and Milosevic found it useful to arm and empower the radical militias, led by Arkan, Vojislav Seselj, and others, to bolster his campaign in Croatia. The Yugoslav army that remained was hardened by its initiation into extreme bloodshed (committed on both sides in the Croatian war), and by its association with the extreme militia leaders now armed and emboldened by the support of the Milosevic government. The bloodshed culminated in the annihilation of the city Vukovar and the atrocities that followed upon it.[16]

The arming of the militias, the financing of them through bank fraud and other schemes, and the sending of the militias first into Croatia and then into Bosnia, became the linchpin for instrumentalizing the genocide in Bosnia. According to the Serbian dissident magazine *Vreme,* there were more than forty major militia groups operating from Serbia, crossing the Drina river into Bosnia to carry out atrocities against civilians, and bringing looted property back into Serbia. None of this could have happened without the cooperation of the Yugoslav secret police and the Yugoslav army. In addition to organizing the killing and expulsion of civilians and the expropriation of their property, these militias were vital for another task: the intimidation and, if necessary, liquidation of any local Serbs who refused to participate in the attack on the non-Serb population. By forcing as many Serbs as possible to engage in the atrocities, the organizers guaranteed that complicity would be spread throughout a wide section of the population who would, thereafter, have a vested interested in denying what happened and in obstructing investigations into the atrocities.[17] As the property of non-Serbs was distributed to the local Serb population, the circle of complicity and solidarity was further strengthened.

Among the major militia figures, several had three bases of support: organized crime; the Serbian bishops; and the Milosevic-controlled secret police. Arkan (Zeljko Raznjatovic), who claims credit for beginning the "ethnic cleansing" of Bosnia with his attack on Muslim civilians in the eastern town of Bijeljina in March, 1992, was a clear beneficiary of this threefold support. In 1994, Arkan was married to a Serbian folk-pop singer in one of the most extraordinary public events in Serbia since the 1989 Vidovdan celebration. Serbian Orthodox bishops journeyed from Croatia and Bosnia (including areas where Arkan's men had carried out organized atrocities) to preside over a fully mythologized wedding, with Arkan dressed up as a Serbian hero from the Lazar and post-Lazar revolutionary tradition, and with his bride dressed up as the Maiden of Kosovo, the Mary Magdelene figure who in legend had ministered to the fallen and dying Serb soldiers. One of the most fervent supporters of Arkan was Orthodox Bishop Vasilije of the Tuzla-Zvornik region in Bosnia, one of the areas of widespread killings, organized rape, and torture.[18] Arkan was funded by organized crime activities, including a massive bank fraud operation, and throughout 1992 his ties to the secret police network were particularly close.

When the Serbian army and nationalist militias occupied an area in Bosnia, they compelled all Serbian fighting-age men to join the militias and the persecutions. Serbs who resisted were subjected to ridicule, threats, and in some cases immediate killing. The standard tactic, as observed by UN observers who were on the spot but not allowed to intervene, was to broadcast to the Serb villagers that their Muslim neighbors were preparing a massacre. The Serbs would be told to leave, whereupon the village would be shelled and occupied, and the atrocities against the Muslim villagers would begin.[19] A particularly grim example of such reality reversal were charges by Bosnian Serb newspapers and radio stations that Muslims were planning a fourfold crime against the Serbian woman: to remove her from her own family, impregnate her by undesirable [Islamic] seeds, to make her bear a stranger, and then take the infant away from her."[20] These claims, which played upon the Serbian nationalist preoccupation with the Ottoman *devshirme* system as a "stealing of Serb blood," were followed by the commission of precisely that program by Serb militiamen against Bosnian Muslim women.[21]

The local campaigns of "ethnic cleansing" were sometimes planned and organized in local Serbian Orthodox churches, as was the case in Brko, a center of the some of the worst genocidal campaigns of 1992, which included killing-centers, makeshift body disposal operations, and a concentration camp run by Goran Jelisic, who has been indicted for genocide by the International Tribunal in The Hague, and who proudly calls himself the "Serb Adolf." During and after the atrocities, Serbian Orthodox clergy, such as Episkop Slavko Maksimovic of Brko, denied any campaign against the non-Serb population and actually maintained (despite overwhelming evidence to the contrary) that it was the Muslims who attacked the Serbs. [22]

Media control was crucial in further inciting an atmosphere of fear and hatred. For three years, the Milosevic-controlled media in Serbia, and the increasingly nationalist media in Croatia, demonized the other side, with graphic scenes of atrocities and claims that the other group was planning more.[23] Serb radio stations and newspapers in towns like Foca broadcast statements that Muslims were preparing to put Serb women in harems (Bosnian Muslims take only one wife), were already appointing Ottoman-style "viziers" to rule their neo-Ottoman state, and (in complete contradiction to the other claims), that Bosnian Muslims were fundamentalist Islamists who wished to impose Islamic law on all the peoples of Bosnia. Serbian Orthodox bishop Atanasije wrote that Slavic Muslims were part of a chain of primitivism.[24]

The Kosovo ideology and the mythology of *The Mountain Wreath,* which one enthusiast stated was itself "resurrected" on Vidovdan 1989,[25] was a necessary instrument in motivating the atrocities, but as shown above, it was not sufficient in itself. It could work only in conjunction with a media campaign of fear and hatred and with the military and militia instigation of violence and atrocity. Yet the importance of this ideology cannot be underestimated, and it did not end with the 1989 Vidovdan celebration.

The accusation of race-treason and Christ-killing was repeated in increasingly extreme forms by Serbian Orthodox clergy and University of Belgrade academics. Professor Miroljub Jevtic, a specialist on Middle East Studies at the University of Belgrade, propounded the theory that contemporary Slavic Muslims still have on their hands the blood of the Serbian martyrs who died five hundred years ago.[26] This accusation that contemporary Slavic Muslims are responsible for the death of the Christ-Prince Lazar and the other Serbian martyrs of the fourteenth and fifteenth centuries was increasingly important in the furor leading up to and growing out of the passion play commemorations in 1989.

The final twist was added when Serbian religious nationalists wrote that Slavic Muslims suffered from a "defective gene" probably inherited from North Africa that rendered them genetically incapable of reason.[27] This theory, which was advanced in Serbia proper, was picked up with enthusiasm by Biljana Plavsic, the former dean of the Faculty of Natural Science and Mathematics in Sarajevo and a member of the Bosnia-Herzegovina Academy of Arts and Sciences. After leaving her position in Sarajevo and joining the Serb Democratic Party (SDS) of Radovan Karadzic, which had embraced the program of "ethnic cleansing," Plavsic began writing about the "genetically deformed" element in Bosnian Muslims. Addressing the issue that the Bosnian Muslims were also Slavs, or as Plavsic anachronistically put it, "originally Serbs," she wrote:

> That's true [i.e. that the Bosnian Muslims were originally Serbs]. But it was genetically deformed material that embraced Islam. And now, of course, with each successive generation this gene simply becomes concentrated. It gets worse and worse. It simply expresses itself and dictates their style of thinking and behaving, which is rooted in their genes.[28]

This theory of the defective gene carried by subhuman Slavic Muslims was the logical extreme of the ideology of Christoslavism and racial transformation by conversion that was first promulgated in the nineteenth century.

Although rooted in a strand of radical Christoslavist ideology, the "genetic deformation" theory is adopted here not only by Serbian militia leaders and long-time religious nationalists, but by Biljana Plavsic, a formerly respected biologist who had previously subscribed to the multireligious ethos of Yugoslavia. Plavsic is representative of an entire cadre of former members of the urban intelligentsia who, within a period of a few months, converted to violent Christoslavism and a racialist ideology so crude and so blatant that it reveals a complete break with every aspect of the academic ideals and standards of reason they had spent their lives professing. This was the group that led the deliberate attack on the cultural infrastructure of Sarajevo and directed the Serbian army in its burning of the National and University Library in Sarajevo (with more than a million books and 100,000 rare books and manuscripts destroyed); in its annihilation of the Oriental Institute of Sarajevo, with its priceless collection of manuscripts in Ottoman, Persian, Arabic, Bosnian Slavic, and Bosnian Aljamiado (Slavic in Arabic script) and other languages; and in its shelling of the National Museum of Sarajevo. A number of their own former students were killed as they retrieved cultural treasures in the midst of these attacks by the

Serb army.[29] The sudden conversion and subsequent acts of such people indicate just how fragile can be the thread of rationality in the face of a resurgent and militant religious mythology.

In all of this, the Serbian Orthodox Church was instrumental. Serbian religious leaders even held formal rituals to mark the successful "cleansing" of a town of all non-Serb-Orthodox inhabitants. In the Bosnian town of Foca on the Drina, all the Muslims were killed or expelled, and the town was renamed Srbinje (Serbplace). The militiamen who took part in the "cleansing" were given medals named after Milos Obilic, the avenger of Kosovo, and some of them became students at a newly-established Serbian Orthodox seminary in the town. Among other atrocities, including an organized system of "rape-camps," all of the mosques, several of them masterworks of 15th and 16th century Islamic architecture, were dynamited. When asked why all the mosques had been destroyed, the new Serbian nationalist mayor stated that "There never were any mosques in Foca."[30] Similarly, when asked about the mosques of the town of Zvornik, all dynamited by Serb nationalists in 1992, the town's new Serb mayor denied that they had ever existed.[31]

Justification and Denial

The manipulation of sacred time, sacred space, and historical memory that reached a critical mass in the 1989 Vidovdan commemoration became a key element in motivating the "ethnic cleansing" in Bosnia and in denying either that the atrocities took place or justifying that which could not be denied. After the revelations of torture, killings, and other atrocities at the Omarska and Trnopolje concentration camps, the Serbian Orthodox Synod made the following solemn proclamation:

> In the name of God's truth and on the testimony from our brother bishops from Bosnia-Herzegovina and from other trustworthy witnesses, we declare, taking full moral responsibility, that such camps neither have existed nor exist in the Serbian Republic of Bosnia-Herzegovina.[32]

This statement was made at a time when Serbian priests and bishops were stationed right next to the camps. The denial of the Serbian Orthodox Church that the camps existed has been extended in more recent times to an attack on the International Tribunal in the Hague, which is investigating and prosecuting war crimes in the former Yugoslavia. On October 16, 1997, The Association of Writers of Serbia (UKS) published a declaration, signed by sixty Serbian and Bosnian Serb intellectuals, including fourteen members of SANU (the Serbian Academy of Sciences and Arts), and endorsed by Serbian Orthodox Patriarch Pavle. The document was entitled: "Second Declaration on Closure of Process of the Hague Tribunal against Dr. Radovan Karadzic."[33] The Declaration states: "From its illegal founding until today," the Tribunal was and continues to be "exclusively an instrument for the persecution of Serbs." It claims that the Tribunal "cannot hide disgusting crimes that were committed by Muslims and Croats against Serbs." The signatories deem it "obvious that the prime goal of the Tribunal is to compromise, vilify and humiliate the Serbs to the greatest possible extent." At the time this document was issued, the ethnic composition of the indicted war crimes suspects held in the Tribunal's detention unit was: 14 Croats, 3 Muslims and 3 Serbs. The claim was made at a time when there were two trials ongoing at the Tribunal: the one, a trial of Bosnian Croat and Muslim camp officials from the camp at Celebici near Konjic, for abuses against Bosnian Serb civilians; the second, the trial of Bosnian Croat General Tihomir Blaskic for alleged massacres of Muslim civilians in and around the town of Vitez.[34] Thus the Patriarch of the Serbian Orthodox Church endorsed a proclamation claiming that the Tribunal was "exclusively an instrument for the persecution of Serbs" at a time when the major cases were against Croats and Muslims and the vast majority of defendants were non-Serbs, a proclamation that claims the Tribunal is trying to hide crimes committed against Serbs at a time when its most active case was a prosecution for crimes committed against Serbs.

What led the hierarchy of the Serbian Orthodox Church to take a position filled with transparent contradictions was its own religio-national ideology. That ideology is inscribed upon all Serbian nationalist flags in a symbol of the cross formed of the four characters, CCCC, (the Cyrillic "s") that stand for the slogan: Only Unity Saves the Serbs *(samo sloga Srbina spasava)*. This was the symbol in front of which Slobodan Milosevic stood at Vidovdan in 1989 to threaten war. As interpreted by Serbian religious nationalists, the term "unity" does not mean a communal unity where different voices are brought together into a harmony. It means a homogenous unity in which the most extreme and brutal self-proclaimed defenders of Greater Serbia, such as General Ratko Mladic or those indicted for organized rape at Foca, must be supported by all Serbs because they are Serbs and they committed their acts in the name of Serbia.

Figure 1

The animus of the Serbian Orthodox Church toward the International Tribunal is directed against the Tribunal's efforts to distinguish between those who committed or authorized war crimes from those who did not, to direct accountability toward individuals and to reject generic blame leveled against an entire people. In this sense, the Serbian Orthodox Church's attack on the Tribunal for investigating crimes by individual Serbs is part of a position that also includes charges by the members of the Church hierarchy that Serb dissidents who denounced the atrocities were traitors. This homogenizing interpretation of the unity that saves the Serbs, rules out, by its very nature, any self-criticism within the Serbian body politic. [35]

Circles Of Complicity

For three years the military powers of the NATO alliance, through the UN Security Council they dominated, applied a twin policy to Bosnia. On the one hand, they enforced an arms embargo that left the Serb army, which had seized control of the vast majority of arms and equipment from the Yugoslav National army, with a permanent arms advantage and which punished the Bosnian Muslims in particular who had the fewest arms and were in the most vulnerable position. On the other hand, it refused to intervene to stop the killing, thus violating (if the Tribunal's indictments for genocide are valid), the Genocide Convention of 1948, which requires all signatory powers to stop genocide from occurring and to punish it if and when it occurs.

The pretexts given for this policy were several. According to the hypothesis of "age old antagonisms," Bosnians had been killing each other for centuries and it was ingrained in their culture. This constantly-repeated claim had one problem: the massive evidence, throughout Bosnia, of a shared civilization of more than five hundred years. Bosnia, like all of Europe, suffered extreme violence in World War II. But like many civilizations with deep wounds, it had built a common cultural world, despite those wounds, symbolized over the centuries by bridges, libraries, artistic treasures, and the Catholic, Orthodox, Muslim, and Jewish houses of worship build side by side and sharing the same skyline in Mostar and Sarajevo. It was this evidence of a successfully shared five hundred-year-old civilization that Serbian and Croatian religious nationalists targeted for methodical destruction. By destroying the traces of such a civilization they could say that it had never existed in the first place.[36]

The age-old-antagonisms theory is an example of "Balkanism": the notion that the peoples of the Balkans are by nature, genetics, geography, or patterns of history rendered incapable of living with one another and fated to repeated outbreaks of mass killing. Balkanism is itself influenced by an orientalism that can be traced back from Robert Kaplan's popular book *Balkan Ghosts* to Rebecca West, whose *Black Lamb and Grey Falcon,* romanticized and helped make acceptable key assumptions about Balkan peoples and the Turks.[37] Under this view, proximinity to the Balkan Orient has fatally infected Balkan peoples and rendered them incapable of civilization. West popularized the image of an "Ottoman disease" rotting the Balkans from within and Kaplan revived the image for a new generation of readers. The hypothesis of an Ottoman disease is also advanced by present-day Croat and Serb nationalists as a rationale for programs to cleanse the Balkans of their oriental impurities. Polemics between Serb and Croat nationalists commonly entail contests over which nation has done most to protect Christendom from Ottoman defilement, or (when abusing the other) which nation has been most infected by contact with the Ottoman and Islamic world. *Balkan Ghosts* was influential within President Bill Clinton's administration at a tragic moment. In 1993, as members of Clinton's inner circle were reading Kaplan's book, Clinton abandoned his commitment to the "lift and strike" policy, the call for the lifting of the arms embargo (that punished the Bosnians while leaving the Serb and Croat armies with a massive arms advantage) and for offering air support to the Bosnians. To justify the change in policy, Clinton and his secretary of state Warren Christopher began describing the conflict as "age old" and a "problem from hell," best left to burn itself out within a ring of containment. The distinction between perpetrator and victim was lost and the moral claim for halting the killing dissipated.[38]

The work of Jacques Ellul and Bat Ye'or represents a particularly revealing expression of the anti-Ottoman hypothesis. Their work has been influenced by earlier Serbian nationalist historians and has been cited as a vindication by contemporary Serb anti-Muslim polemicists. According to Ellul and Bat Ye'or, Islam (as a civilization) is in its very essence based upon two essential principles: aggressive violence *(jihad)* and parasitic absorption *(dhimmitude)*.[39] It is not that Muslims under certain circumstances have persecuted those of other faiths. Rather, Islam is always and everywhere seeking the annihilation of the religious other. Because its violence is essential, rooted in its very nature, Islam contrasts with the loving nature of Christianity, in which, according to Ellul, persecution is an aberration of the religion rather rather than a necessary and inevitable expression of it.[40]

The essentialism of Ellul and Bat Ye'or has been discredited by scholars of minorities in Islam.[41] Nevertheless, Ellul and Bat Ye'or have been influential in shaping public opinion and public policy in the United States. Bat Ye'or testified before congressional committees investigating "global persecutions" of Christians allegedly carried out primarily by Muslims and communists. The influential Institute of Religion and Public Life invited Bat Ye'or to the United States. The editor of the Institute's journal, Richard John Neuhaus, acclaimed Bat

Ye'or's work, citing with special admiration Bat Ye'or's view that the Arabs, and Islam more generally, developed its cultural ambiance and civilizational treasures "in the midst of conquered peoples feeding off their vigor and on the dying, bloodless body of dhimmitude."[42]

In a discussion largely devoted to Ottoman Islam, Bat Ye'or writes of the officially recognized non-Muslim *(dhimmi)* communities under Islam:

> The oblivion which surrounds the *dhimmi* past is not accidental; it reflects the abolition of *dhimmi* history. The annihilation of a community transfers its cultural heritage—civilization, arts, and sciences—to the dominating group. Cultural imperialism accompanies territorial imperialism; culture, monopolized by the authorities, becomes an additional instrument of domination and alienation. In fact, the *umma* claims a monopoly of culture: the *dhimmis'* languages are banned, relegated to the liturgy; their monuments, testimony to their civilizations' greatness are destroyed or Islamized.[43]

The claim is one of a timeless, unchanging violence. Much of it is counterfactual. In the case of Islamic al-Andalus, for example, not only was Hebrew not banned or "relegated to the liturgy" under Islamic rule, but, on the contrary, it was in al-Andalus and elsewhere in the Islamic world that Hebrew poets developed a secular love lyric for the first time, in what is generally referred to as the "golden age" of Hebrew poetry.[44]

In the Balkan context, the full danger of Bat Ye'or's claim lies in the assertion that "their [the *dhimmi* communities] monuments, testimony to their civilizations' greatness are destroyed or Islamized." This claim reflects a persistent feature of radical Serbian religious nationalism. The claim was revived with particular vehemence during the conflict in Kosovo that began in the early 1980s, with charges that the Ottomans and the Albanian Muslims had destroyed the sacral heritage of Serbs. Of course there were many cases of destruction or Islamization of Christian monuments during the centuries of Ottoman rule. But the same Ottomans reestablished the Serbian Orthodox Patriarchate and authorized the renovation and construction of hundreds of Christian and Jewish monuments. The monasteries through which the relics of Lazar passed in 1989 survived five hundred years of Ottoman and Albanian rule. They testify to both the magnificence of medieval Serbian culture and to its preservation under Islam. In the area of the self-declared Republica Srpska, however, not one Islamic monument, from among an estimated thousand mosques, *tekkes* (Sufi centers), schools, and *turbes* (monumental tombs) survived three years of Serbian religious nationalist rule from 1992 to 1995.

On July 11, 1995, the United Nations Protection Force (UNPROFOR) handed over the declared "safe area" of Srebrenica to the forces of Serb General Ratko Mladic. Over a period of three years, Mladic's Serb army and Serb irregulars had developed a consistent record of organized atrocities in the civilian areas they had taken. For almost as long, Serb nationalist media had announced its inention to punish the Muslims of Srebrenica. Yet French General Bertrand Janvier and UN Special Envoy Yasushi Akashi dismissed warnings that the Serb army and paramilitaries would harm the civilian population if Srebrenica were turned over to them. Janvier and Akashi blocked all efforts to use serious air support to save Srebrenica and insisted that handing it over to the Serb army would not result in war crimes. From July 11 to July 14, approximately eight thousand unarmed captives from Srebrenica were tortured and exterminated, in some cases in the view or hearing of Dutch UNPROFOR soldiers, and disposed of in mass graves throughout eastern Bosnia.[45] Srebrenica culminated three years of appeasement of "ethnic cleansing" in Bosnia. The enormity of both the betrayal of the "safe area" by the UN leaders and the atrocities that followed forced NATO into more resolute action. For three years the Serb nationalist forces had carried out atrocities in Bosnia with impunity. After three weeks of air strikes and an assault by Croat and Bosnian ground troops, the Serb nationalist siege of Sarajevo was broken. A peace plan was signed in Dayton, Ohio, and three years of organized "ethnic cleansing" in Bosnia came to an end.

The violence then returned to the land from which it gains its symbolic power. For twelve years, the Albanian majority in Kosovo had endured systematic repression, including a de facto apartheid system of rule and institutionalized use of mass torture. The Albanian resistance had been nonviolent, but as the repression continued to intensify and as the world ignored the situation of the Kosovar Albanians, the non-violent movement was discredited. The influence of the Kosovo Liberation Army (KLA) began to grow. In retaliation for KLA attacks on Serb police, Serb forces began carrying out massacres of civilians. By 1999, the Serb army, secret police, and paramilitary terror units were working in Kosovo as they had worked together in Bosnia. In the early spring of 1999, Serb paramilitaries began burning mosques in western Kosovo and destroying entire Muslim historical districts. After the failure of negotiations with Serbia, NATO began organized air strikes and the Serb military intensified the atrocity program it had perfected earlier in Bosnia. More than a million Albanians were driven out of the country and thousands were killed, fulfilling the pledges to clear the

Albanians out of Kosovo that had been made since 1989 by all the major factions of political leadership in Serbia. Ultimately, the NATO action forced Serbian forces to leave Kosovo and the Albanian refugees returned in a surprisingly short time.

Those who opposed NATO's post-Srebrenica policy of using military force in the Balkans argue that it was not needed. They claim that more negotiations should have been pursued with the Milosevic regime during the Kosovo crisis. They argue that a strong dissident movement in Serbia was gaining strength before the Kosovo air strikes. Before we can responsibly take a position on the issue of the use of NATO force, we must understand the depth and scope of radicalization in Serbia. From 1987 to 1989, the Milosevic regime, with the help of the leadership of the Serbian Orthodox Church, manipulated the Kosovo myth to secure its own power. For a time there was indeed a strong dissident movement. Within a few years, however, Milosevic was no longer directing Serb nationalism, he was following it. He had used the Kosovo mythology to crush the dissent, but in doing so, he had created something that was no longer in his control: an ideology of genocide that had gained its own critical mass of economic, religious, political, and social motivations and had taken on a life of its own.

Opponents of the use of force against the Serbian military apparatus point to the hundreds of thousands demonstrating against Milosevic in 1996 and 1997 as evidence that Serbia had a strong dissident movement and that the use of force damaged that movement. The vast majority of demonstrators at that time, however, were not protesting the regime's policy of "ethnic cleansing" but rather the failure to carry it out successfully. The two major leaders of the dissident movement had been among the leaders of the extreme nationalist element in Serbia.[46] In Bosnia, Serbia and Montenegro, the bishops of the Serbian Orthodox Church, with the exception of Bishop Artemije, were and continue to be committed to radical Serb nationalism. By 1999, Serb military forces were moving on the province of Kosovo with the same kind of determined coordination and open ideology of "ethnic cleansing" they had used in Bosnia. To have followed the Bosnia model of further negotiations, reliance on UN guarantees or the promises of the Milosevic regime may well have ended in a repeat of the Srebrenica genocide in Kosovo, on a larger scale, with incalculable long term consequences for peace and security in southeast Europe, with more than a million refugees living in camps outside Kosovo, survivors of unspeakable violence, passing on both the horror they survived and the dream of return to new generations.

Future decisions regarding policy toward the Balkans should take into consideration the Kosovo mythology, how it was manipulated and continues to be manipulated, and the way in which those who manipulate it one day become servants of the mass psychology they helped create, the next day. To adequately acknowledge the role and power of Kosovo mythology entails a recognition that religion is not necessarily confined to the self-conscious articulations of private faith or piety but has social aspects, mediated through symbols and myth, that can act, with massive power, upon a society as apparently secularized as the communist Yugoslavia of 1989. It remains to be seen whether, after such destructive use of the Kosovo legacy, the Serbian Orthodox Church and Serbian society will retrieve a constructive vision of the Kosovo story.[47]

Notes

1. The argument in this essay is conveyed in more detailed form in Michael A. Sells, *The Bridge Betrayed: Religion and Genocide in Bosnia* (Berkeley: University of California Press, second edition, 1998). The documentation on the human rights violations and the International Tribunal Indictments for genocide, crimes against humanity, and grave breaches of the Geneva Accords is voluminous. I have dedicated a World Wide Web site to background documentation on the specific human rights reports, war-crimes reports, and other evidence: http://www.haverford.edu/relg/sells/reports.html.

   In this essay I focus almost exclusively on the role of Serbian religious nationalism in the justification and motivation of genocidal acts in Bosnia. Such a focus is not in any way an attempt to lessen or deny the responsibility of Croatian religious nationalism, which is treated in Chapter 5 of *The Bridge Betrayed*. Nor is the argument presented here in any way intended to deny the importance of economic, social, and political factors in the disintegration of Yugoslavia, or to make a claim as to which factor is most important. The goal is simply to show that religious nationalism was an important, indeed, critical factor in the genocide.

2. For human rights reports and war-crimes data on Kosovo see http//www.haverford.edu/relg/sells/reports.html. The site includes the program of the Serbian Radical Party of Vojislav Seelj (Miloevic's governing partner in 1999) for the systematic annihilation of Kosovar Albanians, a detailed program adopted in 1991 and supported in four resolutions of the Serbian Unity Congress, a U.S. lobby supporting the greater Serbia project.

3. See Thomas Emmert, *Serbian Golgotha: Kosovo, 1389* (New York: East European Monographs, 1990) and Wayne Vucinich and Thomas Emmert, *Kosovo: Legacy of a Medieval Battle* (Minneapolis: University of Minnesota, 1991).

4. See Alexander Greenawalt, "The Nationalization of Memory: Identity and Ideology in Nineteenth Century Serbia" (Princeton University Bachelors Thesis, April 15, 1994, and Milorad Ekmecic, "The Emergence of St. Vitus Day," in Vucinich and Emmert, *Kosovo: Legacy of a Medieval Battle,* p. 355. For an artistic representation of Lazar's last supper, modeled precisely on Renaissance paintings of the last supper of Jesus, see Ljubica Popovich in Vucinich and Emmert, *Kosovo: Legacy of a Medieval Battle,* Fig. 21, p. 287.

5. Bishop Petar II Petrovi, *The Mountain Wreath (Gorski vijenac),* translated and edited by Vasa Mihailovich (Irvine, Calif.: Charles Schlacks Jr., 1986). This edition contains facing Serbian and English versions of the work.

6. For the *kum* ceremony and blood feud, see Christopher Boehm, *Blood Revenge: The Enactment and Management of Conflict in Montenegro and Other Tribal Societies* (Philadelphia: University of Pennsylvania Press, 1984).

7. Ivo Andri, *The Development of Spiritual Life in Bosnia under the Influence of Turkish Rule* (Chapel Hill: Duke University Press, 1990), pp. 20 ff. This is the translation of Ivo Andri, *Die Entwicklung des geistigen Lebens in Bosnien unter der Einwirkung der türkischen Herrschaft.,* doctoral dissertation, presented to the Dean of the Faculty of Philosophy at Karl-Franz University in Graz, Austria, May 14, 1924 .

8. See Ivo Andri, *The Bridge on the Drina,* translated from the Serbo-Croat by Lovett F. Edwards (New York: Macmillan, 1959; Chicago: University of Chicago Press, 1977) from *Na Drini uprija.* See also Ivo Andri, *The Development of Spiritual Life,* cited above, passim. For specific examples of how Andri builds the theme of the "stealing of Serb" blood into *The Bridge on the Drina,* see Sells, *The Bridge Betrayed,* pp. 45-50.

9. See Sava Pei, *Medieval Serbian Culture* (London: Alpine Fine Arts Collection, UK, 1994). See also the collection of essays, sumptuously illustrated, *Kosovo,* compiled and produced by William Dorich, edited by Basil Jenkins (Alhambra, Calif.: Kosovo Charity Fund '92 of the Serbian Orthodox Diocese of Western America, 1992).

10. "It is no exaggeration to say that planned GENOCIDE [emphasis original] is being perpetrated against the Serbian people in Kosovo! What otherwise would be the meaning of 'ethnically pure Kosovo' which is being relentlessly put into effect through ceaseless and never-ending migrations." Appeal by the Clergy in Gordana Filipovi, *Kosovo: Past and Present* (Belgrade: Review of International Affairs, 1989), pp. 355-60. The capitalization of GENOCIDE is in the original. The Serbian Church claims of genocide in Kosovo continued in 1987 and 1988, see *idem,* pp.360-63 and the *American Srbobran,* 2 November 1988.

11. Amnesty International, *Yugoslavia: Ethnic Albanian Victims of Torture and Ill-treatment by Police* (New York, 1992). Cf. *Helsinki Watch* reports on Kosovo for the years 1986, 1989, and 1990; and see Branka Maga, *The Destruction of Yugoslavia: Tracking the Break-up 1980-92* (London: Verso, 1993), pp. 49-73.

12. "Memorandum on the Position of Serbia in Yugoslavia" (Belgrade, 1986). The document was authored by members of Serbian Academy of Sciences and Arts, but the names were not made public and the Manifesto was never published, but leaked to nationalists in the media.

13. Muharem Duriand Mirko Cari, *"Kako srpski nacionalisti odmazu srpskom narodu i sta prati kosti kneza Lazara"* (How Serbian Nationalists Are Avenging the Serbian People and What Accompanies the Relics of Prince Lazar), *Politika,* Sept. 17, 1988, p. 7. Cited and translated by Norman Cigar, *Genocide in Bosnia: The Policy of "Ethnic Cleansing" in Eastern Europe* (College Sta-

tion: Texas A&M University Press, 1995), p. 35. Cf. Milan Miloeviand Velizar Brajoviin *Vreme* 145 (4 July 1994): "At about the same time, the Serbian Orthodox Church carried the relics of Grand Duke Lazar (the leader of the Kosovo battle) around the Serb lands and religious services were held over the remains of the victims of genocide of a half a century ago that were retrieved from mass graves for that purpose. "

14. Ante Pavelic lived a long, boastful life in Spain, and his minister of the interior, Andrije Artukovi, who drew up the laws for the annihilation of the Jewish community in Croatia, was sheltered in the United States for decades. Mark Aarons and John Loftus, *Unholy Trinity* (New York: St. Martin's Press, 1991) and Howard Blum, *Wanted: The Search for Nazis in America* (New York: Touchstone, 1977).

15. The writings of politician Vuk Drakovi, in particular his *No.* were effective in inciting hatred against all Croats and Muslims. Drakovi portrayed Muslims as Serbs who betrayed their race by converting to Islam and, within the context of World War II, as sadistic monsters.

16. For a good account of the Bosnian tragedy in the wider context of the Yugoslav wars, see the video series "Yugoslavia, Death of a Nation" (BBC/Discovery, 1995) and the accompanying book, Laura Silber and Allan Little, *Yugoslavia: Death of a Nation* (New York: TV books, 1986).

17. See U.S. Department of State, "War Crimes in the Former Yugoslavia: Submission of Information to the United States Security Council in Accordance with Paragraph 5 of Resolution 771 (1992)," *U.S. Department of State Dispatch,* 4th report, 9 May 1992 (incident no. 12); For other examples, see Norman Cigar, *Genocide in Bosnia,* p. 84.

18. See the three articles in *Vreme News Digest* 178, 27 February 1995: Alexander Ciri, "Turbo Land: Machine Gun Wedding (with Singing)"; Dejan Anastasijevi, "Zeljko Raznjatovic Arkan: The Groom," and idem, "Ceca Velikovi: The Bride." See also Roger Cohen, "Serbia Dazzles Itself: Terror Suspect Weds Singer," *The New York Times,* February 20, 1995; and John Kifner, "An Outlaw in the Balkans Is Basking in the Spotlight" *The New York Times,* November 23, 1993. For a particularly thorough case study of "ethnic cleansing," see the report on Zvornik by Tretter, Müller, Schwanke, Angeli, and Richter, "Ethnic Cleansing Operations" in the Northeast Bosnian City of Zvornik from April through June 1992." The study was prepared under the auspices of the Ludwig Boltzmann Institute for Human Rights, with the encouragement of Cherif Bassiouni, head of the Commission of Experts that was established pursuant to Security Council Resolution 780 (1992). In the Final Report of the Commission (UN Doc. S/1994/674) the report of BIM was cited as an exemplary study on "Ethnic Cleansing" and published as an annex (UN Doc. S/1994/674/add.2 (vol.I) December 1994). The full report is available on the war-crimes reports page at http://www.haverford.edu/relg/sells/reports.html.

19. See the eyewitness testimony of UNHCR official José María Mendiluce, *Vreme News Digest ,* 170, 26 November, 1994.

20. Roy Gutman, *Witness to Genocide* (New York: MacMillan, 1993), Preface, p. x. Cf. Vamik Volkan, *Blood Lines: From Ethnic Pride to Ethnic Terrorism* (New York: Farrar, Straus and Giroux, 1997), pp. 75-80.

21. See the historic International Tribunal indictments for organized rape, torture, and sexual slavery committed in the town of Foa at www. haverford.edu/relg/sells/reports.edu. This is the first indictment in International Tribunal his-

tory that focuses upon organized rape as a crime of war. In March, 1998, the first of the Foa indictees turned himself in for trial at The Hague.

22. For details of the genocide indictment against Goran Jelisifor crimes at Brko, see: http://www.haverford.edu/relg/sells/reports.html. For an recent account of the "ethnic cleansing" of Brko, based on evidence from excavations of mass-graves, see Scott Peterson, "The Town Where Truth is a Victim of Ethnic Hatred," *The Daily Telegraph,* January 23, 1996, p. 11: "The result was a massacre of thousands of Muslims and the ethnic cleansing of the town in north-east Bosnia, which Serbs have controlled since the spring of 1992. Details of Brko's primary mass grave, revealed yesterday following an investigation by The Daily Telegraph, and of other killing fields in the town, make clear that Serbs were responsible." Peterson goes on to write:

> The "cleansing" of Brko began in the town's Serb Orthodox Church, several weeks before the Serb onslaught. Witnesses say meetings were held at night and street lights were turned out to protect identities. Serb paramilitary groups also began forming. A Muslim refugee said: "We all knew that Serb guys were going to Serb villages for training." The refugees say the Serbs attacked in waves. In early May, local Serb extremists began rounding up non-Serbs for detention camps. Then came soldiers loyal to the notorious "Arkan", who "cleansed" towns in Bosnia under orders from Belgrade, the Serb capital. They were followed by outside soldiers wearing red berets and, finally, Serb units from their stronghold of Banja Luka."

In the same article, Episcop Maksimoviis quoted as claiming that:

> The Muslims started leaving, destroying everything they were leaving behind. The Serbs didn't leave this town because they felt they were here in their homeland, in the land of their fathers. So many people were killed here because the Muslims withdrew to the suburbs from where they shelled the town.

Cf. Sonia Bakari, "NATO troops arrest Bosnia's self-styled 'Serb Adolf'", AAP Information Services Pty. Ltd. , January 22, 1998.

23. See Mark Thompson, *Forging War: The Media in Serbia, Croatia, and Bosnia-Hercegovina* (London: Article 19 International Centre Against Censorship, 1994).

24. Atanasije Jevti, cited in the Serbian Orthodox Church publication *Glas Crkve,* cited by Cigar, *Genocide in Bosnia,* pp. 31-32.

25. For the resurrection of Njegoin 1989, see Alek Vukadinovic, ed., *Kosovo 1389-1989: Special Edition of the Serbian Literary Quarterly on the Occasion of 600 Years since the Battle of Kosovo,* (Belgrade: Serbian Literary Quarterly, 1989), p. 79.

26. See H. T. Norris, *Islam in the Balkans* (Columbia: University of South Carolina Press, 1993), 295; and Norman Cigar, *Genocide in Bosnia,* p.29. More recently, Jevtihas spelled out the implications of his view that contemporary Slavic Muslims are guilty of the blood of Lazar and the early Serb martyrs:

> If you want to destroy a Turk, you must destroy his every part. If you do not do this, you risk that he moves about like a whole Turk, that is the whole of Bosnia, and becomes dangerous like the whole of Bosnia. ... The only remedy would be to completely destroy each "part of the Turk's body."

Cited in *Vreme News Digest,* 21 November 1994.

27. Serbian religious nationalist Drago Kalaji was one of the proponents of this theory. Kalaji claimed that Slavic Muslims did not belong to Europe, that their

culture is an unconscious expression of "semi-Arabic subculture," and that the Slavic Muslims of Bosnia inherited an inferior "special gene" passed on from North African Arabs by the Ottomans. Kalaji was a mentor for the militia known as the "White Eagles" *(beli orlovi)* , associated with some of the most inhuman atrocities in Bosnia and commanded by a historian on Kosovo, Dragoslav Bokan, and Mirko Jovi, the chairman of the Serbian People Renewal Party. See DragoKalaji, "Kvazi Arapi protiv Evropljana" (Semi-Arabs versus Europeans), *Duga,* Sept. 13-19, 1987, pp. 14-15; translated and cited by Norman Cigar, *Genocide in Bosnia,* p. 26. For the genetically caused flaws supposedly resulting from this "special gene" of Ottoman soldiery, see Cigar, *Genocide in Bosnia,* pp. 26-27. In a September 1995 issue of *Duga,* Kalaji also celebrates Serb army destruction of Bosnian cities, claiming that since Homer, true Europeans have hated cities. For a critique of the anachronism behind the notion that pre-Ottoman Bosnian Slavs were "Serbs" and a critique of common fallacies concerning conversion and ethnicity in medieval Bosnia, see John Fine, *The Bosnian Church: A New Interpretation* (Boulder: East European Quarterly, 1975).

28. Biljana Plavi, *Svet,* Novi Sad, September 1993), cited and translated by Slobodan Ini, "Biljana Plavi: Geneticist in the Service of a Great Crime," *Bosnia Report: Newsletter of the Alliance to Defend Bosnia-Herzegovina* , 19, June— August, 1997, translated from *Helsinska povelja* (Helsinki Charter), Belgrade, November 1996.

29. Other members of the academic elite in Bosnia to join the Serbian Christoslavic movement include: Nikola Koljevi, former professor of English and noted Shakespeare scholar; Aleksa Buha, former professor of philosophy; Radovan Karadi, psychiatrist and poet; and Vojislav Maksimovi, former professor of Marxism and a major suspect in the annihilation of the Muslim community in Foa and the "ethnic cleansing" of the University of Banja Luka. All these academicians lived and practiced in Sarajevo. The psychoanalytic parallel to Plavsi's theory of genetic deformation was the theory held by Jovan Rakovi, the mentor of Dr. Radovan Karadi, who maintained that Muslim use of ablutions before prayer indicated the "anal analytic" nature of Muslims as a people. See C. Bennett, *Yugoslavia's Bloody Collapse: Causes, Course and Consequences* (New York, New York University Press, 1995), pp.126-29.

30. See the account in the *Cleveland Plain Dealer,* 2 April 1995.

31. Carol Williams, *New York Times,* 28 March 1993; and Roger Cohen, *New York Times,* 7 March 1994, "In a Town 'Cleansed' of Muslims, Serb Church Will Crown the Deed."

32. See "The Extraordinary Session of the Holy Episcopal Synod of the Serbian Orthodox Church in Response to the False Accusations against the Serbian People in Bosnia-Herzegovina," *Pravoslavni misionar;* June 1992, pp. 250-51, cited by Norman Cigar, *Genocide in Bosnia,* p. 89; See also the "Memorandum of the Holy Episcopal Synod's session of May 14-20, 1992," *Pravoslavlje,* June 1, 1992, p. 2, in Cigar, *Genocide in Bosnia,* p. 78. Cigar's book offers the most detailed investigation available of the role of the Serbian Orthodox Church in the Bosnian genocide.

33. Srpska Republika News Agency (SRNA), 97-10-16; Agence France Presse October 16, 1997, "Sixty Serb intellectuals plead for Radovan Karadi, " The account by SRNA (Serbian Republic News Agency) states that His Holiness, Patriarch of the Serbs, Pavle, gave his blessing for the Declaration, signed by sixty intellectuals. Fourteen members of the Serb Academy of Science and Art

(SANU) were among the signatories who wanted to "inform domestic and international public of truth, of maintaining of the international legal order and recognition of the Serbian people as an equal member of the international community." Cf. *Naa Borba,* October 18, 1997. Translation reposted from Tribunal Watch; the Serbian original can be found at the following web address: (http://206.14.50.15/arhiva/Okt97/1810/1810_20.htm) *Naa Borba,* October 18, 1997. The language of the declaration was picked up and broadcast by Radio Sveti Jovan (Radio St. John) in Pale, a station backed by the Serb Orthodox Church. See the January 16th NATO/UNHCR joint press conference in Sarajevo, where spokesman Alex Ivanko commented upon the broadcast, which also praised the allegedly persecuted Dr. Karadi, indicted on multiple counts of genocide, as a "man of Christ."

34. For the Vitez and Celibii trials, see the reports from Tribunal Update, for the period from September 1997 to March 1998. Tribunal Update reports can be found at: http://www.demon.co.uk/iwpr. The reports are a service of The Institute for War & Peace Reporting (IWPR).

35. When the militant nationalist and author of anti-Muslim hate tracts, Vuk Drakovi, finally found the atrocities in Bosnia committed by Serb militias even too much for him to bear and criticized the "ethnic cleansing" of Trebinje, he was attacked by Serbian Orthodox Bishop Atanasije as a traitor.

36. András Riedlmayer, *Killing Memory: Bosnia's Cultural Heritage and Its Destruction* (Haverford: Community of Bosnia Foundation, 1994); A. Riedlmayer, "The War on People and the War on Culture," *The New Combat,* Autumn, 1994: pp.16-19; B. Bollag, "Rebuilding Bosnia's Library," *The Chronicle of Higher Education* (January 13, 1995): A35-A37; *Warchitecture* (Sarajevo, OKO – graphic-publishing house, 1994); Karen Detling, "Eternal Silence: The Destruction of Cultural Property in Yugoslavia," *Maryland Journal of International Law and Trade* 17 (Spring 1993): 41-74. See also the essay by the Serbian architect who served as mayor of Belgrade 1982-86 and was kept under house arrest for his opposition to radical Serb nationalism: Bogdan Bogdanovi, "Murder of the City," *New York Review of Books* Vol. 51, No.10 (27 May 1993), p. 20. For a survey of Bosnian artistic monuments before their systematic destruction, see M. Filipovi, ed. *The Art in Bosnia-Herzegovina (The Art Treasures of Bosnia and Herzegovina),* (Sarajevo: Svjetlost, 1987); and M. Filipovi, ed. *Yugoslavia,* (Sarajevo: Svjetlost, 1990).

37. Robert Kaplan, *Balkan Ghosts: a Journey Through History* (New York: St. Martin's Press, 1993), and Rebecca West, *Black Lamb and Gray Falcon* (New York: Viking Press, 1941). For an excellent analysis of the influence of Rebecca West on Western reporting of the Bosnia tragedy, see Brian Hall, "Rebecca West's War," *The New Yorker,* April 15, 1996, pp. 74-83. For his caricature of Bosnian Muslims Kaplan drew on material from West and also from Joseph Brodsky's essay "Reflections (Byzantium)," *The New Yorker,* Oct. 28, 1985, p. 47, reflection number 9. See also reflections number 23, 44, 33, and 43. Brodsky's reflections supplied the vital metaphors of filth used by Kaplan in his depiction, metaphors that fit well the Serbian religious nationalist desire for cleansing.

38. Although Kaplan's work represents an extreme of ethnoreligious caricature, stereotypes are common in U.S. policy debates over the Balkans. Thus the Foreign Policy Research Institute of Philadelphia, a group that publishes widely in op-ed columns, distributed an address by Robert Strausz-Hupe, the institute's founder and president emeritus, defining the Serbs, Croats, and Muslims as

peoples, and then declaring that "These are three groups destined by their own inclinations to tear at each other without mercy and without any regard for the rules, except of course, the rule of superior force." See Robert Strausz-Hupe, "Bosnia; a Summing Up," FPRI, 11 February 1998.

39. "Bat Ye'or" is the poetic pseudonym ("Daughter of the Nile") taken by Gisele Littman, an emigrant from Egypt living now in Switzerland. The late Jacques Ellul was a French Protestant theologian and social critic. See Bat Ye'or, *The Dhimmi: Jews and Christians under Islam* (Madison: Fairleigh Dickinson University Press, 1985), translated by David Maisel, Paul Fenton, and David Littman, with a preface by Jacques Ellul, first published as *Le Dhimmi: Profil de l'opprimé en Orient et en Afrique du Nord depuis la conquête arabe* (Paris: Edition Anthropos, 1980). Bat Ye'or, *The Decline of Eastern Christianity under Islam: From Jihad to Dhimmitude, Seventh-Twentieth Century*, with a preface by Jacques Ellul, translated from the French by Mirian Kochan and David Littman (Madison: Fairleigh Dickinson University Press, 1996), first published as *Les Chrétientés d'orient entre jihâd et dhimmitude. VIIe-XXe siècle* (Les Éditions du Cerf, Paris, 1991).

40. See Jacques Ellul's preface to *The Decline of Eastern Christianity Under Islam:*

> It will probably be said that every religion in its expanding phase carries the risks of war, that history records hundreds of religious wars and it is now a commonplace to make this connection. But it is, in fact, "passion"— it concerns mainly a fact which it would be easy to demonstrate does not correspond to the fundamental message of the religion. This disjuncture is obvious for Christianity. In Islam, however, *jihad* is a religious obligation. It forms part of the duties that the believer must fulfill; it is Islam's *normal* path to expansion [emphasis Ellul's]. (pp. 18-19)

One could argue that "passion" does correspond to the fundamental message of Christianity and, in the case of Bosnia, it was a particular presentation of the passion of Christ and the passion of Lazar, a presentation commonly called the "Serbian Golgotha," that anchored the ideology of "ethnic cleansing" for Serb religious nationalists. But, just as Islam is not fated always and everywhere to interpret *jihad* as aggression and war, so Christianity is not always and everywhere fated to interpret the passion as a pretext for the extermination of those allegedly responsible for it, despite the tragic examples of such interpretations in the past. If Christianity and Islam are viewed as unchanging and incapable of change, then indeed, the generalizations made against Islam by Ellul and Bat Ye'or would also apply to Christianity, and both religions would be reduced to vehicles of war and violence.

41. For one exposé of the fallacies in the work of Bat Ye'or, see Vera Basch Moreen, review of *The Dhimmi*, in *Middle East Studies Association Bulletin* 20 (1986), pp. 62-64.

42. Richard John Neuhaus, "The Public Square," *First Things* 76 (October 1997), pp. 75-93.

43. Bat Ye'or, *Decline*, pp. 258-59. Jovan Cviji, *La Péninsule balkanique: Géographie humaine* (Paris: Armand Colin, 1918).

44. See Samuel ha-Nagid, *Selected poems of Shmuel HaNagid* , translated from the Hebrew by Peter Cole (Princeton: Princeton University Press, 1996); Ross Brann, *The Compunctious Poet : Cultural Ambiguity and Hebrew Poetry in Muslim Spain* (Baltimore : Johns Hopkins University Press, 1991); and Raymond Scheindlin, *Wine, Women, & Death : Medieval Hebrew Poems on the Good Life* (Philadelphia: Jewish Publication Society, 1986).

45. See David Rohde, *Endgame: The Betrayal and Fall of Srebrenica* (New York : Farrar, Straus and Giroux, 1997). See also The Report of the Secretary General Pursuant to General Assembly Resolution 53/55 (1998): Srebrenica Report, par. 467-468:

> 467. The tragedy that took place following the fall of Srebrenica is shocking for two reasons. It is shocking, first and foremost, for the magnitude of the crimes committed. Not since the horrors of World War II had Europe witnessed massacres on this scale. The mortal remains of close to 2,500 men and boys have been found on the surface, in mass grave sites and in secondary burial sites. Several thousand more men are still missing, and there is every reason to believe that additional burial sites, many of which have been probed but not exhumed, will reveal the bodies of thousands more men and boys. The great majority of those who were killed were not killed in combat: the exhumed bodies of the victims show large numbers had their hands bound, or were blindfolded, or were shot in the back or the back of the head. Numerous eyewitness accounts, now well corroborated by forensic evidence, attest to scenes of mass slaughter of unarmed victims.
>
> 468. The fall of Srebrenica is also shocking because the enclave's inhabitants believed that the authority of the United Nations Security Council, the presence of UNPROFOR peacekeepers, and the might of NATO air power, would ensure their safety. Instead, the Serb forces ignored the Security Council, pushed aside the UNPROFOR troops, and assessed correctly that air power would not be used to stop them. They overran the safe area of Srebrenica with ease, and then proceeded to depopulate the territory within 48 hours. Their leaders then engaged in high-level negotiations with representatives of the international community while their forces on the ground executed and buried thousands of men and boys within a matter of days.

   The full report can be found at http://www.haverford.edu/relg/sells/reports/ UNsrebrenicareport.htm.

46. Zoran Djindjic, the leader of the Democratic Party, was a supporter of the "ethnic cleansing" in Bosnia. Vuk Draskovic, the leader of the Serbian Renewal Party, was one of the original instigators of the movement of ethnoreligious hate in Bosnia and his party has long fervently supported the expulsion of Kosovar Albanians from Kosovo. In addition, Vojislav Seselj, arguably the most popular politician in Serbia, who is believed to have defeated Milosevic's candidates for president of Serbia but to have been cheated out of his victory by vote fraud, was an active leader of the most notorious militias in Bosnia as well as a supporter of systematic annihilation of the Kosovar Albanian community. See the Kosovo program of Seselj's Serbian Radical Party posted at http://www.haverford.edu/relg/sells/reports.htm. For the role of Draskovic, see Norman Cigar, *Genocide in Bosnia* (College Station: Texas A & M University Press, 1995).

47. The genuine opposition in Serbia, although marginalized by the major actors in society, has been consistently courageous and honest. For a brilliant analysis of the radicalization of Serbian society and the widespread complicity in "ethnic cleansing," see Natasha Govedic, "The Forging of Schizophrenia: An Interview with Zarana Papic," *Zarez* (Zagreb), 11 May 2000. Zarana Papic is a prominent Serbian feminist and member of the Belgrade circle Women in Black. A translation of the interview is available at http://www.bosnia.org.uk.

PART II

SURVIVAL: RESCUERS AND VICTIMS

– Chapter 9 –

THE ABSORPTION OF ARMENIAN WOMEN AND CHILDREN INTO MUSLIM HOUSEHOLDS AS A STRUCTURAL COMPONENT OF THE ARMENIAN GENOCIDE

Ara Sarafian

"... [T]he orders from Constantinople were that no Armenian man was to escape. But the government was not so determined in its efforts to exterminate the women ..., ... Some women and girls did so give themselves up and saved their lives by entering Moslem harems."[1]

Introduction

Most Armenians in the Ottoman Empire were murdered in 1915. In 1916 two British authors articulated the first academic thesis on the systematic nature of these killings: first, Armenian conscripts were liquidated in the Ottoman army; then, Armenian community leaders were rounded up and killed; finally, the remaining Armenian population was "deported." These deportations entailed forced marches accompanied by deprivations, individual killings, and general massacres.[2] Yet, the evidence at hand shows that a large number of Armenians were also "abducted," "carried off," or "converted to Islam" during this period. This paper argues that the fate of this latter class of Armenians was part of the same genocidal calculus as those who were murdered.[3]

The absorption of Armenian women and children into Muslim households was a genocidal act as defined by Article 2 of the United Nations' Convention on the Prevention and Punishment of the Crime of Genocide (12 January 1951). According to this Convention, genocide is defined as any one (or combination) of the following acts "committed with the intent to destroy, in whole or in part, a nation, ethnical, racial or religious group, as such: (a) killing members of the group; (b) causing serious bodily harm to members of the group; (c) deliberately inflicting on the group conditions of life calculated to bring about its physical destruction in whole or in part; (d) imposing measures intended to prevent births within the group; (e) forcibly transferring children of the group to another group."[4] The Armenian genocide of 1915 was composed of a combination of above acts. Deportations were the most visible aspects of the Armenian Genocide, but they were not only a means of killing a large number of Armenians through forced marches, starvation, and outright massacres. Deportations were also a means of weakening certain elements of these convoys, invariably young women and children, for absorption into Muslim households. These young women and children were rendered prime candidates for absorption into Muslim households after they were isolated from their families and terrorized during the forced marches and executions of their elders.

A number of recent works have looked at the fate of Armenians who were not killed in 1915 but transferred into Muslim households.[5] These studies have tended to look at the motivation of individual Muslim hosts in adopting their charges, the treatment afforded to these victims, and the effects of these years on the future lives of survivors. However, there has not been a sustained discussion of the scale, formal context, and manner in which tens of thousands of Armenians were transferred and absorbed into Muslim households. Today, the archival testimonies of American consular and missionary observers, as well as Armenian survivors themselves, can be used effectively to construct four categories of how Armenians were transferred and absorbed into Muslim households after the summer of 1915.[6] These were (1) "voluntary" conversion of individuals in the initial stages of the 1915 persecutions; (2) selection of individual Armenians by individual Muslim hosts for absorption into Muslim households; (3) distribution of Armenians to Muslim families by government agencies; (4) the use of Ottoman government sponsored orphanages as a direct means of assimilating Armenian children.

Mass Conversions: An Overview (1915-16)

The number of Armenians who were converted to Islam can be illustrated by the more impressionistic accounts of well placed commentators in different regions of the Empire. If one takes such estimates seriously, between 5 and 10 percent of Ottoman Armenians were converted and absorbed in Muslim households in the course of 1915. This translates to a figure of between one hundred thousand to two hundred thousand people. The more qualitative statements, along with these general appraisals, point out that the bulk of converts were women of child-bearing age and children. Dr. Clark, for example, who was an American missionary in Sivas, reported that around 1,000 of 25,000 Armenians had become Muslim in the summer of 1915 to evade "deportations" organized by the Ottoman government.[7] Further to the north, Dr. J. K. Marden stated that 1,500 Armenians converted while 11,500 were deported from Marsovan.[8] Dr. George E. White, the president of Anatolia College (Marsovan), gave a similar figure for the Marsovan deportees (1,200 converts). He qualified this number as mostly women and children.[9] American consular officials in the interior of the Ottoman Empire also recorded similar results regarding the destruction of Armenians, as well as the mass conversion and absorption of women and children into Muslim households. In Samsoun, on the Black Sea coast, Consular Agent William Peter reported that all Armenians were deported from that city, except for 150 families who had become Muslim.[10] Leslie Davis, the American consul at Harpoot, stated that thousands of Armenians were converted and kept in Muslim households in his consular region.[11] The American consul at Aleppo, Jesse Jackson, reported that the last three hundred to four hundred Armenian families in Aintab were given a clear choice between conversion and deportation.[12] A year later, in a private letter to his wife, Jackson reiterated that thousands of Armenians who had been spared the first wave of deportations were forced to become Muslims or again face deportation.[13] Charles Allen, American Consular Agent in Adrianople, concluded that Armenians were being forcibly converted to Islam as a "method of securing the disappearance of the Armenian race."[14]

Regarding the mechanics of absorption, the targeted individuals were given new names, converted to Islam, and absorbed as members of individual families. Henry Vartanian's widowed mother and four siblings, for example, who were protected by a Turkish friend, were required to go to a judge in Sivas city council, renounce their Christian faith, and declare their adherence to Islam. Once their conversion was confirmed, they were given new names, registered with the authorities, and issued new identity papers. Henry Vartanian (aged 9) thus became Abdul Rahman Oghlu Assad. He was circumcized by a Muslim cleric and started to go to a Turkish school.[15]

The Children of Trebizond[16] and Leon Surmelian's Story

The Ottoman government was the controlling center in the destruction of Armenians in 1915. The Armenian population of Trebizond, for example, comprised of around one thousand households,[17] was destroyed within a matter of a few weeks. The main organiser of the genocide in this town was Nail Bey, who was sent from Constantinople to supervise the annihilation of Armenians.[18] The bulk of Trebizond Armenians were deported in five convoys on July 1, 3, 5, 7, and 18, 1915.[19] According to Oscar Heizer, the American consul at Trebizond, most of these Armenians were killed by their guards shortly after leaving Trebizond.[20] Nail Bey was also responsible for closing an orphanage set up by the governor of Trebizond, Jemal Azmi Bey, and the Greek archbishop (Krisantos). This orphanage had been set up to save Armenian children from deportation (*i.e.*, Armenian girls under fifteen, boys under ten, and a number of older caretakers).[21] By July 6, 1915, the orphanage housed approximately three thousand children under the supervision of a mixed Greek and Turkish committee.[22] The local American school was also turned into an orphanage and included 300 Armenian children and infants.[23] These children were left behind by their parents who were marched away and killed in the July convoys.[24] According to Oscar Heizer, all orphanages were closed down on the orders of Nail Bey. Some of the children were drowned at sea; some boys were sent to farmers at Platana; a number of the older women caretakers were turned into concubines in Trebizond; and some children were distributed to the general Muslim population.[25] Heizer related the fate of several former pupils of the American Mission School in Trebizond in detail. These children were placed with Muslim families and assimilated as Muslim Turks within a matter of a few weeks.[26]

Leon Surmelian, a native of Trebizond, provides a detailed account of his experiences. His narrative is one example of the manner in which thousands of Armenian children were separated from their parents and dispersed to Muslim households. Surmelian was an eight-year-old child of a well-to-do Armenian family from Trebizond. When the Ottoman authorities announced the imminent deportation of Armenians from that city, his parents placed him in an American orphanage (probably the one mentioned above).[27] When this orphanage was closed, by the same authorities who despatched Armenian adults to their deaths, Leon was taken away by a Greek friend of the Surmelian family. However, the authorities sought him out and the Greek lawyer was ordered to hand Leon over to them. Leon was placed in a house with hundreds of other Armenian children and women caretakers. After a few days these women and children were taken to the Armenian prelacy building in Trebizond where they were joined by children from other orphanages (which were presumably closed by the government). The following day, these children had their names read off an official list, their numbers counted by a commissioner of police, and they were marched out of the city. The convoy was much abused by its escort and several members of the party were killed because they could not keep up with the rest. Two days later, when the convoy reached Jevizlik, the boys were separated from the women and girls, who proceeded on their march. The boys were then exhibited before the local government building by the sub-governor (kaimakam) of Jevizlik and adopted by ordinary Muslims.[28]

Leon was adopted by an irregular soldier on the second day, and the secretary at the sub-governor's office recorded Leon's adoption. One of Leon's friends, Michael, was adopted by a coffeehouse owner in Jevizlik, while another, Nurikhan, was adopted by a local scribe. Michael's new father wanted his adopted son to disassociate himself from other adopted Armenians, forget his past, and become a Turk. Nurikhan's adoptive father did not share the same sentiment; he had adopted Nurikhan simply to save the boy's life. Leon, after his guardian entrusted him to a temporary caretaker, took advantage of the situation, returned to the sub-governor, and found a better family to adopt him! His new guardian was Osman Agha, a wealthy merchant, who gave him a Muslim name, Jemal, and took him to his village. Leon was well received by Osman Agha's family and the village population, but was soon alarmed when he was informed of his imminent conversion to Islam. He escaped from Jevizlik and found shelter with local Greeks.[29]

It is significant that the Ottoman authorities, who were responsible for the deportation of Armenian adults in Trebizond, were also responsible for the "special" treatment of children like Leon

Surmelian. These same authorities were obviously implementing a single policy of destruction. At each stage, as the state implemented a complex deportation and absorption program, Ottoman officials and policemen kept accounts of people in their charge. Ottoman bureaucrats compiled specific lists of people for each deportation convoy; Ottoman policemen ensured that these individuals were assembled in the deportation convoys as planned; Ottoman gendarmes marched these deportees out of Trebizond. These same gendarmes apparently had the authority to kill their charges, as a matter of discipline, if not policy. Those killed were, presumably, also accounted for by other officials further down deportation routes. In the case of Surmelian, the gendarmes passed him and a number of other Armenian boys, to the sub-governor of Jevizlik and his assistants, who publicly scattered the boys to Muslim families, keeping a record of their activities.

Consul Leslie Davis: Picking Armenians

The American Consul at Harpoot (Kharpert), Leslie Davis, also witnessed the passage of thousands of Armenian deportees through his consular region in the summer of 1915. Harpoot was on a major artery of the so-called deportation routes to the deserts of Syria. Some of his observations concerned the condition of Armenian deportees arriving from further north. Davis noted that there were no men to speak of in these convoys, and the remaining members were much abused, starved, and exhausted.

> There were parties of exiles arriving from time to time throughout the summer of 1915, some of them numbering several thousand. The first one, who arrived in July, camped in a large open field on the outskirts of the town, where they were exposed to the burning sun. All of them were in rags and many of them were almost naked. They were emaciated, sick, diseased, filthy, covered with dirt and vermin, resembling animals far more than human beings. They had been driven along for many weeks like herds of cattle, with little to eat, and most of them had nothing except the rags on their backs. When the scant rations which the Government furnished were brought for distribution the guards were obliged to beat them back with clubs, so ravenous were they. There were few men among them, most of the men having been killed by the Kurds before their arrival in Harput. Many of the women and children also had been killed and very many others had died on the way from sickness and exhaustion. Of those who had started, only a small portion were still alive and they were rapidly dying.[30]

The gendarmes leading these deportation convoys were clearly not accountable for the condition of their charges. While they did not allow Armenians to leave deportation convoys alive, or to receive external aid from American missionaries nearby, they did allow Muslims to approach these same convoys to pick out and take away women and children.[31] Davis stated that many Turks from Harpoot even visited deportation convoys with doctors in order to select Armenians ("the prettiest girls") for their purposes.[32] In one case which Davis investigated, Siranoush Hoghgroghian from Erzinjan was found living with a Turkish officer in Harpoot. Davis noted that Siranoush was "well developed for her age and was a comparatively good looking girl but was beginning to show the marks of the life she was living. Young as she was, we noticed that she appeared to be pregnant." She was twelve or thirteen years of age. Davis confirmed that Siranoush's case was one of thousands of similar instances that had occurred "where no missionary or foreign official could do much to help these unfortunate people."[33] Again, one can discern from Consul Davis's reports that deportations were not simply carried out to exterminate every Armenian in the Ottoman Empire, but also to allow a large number of individuals to be absorbed as Muslims.

Stella H. Loughridge: Farming Out at Cesarea, 1916

The Ottoman government's assimilationist policy was still being implemented in the summer of 1916, a year after the main deportations had started. The case of Talas is a good example. Here, a number of Armenian women and children, who were allowed to remain with American missionaries in 1915, were sought out and publicly victimized by government officials. Stella H. Loughridge, an American missionary in Talas, recorded the fate of a few Armenian women and children who were left in her care. Once more, Ottoman state officials gave Armenian women and girls the option of deportation or conversion. The authorities closed down the American girls' school in Talas and moved the students to a temporary government orphanage in the city.[34] Then the older girls and women were pressured to convert to Islam or be deported. The women who converted were dispersed in surrounding villages.[35] Several were reportedly married off to Turks. Children belonging to these older women were put into Muslim orphanages and given away for adoption. The two older children of Toona Mihran Effendi's wife were placed in a Turkish orphanage: One child was subsequently adopted by the civil governor of Cesarea, and the other by a prominent Turkish doctor of that city. The mother was allowed to keep her youngest child, an infant, with her.[36] After Ottoman officials disposed of the older Armenian women they proceeded to pressure the younger schoolgirls to convert or be deported. The Talas example shows the continuity in the Ottoman government's genocidal policy even a year after the summer of 1915. The state remained persistent in implementing such policies and seeing such policies through.

Harriet J. Fischer: Government Orphanages

The Ottoman government also organized special orphanages for the direct assimilation of Armenian children under its auspices. These orphanages, unlike the aforementioned temporary holding points in Trebizond and Cesarea, were used as fixed locations for the assimilation of Armenian children. Harriet Fisher reported that one such orphanage had nearly 1,000 Armenian children and was run by Halide Hanoum (who later became the Turkish nationalist author Halide Edip Adivar). Halide Hanoum confided to Ms. Fischer that the children in her orphanage were Armenian and were all converted, given Muslim names, and assimilated as Muslims.[37] We have very little information on these orphanages from American sources because they were located in areas where American consuls and missionaries would not ordinarily come across them. However, there are accounts by Armenians who, young as they were, survived such orphanages and narrated their experiences in later years. Yeranouhi Simonian, for example, came from an Armenian family from Adana. Her family was deported to a concentration camp at Ras ul Ain before being exterminated. However, Yeranouhi was taken to a mobile orphanage containing 250 Armenian and Muslim children. Her narrative of orphanage life recounts the care taken to look after the inmates, and the persistent attempts of the orphanage authorities to assimilate the Armenian children as Muslims. They were all converted, given Muslim names, and expected to conform to their new surroundings.[38] The Ottoman government's attempts to take direct charge of Armenian children and to assimilate them in government-run orphanages was the most direct example of the state's assimilationist policies.

Conclusion

While a lot more work still needs to be done, this paper has already cited sufficient evidence—almost all from American consular and missionary sources in the Ottoman Empire—that there was a mass transfer of Armenians into Muslim households in 1915, and that this transfer was a major element in the genocidal designs of the Ottoman state. This can be seen in the scale on which Armenians were absorbed into Muslim communities, as well as the geographical prevalence, chronological scope, and the agency of Ottoman officials in managing these transfers.

The Ottoman central authorities organized the destruction of Armenian social structures in the early stages of the genocide (*e.g.*, through the murder of young men, community leaders, and family heads) and proceeded with a deportation program which not only led to the death of most Armenians in the Ottoman Empire, but also yielded ideal candidates for absorption into Muslim households. The religious conversion of these remnants, invariably young women and children, was the final step in their absorption into the general Muslim population. Muslim families which acted as guardians and participated in the conversion of Armenians at this time, also acted as agents for the Ottoman central authorities and their genocidal designs.

At the end of World War I, between the capitulation of the Ottoman Empire and the rise of a new Turkish nationalist movement under Mustafa Kemal Ataturk, a number of American and Armenian organizations made a concerted effort to collect as many of these Armenian orphans as possible. During this brief interim, less than 20,000 Armenian people were collected from different parts of the Ottoman Empire.[39] There was much resistance to this exercise and some areas never yielded a single Armenian woman or child. The vast majority of the victims of the genocide were lost forever in the aftermath of WWI.

Notes

1. Rev. Riggs, *Days of Tragedy in Armenia: Personal Experiences in Harpoot, 1915-17,* Ann Arbor: Gomidas Institute, 1997, p. 98.

2. James Bryce and Arnold Toynbee, *The Treatment of the Armenians in the Ottoman Empire, 1915-16: Documents Presented to Viscount Grey of Falloden by Viscount Bryce,* London, 1916, and, *Key to Names of Persons and Places Withheld from Publication in the Original Edition of "TheTreatment of Armenians in the Ottoman Empire, 1915-16: Documents Presented to Viscount Grey of Falloden by Viscount Bryce" Miscellaneous No. 31* (London: Sir Joseph Causton and Son, 1916)

3. Regarding the premeditated nature of the genocide of Ottoman Armenians, see Vahakn N. Dadrian "The Armenian Genocide and the Pitfalls of a 'Balanced' Analysis in *Armenian Forum: A Journal of Contemporary Affairs* (Princeton, N.J., Number 2, Summer 1998), pp. 73-130.

4. See Leo Kuper, *Genocide: Its Political Use in the Twentieth Century,* New Haven: Yale University Press, 1982, pp. 210-14.

5. Donald E. Miller, and Lorna Touryan-Miller, *Survivors: An Oral History of the Armenian Genocide* (Berkeley: University of California Press, 1993); Donald E. Miller, and Lorna Touryan-Miller, "Women and Children of the Armenian Genocide" in *The Armenian Genocide: History, Politics, Ethics* (Richard G. Hovannisian, ed.), (New York: St. Martin's Press, 1992, pp. 152-172; Richard G. Hovannisian, "Intervention and Shades of Altruism During the Armenian Genocide" in *The Armenian Genocide: History, Politics, Ethics* (Richard Hovannisian, ed.), St. Martin's Press, 1992, pp. 173-207; Elise Sanassarian, "Gender Distinction in the Genocidal Process: A Preliminary Study of the Armenian Case," *Holocaust and Genocide Studies,* Volume 4, No. 4, pp. 449-461, 1989.

6. The present paper has been based on a large number of sources (see below), though we have limited citations in this article mainly to a select number of key American sources. For American consular records, see State Department, Record Group 59, *The Internal Affairs of Turkey 1910-1929,* National Archives, Washington D.C. (hereafter cited as RG 59)and RG 84, Record of Foreign Service Posts of the Department of State, Consular Posts, National Archives, Washington, D.C. For American missionary archives, see the American Board of Commissioners for Foreign Missions, Houghton Library, Harvard University (hereafter cited ABC). Memoirs consulted for this paper: Kerop Bedoukian, *The Urchin: An Armenian's Escape,* [c. 1977]; Elizabeth Caraman, *Daughter of the Euphrates* (New York: Harper & Bros. Pub., 1939); Khoren Davidson, *Odyssey of an Armenian of Zeitoun* (New York: Vantage Press, 1985); B. Donabedian, (ed.), *Tsayn Darabelots* (Paris: Hagop Diwrabian Printing Press, 1922); Elise Hagopian-Taft, *Rebirth* (New York: New Age Publishers, 1981); Srpoohi Christine Jafferian, *Winds of Destiny: An Immigrant Girl's Odyssey* (Boston, Mass.: Armenian Heritage Press, 1993); Misag Khralian, *Palahovid. Hayreni Hishadagaran* (Sofia: Masis, 1938); Dirouhi Kouymjian-Highgaz, *Refugee Girl* (Watertown, Mass.: Baikar Publiations, 1985); Aurora Mardiganian, *Ravished Armenia* (American Committee for Armenian and Syrian Relief, 1918. Facimile republication New York: J.C. & A.L. Fawcett, 1990); Ramela Martin, *Out of Darkness* (Boston, Mass.: Zoryan Institute, 1989); John Minassian, *Many Hills Yet to Climb: Memoirs of an Armenian Deportee* (Santa Barbara, CA: Jim Cook Publisher, 1986); Anna G. Mirakian, *Verker ou Tsaver* (Beirut: Armenian Catholicosate of Cilicia, 1960); Bertha

Nakashian-Ketchian, *In the Shadow of the Fortress: The Genocide Remembered* (Boston, Mass.: Zoryan Institute, 1988); Khachadoor Pilibosian, *They Called Me Mustafa* (Watertown, Mass.: Ohan Press, 1992); K. Siwrmenian, *Yerznga* (Cairo: Sahag-Mesrob Press, 1947); Yeranouhi A. Simonian, *Im Koghkotas* (Beirut: Armenian Catholicosate of Cilicia, 1960); Leon Z. Surmelian, *I Ask You Ladies and Gentlemen* (New York: E. P. Dutton & Co. Inc. 1945); Douglas Y. Haig, *Armenian Resolve to Survive Turkish Genocide*, [no info.: 1997].

7. Report by Dr. C. E. Clark of Sivas, dated Constantinople, May 31, 1916, in Philip Hoffman to Secretary of State, dated American Embassy, Constantinople, 12 June, 1916, RG 59, 867.4016/288.

8. Statement by Dr. J. K. Marden of Marsovan [no date] in Maurice Francis Egan to Secretary of State, dated American Embassy, Copenhagen, July 32, 1916, RG 59, 867.4016/292.

9. George E. White, *Report on Turkish Atrocities in Marsovan*, 4/10/1918, James L. Barton (comp.) Ara Sarafian (ed.), *"Turkish Atrocities:" Statements of American Missionaries on the Destruction of Christian Communities in Ottoman Turkey, 1915-1917* (Ann Arbor: Gomidas Institute, 1998), document number 7.

10. William Peter to Ambassador Morgenthau, dated Samsoun, July 10, 1915, Papers of Henry Morgenthau (Sr.), Library of Congress (Manuscripts Division), Washington, D.C., Reel 7/619; National Archives, Washington, D.C., Record Group 84, Records of Foreign Service Posts of the Department of State, Consular Posts: Samsoun, Turkey, Miscellaneous Documents, c49, c8. 1, 1915, Box 5. Also see Raymond Kévorkian and Ara Sarafian, "Documents consulaires americains sur la deportation des armeniens de Samsoun pendant la Premiere Guerre mondiale" in *Revue d'histoire armenienne contemporaine: annales de la bibliotheque Nubar de UGAB*, (Paris) vol. 1, 195, pp. 101-127.

11. *Davis, American Consul, Formerly at Harput, Turkey, on the work of the Consulate at Harput Since the Beginning of the Present War* (dated New York, February 9, 1918) in Ara Sarafian (comp.), *United States Official Documents on the Armenian Genocide: The Central Lands* (Boston, Mass.: Armenian Review, 1995), p. 80.

12. Jesse B. Jackson to Henry Morgenthau, report dated Aleppo, February 8, 1916 in Ara Sarafian, *United States Official Documents on the Armenian Genocide: The Lower Euphrates* (Boston, Mass.: Armenian Review, 1993), document number 117.

13. Jesse B. Jackson to Mrs. Jackson, private letter dated Aleppo, September 3, 1916 in Ara Sarafian, *United States Official Documents on the Armenian Genocide: The Lower Euphrates* (Boston, Mass.: Armenian Review, 1993), document number 119.

14. Charles E. Allen to G. Bie Ravndal, report dated Adrianople, March 18, 1916 in Ara Sarafian (comp.), *United States Official Documents on the Armenian Genocide: The Peripheries* (Boston, Mass.: Armenian Review, 1994), document number 39.

15. Henry Vartanian, quoted in Donald E. Miller, and Lorna Touryan-Miller, *Survivors: An Oral History of the Armenian Genocide* (University of California Press, 1993), p. 146.

16. For a general account of the Armenian Genocide at Trebizond, see Suakjian, Kevork Yeghia, *Genocide in Trebizond: A Case Study of Armeno-Turkish*

Relations During the First World War, Ph.D. thesis (Political Science), University of Nebraska (Lincoln), 1981.

17. According to the 1912-13 census of the Armenian Patriarchate of Constantinople, the city of Trebizond and its environs, including 36 villages inhabited by Armenians, had a combined Armenian population of 20,158 Armenians. Raymond Kévorkian and Paul B. Paboudjian, *Les Arméniens dans lémpire ottoman a la veille du génocide* (Les Éditions d'Art et d'Histoire ARHIS: Paris, 1992), pp. 57, 187-191.

18. Oscar Heizer Heizer, reports number 14, 15, 18, 24 in Ara Sarafian (comp.), *United States Official Documents on the Armenian Genocide: The Peripheries* (Boston, Mass.: Armenian Review, 1994). Both [Yenibahcheli] Nail Bey and Jemal Azmi Bey were condemned to death by an Ottoman court martial on 22 May 1919. See Krieger (Krikor Gergerian), *Yozgadi Hayasbanoutian Vaverakragan Badmoutiun* (Documentary history of the Armenocide in Yozgat) (New York, 1980), p. 251.

19. Oscar Heizer to Ambassador Morgtenthau, despatches dated June 10, July 10, and July 28 in Ara Sarafian (comp.), *United States Official Documents on the Armenian Genocide: The Peripheries* (Boston, Mass.: Armenian Review, 1994), reports number 14, 15, 18. Suakjian, *idem., p*p. 132-136.

20. Oscar Heizer, reports number 18, 24, *idem*. According to Suakjian, 25 percent of Trebizond Armenians survived the genocide. See Suakjian, *idem*, p. 141.

21. Oscar Heizer Heizer, *idem.*, report number 24; Kevork Yeghia Suakjian, p. 133.

22. Oscar Heizer, *idem.*, reports number 9, 18.

23. Oscar Heizer, *idem.*, report number 9.

24. Oscar Heizer, *idem.*, report number 9.

25. Oscar Heizer, *idem.*, reports number 14, 15, 18, 24. Not all children were prepared for absorption. Most were actually killed in groups. Heizer states (in report number 24) that "Many of the children were loaded into boats and taken out to sea and thrown overboard. I myself saw where 16 bodies were washed ashore and buried by a Greek woman near the Italian Monastery." Lieutenant Said Ahmed Moukhtar Ba'aj, who was in Trebizond in July 1915, also stated that: "The infants in the care of the American consul in Trebizond were taken away with the pretext that they were going to be sent to Sivas where an asylum had been prepared for them. They were taken out to sea in little boats. At some distance out, they were stabbed to death, put in sacks, and thrown into the sea. A few days later their little bodies were washed up on the shores of Trebizond." See British Foreign Office document number 371/2781 quoted by Christopher Walker, "British Source on the Armenian Massacres, 1915-16" in *The Crime of Silence: The Armenian Genocide*, The Permanent People's Tribunal, prefaced by Pierre Vidal-Naquet (London: Zed Books Ltd., 1985).

26. Oscar Heizer, *idem.*, report number 18.

27. Leon Z. Surmelian, *I Ask You Ladies and Gentlemen* (New York: E. P. Dutton & Co. Inc., 1945), pp. 67-68.

28. *Ibid*, pp. 68-79.

29. *Ibid*, pp. 81-88.

30. *Report of Leslie A. Davis, American Consul, Formerly at Harput, Turkey, on the work of the Consulate at Harput Since the Beginning of the Present War* (dated New York, February 9, 1918) in Ara Sarafian (comp.), *United States Official Documents on the Armenian Genocide: The Central Lands* (Boston, Mass.: Armenian Review, 1995), documents number 11, p. 79.

31. For descriptions of the condition of refugees passing by Harpoot (Kharpert) from the north, see Leslie Davis to Henry Morgenthau, dispatch dated Mamouret-ul-Aziz (Harput), July 11, 1915 in Ara Sarafian, *idem.*, documents number 5 and 11; Rev. Henry H. Riggs, *Days of Tragedy in Armenia: Personal Experiences in Harpoot 1915-17* (Ann Arbor, Mich.: Gomidas Institute, 1997), pp. 145-153; Mary W. Riggs "Report on the Turkish Atrocities. The Treatment of Armenians by Turks in Harpoot," *in* James L. Barton (comp.) Ara Sarafian (ed.), *"Turkish Atrocities:" Statements of American Missionaries on the Destruction of Christian Communities in Ottoman Turkey, 1915-1917* (Ann Arbor: Gomidas Institute, 1998), document number 3; Dr. Tacy W. Atkinson, "Report on Turkish Atrocities in the Harpoot District," in James L. Barton (comp.), *idem.*, document number 4; Ruth A. Parmelee "Report on Turkish Atrocities. Massacre Conditions at Harpoot," in James L. Barton (comp.), *idem.*, document number 5; Isabelle Harley, "Report on Turkish Atrocities," in James L. Barton (comp.), *idem.*, document number 6.
32. *Report of Leslie A. Davis, American Consul, Formerly at Harput, Turkey, on the work of the Consulate at Harput Since the Beginning of the Present War* (dated New York, February 9, 1918), *idem.*, p. 79.
33. *Ibid*, p. 80.
34. See Stella N. Loughridge to James L. Barton report (October 16, 1917), dated Talas, June 12, 1916; *Statement of Happenings in Turkey of Stella N. Loughridge, Missionary of A.B.C.F.M. Stationed at Talas*, ABC 16.9.3/43/165. A second American missionary, Theda Phelps, gave similar details of this last remaining group of Armenians in the Talas region, see Theda Phelps to Keghani, letter dated Talas, June 12, 1916 in ABC 19.9.3/44/471. Also see Theda Phelps "dear friends letter" dated Talas, June 12, 1916, ABC 16.9.3/44/473.
35. Theda Phelps "dear friends letter" dated Talas, June 12, 1916, ABC 16.9.3/44/473. The distribution of Armenian women and children in Muslim villages is a common theme in many missionary accounts. We have already noted Leon Surmelian's experience in Jevizlik. One could find similar examples elsewhere. Dr. Marden, for example, also reportedly stated that a number of Armenian women and children were distributed in the Angora vilayet in the summer of 1915. See Dr. William Dodd to Henry Morgenthau, letter dated Konia, May 6, 1915, in National Archives, RG 59, 867.4016/71 and Papers of Henry Morgenthau (Sr.), Library of Congress, Washington, D.C., Reel 7, pp. 557-558
36. See ABC 16.9.3/43/165; ABC 16.9.3/44/473
37. Harriet J. Fischer "Report on Turkish Atrocities. Conditions at Adana, Northwestern Syria," in James L. Barton (comp.), *idem.*, document number 16.
38. Yeranouhi A. Simonian, *Im Koghkotas* (Beirut: Armenian Catholicosate of Cilicia, 1960.)
39. Madteos M. Eblighatian, *Azkayin Khnamadroutiwn: Unthanour Deghegakir Arachin Vetsamya, 1 Mayis 1919–31 Hogdemper 1919*, Constantinople: M. Hovagimian Publication, 1920. Facimile republication, Lebanon: Armenian Catholicosate of Cilicia, 1985.

– Chapter 10 –

TRANSCENDING BOUNDARIES
Hungarian Roman Catholic Religious Women and the "Persecuted Ones"

Jessica A. Sheetz-Nguyen

Margit Slachta (1884-1974), Hungarian founder of the Roman Catholic female religious congregation the Society of the Sisters of Social Service, coupled zeal for social justice with religious convictions in rescue and relief efforts between 1939 and 1945 for Jewish families whom she called the "persecuted ones."[1] She protected Slovakian and Hungarian Jews with the assistance of her religious community and a large network of lay Catholic women spiritually associated with the Sisters of Social Service. She also collaborated with a circle of Jewish women, the Hungarian Jewish Welfare Bureau, and various relief agencies.[2] In the years immediately following the Second World War, she raised awareness of the considerable contribution of Protestant churches in rescue efforts. This suggests that she probably collaborated with their relief efforts as well.[3] The rescue efforts of Margit Slachta and the Sisters of Social Service provides a case study of an exceptional group of altruistic women. As women of the Church, they stretched the boundaries of their duties as Christians by interpreting the Gospel liberally and challenged government policies with regard to restrictive anti-Jewish legislation through the press and in public and clandestine activities.

Undoubtedly, the gulf between Judaism and Christianity, constantly reinforced over the centuries by the teachings and practices of the Roman Catholic and Protestant churches, poses a barrier to understanding the horrors of the Shoah, a Hebrew word signifying the "catastrophe" wrought by the destruction of European Jewry.[4] The debate surrounding the ways in which the Roman Catholic Church shirked or accepted responsibility for the Shoah frequently focuses on the lack of an outright public condemnation of the Nazi atrocities by Pius XII (1939-1958). Since the focus of the debate has been on the largely male hierarchy of the Church, few have explored the grassroots responses of women, particularly religious women, to Nazi atrocities.[5] Moreover, many have overlooked the important connections between the spiritual and communal powers imparted by life in a religious community and the social activism exhibited by religious women. This oversight is due in part to the fact that histories of women religious have been obscured by studies of the Roman Catholic Church hierarchy.[6] The following study focuses on religious women who, through their faith in God and their strong adherence to a tradition of Christian altruism, resolved to cross personal, social, political, and spatial boundaries without taking account of real threats to their own persons. Simultaneously, this study highlights the ways in which Jews or the "persecuted ones" crossed spiritual, social, and psychological boundaries in order to preserve human life. Transcendence of these boundaries would not have been necessary if antisemitism had not been part of the Nazi ideology. Nor would the transcendence have been possible if the groundwork for Christian social action had not been laid a quarter century earlier in Hungary by Margit Slachta.

Prologue to Social Justice Activities During the Shoah

Margit Slachta was born in Kassa, Hungary (Kisice, Slovakia) in 1884. As a young girl she left Hungary with her parents for the United States, where they lived for a short period before returning home.[7] She earned a secondary education degree in German and French languages from a Catholic training school in Kalosca. There she met Carlotta Koranyi, a Hungarian activist, who instilled in her a concern for the condition of working women and their children.[8] They met again in Berlin where both learned organizational skills for "collective action" based on "political fronts." After her professional training, Slachta formed the Union of Catholic Women, an organization that promoted the female franchise in Hungary.[9] As a result of her campaign work on behalf of the franchise, Slachta became the first woman elected to the Hungarian Parliament. In the

parliamentary chambers her speeches focused on the social conditions of women and children and state responsibility for their welfare.[10] Slachta's broadly based left-of-center political sympathies and
her practical training shaped her future political struggles and suc-
cesses and made her a widely known political figure in Hungary.[11]

Slachta contended that *Rerum Novarum*, the 1891 encyclical
issued by Pope Leo XIII (1878-1903), had inspired her to become
engaged in social issues.[12] She joined the Society of the Social Mission, a religious community founded by Edith Farkas, in 1908.[13]
Slachta's vision of a religious community differed from that of
Farkas. On 12 May 1923 she instituted a new community in
Budapest,[14] where Hungarians would come to know the Sisters of
Social Service as the "Grey Nuns" because of their simple grey religious habit.[15] Slachta wrote that the religious life "frees the heart,
lifts it beyond the sphere of human power, and detaches it from
that power."[16] This vision shaped the way in which Slachta
designed her religious community to meet contemporary problems
as well as those of the future through work among the poor.[17]

Roman Catholic religious women entering the contemplative
life took perpetual, or lifelong vows, of poverty, chastity, and obedience, which entailed prayer, fasting, celibacy, and social isolation.[18] Members of Slachta's community, which was apostolic
rather than contemplative, did not take perpetual vows; they took
simple vows which they renewed annually. Another distinction
made between nuns who lived in a convent and members of religious congregations who lived in groups of two or three in separate
dwellings relates to the vow of poverty that required non-cloistered
religious to serve the poor in body and spirit. Unlike cloistered sisters, members of Slachta's congregation were not required to leave
their work for prayer three times a day to say the Divine Office.
They regarded their work as prayer and obedience to their superior
as their form of confinement.[19] Slachta's writings expressed her
vision of the society's apostolic mission in the following way:

> The Society exposes its members to various types of work, sending them
> on untrodden paths, entrusting them with troublesome problems of
> today and even of tomorrow. In their field of work there are no written
> paragraphs, no repetitions, no trenches. Here everyone realizes her per-
> sonal deficiency and experiences daily that she has no life *without the
> spirit of wisdom, understanding, knowledge, counsel, piety, fortitude,
> and fear of the Lord.*[20]

Both contemplative and active orders likened their vows to the spiritual commitment made by brides. According to Slachta:

The idea that the soul should offer itself to Almighty God with the love of a spouse, is as ancient as the Church. External forms need to change according to the demands of the times. The essence of the commitment to God has remained the same.[21]

Slachta shaped the professional training program in her community by using her social work practices as an opportunity for collective action, and by educating the sisters in her spirituality . Under Slachta's leadership the Sisters of Social Service opened professional training schools for social work in Budapest and in the Transylvanian city of Cluj. Both schools flourished. Most of the women attending these programs were twenty years of age or older and had been engaged in social action movements. Some students joined Slachta's religious community; others affiliated themselves as members of a lay association. Instructors frequently related the coursework, which included studies in rhetoric, public speaking, lobbying, and collective action, to important social questions of the day.[22]

After professional training, the women were sent to posts where they were most needed, usually in rural Hungary.[23] Since the religious congregation had selected social work as its charism or mission, the community provided nursing, midwifery services, and care for orphans. The Sisters of Social Service were professional women who were married to the cause of social justice. They were not idealists working from some abstract and utopian worldview. Nonetheless, they placed contemporary problems within a spiritual framework. Slachta's prayerful reflections on the grace of God suggest that without the powers imbued in her through her deep spirituality, all work, particularly rescue work, would have been impossible.[24]

Theological Commitments

To save lives, religious women and Jewish individuals found it necessary to cross spiritual boundaries. It demanded a degree of risk-taking on the part of the religious women and the Jewish people whom they set out to help. Sociological and historical studies of human behavior, particularly altruistic behavior, may partially explain the ways in which religious beliefs guided the choices made by members of the Sisters of Social Service. Feminist sociologists Carol Diem and Debra Friedman posit that individuals make choices based on personal values, which in turn result in social action. Agency or the ability to act derives its efficacy from the actor's desire to attain ends deemed most consistent with personal values. Actions, however, involve individual choices that are subject to external and internal constraints. Institutional constraints or costs to personal well-being may shape these choices.[25] When an individual makes a choice that flies in the face of external and internal constraints, we might say they are transcending, or perhaps crossing, boundaries.[26]

Margit Slachta turned to the Gospel for teachings on Christian *agape*, or love of one's neighbor, and argued that these lessons were diametrically opposed to principles of Nazi ideology or what she considered to be neo-pagan materialism.[27] A Christian ethos guided her responses in the role she assumed as head of the Sisters of Social Service. Slachta wrote, "I stand without compromise, on the foundation of Christian values; that is, I profess that love obliges us to accept natural laws for our fellow-men [women and children] without exception, which God gave and which cannot be taken away."[28] Her spiritual writings generally integrate the concepts of salvation through faith and good works. Her trust in and understanding of God permitted Slachta to demonstrate these beliefs in the world of politics.[29]

By the time Slachta began to comment on the threats imposed by National Socialism, the Nazis had succeeded in gaining control of Europe through military conflict and brutal intimidation. The Nazis also empowered like-minded collaborators to dictate political and social values and to command scarce economic resources. National Socialism, Slachta argued, manifested its egocentricity in its zeal for power and control. Fear of God and a recognition of God's love were notably lacking from this coarse and simplistic ideology. This egocentric belief system created and engendered social divisions, forcing individuals to abandon the teachings of the church and the values of the community. This ideology promoted competition and a struggle for power and control over scarce resources and explained one of the causes for war. Slachta argued that this insidious belief system denied the existence of the Supreme Being and overlooked Biblical teachings that validated the human and spiritual identity of every human.[30] During the Shoah, Slachta's doctrinal and spiritual perspectives inspired her to lead those willing to listen, those willing to be taught, and those willing to act, to transcend spiritual, cultural, and social boundaries that so impair human judgment.

Transcending the Boundaries of Theological Commitments

Governments sympathetic to the Third Reich legally disenfranchised, socially isolated, and ultimately eliminated as many Jews as possible from Europe. Under the Vienna Awards of 1938 and 1940 the Nazis returned lost pieces of territory from Czechoslovakia and Romania (signed away in 1919 under the Treaty of Trianon) as a tribute for support from Hungarian Regent Miklós Von Horthy (1868-1957).[31] The advance of Nazi troops into Poland in September 1939 catalyzed the eastward migration of Jewish families.[32] The new political boundaries stretched to include age-old communities of non-Hungarian Jews. As the population of foreign Jews increased, the dynamic served as a pretext (among radical anti-semitic factions in the Hungarian Parliament) for the passage of anti-Jewish laws.[33] In a bid to mimic the anti-Jewish policies of the Third Reich, the Commissioner of Carpatho-Ruthenia, Miklós Kozma, began a roundup of Jewish dissidents in the newly acquired territory.[34] In November 1940 the government made its first arrests among Jews with leftist sympathies, charging them with ignoring vital national interests, spying, collaborating with the enemy, and encouraging dissent. If police could not find an infraction of the law, they launched trumped-up charges.[35] Of course these Jewish men had families whom they were trying to support. Slachta identified these men and their families as the "persecuted ones." Moreover, some Jews had heard rumors and understood that they were threatened with slow and painful starvation or death in the gas chambers should they be deported and sometimes felt it necessary to renounce their centuries-old faith tradition in order to survive.

The 1940 Vienna Awards (which ceded part of Transylvania to Hungary) removed the requirement for travel visas between Budapest and Cluj and facilitated communication and travel between the sisters' motherhouse in Budapest and a large community living in Cluj, Transylvania. The distance between Cluj and Budapest was about a five to six hours by train.[36] The motherhouse began receiving calls for help from Cluj. These appeals drew Slachta into direct contact with the Jewish families of Csíkszereda, who had been deported to Körösmezö near the Polish border.[37] The families had been forced to move twice before. Now destitute, they had no means for escape; they either had to go into the Russian woods, only to face the viciously antisemitic Ukrainians, or remain in the camps. Slachta visited the detention centers and transfer points in Northern Transylvania and wrote summaries of her observations. She gathered information from police officials and clerics and acted as an intermediary between the families and petty bureaucrats. Repeatedly, the same pattern occurred. The sisters received an appeal from a family, usually through a woman because the men were already in labor camps, and then Slachta appealed to the local clergy for help.[38]

Just as the Sisters of Social Service crossed spatial boundaries by coming to the aid of the "persecuted ones" in the new outlying provinces of Hungary, the sisters also tried to encourage other Hungarian Christians to cross cultural and spiritual barriers through their educational efforts. Slachta familiarized Hungarians with her sympathies for the Jewish cause as early as 1940 through her monthly paper, *The Voice of the Spirit*. The bulletin served as a mouthpiece for Slachta's spiritual and political views and to that end, Slachta used the paper to organize women for political action.[39] The community distributed this newspaper, which published information about religion classes, fundamental Christian values, and a film and lecture series advocating toleration and support for persecuted Jews.[40] Relying on modern technology to extend their message, the series were offered in more than fifty Hungarian towns with three to four thousand people in attendance. Slachta required the sisters to memorize the text of the film—usually on the life and papal encyclicals of Pius XII — and to teach its principles to outstanding Hungarian women of all ages. The sisters taught that the Christian principle of universal love was an antidote to Nazi principles. And they professed Slachta's teachings that although "nation and race were the thoughts of God," these Nazi principles sowed the seeds of division. Moreover, the sisters taught that the profane and terrible atrocities were not the will of God but Godless acts.[41]

These overt acts of support would not go unnoticed by the government. After the Catholic Women's Union, a political organization formed by Slachta in the thirties, published a controversial article, "Why We Catholic Hungarians Cannot Join the Arrow Cross" by the Pierest priest Gyorgy Balanyi, *The Voice of the Spirit*, which enjoyed a much larger circulation, followed suit. The Arrow Cross, Hungary's version of the Nazi party, arrested Father Balanyi and charged him with treason. The government also censured Slachta and warned her publishers against printing the second installment of the article.[42] Undeterred by government threats, Slachta used the *Voice of the Spirit* to remind Hungarian women that while all families suffered under wartime conditions, obviously Jewish families suffered more. Slachta urged Hungarian women to reach out to Jewish refugees, particularly to families in which the fathers, husbands, brothers, and sons had been forced into labor camps:

> *Dare to rid* your heart of ignorance, unlovingness, and hatred in this deadly serious age, *dare to accept* deep in your heart another mother and her son as your fellow human beings, *dare to bear* her pain and help her to carry her cross.[43]

Slachta urged women to encourage their fathers, brothers, husbands, and sons who were in the military or in charge of the forced labor camps to treat their charges with Christian gentleness. Slachta reminded Hungarian Catholic women that they would hope for the same if their relatives faced a similar fate. After this article was published, government officials reprimanded her publication for being unpatriotic. Slachta was only a short step from being condemned as a traitor.[44] The *Voice* was ultimately suppressed with the arrival of Nazi troops.[45]

Slachta had no reluctance to cross the political borders between Hungary and the "Catholic state," Slovakia, to aid Jews facing deportation between 1942 and 1943. In her letters to the Hungarian Roman Catholic Church hierarchy, Slachta urged Hungarian bishops to share a commitment to Christianity that embraced the ideal of love of one's neighbor. She urged them to act "against this Satanism." Anticipating the bishops' reluctance to assist her because they believed that they should not become involved in the internal political affairs of a neighboring state, Slachta wrote, "Surely there are no political frontiers before God."[46]

In the spring of 1943 the Archbishop of New York, Francis Spellman (1889-1967), arranged an audience for Margit Slachta with Pius XII (1939-1958).[47] In recounting her experience she wrote that her hands were clammy when usually they were dry and "tears were welling up in my eyes." She attributed her anxiety to the gravity of the situation, meeting with the Pope, carrying a message of anguish and woe, and asking for him to intercede. When the Pope entered the room he asked her to be seated, while he remained standing. Then Slachta told him that she represented 20,000 people, the Slovakian deportees, who were facing untimely deaths. Slachta set forth a proposal to rescue the Jews. She asked the Pope to provide food and shelter for the Jews in detention camps, thereby alleviating the need for deportations.[48] Pius XII agreed with that her proposal was a sound idea. Slachta wrote:

> He [Pius XII] listened to me all the way through. He expressed his shock. I can say the following: he listened to me but said very little. I will never forget the way he looked at me. It was deep, deadly serious and beneficent. I felt deeply moved that evening and even the next day.[49]

The Vatican secretary recorded the following observations about the meeting:

> The Holy See has done and is doing all that which is in its power on behalf of the Jews, in all the areas where they are the object of odious

measures; and particularly, in regard to the case at hand, on behalf of the Slovak Jews.[50]

Some have argued that Slachta's visit to the Pope helped to delay the 1943 deportations in Slovakia.[51] In the weeks following her audience with the Pope, the Slovakian bishops had a change of heart from previous years when they were in close collaboration with the Tiso government.[52] The bishops published a letter containing strong language favoring the basic human rights of the Jewish detainees. At Sunday Masses throughout Slovakia, priests read the letter to the faithful. Yet, although papal representatives may have been working behind the scenes to shape the text of these letters, Pius XII never publicly condemned the atrocities.[53]

The Slovakian Catholic hierarchy had particular concerns for those Jews who had taken steps to convert to Catholicism by being baptized. A similar situation arose in Hungary. Catholic baptism is the sacrament by which an individual becomes a Christian and a member of the Church. Although baptism in the Roman Catholic Church is usually celebrated for infants at the request of their parents, baptism presented itself as a life-saving option for some Hungarian families, adults as well as children.[54] A move to convert Jews was placed in motion by the Holy Cross Society, an organization specifically organized in the late 1930s to protect and advance the interests of Jews who had converted to Catholicism.[55] During the war, the Holy Cross Society in conjunction with the Sisters of Social Service baptized Jewish families to safeguard their lives until they could find a means of escape. While most Jews did not accept the sacrament for spiritual reasons, they realized that by being baptized they could achieve a degree of political protection from Nazi-led persecution.[56] In the early years of the war the Sisters of Social Service, the Holy Cross Society, and eighty lay helpers provided religious instructions for baptism throughout the day and into the night at various locations throughout Hungary. Reportedly the sisters and the Holy Cross Society baptized over 10,000 people.[57] Naturally, the Hungarian government did not sanction this, and as early as 1943 several priests were charged with illegal baptisms.[58]

Anti-Jewish laws requiring Jews to mark their homes with the Star of David prompted the Sisters of Social Service to visit the marked homes, bringing food, clothing, and medicine, and encouraging baptism. Acquiring baptismal certificates for Jewish families certainly required cooperation from parish priests, men who clearly understood the consequences of their actions. Sister Natalie Palagyi[59] recounted that she asked Vicar General Monsignor Witz to permit her to baptize interested parties. At first, Monsignor Witz rejected her proposition. Sister Natalie rephrased her question. "If we would do it, would you prohibit it?" Monsignor Witz replied, "No." To carry out the plan, Sister Natalie recruited neighboring parish priests who were willing to cooperate with this project. First, parish priests stopped marking "deceased" on the baptismal certificates of parishioners who died. Next, the sisters matched the certificates of the deceased with Jewish candidates of similar ages. Then the sisters copied the name and year from the old certificates onto new certificates. Finally, the sisters returned to the Jewish families in order to give them their baptismal certificates and in some cases to perform the ceremony. The Roman Catholic Church held that those who had received the sacrament with honest intentions were legitimately baptized. The act of supplying baptismal certificates to their Jewish neighbors created a crisis of conscience for some lay and religious Catholics. In the confidential and enclosed space of the confessional, the confessor's response to a sister's report about her baptizing activities was: "In the case of doubt: charity has precedence."[60]

Taking Roman Catholic religious instructions or participating in the ceremony of baptism was obviously a deeply personal choice. While some Jews were actually baptized, others were never baptized, particularly during the siege of the Jewish community in Budapest in the late spring of 1944, but simply received a Roman Catholic baptismal certificate.[61] Because of the critical nature of the situation for Jews, some members of the Catholic and Jewish communities arrived at an understanding on a very personal and spiritual issue. Only a few years earlier this cooperation would have been unimaginable.

Nazi troops rolled into Budapest on 19 March 1944. Regent Horthy transferred power to the pro-Nazi Sztójay government.[62] The mastermind of the deportation and transportation process, Adolph Eichmann (1906-1962), arrived in tandem with the troops to oversee the clearing action ironically named Margarete I.[63] Clearing actions in Hungary began in the north; the first deportations occurred within a month. This horrific event was marked by the departure of ninety-two trains from Kassa, Slachta's hometown, for Auschwitz.[64] The news caused alarm and marked the end of most public Christian support for Jewish families. Margit Slachta and the Sisters of Social Service proved the exception.[65]

Slachta called the sisters together for a general retreat at the novitiate-training center in Oradea, Transylvania.[66] Before leaving Budapest for the retreat, however, Slachta set up the motherhouse as a safe haven and placed it under the auspices of the Swedish Red Cross.[67] Perhaps Slachta selected Oradea because the site was far enough away from the hustle and bustle of Budapest. Oradea, situated in close proximity to the clearing action, had a large Jewish population; perhaps she selected the site because it was centrally located and had facilities large enough to shield those fleeing persecution. The retreat lasted several weeks as groups of thirty to fifty sisters from across Hungary arrived every other week. In the silence of the retreat, Slachta implored the sisters to consider the gravity of the situation facing the Jewish community in the following way:

> Is it the conviction of every Sister of Social Service that a moral organization can be safe for the future only when it lives up to its moral convictions? Are we willing in the name of fraternal love to take the risk of being interned, or carried away, of the Community being dissolved, or even of losing our own lives? If so, even if all these things were to happen, yet if in the soul of every Sister of Social Service, the ideals of Christianity still live, then the Community will be found worthy to have a future and will deserve life even if only one Sister of Social Service were left alive. What does it help us if our work, our property, our lives are left to us but when we come to give account we have to hide our face shamefully before the eyes of God.[68]

The retreat had deep personal implications for a sister named Judit Fenyvesi, a Jewish convert. The Sisters of Notre Dame de Sion, a nineteenth-century Roman Catholic female religious congregation founded by Jewish women, had inspired Judit to convert to Roman Catholicism in 1938. In succeeding years the Sisters of Notre Dame de Sion encouraged her to pursue training at the Sisters of Social Service school in Cluj. While there, Judit lived in a student hostel that was opened by the Sisters of Social Service. Close friendships formed between Judit and her instructors. Still, close friendships do not always instill vocations for the religious life. Despite her admiration for the Sisters of Social Service, Judit continued to hold to her call to join the Sisters of Notre Dame de Sion. Moreover, Judit's mother, an observant Jew, objected to her conversion to Roman Catholicism. Her mother hoped that Judit would marry and have a family of her own. Times had changed, however. March 1944 was no time for the youthful dreams of a Jewish woman or her mother.

As the pro-Nazi government forced all Jewish people into the ghettoes and the clearing actions drew closer to Cluj, the Sisters of Social Service feared for Judit's life. On 5 April, the day on which all Jews in Hungary were forced to wear the yellow star of David, Justinian Cardinal Serédi attempted to negotiate better terms for

Jewish converts but he was allowed only one concession. Prime Minister Sztójay made an exception for priests, nuns, and lay church officials of Jewish background.[69] The Sisters of Social Service advised Judit to begin the process of taking her vows in order to ensure her safety. The problem of her mother's consent, however, loomed large. The Sisters of Social Service sent a priest to discuss these matters with Judit's mother in Salonata. Considering the circumstances facing all Jews in mid-April 1944 in Transylvania, Judit's mother gave her daughter permission to join the congregation, transcending a boundary that neither she nor Judit could have envisioned crossing five years earlier. Judit's mother told the priest that if her daughter ever wished to return home, she was welcome. With her mother's approval and Judit's consent, the Sisters of Social Service took Judit to the novitiate house in Oradea. The sisters waived her novitiate training and immediately received Judit into the order. So, instead of taking the habit of the Sisters of Notre Dame de Sion, Judit was measured and fitted with the habit of the Grey Nuns.[70]

Sister Judit had taken her vows by the time Sister Margit Slachta arrived for the planned retreat. Clean sweeps had already been made of all people of Jewish origin in Northern Transylvania. The Jewish victims were loaded onto trucks and brought to central detention centers. Sister Judit Fenyvesi revealed how Slachta had instructed the sisters to take in as many Jewish families as possible. Slachta said, "they are God coming to us." Slachta believed that "there was no other choice at that moment for Christians. The Sisters of Social Service could do nothing other than save lives, even at the cost of their own lives."[71]

Sister Judit began to fear for her mother and sister. Other members of her community advised Sister Judit to make an appointment with Slachta and to seek her advice. Apparently, Slachta was quick to answer, having witnessed similar scenarios many times before. She told Sister Judit, "dress as a peasant woman. Go to Salonata and smuggle your family out as soon as possible."[72] Slachta promised that the sisters would find safe hiding places for her relatives and supply them with baptismal papers. Unfortunately, Sister Judit's mother and sister had already been loaded onto trains bound for the detention center in Oradea. Although the first plan was stymied, the sisters came up with a new strategy to smuggle Sister Judit's family out of the camp via a garbage truck. To relay the plan to her family, Sister Judit entered the detention camp through a favor supplied by friends of the camp commander. Although Sister Judit knew the day and time of the garbage truck's

scheduled arrival and departure and she watched the truck enter
the camp from a concealed hiding place, she never saw its return.
Neither did Sister Judit ever see her family again; they perished at
Auschwitz.[73] Sister Judit recalled her meeting with Slachta and
described the succeeding series of events as a "personal encounter
in a very tragic moment."[74]

In June 1944 the mayor of Budapest passed a decree forcing all
Jews (whether they held a baptismal certificate or not) to move into
specially assigned apartment buildings.[75] After the Jews settled in,
armed guards prevented them from leaving the ghetto. All buildings
were marked off limits to visitors.[76] Under these circumstances,
Slachta received approval from ecclesiastical authorities for sisters
to dress in regular street garb so they could enter the ghetto without notice and continue their regular visits to Jewish families. The
sisters hid food and medicines for the families in their garments.[77]
They also shuttled Jews in and out of the city in the dark of night.
If they were from a rural village, the sisters smuggled them to the
city. If they were from the city, the sisters smuggled them to a rural
village. The sisters devised this strategy in hopes of relieving neighbors of the responsibility of identifying newcomers, should authorities question them. If asked about the identity of a refugee, city
dwellers and rural residents alike could easily deny knowing anything about the individual in question.[78]

In July transports began to depart from Budapest. Most who
witnessed the passage of the trains knew the passengers were bound
for labor camps in Poland. The sisters and lay women performed
corporal works of mercy by providing the deportees with water and
food at transit points along the way.[79] These acts were highly visible and public shows of solidarity with the "persecuted ones."[80]
Although some members of the Sisters of Social Service were in
danger, they continued their rescue activities. Most sisters refused
to leave Budapest. In the autumn members of the Arrow Cross
caught Slachta off guard and brutally beat her.[81] In December, a dis-
gruntled employee of the sisters reported the Sisters of Social Service for hiding Jewish refugees in their home for women. The
following day, the Arrow Cross arrested Social Service Sister Sara
Salkahazi, who operated the refuge, along with a religion teacher
and six refugees.[82] The armed thugs took the women away from
the home and executed them. A passerby found Salkahazi's remains
"shot full of holes" lying on the riverbank several days later. The
warning was clear enough to Slachta and prompted her to seek
refuge in a Carmelite convent, where she remained until the Soviet
Army arrived and liberated Budapest in the early spring of 1945.[83]

Concluding Remarks

Margit Slachta's formative years and spiritual commitments laid the groundwork for the social justice strategies that proved fundamental to the life of her religious congregation. The members of this women's religious community gave strength to each other, allowing the individuals to extend their humanity beyond anything they could have anticipated before the beginning of the Second World War. To say that their activities were overlooked by government authorities or the hierarchy of the Roman Catholic Church because they were women would be a misstatement. In fact, because their vows required them to serve the poor by performing works of mercy they were a very visible part of social life in Budapest. Therefore, when Slachta made public appeals for assistance for the "persecuted ones," the call for help could hardly go unnoticed.

On a more private level, the question of baptism was an essential part of rescue activities. Baptism required Christians and Jews to face a crisis of conscience, but ultimately to transcend their doctrinal differences. In doing so, Christians identified with the needs of the downtrodden, and Jews accepted heretofore unacceptable offers in an effort to save their lives. Although both parties participated in the baptismal process, the crisis of conscience, to be sure, remained. At war's end, some of those who held the baptismal certificates and had managed to avoid the later persecutions returned to thank the sisters for saving their lives.[84] Through their collective efforts, standing in solidarity with Jewish friends, neighbors, and strangers, the Sisters of Social Service were able to save the lives of some of the "persecuted ones." The sisters could not, however, protect the victims from the pain caused by the loss of Jewish family members.[85] Yad Vashem, the Holocaust Martyrs' and Heroes' Remembrance Authority, honored Slachta[86] as a Righteous Gentile for her dedicated efforts.[87]

Notes

I wish to thank Sister Natalie Palagyi and Sister Judit Fenyvesi, both Sisters of Social Service, for their poignant and personal chronicles of rescue activities during the Shoah. I am also in debt to Dr. Bela Piascek who translated archival documents from Hungarian to English for this study and to Pal-Foti Friedlander for his personal interview in which he shared his knowledge of Margit Slachta and his experiences of Christian rescue and relief efforts for labor service men orchestrated by Pastor Gabor Stezhlo.

A version of this chapter was presented to the Political Science Seminar convened at the Erasmus Summer Institute, which was sponsored by the Pew Foundation and Notre Dame University at St. Edward's University, Austin, Texas, June 1999. I wish to thank Political Science Seminar leader Professor Clarke Cochran, Anita Houck from the Literature Seminar, and the seminar participants for their helpful comments and suggestions.

1. Margit Slachta, "What the Church Did for Persecuted Jewish People," speech to the Hungarian Parliament, 16 April 1947, trans. Dr. Bela Piascek; and "Some Early History," *Sisters of Social Service Newsletter*, 11 (1991): 1, Sisters of Social Service Archives, Buffalo, New York (hereafter cited as SSSA). Additional sources for this chapter include oral history interviews and archival materials from the Sisters of Social Service, Buffalo, New York. Tamás Majsai translated a large body of Slachta's correspondence from Hungarian to English. His translations are helpful and provide a substantial amount of background material on Slachta. See Tamás Majsai, translator and compiler, "The Deportation of Jews from Csíkszereda and Margit Slachta's Intervention on their Behalf," *Studies on the Holocaust in Hungary*, ed. Randolph L. Braham (New York: Columbia University Press, 1990). The Sisters of Social Service in Budapest hold the bulk of Margit Slachta's papers. A member of the congregation recently completed a biography, in Hungarian, on Sister Margit Slachta.

2. A group of lay women associated with the Sisters of Social Service remained politically and spiritually committed to the work of the Sisters of Social Service. Lay women provided material support, including food and shelter for refugees. Sister Judit Fenyvesi (1923-), Sister of Social Service, telephone interview by author, April 1997, Buffalo, N.Y.-Milwaukee, Wisc.

3. In this 1947 speech to the Hungarian Parliament Slachta stated, "I might mention that I am only speaking about the Catholic role in protecting the persecuted ones. It would be worthwhile to bring up the role of the Calvinist and Evangelical Churches and their work to the Assembly. [Many were also assisted] under the leadership of Arias, Josef Elias who was the soul of the Good Shepherd movement and [whose churches] functioned in an outstanding manner." Slachta, "What the Church Did for Persecuted Jewish People," 16 April 1947. For additional accounts of intercessory activities by the Christian community see Haim Genizi and Naomi Blank, "The Rescue Efforts of Bnei Akiva in Hungary During the Holocaust," ed. Aharon Weis, *Yad Vashem Studies*, vol. 23 (Jerusalem: Yad Vashem, 1993), 192-3; Gabor Sztehlo, *In the Hands of God*, trans. Judit Zinner (Budapest: Gabor Sztehlo Foundation, 1994).

4. "Shoah" rather than "Holocaust" is used by some scholars to denote the catastrophic destruction of European Jewry during World War II. The term is used in Israel. The Knesset (the Israeli Parliament) has designated an official day, called Yom ha-Shoah, to commemorate the Shoah or Holocaust. For a glossary

of terms relating to the Shoah see http://fcit.coedu.usf.edu/holocaust/resource/glossary.htm.

5. See *Cries in the Night*, a collection of essays exploring the role played by Roman Catholic religious and lay women during the Shoah. J. Michael Phayer and Eva Fleischner, *Cries in the Night: Women Who Challenged the Holocaust*, foreword by Nechama Tec (Kansas City: Sheed and Ward, 1997).

6. Gerda Lerner and Jo Ann Kay McNamara make significant inroads on this subject. Both agree that feminism offers the best perspective from which to develop case studies in the history of women religious. Even in this context, however, the history of women will remain abstract and utopian until scholars examine the charisms or practices of various orders. Lerner argues that only women organizing on behalf of women could generate truly liberating thought. Her study illuminates the ways in which religious women transformed their ideas into action through work within religious communities. See Gerda Lerner, "Female Clusters, Female Networks, Social Spaces," *The Creation of a Feminist Consciousness: From the Middle Ages to 1870* (New York, Oxford University Press, 1992), 220-1. For a general discussion of Roman Catholic women's religious congregations in the church from 1797 to the present, see Jo Ann McNamara, "The Feminine Apostolate," *Sisters in Arms: Catholic Nuns through Two Millennia* (Cambridge: Harvard University Press, 1996), 601-44.

7. "Sister Margaret Slachta Dies; Champion of Rights," *Buffalo Evening News*, 7 January 1974.

8. Giancarlo Rocca, "Slachta, Margit," *Dizionario degli istituti di perfezione*, trans. J. P. Donnelly, 9 vols. (Roma: Edizioni paoline, 1974), vol. 8, col. 1554.

9. The Catholic women's political party was later known as the Party of Christian Women. Ibid., 8: 1555.

10. "Some Early History," *Sisters of Social Service Newsletter*, 11 (1991): 1, SSSA.

11. Pal-Foti Friedlander interview by author, 13 September 1994, London. In a speech to the Hungarian Parliament after the war, Slachta claimed that she was "non-partisan." Slachta's account reflected shifting and risky political boundaries associated with the pending installment of the Communist government. Slachta, "What the Church did for Persecuted Jewish People," 16 April 1947.

12. Leo XIII (1810-1903), whose pontificate began the modern age of Roman Catholicism, composed *Rerum Novarum*, the first modern papal statement on social and economic theory. Eighty-eight statements on political theory and practice and the condition of labor followed this path-breaking document. The encyclical, articulating the Roman Catholic Church's position on just wages and trade unions, was of such great significance that it earned him the honorary title of the "workers' pope." "Leo XIII," David Crystal, ed. *The Cambridge Biographical Encyclopedia* (Cambridge: Cambridge University Press, 1995), 564.

13. Margit Slachta, *From the Hermitage of the Desert to the Center of Life*, trans. Sister of Social Service Alice Slachta (1933-38; reprint, Buffalo, NY: Sisters of Social Service, n. d.), 15, SSSA.

14. The clerical president of the Society of Social Sisters was Bishop Count Janos Mikes (1923-1948). It was, however, under the leadership of Slachta that the Sisters of Social Service was able to establish itself in five countries to provide qualified social workers to women and children. Maria Schmidt, "Action of Margit Slachta to Rescue Slovakian Jews," *Danubian Historical Studies* 1 (1987): 58; Rocca, "*Servizio Sociale, di Buffalo, USA,*" *Dizionario degli istituti de perfezione*, 8: 1434-5.

15. Dr. Bela Piascek, interviews by author, February-March 1996, Marquette University, Milwaukee, Wisconsin. Dr. Piascek was a child-resident of Budapest between 1938 and1944 and immigrated to the United States with his parents in 1952.

16. Margit Slachta, *In the Mission of Sanctifying Love*, trans. Sister Alice Slachta (1933-1938; reprint Buffalo, NY: Sisters of Social Service, n. d.), 59-60, SSSA.

17. Slachta, *From the Hermitage of the Desert to the Center of Life*, 15.

18. Lerner, *The Creation of a Feminist Consciousness*, 220-1; McNamara, "The Feminine Apostolate," *Sisters in Arms*, 601-44.

19. Catholic Truth Society, *The Sisters of Charity of St. Vincent de Paul*, vol. 108 (London: Catholic Truth Society, 1916), 10-25. For an explanation of the relationship between political activism and changes in canonical laws among communities of women religious see Lynn Jarrell, OSB, JCD, "The Development of Legal Structures for Women Religious between 1500 and 1900: A Study of Selected Institutes for Religious Life for Women," *U.S. Catholic Historian* 10 (1992): 25-37. For canonical distinctions between consecrated nuns and members of third order communities see James A. Coriden, Thomas J. Green, and Donald E. Heintschel, eds., *The Code of Canon Law* (New York: Paulist Press, 1994), 535.

20. Slachta, *From the Hermitage of the Desert to the Center of Life*, 15.

21. Ibid., 1.

22. Fenyvesi interview by author, April 1997, Buffalo, N.Y.-Milwaukee, Wisc.

23. Ibid.

24. Although Margit Slachta met resistance from some members of the Church hierarchy, she was never in prolonged conflict with the Church. Sister Natalie Palagyi contended that Slachta was never disappointed by the Church. Sister Natalie wrote, "I wish to see no conflict between Sister Margaret and the Church. It was never a conflict." Sister Natalie Palagyi, Sister of Social Service letter to author, 15 February 1996.

25. For a sociological view of women's choices see Debra Friedman and Carol Diem, "Feminism and the Pro- (Rational-) Choice Movement: Rational-Choice Theory, Feminist Critiques, and Gender Inequality," *Theory On Gender/Feminism On Theory*, ed. Paula England (New York: Aldine de Gruyter, 1993), 91-2. See also Friedman and Diem, "The Importance of Altruism and the Interdependence of Utilities: Reply to Folbre," *Theory On Gender/Feminism On Theory*, 332(6. For a critical analysis of behavior within groups and the ways in which values may be "spatially" defined and communicated see Anthony Giddens, *The Constitution of Society* (Berkeley: University of California Press, 1984), 3-6; Anthony Giddens, *Politics, Sociology and Social Theory: Encounters with Classical and Contemporary Social Thought* (Cambridge: Polity Press, 1995), 265-8.

26. The ways in which ethical values shape these personal choices are illustrated in Nechama Tec's study, *When Light Pierced the Darkness*. Tec describes a variety of personalities or character traits associated with altruism as exhibited by Christian and non-Christian rescuers living in Poland during the Shoah. Nechama Tec, *When Light Pierced the Darkness: Christian Rescue of Jews in Nazi-Occupied Poland* (New York: Oxford University Press, 1986), 150-2.

27. In John's Gospel Jesus exhorts his followers to "love one another as I have loved you." John 15.12-13 NAB.

28. Majsai, "The Deportation of Jews from Csíkszereda," 119.

29. Slachta, *From the Hermitage of the Desert to the Center of Life*, 15.

30. Sister Margit Slachta, *Voice of the Spirit*, 15 May 1943 as reprinted in *Highlights of the First Fifty Years of the Society of the Sisters of Social Service*, comp. Sister Natalie Palagyi (Buffalo, NY: Sisters of Social Service, 1973), 82, SSSA.

31. The Treaty of Trianon was negotiated in 1920. Hungary lost about two-thirds of its territory and half of its population. The treaty ceded lands from Slovakia and Carpatho-Ruthenia to Czechoslovakia. The treaty also ceded lands from Transylvania and part of the Banat Region to Romania. The treaty ceded lands from Croatia-Slavonia and the remainder of the Banat Region to Yugoslavia, lands from the Gurgenland Region to Austria, and small sections of territory to Italy and Poland. See also Pal-Foti Friedlander, "The Horthy Phenomenon," *Association of Jewish Refugees Newsletter*, January 1994, 3. For a recent account of the activities of Admiral Horthy from the settlement at the Treaty of Trianon to his discharge as regent of Hungary in 1944 see Thomas L. Sakmyster, *Hungary's Admiral on Horseback: Miklós Horthy, 1918-1944* (New York: Columbia University Press, 1994).

32. Between 1933 and 1938 Hungary received over 3,000 Jews from Germany. This resulted from the expulsion of Jews from Poland, Romania, Slovakia, and the Sudetenland. Martin Gilbert, *Atlas of the Holocaust* (New York: Macmillan Co, 1982), 23-43. After the Munich and Vienna Awards, Hungary added another 250,000 to its Jewish population of 400,000; 75,000 Jews in former Slovakian territory, 25,000 in the Backa basin of Yugoslavia, and 150,000 Transylvania, for a total of 650,000 in Greater Hungary. Lucy Dawidowicz, *The War Against the Jews, 1933-1945* (New York: Bantam Books, 1986), 381. For an overview of the historical effects of demography, geography, and shifting political boundaries on this complex region see Erno Lazslo, "Hungarian Jewry: Settlement and Demography, 1735-38 to 1910," *Hungarian-Jewish Studies*, ed. Randolph Braham (New York: World Federation of Hungarian Jewry, 1966), 61-137.

33. Randolph Braham argued, "The *Gleichschaltung* in Northern Transylvania as in the other territories acquired through the cooperation of the Third Reich in 1938-39 was a clear indication that Hungary was ready to embrace the New Order for Europe envisioned by Hitler." Randolph Braham, *The Politics of Genocide: The Holocaust in Hungary*, 2 vols. (New York: Columbia University Press, 1981), 1: 172.

34. Miklós Kozma was a leading figure in the counter-revolutionary movement from the end of 1918 and one of the leaders of the National Defense League. From 1935(1937 he was Minister of the Interior; from 1939 to 1941, he was Commissioner of Internal Affairs of Kárpatátalja. According to Jenö Levai, the Ministry of Internal Affairs was the center of the antisemitic struggle within the Hungarian Government. Jenö Levai, *Hungarian Jewry and the Papacy: Pope Pius XII Did Not Remain Silent*, trans. J. R. Foster (London: Sands & Co., 1967), 23; Majsai, "The Deportation of Jews from Csíkszereda," 132.

35. For an excellent analysis of Hungarian police actions in the new territories see Mária Schmidt, "Provincial Police Reports: New Insights into Hungarian Jewish History, 1941-1944," *Yad Vashem Studies*, ed. Aharon Weiss, vol. 19 (Jerusalem: Yad Vashem, 1988): 233-68.

36. Fenyvesi interview by author, April 1997, Buffalo, NY-Milwaukee, WI. See Bela Vago, "The Destruction of the Jews of Transylvania," *Hungarian-Jewish Studies*, Randolph Braham, ed. (New York: World Federation of Hungarian Jews, 1966), 173.

37. Majsai, "The Deportation of Jews from Csíkszereda," 116.
38. For a more detailed account of Slachta's rescue efforts in Transylvania and Slovakia see Jessica A. Sheetz, "Margit Slachta's Efforts to Rescue Central European Jews, 1939-1945," *Cries in the Night: Women Who Challenged the Holocaust*, ed. J. Michael Phayer (Kansas City: Sheed and Ward, 1997), 42-64.
39. Sister Natalie Palagyi, *The Dove*, typescript mimeograph (Budapest: Sisters of Social Service, 1946), 9.
40. Titles of her articles include the following: "The Brother," "The Soul's Voice," "A World View Credo," all of which emphasized fundamental Christian values. Majsai, "The Deportation of Jews from Csíkszereda," 117.
41. Palagyi, *The Dove*, 8-9.
42. Slachta, "What the Church Did for Persecuted Jewish People," 16 April 1947.
43. Braham, *The Politics of Genocide*, 2: 1030; New Year Letter, *The Voice of the Spirit*, 10 (January 1943): 1; Majsai, "The Deportation of Jews from Csíkszereda," 118.
44. Ibid., 9.
45. Palagyi, *The Dove*, 9.
46. Margit Slachta to Bishop of Kalocsa, 27 April 1942, as cited in Mária Schmidt, "Margit Slachta's Activities in Support of Slovakian Jewry, 1942-1943," *Remembering for the Future: Jews and Christians During and After the Holocaust*, 3 vols. (New York: Pergamon Press, 1989), 1: 208.
47. Mária Schmidt, "Action of Margit Slachta to Rescue Slovakian Jews," *Danubian Historical Studies* 1 (1987): 57. For more information on the role of Francis Spellman during the Second World War see John Cooney, *The American Pope: The Life and Times of Francis Cardinal Spellman* (New York: Times Books, 1984).
48. John F. Morley, *Vatican Diplomacy and the Jews During the Holocaust, 1939-1943* (New York: KTAV Publishing House, Inc., 1980), 91.
49. Slachta's own essay, typed original, 13 March 1943 in the possession of Ilona Mona, as cited in Schmidt, *Remembering for the Future*, 209.
50. Morley, *Vatican Diplomacy and the Jews During the Holocaust, 1939-1943*, 91.
51. Majsai, "The Deportation of Jews from Csíkszereda," 117.
52. Although Slovakia was proclaimed an independent country, it was essentially a German satellite. Largely Catholic, Slovakia was under the aegis of a Catholic-led government and headed by Monsignor Josef Tiso. Tiso and his associates, Vojtech Tuka and Alexander Mach, had dedicated themselves to making Slovakia a "model Catholic state." Morley, *Vatican Diplomacy and the Jews During the Holocaust: 1939-1943*, 72. Between March 1942 and July 1942, 60,000 people (60 percent of the Jewish population) were deported from the Republic of Slovakia. Leni Yahil, *The Holocaust* (New York: Oxford University Press, 1990), 89.
53. Braham lists the following reasons why Pius XII never spoke out against the atrocities: Pius XII was concerned about the welfare of Germany's 20 million Catholics; the Pope had an affection for the German people and culture; the Pope regarded Bolshevism as a greater danger than anything posed by the aggressively anti-Jewish policies of the Nazi government. Braham, *The Politics of Genocide*, 2: 1066.
54. In 1944 the Papal Nuncio, Angelo Rotta, sent diplomatic messages to the Royal Government requesting special protection for Jewish converts. The Royal Government responded, "The Royal Government is examining these

plans sympathetically and as soon as they reach the stage of being put into effect it will see that baptized Jews are given some of the first opportunities to emigrate." 331/Res. Pol. 1944, Levai, *Hungarian Jewry and the Papacy: Pope Pius XII Did Not Remain Silent*, 22-3.

55. Braham, *The Politics of Genocide*, 2: 1050-1.

56. Palagyi, *The Dove*, 11.

57. Ibid.; Braham, *The Politics of Genocide*, 2: 778.

58. See the case of Jozsef Ambrus, a priest charged with illegal baptisms, as well as a list of rescue and relief activities by other Christians in Uri Asaf, "Christian Support for Jews," *Studies on the Holocaust in Hungary*, ed. Randolph Braham (New York: Columbia University Press, 1990), 68.

59. Sister Natalie Palagyi (1910-) joined the Sisters of the Social Service in 1927. Margit Slachta was Sister Natalie Palagyi's formation director. Sister Natalie remained in Budapest throughout the war and immigrated to the United States with Slachta in 1949. Sister Natalie Palagyi, Sister of Social Service letter to author, 5 January 1994.

60. Sister Natalie Palagyi interview by author, April 1997, Buffalo, N.Y.-Milwaukee, Wisc.

61. Palagyi interview by author, April 1997, Buffalo, N.Y.-Milwaukee, Wisc.

62. Braham, *The Politics of Genocide*, 1: 400-17; Moshe Y. Herczl, *Christianity and the Holocaust of Hungarian Jewry*, trans. Joel Lerner (New York: New York University Press, 1993), 180-91.

63. Margarete is the German name for Margaret in English or Margit in Hungarian. Levai, *Hungarian Jewry and the Papacy*, 18-9.

64. Kassa had one of the largest Jewish communities in Hungary and acquired the dubious distinction of becoming the transfer point from which deported Jews were handed over to the Germans. Braham, *The Politics of Genocide*, 1:545-7; 2:674.

65. Braham, *The Politics of Genocide*, 2:924-6; Levai, *Hungarian Jewry and the Papacy*, 17.

66. The Transylvanian branch of the Sisters of Social Service owned the Oradea novitiate. It was situated on a large piece of property and surrounded by flower and vegetable gardens. The Transylvanian province trained their novices at this site. The Sisters of Social Service also ran a large home for aging Hungarians at this site. Fenyvesi interview by author, April 1997, Buffalo, N.Y.-Milwaukee, Wisc.

67. Palagyi, *The Dove*, 10.

68. Ibid.

69. Braham, *The Politics of Genocide*, 2:1033.

70. Palagyi, *The Dove*, 10.

71. Fenyvesi interview by author, April 1997, Buffalo, N.Y.-Milwaukee, Wisc.

72. Ibid.

73. Ibid.

74. Ibid.

75. Herczl, *Christianity and the Holocaust of Hungarian Jewry*, 218.

76. Ibid.

77. Palagyi, *The Dove*, 11.

78. Fenyvesi interview by author, April 1997, Buffalo, N.Y.-Milwaukee, Wisc.

79. Braham, *Politics of Genocide*, 2: 1032.

80. Of the 435,000 Hungarian Jews deported to Auschwitz from 15 May to 8 July 1944, approximately 10 percent were selected as fit for labor. Some were

retained to work, others were sent to Bergen Belsen, Buchenwald, Dachau, Mauthausen, Grossrosen, Günskirchen, Neuengamme, and Ravensbrück. Braham, *The Politics of Genocide,* 2:676, 685.

81. Schmidt, "Margit Slachta's Activities in Support of Slovakian Jewry," 1:210.
82. Sara Salkahazi worked for two years as a government social worker among Jewish families during this era of repression "A Victim of Fraternal Charity," (Buffalo, New York: Sisters of the Social Service, n. d.), SSSA.
83. Palagyi, *The Dove,* 11-13.
84. Sister Natalie Palagyi interview by author, December 1995, Buffalo, N.Y.-Milwaukee, Wisc.
85. Herczl, *Christianity and the Holocaust of Hungarian Jewry,* 180.
86. After the war Slachta was re-elected to the Hungarian Parliament. When she found herself at odds with the Hungarian government, now under a Communist regime, her community urged her to leave Hungary. She was smuggled in a hay wagon to a remote part of the Austro-Hungarian border where she crawled under a barbed wire fence to the West. Slachta immigrated to the United States in 1949 and died in Buffalo, New York, in 1974. Sister Natalie Palagyi, letter to author, 5 January 1994.
87. Asaf, "Christian Support for Jews," 99. In 1978 Yad Vashem in Jerusalem recognized twenty-seven Hungarians as Righteous Gentiles. Margit Slachta was honored with Yad Vashem's highest awards, including a medal, a certificate of honor, and the right to plant a tree on the avenue of the Righteous at Yad Vashem. Braham, *The Politics of Genocide,* 2:1011, n. 5.; 2:1053, n. 6.

Chapter 11

DENIAL AND DEFIANCE IN THE WORK OF RABBI REGINA JONAS

Katharina von Kellenbach

Regina Jonas, born in Berlin in 1902, was the first ordained female rabbi in the Jewish tradition. Her efforts to attain equal rights in the synagogue coincided with the gradual destruction of Jewish life in Germany. She fought valiantly against religious and cultural restrictions imposed on women just as the German state deprived her of her rights as a Jew and a human being. Her faith in God's benevolence and commitment to a just and egalitarian future, as well as her stubborn and relentless pursuit of her vision helped to break down the objections to women's rabbinate. It also prepared her for her rabbinic work in wartime Berlin and the ghetto-camp of Theresienstadt. Her religiously based inner strength allowed her to challenge a Jewish community initially hostile to her aspirations and sustained her defiant stance toward the crushing forces of Nazi antisemitism.

The first part of this article will look at Jonas' struggle to gain recognition as an ordained female rabbi, and compare her to Protestant women who were simultaneously challenging the churches to ordain women into the ministry. It is one of the ironies of history that the social repression, antisemitic persecution and military aggression of Nazi Germany inadvertently opened professional opportunities to women. Although Rabbi Jonas was never officially installed in a congregation, her rabbinic duties steadily expanded as she was called upon to preach and provide pastoral care in senior citizen homes, institutions for the handicapped, schools and hospitals, and later in congregations left without rabbinic guidance. The second part of this article examines her sermons, articles and pastoral work as a form of resistance to Nazi antisemitism which assaulted Jews spiritually, economically and physically. Her message of steadfast faith in God and responsibility for the welfare of fellow human beings empowered people to preserve their dignity as Jews and helped to confront the brutal reality of daily life.

Jonas' Rabbinic Career

Few people know about Jonas' existence or her rabbinic career. She graduated from the *Hochschule für die Wissenschaft des Judentums* in December of 1930. Although she had completed the exact same education as her male colleagues, she was denied ordination. Her master's thesis on Jewish religious law (halakhah), "Can a Woman Hold Rabbinic Office?" which affirmed the legal ability of women to perform most of the functions of a modern rabbi was accepted by her professor of Talmud, Eduard Baneth. However, Baneth died before her oral examinations, which were a prerequisite for a *semikhah* (ordination). His successor, Professor Hanokh Albeck, refused to have anything to do with the ordination of "girls."[1] Jonas received only a diploma as an academic teacher of religion, but immediately began to preach sermons in small synagogues[2], lectured on women's ability to become rabbis,[3] and lobbied individual rabbis and rabbinic organizations to grant her full rights as a rabbi. Rabbi Leo Baeck supported her in her quest for ordination. She had been one of his students at the *Hochschule.* Upon graduation, he handed her an additional diploma certifying her successful completion of his homiletics course and attesting her skills as a preacher. It was probably Leo Baeck who arranged for Max Dienemann, the liberal rabbi of Frankfurt/Main, to examine her orally and to sign a *Hatara Hora'a* (permission to teach, i.e., certificate of ordination) five years after her graduation from the *Hochschule.* Thus, in December of 1935, one month after the Nuremberg laws revoked her citizenship rights as a Jew in Germany, Jonas could officially claim the title of a rabbi. In a letter of December 31, 1935, Leo Baeck congratulated her and gave her his blessings:

> May you be allowed to possess continual satisfaction and fulfillment of all your hopes in this position which you have achieved, yes almost conquered. I have been appraised about the exam by Dr. D[ienemann]. To my delight I have heard that he seriously examined you and that you

passed the exam well. I will tell you in the coming days when we can meet. And then I want you to tell me all about it.[4]

His wife, Natalie Baeck, added: "Receive my most cordial congratulations from me also. I greatly share your joy, that you have finally achieved your goal after so much labor."[5]

But despite this momentary triumph, Jonas was immediately confronted with new restrictions. Because Dienemann's ordination was only a private *semikhah,* the Berlin Jewish community board was not prepared to employ her as a congregational rabbi. They hired her as a teacher of religion (first in public and, later, in private Jewish schools) and as a chaplain to "carry out rabbinic-pastoral care (*rabbinisch- seelsorgerische Betreuung*) in the social institutions of the community."[6] Her chaplaincy sent her to homes for the elderly, Jewish welfare and youth institutions, institutions for deaf-mutes, various state hospitals as well as the Jewish hospital in Berlin.

Her determination to break the patriarchal bounds of the synagogue was couched in religious language which emphasized God's will and minimized her own initiative. Writing for the liberal journal, the *Central Verein Zeitung,* about her decision to become a rabbi, she cited her "faith in the divine calling and my love for human beings. God has buried abilities and callings into our hearts without asking for the gender. Therefore, everybody, regardless whether man or woman, has the duty to work and generate according to the gifts which God has given to him (sic). When one sees things this way, one takes men and women as what they are: as human beings."[7] Her faith asserted God's omnipotence and called for complete trust in his invisible and incomprehensible ways. In 1939, Jonas summarized the "central doctrines" of Judaism the following way:

> The acceptance of God and his omnipotence; the most profound humility before his actions which remain unknowable to us human children to the last, always a marvel for the searching and penetrating human mind and which can only be sensed; pure and ultimate trust in his eternal fatherly benevolence, which will guide the destiny of the mortal from darkness to light, from confusion to clarity.[8]

Jonas understood her long and often lonely struggle for recognition as a rabbi as part of a larger divine plan which transcended the present. Although ultimately ignorant of the overall divine design, she believed it to be a person's responsibility to strive and live according to God's will. In Jonas' interpretation, the God of Israel commanded justice and equality for all of humanity. She saw

herself as an instrument in a larger drama of establishing God's justice on earth. She presented the "difficulties and disappointments"
(Mühsal und Enttäuschung) which were part of her "fate to be the
first woman in her profession" as part of the "human fulfillment of
duty" which should not be "romanticized." [9] Her conviction that
the struggle for equality was God's will sustained Jonas more than
any movement, such as the women's movement. As the Swiss feminist women's magazine *Berna* noted with some regret, Jonas
"never belonged to or was close to a movement" although "according to her opinions on the equality of the sexes, women's careers
and women's education, we may most definitely count her as one of
us."[10] Jonas' determination and strength to resist gender oppression
resulted from her religious faith.

To the dismay of other Jewish liberals, she denied any conflict
between her egalitarian principles and the Jewish rabbinic tradition. Her halakhic thesis on the ordination of women, which cites
many of the restrictive laws and customs sustaining women's
silence, legal inferiority, and secondary status in the rabbinic tradition, concludes: "Halakhically, almost nothing opposes investing
women with the rabbinic office other than prejudice and unfamil-
iarity."[11] She claimed the Jewish rabbinic tradition as an ally in her
fight for women's equal rights and rebutted laws, customs, and
individual statements bolstering women's inferiority by citing
examples of exceptional Jewish women or women-friendly rulings
and opinions. Her denial of patriarchal restrictions in the rabbinic
tradition led to harsh criticism. An editorial commentary on the
"Women's Page" of the *Israelitisches Familienblatt* in 1931, which
reported on a lecture by Jonas on the ordination of women, shows
just how controversial her position was:

> One must not argue like that. One may say: New times require new
> institutions, including the female rabbi. One may say: neither we nor
> many valuable rabbis keep the tradition anyway—why then should we
> be especially prevented from ordaining women as rabbis, if we want
> and think we must do so. But one can NOT say: women as rabbis—that
> is in the spirit of Talmud and Torah.
>
> One can call on whoever but not on individual sentences and exam-
> ples from a book which one otherwise does not respect, before an audi-
> ence which has long denied this book the right to regulate our communal
> life. One may not call on the Talmud, of which everyone knows that it
> would have prohibited even such a profane women's lecture—even if
> these individual quotes were true. Even then one should have the
> courage *(Mut zur eigenen Courage)* to say: whether the Talmud allows
> or prohibits this, has little significance for me and the audience which
> employs me as a rabbi. We consider the female rabbi a requirement of
> our time. *Basta*

But to pull sentences from the Talmud against the spirit of the Talmud is unfair.[12]

Jonas' interpretation of Torah, Talmud, and halakhah in support of women's religious equality was unpopular on both the right as well as the left, among more conservative religious Jews as well as in more liberal circles. But she remained undeterred and insisted that women's rabbinate could be justified halakhically and did not break with traditional religious principles or rabbinic authority. Except for the role of witness, Jonas could not find any explicit prohibitions which would prevent women from assuming religious leadership and she believed deeply that neither God nor the core beliefs of Judaism discriminated on the basis of gender. By refusing to let patriarchal restrictions define her place in the synagogue, she became the first woman to hold a claim on the title (and job) of a rabbi.

There is no telling how her career would have developed, had the Nazis not wreaked havoc in Germany. Her persistence and accomplishments as a lecturer, preacher, teacher and pastoral counselor might well have earned her the recognition and congregational appointment she wanted so desperately. Instead, it was in part the chaos and brutality unleashed by the Nazis that helped break the determination "of the Berlin Jewish Congregation *(Jüdische Gemeinde)* ... not [to] assign her to preach in a regular congregational synagogue."[13] Like Guttmann, another former colleague, Dr. Israel Lehmann, insisted that she was never allowed to preach in a synagogue, but worked "merely [as] a preacher in an old age home, what is done in the U.S.A., usually by student rabbis."[14] However, their recollections are only partially correct, because Rabbi Jonas' abilities as a rabbi were acutely needed as the economic and social strangulation of the Jewish community in Berlin heightened. Her contract of 1937 allowed the Berlin community board to give Jonas greater responsibilities and employ her "in other areas *(anderweitig)* in the service of the community according to her abilities and performance." When more and more congregations were left without a rabbi because of arrests, deportations, or emigration, Jonas' rabbinic duties expanded. In 1940, the Reichsvereinigung der Juden in Deutschland assigned her as a congregational rabbi to Woltersdorf, a congregation including twenty-one suburbs. She was probably unable to fill this position because many members had left or had been deported and because she could not travel the long distances from Berlin on a regular basis.[15] By 1941, she traveled and substituted for rabbis in congregations in Frankfurt, Wolfenbüttel, Bremen, and Stolpe as well as in some synagogues in Berlin.[16] Thus, Jonas' rabbinic responsibilities increased as Jewish religious institutions strained to counter the Nazi assault and began to use all available resources, including the female rabbi.

Women's Congregational Work

Jonas increased visibility as a religious leader in congregations was not unique to the Jewish community. A similar process occurred in the Evangelical Churches where ordained women, who had previously been denied congregational appointments, were also allowed to work as congregational ministers in order to substitute for male ministers who had been drafted or imprisoned. This development confirms the general phenomenon during wartime, that women move into civilian positions as men get involved in military duties. A comparison of Protestant women's ordination to Jonas rabbinic career helps explain the paradoxical impact of war on professional opportunities for women.

Like Jonas, Protestant women had been graduating with academic degrees in theology beginning in the twenties and thirties and demanded employment in the Evangelical churches. They were, like Jonas, initially denied ordination and quietly employed in a variety of undefined, mostly teaching-related positions. But eventually, various regional churches of the German Evangelical Church created a new separate and inferior theological office for women. This office emphasized the essential difference between men and women, and was variously called vicar *(Vikarin)*, minister's aid *(Pfarrgehilfin)* or assistant minister *(Hilfspfarrerin)*.[17] Women were not ordained but "blessed in;" their ministry was restricted to women, youth and children; women were not to preach to men or have authority over them; only unmarried, celibate women could perform as vicars, and their employment ended with marriage; their office was to be supportive and subordinate to the male and supplement his role as minister.[18]

As the soon as the National Socialist party assumed power, this separate and inferior office of women's ministry was rescinded in some churches, such as Hamburg and Bavaria. Most Nazis embraced a sexist and patriarchal policy advocating "Aryan" women's biological role as mother and wife. They opposed women's employment and the "liberal (Jewish) individualism" of the Weimar Republic which had encouraged women to enter the universities and embark on professional careers. Some of the early laws designed to eliminate the alleged Jewish influence in German society also restricted non-Jewish women's education and professional roles. For instance, the law of April 1933 against the "Overcrowding of German Schools and Universities" restricted Jewish enrollment to 1.5 percent and imposed a quota of 10 percent on female non-Jewish students. Similar laws restricting and prohibiting Jews from practicing law, medicine, dentistry, etc., also regulated non-Jewish women's involvement in these professions. Non-Jewish women were removed from the civil service (June 1933), from medical practice (May 1934) and from legal professions (December 1935).[19] This "new spirit" of 1933 was adopted in some churches, such as the Hamburg synod, which reversed its earlier acceptance of women theologians and flatly stated: "According to scripture and confession the spiritual office is a male office. There is no more room for the law of November 8, 1927, concerning theologically educated women in the church of Hamburg, which grew out of an obsolete understanding of women's paid work."[20] In Cologne, a group of more progressive vicars were summarily fired in 1933.[21] Other churches kept the office of the vicar but severely restricted their work (and pay) to a subordinate role helping the male minister and serving only the spiritual needs of women, children and youth. No vicar was allowed to officiate in a congregation.

But despite this initial purge of professional women, the Nazi government began to actively recruit politically docile women into the labor force by 1936 in order to meet shortages in virtually all areas of German economy. Once the war began in 1939, the Nazis adjusted their patriarchal rhetoric of women's exclusive role as mother to the needs of a growing war economy.[22] The Nazis' explicit anti-feminist policy and legislation did not retard the growth of women's employment. Instead, "Aryan" Christian women experienced greater independence and moved into all areas of the workforce. The churches followed suit. By 1939, female vicars began to substitute for men and served as ministers in congregations where the male ministers had entered military service. Although the legal restrictions on women's ministry remained in effect they were routinely and systematically violated.

The majority of vicars were affiliated with the Confessing Church which had formed over the introduction of the Aryan Paragraph in 1933 and stood in opposition to National Socialism. While some in the Confessing Church supported full ordination rights for women, the majority did not.[23] Despite the vicars' repeated petitions to legalize their status, the synod of the Confessing Church in 1942 reached only a disappointing compromise. It recognized women's *de facto* equality "in times of emergency when the proper sermon of the Gospel from the mouth of a man has become silent,"[24] but denied women's equal rights in principle and upheld all previous restrictions. Women were allowed to work in all aspects of congregational ministry under severe war conditions, albeit at a fraction of a man's salary, but were expected to hand over their congregations upon the return of the male minister. For many female vicars, the end of the war was a traumatic experience. One vicar for whom "the war brought ... the greatest and most beautiful [service] ever given to me by life" recalls that when "the minister whom I had replaced came back and could take on his congregation by himself again ... I left a piece of my heart and a lot of my life force behind."[25] Ironically, for many vicars the war became the best time of their lives. It gave them the opportunity to work as autonomous, independent congregational ministers. As soon as the state of emergency due to the war ended, so did their ministry.[26] Once again, women were only allowed to work in social institutions, hospitals, prisons, and schools. They had to wait until the 1960s before the issue of women's congregational ministry was taken up again.

It is, of course, a moot point to ask whether Rabbi Regina Jonas would have been allowed to continue working as a congregational rabbi after the defeat of National Socialist Germany, since neither she nor her community survived. But the example of Protestant ordained women who achieved a measure of recognition during wartime crisis only to be dismissed shortly afterwards should give pause. It raises troubling questions about the impact of war on women's professional advancement. Surely, nobody would argue that the Nazi antisemitism which ended in the Holocaust served Jewish or non-Jewish women and that the Nazis, so to speak, helped Jonas' rabbinic career. But it remains a fact that professional women in Germany witnessed a greater demand for their skills and that their professional lives expanded because of and despite the chaos and destruction unleashed by the Second World War. While non-Jewish women filled the vacancies left by soldiers, the war against the Jews thrust Jewish women into leadership positions because it forced Jewish men out of their accustomed professional lives into unemployment, exile, displacement, or imprisonment. Hans Hirschberg remembers that "after Kristallnacht in November 1938, she [Jonas] preached in various synagogues in Berlin, often replacing rabbis who were thrown into concentration camps or had emigrated." [27] But this was a hollow victory and certainly not the kind of recognition Jonas had hoped and fought for so persistently during the early years of her career. Although she continued to insist on the essential equality of women, resisting the increasingly vicious and life threatening assaults of Nazi antisemitism and helping her Jewish community to survive began to dominate her work.

Denial of Genocidal Reality as Defiance

Was Jonas' religious message of perseverance, trust and courage an act of defiance of the Nazis or a form of escape, a fateful refusal to accept the severity of the genocidal threat? As far as the evidence goes (which Jonas deposited into the Jewish archives before she was deported), Jonas did not join an underground movement or participate in any organized effort to obstruct or sabotage the Nazi death machine. She understood her resistance to Nazi antisemitism as an extension of her rabbinic role. Her message of faith in God, love of humanity, and hope in the future contradicted Nazi reality, which decreed the falsehood of the Jewish faith and the diabolic nature of Jewish culture, and which enacted hatred of Jewish people.

Her sermons were especially noted for their ability to provide solace, to renew trust in God, and to bolster people's spirits. In a letter dated January 18, 1941, a congregation in Gardelegen complimented the *Reichsvereinigung* for sending such an outstanding preacher "who knows how to handle broken and despairing hearts, to elevate them, and to inspire and excite them with the wealth of her learning *(Anregungen)*."[28] In another letter of 1941, a woman thanked Jonas for a sermon which was "consolation and encouragement. ... Through your warm and cordial words, which are so healing for people, I have found new courage and new strength to continue with greater fervor my work which is certainly not easy work and requires iron nerves."[29]

Jonas redefined the profession of the rabbinate with traditionally female values and duties. In a letter written to Leo Baeck in 1940 and forwarded by him to Rabbi Jonas, a woman praises Jonas who "in her sincere rabbinic motherly way *[aufrichtigen rabbinisch mütterlichen Art]* did me a great service, so that I don't know how I can ever thank her. It has now been proven to me that Jewish humanism *(Humanität)* is not an empty phrase but a reality, and I will contribute my part that this magnanimous deed will not remain hidden."[30] Jonas took care of her "congregation," which typically consisted of people who were twice if not triply oppressed: the elderly who were often female, the sick, and the handicapped. She did not limit her pastoral care to the spiritual needs of her elderly congregants, but provided for their physical ones as well. Several letters from various European cities as well as from China and North America thanked her for taking care of elderly relatives (mostly parents) and asked her to help them materially as well as spiritually. For instance, Jonas approached the American Joint Distribution Committee to pressure an emigre in New York to "send regular financial aid for his ailing mother;"[31] she found food and clothing for people through the Jüdische Winterhilfe; organized gift giving for patients during Hanukkah; arranged book deliveries to patients in hospitals by the Kleiderkammer; helped to place an ailing grandfather in a senior citizen home; and assisted another person without family support upon his release from the hospital.[32] She raised funds for the Jüdische Winterhilfe and admonished her listeners and readers that charity is a very important *mitzvah* and that those who were emigrating should share as generously as possible with those forced to remain.[33]

While all remaining German Jews existed under extreme conditions and constant threats to their lives, senior citizens were especially vulnerable. They were unable to secure their survival by proving their worth as workers and by "organizing" the necessities of life. They were perceived as a drain on shrinking economic resources and as a burden on the community. Furthermore, many of these remaining seniors were elderly women who faced additional pressures because of their gender. As Marion Kaplan pointed out, for a number of reasons more men than women left Germany in time and "the statistics, memoirs, and interviews all give the impression that the Nazis, whose propaganda trumpeted the threat of Jewish men as rapists, thieves, and crooks, murdered a high percentage of elderly Jewish women."[34] Like many unmarried women, Jonas herself lived with and cared for her own mother.[35]

Her sermons often emphasized the obligation to care for the elderly and the sick. Contrary to Nazi ideology which advocated the health of the *Volksbody* by eliminating the weak and unhealthy, Jonas preached the sacred obligation to stand by the weaker members of the community. The Jewish religion, she argued in a 1938 lecture organized by WIZO (Women's International Zionist Organization), "is a rejection of peace and comfort. ... Religious life means practicing concern and love for the helpless and the burdened."[36] For Jonas, religion was not a withdrawal from the problems of the world, but an obligation to become involved in the welfare of the people. "The solemn service of God is that of the neighbor, and the most sacred service is that performed for the most downtrodden, those struck by misfortune, the helpless, fearful, worried, the person who despairs of life."[37] In another lecture she maintained that the fundamental message of Judaism was summarized in the first sentence of the Bible:

> In the beginning God created heaven and earth. Here faith becomes a mandate, the requirement of human beings to sustain the earth and to establish the rule of God in the world. ... Learning is a commandment which applies to men and women in the same way. Learning, however, is not pure theory. At the end of learning lies the deed.[38]

For Jonas the religious life was an activist life and she used her religious office to activate and energize her listeners on behalf of the most vulnerable.

Her deportation to Theresienstadt in the fall of 1942 did not affect her basic message. In a sermon held in Theresienstadt and attended by the well known psychiatrist Victor Frankl, she denounced the bio-eugenic vision of the "survival of the fittest" which the Nazis put into perverse practice in their euthanasia program and their genocidal policies in the ghettos, concentration, and death camps. Jonas compared the care for the mentally handicapped, the senile and the "degenerates" to the care of the stone tablets which Moses received on Mount Sinai. Just as the load of the stone tablets was carried along on the arduous journey through the desert, so the weak members of the people of Israel may not be abandoned as a burden. She affirmed the dignity of each human as God's creation whose handicap may inconvenience the community but who must not be deserted. The community, in her view, was responsible for the least of its members. It could not secure its survival by forsaking its elderly, handicapped, and ill. To do so, she maintained, meant forsaking God. Jonas strongly resisted the reduction of life to the survival of the fittest and worked strenuously to uplift and save the weakest.[39]

She defied genocidal reality by denying it the power to define her faith and interactions with people. Her sermons, lectures and chaplaincy work attempted to impose a different, humane, Jewishly affirmative reality onto people's daily experience of dehumanization, harassment, starvation, and death. Where people despaired, Jonas preached hope; where people were full of cynicism and bitterness, she preached the love of God and humanity; where people scrambled against each other to survive, she preached the sacredness of the weak. By repudiating the reality of despair, cynicism, and the selfish fight for survival she attempted to reverse the values which the Nazis inflicted on the Jewish community and to enable people to transcend the narrow confines of Nazi actuality.

In Theresienstadt, Jonas lectured and preached as part of the Freizeitgestaltung, the office of "leisure time activities." This office operated on a similar premise of denial as defiance by providing inmates with opportunities to escape the dreary misery of their lives by attending opera productions, theater performances, concerts, poetry readings, and philosophical soirees. The Freizeitgestaltung created temporal islands of humanism, culture and education, which would give people the energy to face the hostile environment again. The paperwork generated by the inmates of Theresienstadt (and housed today in the Jewish Archive in Prague) is an astounding monument to this strategy of defiance by denial. The "self-government" of Theresienstadt succeeded in creating a "normal" reality, sustained by a formidable bureaucratic apparatus that was designed to keep the threat and chaos of total destruction at bay.

This attempt to maintain a sense of normalcy in the face of genocide has been criticized by some historians as a self-defeating attitude. In the ongoing debate about what constitutes Jewish resistance to the Holocaust, this strategy has been faulted as an impediment to military resistance. According to historian Marrus, most rebellions occurred only after people realized that "all Jews were doomed and that there was no hope at all. Up to that point, even those disposed to resistance usually acted cautiously."[40] As long as people effectively denied the full hopelessness of their situation, it appeared wiser to cooperate rather than to provoke the Nazis' wrath—and thus inadvertently to ensure the smooth execution of the Final Solution. On the one hand, Regina Jonas' sermons of faith and trust in God's transcendent will and unknowable plans for the future blinded people from seeing that there was no future and that the time for open rebellion had come. On the other hand, her message of hope, solidarity, and perseverance was an act of defiance against the Nazis because it enabled people to retain their dignity and preserve their humanity in the face of an enemy intent as much on dehumanizing as on killing. Since the Nazis were determined to destroy Jewish people spiritually as well as physically, Jonas' work can be seen as an example of spiritual resistance. While it did not stop the machinery of destruction, it successfully helped people to withstand the Nazis' attempt to turn Jews into subhuman vermin and to destroy their humanity.

Regina Jonas was deported to Auschwitz on October 12, 1944, along with her sixty-eight-year-old mother, and was presumably killed. Most if not all of her sick, elderly, and handicapped flock perished as well. But her faith denied the Nazi regime the power to define her existence, to change her belief, or to abandon her faith in humanity. I want to end with Jonas' own words, the only written words available from her time in Theresienstadt. The text is a short meditation on a Biblical verse which she submitted as a dedication honoring the efforts of Karl Hermann, who recorded and memorialized the work of the Freizeitgestaltung. This dedication is not dated, but was presumably written close to the mass deportations from Theresienstadt to Auschwitz in September and October of 1944. She referred to the biblical story in Numbers where the king of Moab commissions Balaam to curse the people of Israel. Balaam, however, cannot pronounce the curses as long as God blesses the people. When the King of Moab pressures him to curse the people, he ends up blessing them. Jonas quoted Numbers 22:12, "You shall not curse the people, for they are blessed," and commented:

> Our Jewish people have been sent by God into history as "blessed." To be blessed by God means to give, wherever one steps, in every life situation, blessing, kindness, faithfulness, humility before God, selfless and devoted love to his creatures sustain this world. To erect these fundamental pillars of the world was and is Israel's task. Man and woman, woman and man have taken on this task with the same Jewish devotion. We strive toward this ideal in our grave and trying work in Theresienstadt ... to be servants of God, and as such to be transported from earthly into eternal spheres. May all of our work, which we strove to perform as servants of God, be a blessing for Israel's future and for that of humankind.[41]

Notes

1. Alexander Guttmann, "Hochschule Retrospective," in *CCAR Journal* (Autumn 1972), p. 74.
2. The *Israelitisches Familienblatt*, (June 4, 1931) reports that she preached in three small congregations.
3. *Israelitisches Familienblatt*, 45 (November 5, 1931)
4. Letter from Leo Baeck, BA Potsdam, 75 D Jo 1, No. 9, p. 7.
5. Letter from Leo Baeck, BA Potsdam, 75 D Jo 1, No. 9, p. 8.
6. Anstellungsurkunde, BA Potsdam, 75 D Jo 1, No 14, p. 31.
7. Regina Jonas, "Was haben Sie zum Thema Frau zu sagen?" *C.V. Zeitung*, 25 (June 6, 1938), BA Potsdam, 75 D Jo 1 No. 4, p. 63.
8. Regina Jonas, "Häusliche Gebräuche," *Jüdisches Nachrichtenblatt* 18 (March 3, 1939), BA Potsdam, 75 D Jo 1 No. 4, p.8, 8R.
9. Regina Jonas, "Was haben Sie Zum Thema Frau zu sagen?" BA Potsdam, 75 D Jo 1, No. 5, p. 60.
10. Annette Löwenthal, "Die Rabbinerin," *Frauenzeitung Berna* 40/16 (February 10, 1939), BA Potsdam, 75 D Jo 1 No 5, p. 53-54.

11. Regina Jonas, "Kann die Frau das rabbinische Amt bekleiden?" BA Potsdam, 75 D Jo 1, No.3, p. 95.

12. See the bruising critique of her lecture "Können Frauen Rabbiner werden?" on the Frauenseite of the *Israelitisches Familienblatt* 45 (November 5, 1931).

13. Alexander Guttmann, "Hochschule Retrospective," in *CCAR Journal*, p. 74.

14. Dr. Israel Lehmann, letter to me, June 8, 1992.

15. Letter of introduction, dated September 23, 1940, which could not be delivered and was returned. BA Potsdam, 75 D Jo 1, No.1, p.4.

16. For a list of her services, see von Kellenbach, "'God Does Not Oppress Any Human Being.' The Life and Thought of Rabbi Regina Jonas," *Leo Baeck Yearbook* XXXIX (1994), p. 223.

17. hese titles are taken out of the magazine of the *Verband evangelischer Theologinnen* which printed a membership list of 254 names and various professional titles. *Mitteilungen* 5 (1935) 2:pp. 10-16.

18. Dagmar Henze, "Die Geschichte der evangelischen Theologin—Ein Überblick," *Reformierte Kirchenzeitung* 3 (1991), pp. 97-99; Ilse Härter, "Persönliche Erfahrungen mit der Ordination von Theologinnen in der Bekennenden Kirche des Rheinlands und in Berlin/Brandenburg," in *Zwischen Bekenntnis und Anpassung,* Günther van Norden ed, (Köln: Rheinland Verlag, 1985), pp. 193-209; Heike Köhler, "Neue Ämter für neue Aufgaben" *Reformierte Kirchenzeitung* 5 (1991), pp. 165-169. Andrea Bieler, "Zur Professionalisierung kirchlicher Frauenberufe seit Ende des 19. Jahrhunderts: Unterordnung unter männliche Pfarrherrlichkeit oder Aufbruch zu neuen Räumen?" forthcoming, *(Tagungsbericht Arnoldshain*: 1991); Konvent Evangelischer Theologinnen in der Bundesrepublik Deutschland und Berlin (West), eds., *Das Weib schweigt nicht mehr: Katalog zur Ausstellung*, (Kirchenkreisamt Osterhold-Scharmbeck: 1990).

19. Andrea Bieler, "Aspekte nationalsozialistischer Frauenpolitik in ihrer Bedeutung für die Theologinnen," *Darum wagt es Schwestern*, Frauenforschungsprojekt zur Geschichte der Theologinnen, Göttingen, eds., (Neukirchen-Vluyn: Neukirchener Verlag), p. 249. In *Mein Kampf*, Hitler proposed denying women citizenship, anticipating the Nuremberg laws of 1935 which revoked Jewish citizenship: "The German girl is a state subject and only becomes a state citizen when she marries." This proposal did not become law. Trans. John Chamberlain, et. al. (New York: Reynal & Hitchcock, 1940), p. 659.

20. *Das Weib schweigt nicht mehr*, p. 22; Andrea Bieler, "Aspekte," p. 263.

21. Ilse Härter, "Vor politischen und kirchlichen Oberen schreckte sie nicht zurück," in *Junge Kirche*, 11 (1988), p. 608; Andrea Bieler, "Aspekte," pp. 267-268

22. Jill Stephenson, *Women and Nazi Society*, (New York: Barnes and Noble, 1975), p. 178; Andrea Bieler, "Aspekte," pp. 246-249; Dörte Winkler, *Frauenpolitik im "Dritten Reich"*, (Ludwigsburg: Hoffmann und Campe, 1977), p. 53.

23. The Aryan Paragraph had previously facilitated the removal of Jews from state offices, universities, legislature, etc., and was now extended to all offices in the church. The Aryan Paragraph was introduced after a state-mandated election of representatives to church synods, which led to majorities of Deutsche Christen, the National Socialist Christian party, in all but three regional church synods (Bavaria, Württemberg and Hannover). While most non-Jewish Germans acquiesced and supported the Aryan Paragraph as applied to the civil service, some resisted its use to determine church membership. Those ministers and theologians who challenged the state's criterion of race as principal factor for

admission into the church and asserted baptism as the sole constituent of the Christian community founded the *Pfarrernotbund* and begun organizing an independent, underground church in partial defiance of state law and state-sanctioned church administration. The *Verband evangelischer Theologinnen Deutschlands* declared its allegiance to the Confessing Church in October of 1934. They officially informed the head of the National Socialist church Reichsbischof Müller of their decision to refuse allegiance to his administration and to submit only to directives given by the leadership of the Confessing Church. *Mitteilungen des Verbandes evangelischer Theologinnen* 4 (1934), pp. 11-12.

24. Dagmar Henze, "Die Geschichte der evangelischen Theologin-Ein Überblick" *Rheinische Kirchenzeitung* 3 (1991), p. 98.

25. Elisabeth Hahn, "Studentinnengemeinde und Freizeitarbeit," in *Die Vikarin,* Anna Paulsen, ed., (Gelnhausen & Berlin: Burckhardhaus Verlag, 1956), pp. 9, 11.

26. As Ilse Härter recalls, the "last congregational replacement by a female theologian ended in 1948 due to the return of the male minister." Although the new democratic constitution of the Federal Republic guaranteed equality of the sexes (as had the Weimar Constitution), female theologians were removed from office without compensation and the debate over women's ordination was tabled until it was taken up again in the late sixties and early seventies; cf. Waltraud Hummerich-Diezun, "Die Weiterentwicklung der Berufsgeschichte der Theologinnen nach 1945-Ein Überblick," in *Darum wagt es Schwestern,* pp. 263-484

27. ans Hirschberg, quoted in Elisabeth Sarah, "Rabbi Regina Jonas: Missing Link in a Broken Chain," in *Hear Our Voice: Women Rabbis Tell Their Stories,* Sybil Sheridan, ed., (SCM Press, 1994), p, 7.

28. Letter, BA Potsdam, 75 D Jo 1 No. 2, p.53.

29. Letter, BA Potsdam, 75 D Jo 1 No. 2, p. 55.

30. Letter Margaret Saat, (February 28, 1940), BA Potsdam, 75 D Jo 1 9, p. 5

31. Letter, BA Potsdam, 75 D Jo 1 No. 1 pp. 54, 55.

32. These activities are recorded in letters found in BA Potsdam, 75 D Jo 1 No. 2.

33. Rabbiner Regina Sara Jonas, "Häusliche Gebräuche," *Jüdisches Nachrichten-blatt* 18 (March 13, 1939), BA Potsdam, 75 Jo 1 No. 44, p.8 R (note the law which forced the Jews to add the middle names Sara and Abraham).

34. Marion Kaplan, "Jewish Women in Nazi Germany: Daily Life, Daily Struggles, 1933-1939, in *Different Voices: Women and the Holocaust,* Carol Rittner and John K. Roth, eds., (New York: Paragon House, 1993), p. 204; see also Joan Ringelheim, "Women and the Holocaust: A Reconsideration of Research," in *Different Voices,* p. 396.

35. Jonas had lived with her widowed mother throughout her professional life. Her mother supported her career and accompanied her on assignments. Several of her correspondents were acquainted with her mother and asked Jonas to convey their regards or holiday wishes. Mother and daughter were deported together to Theresienstadt on November 5, 1942. During the following two years in Theresienstadt, Regina Jonas was able to safeguard her mother, who was 66 years old when they arrived, although the elderly died in great numbers because of lack of food, space, heat, clothing, and constant disease and harassment. Regina Jonas was able to delay her mother's deportation to the very end. Both of them were on one of the last transports to Auschwitz, leaving Terezin on October 12, 1944.

36. "Ein WIZO Nachmittag," *Jüdisches Gemeindeblatt für Berlin* 26 (June 26, 1938), BA Potsdam, 75 D Jo 1 No 5, p. 16.

37. Rabbiner Regina Sara Jonas, "Häusliche Gebräuche," *Jüdisches Nachrichtenblatt* 18 (March 13, 1939), BA Potsdam, 75 D Jo 1 No. 44, p. 8R.

38. Regina Jonas, "Religiöse Gegenwartsprobleme," *Israelitisches Familienblatt* 25 (June 23, 1938), p. 17, BA Potsdam, 75 D Jo 1 No. 5, p. 18.

39. Telephone conversation with Prof. Dr. Victor Frankl, June 6, 1991.

40. Michael R. Marrus, *The Holocaust in History*, (New York: Penguin, 1987), pp. 135-136.

41. Pamatnik Terezin, Ustredni Kartoteka. Czech Republic.

Chapter 12

A PERSONAL ACCOUNT

Gabor Vermes

I have prayed many times in my lifetime, but never so hard as during the months of January and February, 1945. I was staying in Buda, in the basement of a villa with about a dozen or so ten-to-eleven year old boys, all of us Hungarian Jews. My only precious earthly possession was a large beat-up winter coat, which functioned solely as my blanket, since we did not dare to go outside.

During nighttime, but sometimes at odd hours of the day, lying on my bunk-bed, I often pulled the coat over my head. There and then, the noises of fierce fighting between the Russians and the Germans in the besieged city of Budapest dimmed, nor did any human voice filter through the thick garment of my coat. I was alone with God.

What kind of image did I have of Him as an eleven-year-old child? After all, my family presented me with two different approaches to Judaism. One came from my pious maternal grandfather, who strictly observed Jewish laws, with the exception of dietary ones. As a young recruit to the Austro-Hungarian Army, he had learned to love ham and bacon. Throughout his long life—he died at age ninety-one—he continued both to pray and eat these forbidden foods. I used to wonder whether grandfather had made a pact with God, promising Him strict observance of most of His laws and hoping, as a reward for that, to receive absolution for the one major transgression.

Certainly, in my eyes, grandfather appeared to be a man of no inner doubts. He was a clever self-made man, strong and tyrannical. But toward me, his only grandson, he was always gentle and loving. It was a wonderful adventure to accompany him to the Friday evening services. My grandmother was waiting for us at their apartment, with candles to be lit and a splendid dinner.

Nothing in my life has ever matched the warmth of our big family get-togethers in the same apartment on Passover nights. I worshipped my grandfather, and , if I had any image of God at that young age, it was undoubtedly similar to the Old Testament figure of my grandfather, that is, sturdy, tough, and larger than life.

Living with my parents had, however, given me another perspective on life. The tone was set by my father, totally assimilated and secular, indifferent to any religion, including his own Judaism. He was truly at home with the eighteenth-century French *philosophes,* and the piety of his father-in-law left him cold. We celebrated Christmas at home, simply because my parents did not want my holidays to be different from that of my Gentile playmates. My grandfather would growl when he came to visit and saw the Christmas tree, but other than that, he kept his mouth shut about this issue.

The situation between my father and grandfather was reversed at the time of my *bar mitzvah.* Then, grandfather was in his glory, shepherding me through this experience, while my father stood there forlornly, as the rabbi put a prayer shawl around his neck. The mental photograph of this scene, which happened so many years ago, remains with me as the visual image of polarized attitudes toward religion in my family.

And yet! During the German occupation of Hungary, the news that your life could be saved if you converted to Christianity spread among the Jews of Budapest. My parents and I were among the many Jewish families who flocked to various Catholic churches on Sundays to receive religious instruction. One Sunday afternoon, my mother and I were ready to leave for our designated church, but my father refused to budge from his favorite armchair. To repeated entreaties, his curt response was, "We are not going." It turned out later that baptism saved no one, but this was not known at the time my father refused to proceed to church. My best guess is that, after several weeks of attending church, my ultrasecular father concluded that dying honestly was preferable to living a lie.

Thus, after several sessions at church, my God remained the God of the Jews, whatever the collision between my father's and grandfather's diametrically opposed approaches to religion. However, when I was alone with Him, under my winter coat during the bombardments, my words were not echoing any Hebrew prayers I had learned in school and from my grandfather. Nor were they Christian prayers taught to us by Gabor Sztehlo, the Lutheran pastor who was hiding us.

As I remember them from the distance of over half a century, they were words of an intimate conversation with God. I knew beyond a shadow of any doubt, that He was listening even to my whispers. Although God never responded, His silence seemed to have carried the promise of my survival. And not only mine but also my parents, who were themselves in hiding, somewhere in Pest, separated not only from me but also from each other.

The inner strength I had gained from faith was such that I, who was until tragedy struck a spoiled only child of an upper-middle class family, never sobbed, never even shed a tear. My faith could have moved mountains, but that was not what I would have wanted to do. My wish was so simple that under normal circumstances it might have sounded totally commonplace: to be with my parents, to be just a normal eleven-year-old kid again, good with words but bad with numbers, a hopeless soccer fanatic, who stopped talking for weeks to his best friend Andrew, because he had switched colors and began rooting for the enemy team.

But January and February 1945 were not normal times, and my simple prayers saved me from despair. I am certain that this was also true of my young friends in the basement, though we kept our individual conversations with God private for the most part. Instead, we carried on talks that could either be frighteningly adult about life, death, and persecution, or quite childish, about such subjects as who could keep swearing the longest without repeating himself, about sports or funny aunts and uncles. And, of course, there was always talk about food. In the city under siege, all food supplies were cut, all food stores had been closed, and we were slowly starving.

Occasionally, we formed a small chorus and sang German songs to German officers. Pastor Sztehlo was more afraid of the Hungarian fascists, the Arrow Cross, than of the German army, the Wehrmacht. In order to use the latter as a defensive shield, he intentionally befriended several German officers who came to visit him and his family almost every evening. Posing as Hungarian refugee children, who had fled the advancing Soviet armies in eastern Hungary, we provided occasional entertainment. Luckily, our faces were barely seen by the feeble light of kerosene lamps.

What had brought us to that pass? As late as early 1944, Hungary was still a relatively peaceful haven for Jews. It is true that able-bodied Jewish males were badly treated and often died in labor battalions at the front, but the rest of the Jewish population lived relatively undisturbed. But the Germans, worried about the flagging loyalty of their Hungarian allies, occupied the country on March 19, 1944. And then all hell broke loose. Jews from the countryside were deported mostly to Auschwitz, while those in Budapest were herded into so-called Jewish apartment houses. We had to wear the yellow star any time we left those houses, which could take place only during strictly prescribed hours.

Although forbidden to attend school, we, the children in our Jewish house, filled the time with all kinds of imaginary games, including plans to join the anti-Nazi underground. Our assumed liaison to that underground, a slightly retarded eighteen-year-old young man, seemed to us, ten-and-eleven-year old kids, a very mature-sounding brave warrior. He promised us the delivery of a single hand-grenade. The mere thought of getting one made us ecstatic. Within a few weeks, though, the young man vanished into a labor battalion, and our plans for an armed resistance came to a premature halt.

Our games, hopes, illusions crashed suddenly when in mid-October 1944, the extreme fascists, the Arrow Cross Party, seized power with German help. The killings began. Arrow Cross thugs entered Jewish houses, including ours, at nights, to drag people, mostly old men, women, and children out of their beds. They were then taken to the Danube and shot into the river.

Luckily, my parents and myself had left our house a few days earlier. After my wandering on the streets and hiding out in a warehouse, a kind relative from a mixed Catholic/Jewish marriage took me across the Danube, to a children's home on Bogar Street in Buda, which the Swiss Red Cross had set up for the rescue of Jewish children. There, Pastor Sztehlo greeted me with a friendly smile, which was like unexpected sunshine in the midst of dreadful stormy weather.

We children were constantly occupied at the home. The few adults, also Jews, were teaching us various subjects, and we also played all kinds of fun games. In addition, we had daily Bible-readings of passages both from the Old and the New Testaments. I do not believe that Pastor Sztehlo had our conversion on his mind; rather, he knew that we would gain strength through our immersion in holy texts. He was absolutely right.

For Christmas Eve, I wrote a play, my first and last, which was performed in front of all the kids and the few adults. The center of the plot was a family eating dinner. Real food was served to the young actors and actresses, and, for minutes, the audience heard nothing but the clatter of utensils and the sounds of slow and deliberate eating.

By the next day, the Christmas spirit was in shambles, as the Russians launched an attack from the Buda Hills that transformed our house and adjoining garden into the front line. If we wanted to live, we had no choice but to escape one night, crawling on our bellies as bullets were whizzing by our ears. We then found shelter in the basement of an abandoned villa, the basement of my heartfelt prayers.

Within a couple of weeks, our food situation was getting critical, and lacking hygiene, we were also tormented by lice. Liberation by the Russians came none too soon for us. I still remember the round peasant face of the first Russian soldier, motioning to us at the top of the narrow staircase to come up from the basement to the main floor. There, at the windows, soldiers were shooting at neighboring houses still in German hands.

Soon, it was time to move to yet another place, where we were mostly preoccupied with anguish over the fates of our parents. Both Buda and Pest were liberated, but, because all the bridges had been blown up, no contact existed between the two halves of the city. And yet, one day as we were eating pea soup for lunch, the door opened and my mother walked in. She could not reconcile herself to not knowing what had happened to me, and crossed the frozen Danube by foot three times before she finally found me. The first time the fighting was not yet over, so she had carried her false documents with her, the ones she had used while hiding, should she fall into the hands of the Germans or the Arrow Cross. By the time she found me, the icecover on the Danube was beginning to melt, but we made it safely back to Pest. Miraculously, my father also survived his ordeal, and when we reunited, the tears did finally start to flow.

I could now cockily say that my trust in God's promise paid off. Tragically, this was not the case with many of my young friends who had lost one or both parents. And indeed, bitter disillusionment over apparent divine capriciousness caused many in my generation to embrace either extreme Stalinism or militant secular Zionism. Nor can I characterize my current faith as strong any longer. But as long as I live, I shall admire the little boy I once was, all too sad and wise for his age, who also had an unerring instinct in finding the best, the safest, and the most rewarding path to God.

Part III

AFTERMATH: POLITICS, FAITH, AND REPRESENTATION

– *Chapter 13* –

ZIONIST AND ISRAELI ATTITUDES TOWARD THE ARMENIAN GENOCIDE[1]

Yair Auron

During the later decades of the nineteenth century, the fever of nationalism reached and affected two minority communities: the Armenian *millet* of the Ottoman Empire (a non-Islamic community with a limited autonomous standing) and the Jewish communities in Europe. The Armenians and the Jews were to undergo two remarkably similar processes. They were to be transformed from ethno-religious communities into modern nations, and then, to become victims of monstrous genocides perpetrated by national forces with an indisputable religious coloring: the Armenians were to become the victims of emerging Turkish nationalism and the Jews of German-Nazi nationalism.

This chapter gives an overview and attempts to analyze the attitudes of the Zionist Movement, the Jewish community in Palestine, and the State of Israel towards the Armenian genocide. More importantly, this presentation aims at understanding the seemingly indifferent disposition, and later denial, of the genocide of the Armenian people by the Ottoman Empire during the First World War. Zionist indifference towards the Armenian tragedy will be demonstrated through the analysis of various events and debates which erupted within the Zionist Movement.

This chapter is adapted from a project that we believe is a precursor of its kind, for both presenting the phenomenon and raising inescapably disconcerting moral questions. The analysis will deal with the following issues: Herzl and the Zionist leadership (1894-1904), the controversy between Herzl and Lazare, the controversy in the Jewish press in Palestine in 1909; the Jewish community in Palestine during World War One; the literary reaction; and the attitudes of the state of Israel.

Herzl and the Zionist Leadership: 1894-1904

The first occurrence in Zionist history to make reference to the Armenian people arose in the sharp discord between Theodore Herzl, the founder of the Zionist Organization, and the journalist and political activist Bernard Lazare. Bernard Lazare was a French Jew who for a time saw himself as a member of the Zionist movement; he was one of the first to voice in public impassioned support for Dreyfus.

Herzl's political efforts in the closing years of the nineteenth century were aimed at the Ottoman Empire. He sought to achieve some sort of a diplomatic recognition from the Sultan Abd al-Hamid II. Unfortunately, Abd al-Hamid II was the Ottoman Sultan under whose rule two hundred thousand to three hundred thousand Armenians were killed in 1894 to 1896. Herzl wanted to exploit the Sultan's manifestly failing image in world opinion and the Empire's financial distress. Herzl alluded to the possibility of offering financial assistance, mediating between the Sultan and the Armenians, and of further assistance in improving the Abd al-Hamid image in the Western press after the massacre of the Armenians. Herzl hoped to obtain, in exchange, a charter for the Zionist Movement permitting a Jewish settlement in Palestine.[2]

Did Herzl wish (and if so, to what extent) to make use of the Armenian problem which burdened the Turkish Sultan, in order to promote his Zionist goals? It appears that Herzl did indeed try to make use of it, as a proponent of the Sultan rather than the Armenians, whether as an intermediary or by helping the Sultan in his battle with public opinion.

At Herzl's initiative, the Fifth Zionist Congress, which met in Basel in December 1901, sent public greetings of admiration to the Sultan in order to create sympathy for Turkey. The telegram contains an "expression of dedication and gratitude which all of the Jews feel regarding the benevolence which His Highness the Sultan has always shown them." Earlier, Herzl had praised the Sultan in his opening address to the Congress.[3] Bernard Lazare was incensed at these matters. In the Armenian journal, *Pro Armenia*, Lazare published a short, sharp article, "The Zionist Congress and the Sultan," which attacked the Zionist Congress and Herzl in particular.[4] *Pro Armenia* appeared in Paris from 1901 to 1908. Among the members of its editorial board were Georges Clemençeau, Jean Jaurès, and Anatole France. Clemençeau, who was considered by some to be pro-Armenian, nevertheless abandoned the Armenian cause and broke his explicit promises to them, when he was head of the French government at the end of the First World War. Lazare's decision to publish his article in an Armenian journal was a way of expressing his support for and identification with their struggle:

> The Zionist Congress which gathered in Basel paid honor to the Sultan Abd al-Hamid II. The delegates, or those who present themselves as such, of the most ancient of all oppressed peoples whose history has been written in blood, have sent their blessing to the worst of murderers. They are part of a people, six million of whose brethren groan under the boot of the Czar, not to mention those who are treated like beasts in Rumania, in Galicia, in Persia, in Algier, and even in those countries which consider themselves civilized. They are pariahs, and in great numbers are wasting away through hunger and pain. Every day they are slaughtered and sacrificed [in the original: *en holocaust*] to some Moloch. They are inundated by mud, curses and venom ...

The controversy between Lazare and Herzl at the end of 1901 and the beginning of 1902 is an expression of differences of opinion between people over the means, permissible or impermissible, to achieve their goals.[5] Herzl, who sought political success at almost any price, was not particular about his means. It ought to be mentioned that his efforts, attempts and intercessions with the Turks were in vain and did not achieve their goal. It is possible that they were doomed from the beginning. This tendentious attitude of Herzl toward the Armenian tragedy is neglected, almost completely, in the various biographies written about Herzl.

The Controversy in the Jewish Press in Palestine: 1909

Another interesting and fascinating controversy broke out in Eretz Israel in 1909 over an article by Itamar Ben-Avi, the editor of "Hatzvi," in his paper. Itamar Ben-Avi, "the first Hebrew Child," had lived several years in Paris and was influenced by the discussions about *l'affaire* Dreyfus and "*J'accuse*" of Emile Zola. In 1909, twenty thousand to thirty thousand Armenians had been slaughtered in the area of Adana, in Cilicia.

On May 4, 1909, Itamar Ben Avi published an unsigned editorial entitled "We" *("Anahnu").*[6] The editorial begins thus: "We are
a peculiar people. Yes, We!" The editorial is written in two parts.
The first part relates to the alleged but not proven attempt of Sultan Abd al-Hamid II, two weeks previously, to reestablish control
over the Turkish capital, Constantinople, and to wipe out the
achievements of the "Young Turks."

> But while in all of the countries of Turkey, peoples were shaken by a
> strong national sense, while the "Young Turks" organized as a coura-
> geous band; while the Christians, like the Greeks and the Bulgarians,
> were quick to raise their voices and speak out, by the thousands, to
> strengthen the Armenian and Parliamentary camps, as a united people,
> announcing to Young Turkey that they will act as one to oppose the
> arrogant insurgents, at that time what did we do, we the Jews? Yes, we!
> Alas, nothing.

In the second part of the editorial, Itamar Ben Avi blames the
Jews for indifference to the atrocities which the Turks are committing against the Armenians. In blunt and provocative language,
apparently intentional, he condemns the ego- and ethnocentricity
of the Jews. He also takes exception to the "monopoly of suffering" which the Jews have appropriated to themselves, ignoring the
fact that "there is another people in the world which suffers like
the Jews."

> Another minor comment: we have been told that the Armenian com-
> munity in Jerusalem turned to Rabbi Salant requesting that he encour-
> age the members of his community to contribute a bit of money for the
> pitiful relatives of the Armenians who were slaughtered by the Muslims
> in Adana and its environs. Fifteen thousand Armenians were massa-
> cred, murdered, put to death. Fifteen thousand—and this horrifying
> number means nothing to us! As always with the Jews! Go tell the Jews
> that there are pogroms in Russia, against the Jews of course; go tell them
> that a couple of hundred of their coreligionists have been killed, and you
> shall see what fearsome effect your words have upon them: Jews have
> been killed! The poor Jews! Once again they have been the victims of
> idolatory and barbarism! The pitiful Jews! And at once they will shove
> their hand into their pocket and give generously to aid the survivors.
>
> But go tell them that there is another people in the world which suf-
> fers like the Jews. Go describe to them the sorrows of that people, years
> and years ago, when that very Abd al-Hamid II gave the order and
> three hundred thousand of them were exterminated—an entire nation!
> Go, tell them moreover that only two weeks ago another fifteen thou-
> sand Armenians were taken to the slaughter, wretched Armenians. ...
>
> A slight grimace on their lips, a short heartfelt sigh, and nothing more.
> The Armenians are not Jews, and according to folk tradition the Arme-
> nians are nothing more than Amaleks!

Amaleks? We would give them help? To whom? To Amaleks? Heaven forbid! What Rabbi Salant replied we do not know. But he did not say much, of that we can be sure. And the proof? We today at *Hatzvi*, are initiating a collection for the benefit of the devastated Armenians. We ourselves will give to this effort 10 francs to the wretched who are left, to the widows and orphans, the bereaved, the blind, the lame and the sick. And we call upon all of the Jews in our country to deliver to our editorial offices their donation for the Armenians, the donation of the oppressed to the oppressed, the donation of a people without a country to a people without a country—will the Jews hear us? Will they rise to our call? We shall see!

The Controversy

The editorial staff of *Hatzvi* contributed ten francs to the Armenians, and the workers of *Hatzvi* one franc. The editorial aroused fierce reaction in the Jewish and Eretz Israel press and it was attacked for its style, sharpness and bluntness. But most of the critics attacked *Hatzvi* for slandering the Jews "as the worst enemies of Israel," and for "spreading libel about us." With regard to the content, the critics took exception to the charge that the Jews care only about themselves: The Jews, they said, are taking part in the struggle for freedom and liberation in the world. An additional charge was that the paper had taken anti-Turkish stands which might endanger the Yishuv (the Jewish settlement in Palestine); in this case, taking a stand on the side of the Armenians who were in a conflict with the Turks. *Hatzvi's* position was "baseless persecution, which could only lead to strife and contention between peoples." It is interesting that some of the sharpest reaction were in regard to the Armenians.[7]

Eretz Israel During World War I

The small Jewish Yishuv in Eretz Israel numbered in the beginning of World War I eighty-five thousand people out of the seven hundred thousand people living west of the Jordan River. It was a divided Jewish community. Half of them belonged to the "Old Yishuv" while the other half were Zionists who migrated to Eretz Israel with the start of the Zionist homecoming in 1881. The Jewish people in the world were divided, in loyalty and geographical spread, between the warring empires, and the Zionist Movement officially presented a neutral stand almost until the end of the war. Despite huge difficulties, the Yishuv survived the war years. Its fortune could have been much worse. From that viewpoint, Zionist policy was a success. The Yishuv knew about the annihilation of the Armenians in 1915. Evidence and diaries of that period testify that the people of the Yishuv and its leaders knew what was happening while the events were taking place and feared a similar fate. The fear was evident not only in subjective feelings, but was especially articulated in two events during the war: the expulsion of the Jews of Jaffa in April 1917, and the uncovering of the pro-British spy network (the Nili Group) in October 1917.

There are varying opinions among historians as to the relative weight of the parties—particularly the United States and Germany—who aided the Jews in Palestine during this period.[8] In contrast, some historians emphasize the influence of Jewish public opinion in the world, since Jamal Pasha—who believed that the Jews had great political strength internationally—feared its alleged power.[9]

The Nili Organization and its Attitude Towards the Armenians

The group knows as "Nili" (an acronym of the passage in the First Book of Samuel, 15:29, literally "the Glory of Israel [i.e. God] will not lie," commonly interpreted as "the redemption of Israel will come"), stood out among the people of the Yishuv with its attitude in regards to the Armenian genocide. This pro-British spy network, which comprised fewer than forty members in all, helped the British during World War I by gathering information on the Turkish army. It was uncovered in October 1917, and some of its leading members paid with their lives. The historiography on the "Nili affair" is divided in its assessment of this group's actions. Were these young people, mostly from Jewish agricultural villages, lowly spies or national heroes? The first Jewish underground in the country or traitors? Visionaries or adventurers? Or perhaps all of the above combined?

In the present context, it is important to point out that an empathetic identification with the Armenian tragedy evolved at the time among the top figures of the group. Even though a few reminders of this supportive attitude are recalled from time to time, the first detailed analysis and comprehensive scholarly illumination of it is provided in my study.

Among the leading figures of the Nili group was Avshalom Feinberg, who already in 1907 had written "The Time of Oppressed Peoples,"[10] and in October and November 1915 wrote two reports, both mentioning the murder of the Armenians. The first report was directed to Henrietta Szold, secretary of the United States-based board of trustees of the Experimental (Agricultural) Station at Athlit, which was managed by Aaron Aaronsohn, the leader of the Nili group. It appears to have been the first written reaction from Pales-

tine (although it was actually written in Alexandria) to the destruction of the Armenians in 1915. Under the title "Facts and Worri-
some Rumors," Feinberg asks if the Jews might not be the next
target of Turkish genocide:

> And now new disasters have come about. The Armenians are being
> murdered *en masse*. In Van alone, 35,000 were slaughtered at one time.
> Large numbers of their people in the work brigades are being shot.
> They are being starved and tortured, due, it is asserted, to premeditated
> incitement, which was instigated to take vengeance on the rebels! Sol-
> diers, take fire! And the piles of bodies are food for the crows. In the air
> the question circulates among those who welcome it and those who fear
> it: when will our turn arrive?[11]

Feinberg was full of admiration for the efforts on behalf of the
Yishuv and the Armenians of the U.S. Ambassador to Turkey,
Henry Morgenthau, and of Dr. Otis Glazebork, U.S. Consul General in Jerusalem. Feinberg was aware of the role of the individual
and his influence on the flow of history. He is full of praise for Morgenthau's efforts on behalf of the Armenians:

> It is fair to say that this man has entered human history through the
> front door, by virtue of his approach to the defense of the Armenians. In
> his defense of the Armenians he acted not only as a brave American and
> the valuable Ambassador of a great nation. He also gave of himself.[12]

The second report, sent to a British intelligence officer in Cairo,
includes a "Pro Armenia" section, in which Feinberg reflects on the
Armenian massacre, expressing his emotions and his strong feelings
as a Jew along with sharp criticism of the Christian (and Western)
world, which stood on the sidelines when help and rescue could
have been provided:

> My teeth have been ground down with worry. Whose turn is next?
> When I walked on the blessed and holy ground on my way up to
> Jerusalem, I asked myself if we are living in the modern era in 1915, or
> in the days of Titus or Nebuchadnezzer? And I, a Jew, forgot that I am
> a Jew (and it is very difficult to forget this "privilege"). I also asked
> myself if I have the right to weep "over the tragedy of the daughter of
> my people" only and whether Jeremiah did not shed tears of blood for
> the Armenians as well?!
> Because after all, inasmuch as the Christians—of whom not a few
> sometimes boast that they have a monopoly over the commandments of
> love, mercy and brotherhood—have been silent, it is imperative that a
> son of that ancient race which has laughed at pain, overcome torture
> and refused to give in to death for the last two thousand years, should
> stand up. ... It is imperative that a drop of the blood of our forefathers,
> of Moses, of the Maccabeans who rose up in the scorched land of

Judea, of Jesus who prophesied on the banks of the blue Sea of Galilee, and the blood of Bar Kochba ... that a drop of the blood which was saved from annihilation should rise up and cry: look and see, you whose eyes refuse to open; listen, you whose ears will not hear, what have you done with the treasures of love and mercy which were placed in your hands? What good have rivers of our spilled blood done? How have you realized your high ideals in your lives?

Later on, Avshalom requests, "... please forgive me for the tone of my words, Lieutenant, for in this land I have roots in the past, and dreams for the future, and I have graves here, and a home; I have a mother and a sister, and a new generation in my sister's daughter, a dear small child eight years old (the same age as the Armenian children who were sold ...). Here does my heart bleed, and scream. Forgive me."[13]

An important account of the murder of the Armenians appeared in 1916 in the book *With the Turks in Palestine* by Alexander Aaronsohn (Aaron and Sarah Aaronsohn's brother and also member of Nili) who was then in the United States. Already in November 1915, Aaronsohn had published a short and moving document called "Armenia," urging the Armenians to join the Jews in a common struggle against the Ottoman Empire.[14]

Armenians, my brothers, we have nothing to expect from the nations, we have only to offer our souls and that is of no marked value. The Turks have an army and that counts. Let us give up hope of a salvation brought by others. Let us get up and defy the world that calls itself progressive and just. Let us join hands and stand up for our rights and not beg for mercy. And if it is God's will that we die, if it is written in the book of our destiny that no redemption is possible for us, let us, at least, die with the sweet feeling that our virgins, our old men, our babies, our youths have been revenged. (New York, November, 1915).

Sarah Aaronsohn, another top figure in Nili, personally witnessed, during a journey from Istanbul to Haifa in December 1915, the massacre of the Armenians and told her associates about it. She also referred to the Turkish crimes against the Armenians as she was dying after shooting herself when tortured by the Turks in October 1917.

When Aaron Aaronsohn reached London, in November 1916, he brought his sister's testimony as part of "Pro Armenia" (see the following section).

A sister of the writer traveled from Constantinople to Haifa in the month of December 1915. She was never hysterical before, but since that trip whenever any allusions to Armenians are made in her presence she gets into a fit of hysteria. A few of the things she had actually seen: hundreds of bodies of men, women and babes on both sides of the track and dogs feeding on these human corpses. Turkish women rummaging in the clothing of the corpses in hope of some hidden treasure.

At one station (in Gulek or Osmanieh, the writer can remember no more where it was) thousands of starving, typhus stricken Armenian were waiting for days for a train to carry them southwards. They were lying on the ground near the main track and on the sidings. When the train arrived the engineer, on seeing Armenians on the rails, purposely pushed his locomotive in the mass of Armenians and overran and hurt about fifteen of them. He then triumphantly jumped off his engine, rubbed his hands in joy and called out to a friend of his, "Did you see how I smashed maybe fifty of these Armenian swine?"

The same witness has seen trains arriving packed with 60-80 Armenians in each car when 40 would have over crowded the car, and at the station 10 or 20 dead (of hunger or typhus). Armenians would be thrown out of the car and a respective number of alive Armenians packed in their stead. Needless to say, not even a symbolic effort was made at disinfection.[15]

Eytan Belkind, a Jewish officer in the Turkish Army and a member of Nili, was stationed near Dir a-Zor (today a Syrian town on the border with Iraq), where up to three hundred thousand Armenians who had survived the death marches were annihilated. He described what he saw:

> They ordered the Armenians to gather thorns and thistles and pile them up in a high pyramid. They, then, bound all the Armenians there, close to 5,000 of them, hand to hand, placed them in a circle around the pyramid of thorns and set it alight, with flames rising to the heavens. The cries of the wretched victims burning to death in the huge bonfire could be heard miles away. I fled from the place, unable to watch this terrible sight ... Two days later, I returned there and saw the corpses of thousands of charred human beings.[16]

The leader of the Nili Group was Aaron Aaronsohn, a charismatic, highly educated man with a far-reaching vision. Aaronsohn reacted to, and documented, what happened to the Armenians. He tried to help them until his mysterious death in May 1919. The most important documentation among all the reports and documents and the diary he left—in my opinion—was his intelligence report "Pro Armenia." He submitted that report to the British War Office in November 1916. The British considered the document with high regard and it was sent to the highest levels after being edited (including some deletions) and summarized and having its title changed to "The Turkish Treatment of Armenians." Aaronsohn's report dealt with the key questions relating to the imminent emergence of genocide (even though that precise term was not yet

in use) such as: who knew about it, which part of the Turkish population had participated in the destruction, the role of the Germans
in the genocide, and how the Great Powers reacted. He also provided a critical reading of the account by the Protestant German
pastor, Johannes Lepsius, who had worked on behalf of the Armenians during the early massacres of 1896 and later protested the
widespread acts of destruction perpetrated in 1915 and 1916 in a
report published in Germany in 1916. In his own report, Aaronsohn also expressed his personal, human, and moral reaction to the
murders and looked at it from a Jewish point of view as well.[17]

Another question which he raises is the following:

> It might be asked: what part of the population or of the organized pub-
> lic services was carrying out this wholesale destruction of Armenian life
> and property. The reply is that no class of the Mohammedan popula-
> tion, rich or poor, high or low, young or old, men or women kept away
> from murdering and robbing, which of course does not mean to say that
> every individual Mohammedan is to be blamed, without exceptions. A
> few noteworthy exceptions were reported, cases of individual help ten-
> dered by old Turks are known, but they were very rare, isolated and
> always rebuffed by the Authorities, military and civil.

This passage was deleted from the British report.

Aaronsohn is extremely critical of the Germans and he says,
among other things, that the German mentality arouses wonder.
"The Armenian question was a safe question to tackle with official
Germans and the writer failed on no occasion to start on it, so he
had the opportunity to listen to hundreds of stories proving the cruelty of the Turks, the useless and shameless barbarity, and so on."
Aaronsohn is also shocked by the Germans' exploitation and of the
Armenians' distress, and notes the imperialistic political reasons
for the German approach to the Armenian question. Aaronsohn
sums up "Pro Armenia":

> Looking at it from this angle, would any one who knows something of
> Germans and the long and sometimes crooked way they can go to
> realize their high ambitions, which are in fact nothing less than divine
> missions, would any such man hesitate to say that wiping out the
> thriftiest element in those countries could not have displeased or hurt
> German politics? And would not the Germans themselves, when bet-
> ter fed and in more boisterous spirits than today, have aksed: is this a
> crime? That is arguable, but it is good, farsighted German *realpolitik*,
> is it not? The Armenian massacres are the carefully planned acts of the
> Turks, and the Germans will certainly be made forever to share the
> odium of these acts.

The British also deleted Aaron's accusations against the Germans for doing nothing to stop the barbaric treatment of the Armenians, as well as his fairly detailed treatment of the Lepsius Report.

Literature and Reality: The Massacre of the Armenians as Described in the Literature of Eretz Israel and the Impact of Franz Werfel's *Forty Days of Musa Dagh*

Literature also portrays reality. According to this viewpoint, literature is also a representation of events—a complementary documentation. One can examine, through it, the attitude of the Jewish community of the Yishuv in Eretz Israel toward the Armenian genocide. We have done this by studying expressions about the Armenian tragedy in original literary works and through the reaction to the book *The Forty Days of Musa Dagh* by Franz Werfel.

Feelings about the Armenian massacre appear in only two literary works written in Eretz Israel in the 1920's. One is the trilogy *Until Jerusalem* by Aharon Reuveni. This is a broadly conceived novel about what was happening in Jerusalem during the First World War. It earned lukewarm reviews when it appeared, but was published again in the 1960s when it encountered enthusiastic acceptance and reviews. Reuveni was considered an outsider in his days, both in literary circles and for his political views. The Armenian issue is not central in his work, but the segments dealing with it are most significant.

In a forgotten novel by Shmuel Bass, published in 1928, called *Ara*, its Armenian heroine Ara lives in an Armenian refugee camp near Haifa toward the end of World War I. Through her, the author reviews the Armenian tragedy in great detail and most movingly. Part of the critical reviews of the book when it came out in 1928 contained reservations about the author's dealing with the tragedy of another people.

Franz Werfle's saga, *The Forty Days of Musa Dagh*, tells the story of the inhabitants of the Armenian villages at the foot of Musa Dagh (Mount Moses) in the Cilicia district during the First World War. Gabriel Bagradian, an Armenian expatriate who has lived in France for twenty years, brings his family on a personal visit to Turkey at the eve of the First World War. Political events and the outbreak of war compel him to make fateful decisions. He organizes the villagers in a rebellion against the Turks. The story of the uprising is interwoven with Gabriel's personal story.

Werfel's book shocked millions throughout the world and influenced many young people who grew up in Eretz Israel in the

1930s. For many Jewish youths in Europe, *Musa Dagh* became a symbol, a model, and an example, especially during the dark days of the Second World War. Jews in particular have lauded Werfel's book and have sometimes emphasized the author's Jewishness claiming that "only a Jew could have written this work."

Werfel, it should be noted, completed the book in 1932 after two visits to the Middle East (including Palestine), and was horrified by the Armenian massacre and by its results—the refugees and orphans of the massacre whom he saw in Damascus.[18] When the book first appeared in 1933, Hitler had already come to power; he had *The Forty Days of Musa Dagh* burned together with other important literary works.

The reader of this extraordinary historical novel will find it difficult to believe that the book was written before the Holocaust. The book, unquestionably, raises problematic issues, associations and reminders, and questions of Jewish identity which troubled Werfel himself. The Westernized (assimilated) Armenian (Jew) who comes to lead his people in its time of distress, and the emotional resonance of Mount Moses-Musa Dagh-Massada, are only some of the symbols and allusions which are woven into the book.

Jews and Armenians as victims with a similar fate was a prominent theme in the literary reviews of Werfel's book, together with the recurring question (as in the case of the novel *Ara* mentioned above), "Why does a Jew write about the fate of another people and not about the fate of his own people?" These elements were especially prominent in an article written by Moshe Beilinson, one of the outstanding leaders of the workers' movement in Eretz Israel. The article, entitled "A Glorious Monument to Israeli Alienation," appeared in *Davar* in early 1936.[19] Beilinson took exception to the term "Armenian fate" and claimed that "this term is unjustified."

Beilinson transformed the concept of an "Armenian fate" into a concept of the "fate of Israel." The sad eyes of the Armenian refugee children by which Werfel was so touched, are "Israelite eyes," according to Beilinson. It should also be pointed out that he talks of "Israelite eyes" and the "fate of Israel," not Jewish eyes or a Jewish fate. Beilinson goes further:

> Indeed, it is a book which is entirely Armenian, in which the Jews are not mentioned at all, in which a Christian spirit pervades and the quotations at the beginning of each chapter are taken from the New Testament, which extols the heroic struggle of the Armenian people. It is received by the world as a lamentation and a glorification of the sufferings of the Armenians. But it is not so. Whether the poet consciously sought to do so or not, he has written an Israelite book. Moreover, a Zionist book.

Nonetheless, it is also a book of Israelite assimilation, not merely a book written by an assimilated Jew, but a book of alienation."[20]

The symbol of Musa Dagh was not confined to art. The year of 1942 was a time of deep apprehension for the Jewish community in Palestine, which feared the possibility of a Nazi military invasion of Palestine. The Jewish community in Palestine and its leadership were divided in their view of what needed to be done. Together with thoughts of surrender, defeatism, and helplessness, there were calls for courage, determination, and battle. One proposal was a plan to concentrate all of the Palestinian Jewish defense forces around Mount Carmel and from there to fight the Nazi invader. Known variously as the "Northern Program." "The Carmel Plan," "The Massada Plan," and even as "The Musa Dagh Plan," the program was developed by the leadership of the Jewish defense forces.

Haviv Canaan's book *Two Hundred Days of Fear* relates the testimony of Meir Batz, who was asked to take a central role in organizing the plan. He was told, "We want to turn Mount Carmel into the Musa Dagh of Palestinian Jewry. Our comrades are looking in the mountains for suitable places for defense and sortie. We may turn the Carmel into Massada." That evening he went out to reconnoiter. Batz related, "I will never forget that patrol. The moon smiled down on us with its round face. I imagined to myself the Jewish Musa Dagh which was to ensure the future of the Yishuv, and guarantee its honor."[21] Batz added, "We put our faith in the power of endurance of the Jewish 'Musa Dagh' and we were determined to hold out for at least three or four months."[22]

The associations aroused in Eretz Israel surrounding the battle against a German invasion were of Massada, Musa Dagh, and Tobruk (the North African port city in which a British garrison was besieged by the Germans for over a year in World War II). In the Jewish ghettoes in Nazi Europe we shall see that the example of Musa Dagh was cited more often than Massada. A partial investigation of the subject reveals that for Jewish youth in the ghettoes Massada as a symbol of suicide was less relevant than Musa Dagh, which symbolized struggle and battle with a chance, a faint hope for salvation.

The Bialystock Ghetto, 1943: "The only thing left is to see the ghetto as our Musa Dagh"

The Jewish underground organizations which operated in the ghettoes during the Nazi occupation of Europe debated intensely the purpose and meaning of their struggle, the meaning of their lives and deaths in the harsh reality to which they were subject. From their shocking and fascinating discussions, which highlighted moral and existential Jewish dilemmas, we are left with several records written at the time. One of these is the minutes of a general meeting of Kibbutz Tel Hai, a group of Jewish activist youth in Bialystock, on February 27, 1943.

The minutes of the meeting were buried in Bialystock and recovered after the war. They were published under the title, *Pages from the Fire*. During the discussion, which constitutes an important document for our understanding of the dilemmas faced by organizations of the Jewish ghetto underground, an argument developed over the question of whether to remain in the ghetto or to escape to the forests. Three positions were elucidated in the argument: (a) to remain in the ghetto and to revolt against the Germans ("counter-action") at any price; (b) to rescue; (c) to escape to the forests and to wage armed resistance only if escape proved impossible.

One of the main advocates of "counter-action" and remaining in the ghetto said, *inter alia*, "Our fate is sealed. We are therefore left with only one possibility: organizing collective resistance in the ghetto at any price; to view the ghetto as our 'Musa Dagh,' and to add a chapter of honor to the history of Jewish Bialystock and of our movement."[23] In a letter to Bronka Klevansky, the Jewish resistance contract on the Aryan side, on May 25, 1943, Mordechai Tenebaum wrote, "*Musa Dagh* is all the rage with us. If you read it, you will remember it for the rest of your life. Written by Franz Werfel."[24]

Among the activists of other youth movements Werfel's book was also highly regarded. Inka Wajbort used almost the same exact words in her memoirs when describing the book's impact on the fifteen- and sixteen-year-old members of Hashomer Hatzair (a Zionist-Socialist youth movement), in Sosnowiec in Eastern Upper Silesia, after they read it in the summer of 1941.

> The book passed from hand to hand. ... It completely captivated me. For four full days I was engrossed in the book and could not tear myself away. ... I myself was at Musa Dagh; I was under siege. I was one of the Armenians doomed to death. If I lifted my eyes from the book, it was only to hear the cry—Mama, how could this be? The world knew and kept silent. It could not be that children in other countries at the same time went to school, women adorned themselves, men went about their business, as if nothing had happened. ... And there, a people was annihilated.
>
> Mother knew nothing about Musa Dagh. And that also seemed horrible to me. I was totally shocked by the tragedy and when I finished reading the book and went out to the yard for the first time—it was a summer day, drenched in the afternoon sunlight—I was suddenly overcome by a feeling of joy at my very existence. I was grateful to the Creator for the sunlight and the blue sky, for the vision of two little girls with braided hair jumping rope as they laughingly counted their hops, for the fact that the world still stood. ...

Then I did not deal in comparisons. Then, in the summer of 1941 I did not yet sense that a new Musa Dagh was imminent. That happened later.

In May, 1942, before the deportations from the Sosnowiec region, Mordecai Anielewicz, commander of the Jewish underground in the Warsaw ghetto, came to the Sosnowiec ghetto and reported to the older comrades of his movement about what had already transpired in other regions of Poland, where a significant part of the Jews had already been exterminated. "And so, again, Musa Dagh? And again the world keeps silent?"[25]

And in almost the same words, we have testimony from the Kovno ghetto. Samuel Gringaus, general secretary and later deputy head of the Labor Office in the Kovno ghetto, recalled that following the *Aktion* of February 18, 1942, the ghetto was full of the best books. "It was an odd situation," he said, "that much reading was done in the ghetto, and not only in quiet times. I have seen people in the bunkers during the *Aktionen* reading books whole days. A book such as Franz Werfel's *The Forty Days of Musa Dagh* was passed from hand to hand."[26]

The examples—and there are others—cited above indicate the importance and significance which Jewish youth movements attributed to *The Forty Days of Musa Dagh*, probably before the Second World War and certainly during it. The book was an example, a reference, and to some extent a model to be admired and imitated.

The book was probably read in Yiddish (we know of two Yiddish versions), in Polish and in German. In a study which appeared in 1997, *Hunger for the Printed World: Books and Libraries in the Jewish Ghettoes of Nazi-Occupied Europe*, we find that the most widely read books were Werfel's *The Forty Days of Musa Dagh* and *War and Peace* by Leo Tolstoy among adults, and *The Heart* by Edmond de Amicis among younger readers.[27] Werfel's book raises moral questions and expresses humanist values to which the members of the Jewish youth movements were sensitive, as well as existential uncertainties which were relevant to them. For the members of the Jewish underground, the story of the defense of Musa Dagh was a parable, a model, and a source of inspiration. They equated their own fate with that of the Armenians. In both cases, the persecutor's purpose was the uprooting, the exile, and the physical annihilation of entire communities, and in both cases resistance embodied the idea of an honorable death as a nation, or a chance to be saved as individuals. *Musa Dagh* was relevant because it was a penetrating treatment of the pressing existential and moral questions facing young Jews in those terrible years.

Today, I may be permitted to point out that the young generation in Israel has heard nothing of Musa Dagh and most of them
do not know, to our regret, anything about the genocide of the
Armenian people.

After the Creation of the State

The attitude of the various Israeli governments to the Armenian genocide has been characterized by evasiveness and denial. The State of
Israel has officially refrained from relating to the genocide. A combination of factors connected with Israel's relations with Turkey and
concepts of the uniqueness of the Shoah brought about an almost
total absence of any mention of the Armenian genocide on state television until 1994. Public debate and argument about that official
attitude erupted four times due to some outstanding media events.

In 1978, a film on the Armenian Quarter in Jerusalem was
banned; in 1982, the Israeli government intervened in an international congress on the subject of the Shoah and genocide; in 1989,
Israel was involved in preventing mention of the Armenian genocide
in an American calendar; and in 1990, a TV film produced in the
United States about "A Voyage to Armenia" was banned.

For example we can look briefly at the discussion concerning
the decision to ban the film about the Armenian Quarter. In 1978,
the Israeli Broadcasting Authority decided to produce a documentary film for television about the Armenian community in the Old
City of Jerusalem. The Authority contracted with a private company to produce the film as a co-production. The film script was
approved and an English-language version was planned for distribution abroad. The film included several references to the Armenian massacre during the First World War, primarily the testimony
by several survivors of the genocide of 1915 who resided in the
Armenian Quarter. The film reached the final stages of production
but its screening was prevented and it has never been shown.
Involved in the efforts to prevent the screening of the film were
Turkish officials, their diplomatic mission in Israel, Jews living in
Turkey, activists in the Turkish immigrants' society in Israel, and
the Israeli Foreign Ministry. All of these forces would be involved in
the controversies that came later.

As in the future controversies, the phenomenon which stands
out is the Israeli attitude to "our Holocaust and the Holocaust of
others." Amos Elon, in a series of articles in the respected Israeli
newspaper, *Ha'aretz*, attacked the "demonstrations of hypocrisy,

opportunism, and the moral trepidation within the official bureaucracy of the nation, which ceaselessly reminds the world of our Holocaust while the Holocaust of others is a subject worthy only of political exploitation."[28] About the demand to delete any mention of the events of 1915 from the film, he wrote, "They are like a person who suggests deleting from a movie about the suffering of the Jewish People in the modern era all reference to Germany, the Holocaust or even the Kishinev pogrom." With a certain degree of cynicism, Elon apologizes to his readers for returning to this unfortunate, seemingly marginal subject:

> [A]ll of the great people of conscience, the very image of sorrow, who give speeches at every opportunity and travel abroad to tell everyone they are forbidden to forget—have followed the Armenian affair as though it had taken place on another planet. They were not shocked, they did not open their mouth.

Another phase in the controversy came in 1994 to 1996 over the study program "Sensitivity to Suffering in the World: Genocides in the Twentieth Century" that included the Armenian genocide and the genocide of the gypsies during the second World War and intended to deal later with more current acts of genocide such as those Bosnia and Rwanda. The sore point of the controversy was a lack of full-hearted recognition of the Armenian genocide. Eventually, the program was rejected by the Israeli Ministry of Education. Despite that, the program is being taught in several high schools in Israel without official approval. Two forces led to the rejection of the program: (a) The pressure of the Turkish government and (b) the opposition of several high-powered Jewish groups which were afraid that the program would damage the concept of the uniqueness of the Shoah.

In 1997 there were two other controversies: one about a plan to award professor Bernard Lewis with an honorary citizenship of the Tel-Aviv/Jaffa municipality upon the recommendation of professors from Tel Aviv University, and the other about the nomination of the Israeli ambassador to Turkey.

Conclusion

It is relevant to note that in a field study I am conducting now among students in universities and teachers' colleges in Israel (more than eight hundred students) I have found that the majority of them, by far, defined their degree of knowledge about the Armenian genocide and the genocide of the gypsies as "not at all" or "very little." The degree of ignorance of the Armenian genocide among Israeli Jews is probably much greater than the ignorance of other nations about the Shoah.

What is the significance of this situation? Israel, the national home of the Jews, who were the victims of the most horrendous of all genocidal acts, has a special moral, as well as political, responsibility to place the issue of genocide on the world agenda. Is the Shoah the only subject worthy of learning? I believe that it is essential to develop a greater sensitivity among our youth to the suffering of others and to strengthen universal, humanistic values, which are an integral part of the Jewish tradition. This is what I believe.

The present study has offered the opportunity to examine a general phenomenon, which is separate from both the Armenian genocide and the Jewish aspect, that is: the reactions of the bystanders to the occurrences of mass slaughter. The greater part of my study deals with later reactions, but it is appropriate to note that the great majority of the Yishuv was indifferent and did not relate to the Armenian catastrophe, even though people knew of it while it was happening. The almost total concentration on the Jewish cause—in effect, the Zionist cause—constituted one of the major reasons the leaders of the Yishuv and the Zionist movement ignored or remained indifferent to the Armenian tragedy. As noted, the greater part of the Yishuv had a pro-Turkish orientation. The stands of David Ben-Gurion, Yitzhak Ben-Zvi, the "Hashomer" organization, Poalei Zion and the Socialist International, young Eretz Israel Jews who served in the Turkish Army during World War One, and Ze'ev Jabotinsky can be characterized as indifference. Jabotinsky, who was pro-British, did relate to the Armenian genocide, but his attitude was mainly pragmatic and impersonal.

In those or similar circumstances, human beings do not hold identical views nor behave in a single manner. Those who related, reacted, protested among the Yishuv and the Zionist movement against the Armenian genocide, which caused them to undergo a moral and sometimes explicitly Jewish shock, are characterized by two qualities. First, most of the protesters were born in Palestine. Second, those who reacted to the event were, in one way or another, exceptions—non-conformists, "troublemakers," people with critical views of the Zionist establishment.

In her study, *Eichmann in Jerusalem*, Hannah Ardent describes Adolf Eichmann's last minutes before his execution" "[H]e was summing up the lesson that this long course in human wickedness has taught us—the lesson which could not be verbalized and comprehended—the banality of evil."[29]

Her important, original, and controversial book was rejected by Israeli intellectuals and by the Israeli academic community. Despite its wide publication throughout the world, Arendt's book was not translated into Hebrew. The central claim of the book, which makes it original and important, is the thesis of the banality of evil, that evil is part of the experience of all human existence. There has never been a meaningful discussion of this claim in Israeli society. For years, Israeli society has preferred, out of its own needs and considerations, to place evil on "a different planet," to stress a dichotomous Manichaean world of good and evil and not to see evil (of which the Nazis' deeds are the height) as a diffuse element, existing on different levels—refusing to acknowledge the prevalence of the "banal evil" within its midst. Only in the last decade have different voices begun to be heard within Israeli public opinion.

With all due caution and humility, I would suggest that we consider the concept of "the banality of indifference." The picture which becomes increasingly clear regarding the attitude toward acts of genocide (of which, we emphasize, the Holocaust is the most extreme and unique case in this category) is a picture of the banality of indifference. The reaction of the multitudes located in the space between the perpetrator and the victims is characterized by indifference, conformity, and opportunism. The Jews too, in the circumstances of time and place, do not go beyond this banality, with several exceptions.

The Victims—the Unique and the Universal

Debate continues in the academic community on the characteristics of genocide and the uniqueness of the Shoah. I recognize the unique factors surrounding the Jewish Shoah, creating some significant differences between that event and others of a similar sort. At the same time, a comparison of those events is essential in research, remembrance, and historical consciousness. We need to establish what is identical in these events.

I believe that all the valid reasons for remembering the Shoah are equally valid for remembering the Armenian genocide. Moreover, the Turkish governments that followed the regimes that perpetrated the crimes have denied their having taken place! It is as if German Chancellor Gerhard Schröder denied German crimes during World War II. Recognizing the Armenian genocide, therefore, is of major historical, moral, and educational significance. Knowing the sad past and recalling it are essential conditions—though altogether not sufficient—for the non-recurrence of similar instances in future. Ignoring the Armenian genocide has, of course, a special meaning in view of the fact that the State of Israel regards itself as representing the victims of the Holocaust and its memory. The Shoah constitutes an important and central component in consolidating the Jewish identity in Israel and will continue to be a central element in Israeli identity.

However, I argue that Israelis must hope and work for finding a more suitable balance between the Zionist, Jewish, and universal "lessons" from the Shoah. Even in teaching the Shoah and inculcating the coming generations with its memory, the basic approach has to be that the value of human life is the same for all humans, whether Jews, gypsies, Armenians, or Arabs.

In the Jewish sources we find this sentence:

> Thus was created a single man, to teach us that anyone who destroys a single soul, it shall be written about him as if he has destroyed the entire world, and anyone who saves a single soul, it shall be written about him as if he has saved the entire world. (*Mishna, Sanhedrin, IV, 5*).

This passage was revised in later versions and the phrase "from the People of Israel" was added, no longer to say "anyone who saves" or "destroys a single soul," but rather "anyone who saves or destroys a single soul from the People of Israel." In the editions of the *Mishna* generally available today we usually find the later "amended" version. With all the caution and humility I would propose that we come back to the original version.

The way to work toward this goal is to combine two basic principles which seem apparently contradictory: on one hand, emphasizing the uniqueness of the Shoah; and on the other, even emphatically, relating it to the catastrophes of others and to other genocides in history. There are no contradictions between these approaches; there is, in fact, an accord, a concurrence. This is the integration and synthesis between the unique and the generalized. This integration will add universal, moral, and spiritual significance and power to the remembrance of the Shoah, and to the just Jewish demand that the world never forget. We should not fear that such an integration could create a relativism in regard to the Holocaust, leading to its diminution and to the weakening of its Jewish aspect.

Notes

1. This essay is based on the research project: Jewish/Israeli Attitudes Towards the Armenian Genocide. See now Yair Auron, *The Banality of Indifference: Zionism and the Armenian Genocide* (New Brunswick, N.J., 1999).

2. See Alex Bein, *Herzl: A Biography* (Philadelphia, 1941), p. 198.

3. Bein, pp. 370-373. Previously, in London, in a conversation with the editor of the London *Daily Mail*, he praised the Sultan and his positive attitude toward the Jews, in the hope that his words would be read in Constantinople: "I am fully aware that the Jews have no better friend than the Sultan and that our movement is on the right path." Ibid, p. 296. See also Herzl, opening address to the Fifth Zionist Congress, *Before the Nation and the World*, Vol. II, p. 117.

4. Bernard Lazare, "Le Congress Sioniste et le Sultan," *Pro Armenia*, No. 4 (January 1902), pp. 29-30.

5. Hannah Arendt, "Herzl and Lazare," in *The Jew as Pariah* (New York, 1978), pp. 125-130.

6. *Hatzvi*, Issue 163, May 4, 1896.

7. See among others: *Hapoel Hatzair* issue 14, May 21, 1909 and *Haolam*, issue 18, May 24, 1909.

8. Isaiah Friedman, for example, attributes great importance to the German assistance to the Jewish community in Eretz Israel during the war. See: Isaiah Friedman, *Germany, Turkey and Zionism* (Oxford, 1977); Friedman, "Germany and Zionism, 1897-1918," *Cathedra for the History of Eretz Israel and its Yishuv*, No. 16, 1980, pp. 30-31.

9. See Eliezer Livneh, *Aaron Aaronsohn: His Life and Time* (Jerusalem, 1979), p. 248. Livneh quotes the American historian Frank A. Manuel.

10. *Avshalom (Papers and Letters of the Late Avshalom Feinberg)*, ed. Aharon Amir (Haifa, 1977). Letter from Paris, October 14, 1907.

11. Ibid., pp. 364-365.

12. The report to Henrietta Szold (written originally in French) is in the Archives of the Aaronsohn House.

13. Avshalom, p. 293.

14. Nili Archives, Aara A.1/5. In a short book which Alexander Aaronsohn wrote in 1942, *Sarah: The Flame of Nili*, the first chapter is entitled, "The cry of the Armenians," and contains an excerpt from the document written by Alexander in 1915. See Alexander Aaronsohn, *Sarah: The Flame of Nili* (Tel Aviv, 1965), pp. 11-12.

15. Sarah Aaronsohn's account of events has never been found, and we do not know whether Sarah never wrote the story of her trip or whether it was written and later lost. In any event, it has not survived in written records.

16. See Eitan Belkind, *So It Was* (Tel Aviv, 1977), pp. 115-125 (in Hebrew). In his memoir, written sixty years after the events, he relates that he had written a report on the Armenian massacre at the time it occurred, but the report has not been found.

17. See, inter al., *The Aaronsohn Diaries 1916-1919*, ed. Yoram Efrati (Tel Aviv, 1970), November 17, 1916, and footnotes, pp. 130-131, document 242528, December 1, in file 221220, collection F.O. 3712783. The same report appears again as document 253852, F.O. 3712781, F.O. 3712783, 221220. It seems that it is to this document which Aaronsohn refers in his diary on November 21, 1916: "At 5 to Gribbon, and he reads me the report which he wrote based on my testimony and notes. He has gathered it all very well into 21 pages."

18. Werfel's biographer, Peter Stephan Jungk, argues that Werfel was mistaken when he added a note at the beginning of his book: "The miserable sight of some maimed and famished-looking refugee children, working in a carpet factory, gave me the final impulse to snatch from the Hades of all that was, this incomprehensible destiny of the Armenian nation." In Jungk's opinion, the visit was not in 1929 but in the early part of 1930. See Peter Stephan Jungk, *Franz Werfel: Une Vie de Prague à Hollywood*, (Paris, 1990), p. 339.

19. Moshe Beilinson, "A Glorious Monument to Israeli Alienation," *Davar*, January 22, 1936. The article was also published in the anthology, *Dovrut: For Reading Clubs and Study Groups. A. Beilinson Selections*, (Ein Harod), 1936.

20. Ibid., pp. 93-94.

21. Haviv Canaan, *Two Hundred Days of Fear*, (Mol-Art Publishers, .d.) pp. 244-245. Yehoshua (Josh) Palmon was engaged at the time in training units of undercover soldiers, intended to be used behind enemy lines in the event of an invasion by Rommel. According to Canaan, Palmon and his colleagues thought that if the Germans invaded the country, the Jews of Palestine would be condemned to the same fate as the Armenians in the Ottoman Empire in World War I, i.e., horrific mass slaughter. Ibid., p. 253.

22. Uri Brenner, *Facing the Threat of a German Invasion of Palestine: 1940-1942*, Yad Tabenkin, Research Series, No. 3, 1981, pp. 154-155.

23. Mordechai Tenebaum-Tamaroff, *Pages from the Fire: Dappim Min Hadleka*, rev. and expanded (Yad Vashem, Beit Lohamei HaGettaot, 1984), p. 79, (Hebrew). The person quoted, Herschel Rosenthal, was one of the central figures in organizing the Bialystock underground and Tenebaum's closest friend. He was killed in the August 1943 uprising at the age of 24. Ibid., p. 283.

24. Ibid., p. 138.

25. Inka Wajbort, *Together and Alone in the Face of the Terror*, (Moreshet, 1992), pp. 33-34 (Hebrew).

26. Samuel Gringaus, "Dos Kultur-leben in Kovner," in *Lite*, ed. Mendel Sudarsky et al. (New York, 1951), p. 1955, cited in David Shavit, *Hunger for the Printed Word*, (McFarland, 1997).

27. Shavit, *Hunger for the Printed Wold*.

28. Amos Elon, "Armenia As A Parable: A. Our Holocaust and the Holocaust of Others," *Ha'aretz*, 1978, appeared also in Elon's book, *Looking Back in Consternation*, (Tel Aviv, 1988), pp. 250-260 (Hebrew).

29. Hannah Arendt, *Eichmann in Jerusalem*, revised and enlarged ed., (New York, 1964), p. 252.

– *Chapter 14* –

FAITH, RELIGIOUS PRACTICE, AND GENOCIDE

Armenians and Jews in France following World War I and II

Maud Mandel

In fall 1949, Robert Sommer, a representative of the most prominent administrative body of French Judaism, the Consistoire de
Paris, voiced deep concerns over the future of Judaism in France.
Claiming that 40 to 50 percent of the community's manpower had
disappeared due to the World War II deportations, post-war attempts
to blend into French society, and departures for Israel, Sommer
worried that continued attempts to blend into the surrounding society would decimate French Jewry beyond repair.[1] Other communal
leaders shared Sommer's fears. Indeed in the years immediately
following World War II, Jewish religious and communal leaders
bemoaned the demise of Judaism in France. According to them,
deportations had removed the most observant sectors of the population while post-war attempts to escape Judaism "through conversions
and mixed marriages, through disappearance, evaporation, camou-
flages," as one put it, were forever destroying the community.[2]

This article seeks to assess such claims by tracing the impact
of the Holocaust on Jewish religious practices in France following
World War II. As has been well-documented, the war had severely
disrupted Jewish life in France. Under German occupation and Vichy

---

Notes for this section begin on page 308.

collaborationist rule, Jewish residents faced a wide range of discriminatory legislation restricting their movements, property own-
ership, and civil liberties. Furthermore, as the Nazi attack on
European Jewry evolved, the Vichy government collaborated in the
internment and deportation of approximately seventy-six thousand
Jews, one third of the pre-war population. Of these only about
three percent survived to return to France. Communal life was also
severely damaged, as synagogues, schools, and cultural organizations were systematically closed and dismantled. Foreign-born Jews
who had immigrated to France during the interwar years were hit
the hardest. While antisemitic policies were directed at *all* Jews,
French xenophobia ensured that those policies were most fiercely
enforced against recent arrivals. As a result, immigrant Jews lost property, places of worship, and communal centers and were deported in
larger numbers than native French Jews (over two-thirds of those
deported were foreign born).[3]

If, however, deportations had drastically reduced the size and
diversity of the community, French Jewry was not decimated by the
Holocaust. Indeed, two thirds of the indigenous population survived as did much of the pre-war institutional framework. In addition, once de-Gaulle liberated Paris in August 1944, French Jews
immediately regained the rights of which they had been stripped.
As one French Jewish writer described the moment: "For the first
time in four years, that day we were finally like other people ... we
could call out our names, cry out who we were on the telephone, in
the streets in the stores, and in the restaurants. ... We had returned
to our true identity, to society, to France."[4]

Yet could French Jews return so simply to their pre-war position
in French society? The intended victims of Nazi and Vichy persecution had been attacked at many levels. Not only had they been
uprooted from homes and communities, but they also had faced an
ideological onslaught that had dubbed them unfit to live in their
own society. How, then, did survivors respond to this attack after
the persecutions had ended? Did these four years of persecution
encourage them to question their religious, ethnic, and national affiliations? Did they, as communal leaders feared, flee their ancestral
religion in apprehension of future persecutions? Can we find a direct
link between the Holocaust and the decline of Judaism in France?

To address these questions I will compare post-World War II
French Jews to another population of genocide survivors living in
France, Armenians, who had fled the Ottoman Empire after the disruptions of World War I. During this conflict, the Young Turks had
used the cover of war to deport and murder one and a half million

Armenians, virtually eliminating them from their ancestral lands. Like the Holocaust, the Armenian genocide was an attempt to alter the nature and composition of the existing society. The Young Turk leaders not only dislocated populations that had been in place for centuries but also confiscated Armenian property and desecrated places of worship. Those Armenians who were not killed were forced to renounce all connection with their ethnic and religious heritage. While some survivors escaped the violent onslaught, they only did so by going into exile, leaving their ancestral lands and seeking refuge in the diaspora.[5]

Approximately 65,000 of these survivors ultimately made their way to France where the post-World War I economy necessitated a dependence on immigrant labor.[6] For them, disjuncture and ruptures with the past were far more dramatic than for the post-World War II French Jewish population. Not only had the migration to France transformed the primarily rural, agriculturally-based peasant population into an urban, working-class ethnic minority, but it had also forced them off their ancestral lands and left them to seek refuge in the diaspora.[7] For many, finding a final settlement point took nearly a decade if not longer. Those who settled in France often had spent several years in Greece, Syria, Lebanon, or the former Russian Empire. Arriving as stateless refugees, without passports or visas and with no obvious country of origin, their position in French society was precarious, particularly in the early 1920s when the government had not yet worked out coherent policies for dealing with stateless minorities. With no protection through immigration treaties and no international rights, the first Armenian arrivals in France were utterly dependent on the government's benevolence and their own meager resources. The combination of their precarious position in the polity and their own search for stability set the scene for their integration into French society.

For these Armenian refugees, then, questions of religious, ethnic, and national allegiance were forged from their own past of statelessness, genocide, and exile, a story that differs considerably from that of the post-World War II French Jewish population. Armenians never were persecuted on French soil; French Jews, on the other hand, had been victims of native aggression during World War II. Also, changes in French receptivity to immigrants, as well as changing political, social, and economic conditions, affected those populations differently. It should be clear, however, that in order to make this comparison, the conditions facing the two communities need not have been identical.[8] Although immigration and settlement patterns differed for the two populations as did modes of

integration and communal construction, both addressed remarkably similar dilemmas as they faced the challenges of rebuilding
their disrupted communities within the French context.

For both, the role of religion in communal life was one such
dilemma. As we will see, for both groups, the forces of secularization—so strong in modern France—had a far greater impact on
shaping the religious practices of genocide survivors then the persecutions themselves. Indeed, for both Armenians and Jews, the importance of Christianity and Judaism respectively declined throughout
the twentieth century not because survivors were fleeing their religious heritages in a desperate attempt to escape future persecutions,
but because the impact of secular education and the division of
church and state ensured that survivors would move away from religious distinctions as the line dividing them from the rest of society. If
religious activities declined, however, participation in alternative
forms of ethno-religious institutions increased. Indeed, in neither case
did genocide or the appeals of secular society lead survivors to abandon all links to their ancestral heritages. Rather, for some the persecutions encouraged a greater solidarity and sense of connection,
expressions of which became clear in the secular associations which
continued to multiply in both populations.

1.

In 1948, concerns over the state of Judaism in Paris encouraged
Georges Wormser, the president of the Consistoire de Paris, to conduct an informal survey among his acquaintances. He concluded
that out of every ten young women, two favored mixed marriages,
two favored Jewish marriages, and six were totally indifferent.
Among the men (from twenty-five to thirty-five years old, all former
soldiers or resistors), one had converted and admitted it, one had
probably converted, two were communists—opposed to all religion,
two were a-religious Zionists, three were members of the Consistoire but had no interest in the religion as practiced, and only one
was entirely observant. Based on this "random" sample, Wormser
predicted that "a loss of a minimum of 50 percent is probable."[9]

Leaving aside the relative merits of his poll (which was both
unrepresentative—all participants were drawn from French Jewish
middle-class families—and sexist, since he asked women their marriage preferences while asking men their political and ideological
convictions), Wormser's concern is revealing. Consistoire officials
like Wormser and Sommer feared that French Judaism was in a

spiritual crisis. By pointing to what they considered obvious signs of religious disaffiliation, such as conversion and intermarriage, religious and lay leaders insisted that French Jewry was in the midst of a drastic decline.

Requests from Jewish families to legally change their names particularly worried the local leadership who noted that such requests far exceeded the percentage of Jews in the population. One report indicated that from the end of January to the beginning of April 1945, 110 out of 173 requests for name changes (or two thirds) were made by Jews.[10] Many of these were requested by resistance fighters who wished to maintain the clandestine names they had used during the years of fighting.[11] Nevertheless, Consistoire officials maintained that name changes were the first step toward disaffiliation and full assimilation.

One concerned member, Gaston Hildenfinger, reported in 1947 that name changes posed one of the "most serious and troubling" problems facing French Judaism. After exploring the positions of both those who advocated name changes as a means to avoid further anti-Jewish attacks and those who opposed them on the grounds that they were the first step towards a more radical assimilation, Hildenfinger ultimately encouraged the Consistoire to maintain its traditionally cautious approach towards matters regulated by state policy; if the national government permitted legal name changes, the Consistoire should not interfere. Nevertheless, Hildenfinger could not resist reminding his fellow French Jews of the importance of their names, which he insisted they should wear as a badge of honor. For Hildenfinger, as for most Consistoire officials, names were a symbol of Jewish identity; attempts to mask them could ultimately lead to complete assimilation. "In the near or not so distant future," warned the chief rabbi of France, Isaïe Schwartz, "those of our coreligionists who have changed their names in this way or their children will abandon their faith; abandonment is all the more to fear for we are unfortunately not in a period of deep belief."[12] Concern that French Jews were seeking actively to blend into their surroundings continued throughout the 1950s.[13] In 1954, the World Jewish Congress reported that intermarriage had become widespread, particularly in the provinces where 60 percent of all Jewish families had one non-Jew "among their kith and kin."[14] While some commentators attributed such flight to France's "atmosphere of liberty and a tendency towards assimilation as well as of individualism," most saw the new trend as a radical break from past methods of integration and a direct response to the persecutions of World War II.[15] If previously Jews

had sought to integrate into French society without actively trying
to abandon their Jewishness, recent actions suggested a systematic
flight from their ancestral roots. In an article in *Commentary*,
Arnold Mandel, a French Jewish poet, novelist, and essayist, considered post-war Jewish conversions to Catholicism in an historical
context. According to Mandel, conversion had never been the obvious choice for French Jews anxious to integrate into the surrounding society. Catholicism like Judaism, he insisted, had been
relegated since the time of Napoleon to a religious category only
marginally influential in determining an individual's social position
within the state. Few Jews, therefore, had chosen to adopt the
majority religion. "Assimilation [in France] has never been—except
perhaps in the very first days of Emancipation—a motto inscribed
on a banner. The progressive disappearance of Jewish separateness
came about without conscious choice. It is for this reason that conversions were quite rare among the Jews of France." Since the war,
however, conversions and name changes had become all too frequent. "This is something quite new in [French] history. What distinguished it until quite recently was a natural and spontaneous
kind of assimilation, almost never the result of deliberate resolution."[16] Mandel's outlook for the future remained pessimistic:
"Unless some vital new development appears," he warned, "we
must look forward, it would seem, to the disappearance of organic
Judaism in France."[17]

His fears, however, were exaggerated. Indeed, while a series of
post-war ordinances simplified the process through which individuals could legally change their names, only 2,150 Jews asked to do
so between 1945 and 1957.[18] While it is certainly possible that
some of these requests were made by Jews fearing the return of
antisemitic persecution and anxious to shed an "onerous identity,"
most were requested by Eastern European Jews, the pronunciation
of whose names proved difficult for French tongues.

Statistics on conversions are harder if not impossible to come
by. Nevertheless it is clear that flight from Judaism was not the
wide-spread phenomenon that some feared. Traditionally viewed as
the worst betrayal of Judaism, conversion took on a new poignancy
after the war when a handful of high profile cases bolstered the
communal leadership's concern over the effect of apostasy on their
already diminished numbers.[19] Particularly significant were the stories of children who had survived the war hidden in non-Jewish
homes or in convents and monasteries. While most often these children were returned rapidly to surviving family members, occasionally the Christian households or establishments in which the

children had been hidden had baptized those entrusted to their care.[20] In select cases, the new families refused to return their wards to Jewish agencies, arguing that it would be cruel to remove the children from the environments to which they had grown accustomed. In the most famous of these cases, the Finaly Affair, two boys—Robert and Gerald Finaly—had been baptized by the woman in whose charge they had been placed. Miss Brun, a dedicated Catholic, refused to allow them to rejoin their surviving family members (their parents had died during the war). After many years (during which time Brun resorted to smuggling the boys to Spain to keep them in the Church's grasp) and much public outcry, the Finaly boys were finally reunited with their family, but not before the case had polarized views in France and brought wide-spread attention to the question of baptized Jewish children.[21]

While the Finaly case was the most public of such stories, it was not unique. Immediately after the war, several child-care agencies and other French Jewish organizations began searching the country for such "hidden" children, and in August 1948, the American Jewish Joint Distribution Committee [the Joint] funded a *commission dépistage* to seek out missing children in the provinces. Despite the wide-spread attention of such cases, however, most children were not in danger of conversion. In 1945, the Oeuvre de secours aux enfants (OSE), an international Jewish childcare organization, reported: "The noise made around the future of children at risk of conversion having been placed in an institution or in an religious environment is exaggerated. Out of a total of 10,500 children threatened by extermination, the number of those converted does not exceed forty or fifty."[22] The *commission dépistage* confirmed these small numbers by locating only ten children in the first few months of searching.[23] By March 1949 when they stopped the hunt, the commission had identified a total of 119 cases, 95 of which had been verified.[24]

Despite these small numbers, however, the issue of "hidden children" became immensely important to leaders in all areas of the community. Fearing that such children would add to the numbers of those who were "lost" to Judaism, Jewish organizations dedicated themselves to finding those who had been housed temporarily with non-Jewish families, remaining in contact with them until their parents or nearest relatives could return. The Women's International Zionist Organization (WIZO), for example, had placed nearly two thousand French Jewish children in temporary homes during the course of the war. Worrying that these children had been cut off from their ancestral roots for too long, the French chapter of WIZO began organizing their membership into corps of *marraines,* surrogate mothers or godmothers, whose role it was to stay in contact with the children until homes could be found for them either with relatives or in Jewish orphanages. "The main issue that concerns us now," reported one WIZO newsletter, "is the missing contact that these children have with Judaism." The role of the *marraines* would thus be to provide a connection to Judaism not simply by informing the children of their Jewish roots but by providing them with "a more direct and familial contact." In so doing, WIZO hoped "to establish connections between us and them that are both maternal and spiritual. ... We ask simply that you provide a bit of that maternal love that [the children] have missed and to reintegrate them with your care into the Jewish community." The *marraines,* thus, were to serve as surrogate mothers, providing a living connection to Judaism by providing the love and maternal affection of missing or deported family members and even sending some *gelt* on Hanukah.[25]

Jewish children and war-orphans in particular thus captured the Jewish imagination for several years after the war.[26] According to Marc Jarblum, an Eastern European Jewish immigrant to France active in communal affairs, the "Jewish people" considered these children their own: "They are in some senses the wards of the people of Israel, and they are doubly dear, first as orphans, then as victims of the anti-Jewish barbarism in so far as they represent the remainder of an important fraction of the most traditional Jewish people, those most faithful to its culture, its civilization, and its aspirations."[27] While in reality most surviving children had been reunited with family members fairly quickly after the war, the several thousand children who were orphaned or for extenuating circumstances remained in one of several Jewish institutions took on an importance that far exceeded their numbers.[28] For most of the organizations that played any role in caring for them, saving these children meant more than simply preserving a life, it also meant saving the future of Judaism. As one Zionist childcare agency remarked in a fundraising letter, "[T]he interruption or discontinuation of our work would mean to our children not only the hardships and serious dangers to which abandoned children are exposed, but also their loss to Judaism and the waste of all the efforts we have made in order to strengthen their ties with the Jewish community and Jewish life."[29]

Jewish children, thus, became the focus of those convinced that the war and post-war flights from Judaism had decimated (and were continuing to decimate) their ranks. The sense of crisis was bolstered by the sad state in which Vichy persecutions had left France's rabbinate. Twenty-one consistorial and four non-consistorial rabbis had been lost during the Nazi years, one third of all rabbis. In addition, thirty-five cantors *(ministres officiants)* had perished.[30] Indeed, the situation was so troubling that in May 1946 the Consistoire de Paris' committee on religion described it as "tragic,"[31] and while the rabbinical numbers began slowly increasing, their reduced numbers were felt sorely, particularly in the provinces.[32] By 1956, after some rabbinical losses had been replaced, approximately twenty rabbis worked in Paris and ten in Alsace-Lorraine but only about a dozen in the rest of the country.[33]

For Consistoire officials, the destruction of the rabbinical leadership helped explain the "spiritual crisis" they believed was facing French Jewry.[34] The "State of the Consistoire" report in 1951 noted: "The absence of a spiritual director is too often the sign of the decline of a Community, and currently we regret not only that many of our Associations, formerly rabbinical seats, have only cantors at their head, but also that a large number of our fellow Jews live in areas deprived of all religious organization and find themselves bit by bit detached from Judaism."[35] For communal leaders, then, the Vichy years were directly to blame for the religious malaise that they believed was spreading throughout French Jewry. Deportations, fear, and flight as manifested through intermarriage and conversion, forced baptisms of children, and the destruction of the rabbinate were creating a spiritual crisis among French Jews.

It is important to note, however, that even if the war had a significant impact on French Jewish religious practices, a dwindling interest in organized Judaism was, in fact, a wider phenomenon with roots dating back to the late eighteenth century. Religious observance had consistently declined for both Jews and non-Jews since the Enlightenment, particularly in Paris.[36] Given that the majority of Jews lived in the French capital, the secular instincts of the city had a wider impact on Judaism than on other religions in France. As Paula Hyman has noted regarding the first decades of the twentieth century, "[W]hile religion remained the technical basis for Jewish identity in France, it had clearly lost hold over most French Jews." Indeed, while immigrant religious organizations had flourished during the interwar years, consistorial influence had decreased continually since the separation of church and state in 1906 when it had lost its monopoly over religious life. From then until 1931, therefore, organized Jewish communities dropped from seventy-four to fifty and the number of rabbis dropped significantly as well.[37] While these decreasing numbers can be explained partially by the continual migration of Jews from the provinces to Paris, it is also clear that the daily practice of Judaism was in decline.

The progression of this disaffiliation was certainly aided by the war's disruptions. Statistical accounts for Paris suggest that religious practices among Consistoire-affiliated Jews declined sharply in the post-war years.[38] In 1948, for example, seventy-one benai-mitzvah were performed in Paris compared to 296 in 1926. Similarly, the number of consistorial marriages dropped dramatically in the first decade after World War II. While in 1947, 440 such marriages were performed, the number dropped consistently thereafter and by 1953 had reached an all time low of 253.[39] Moreover, the numbers of children enrolled in religious instruction consistently dropped throughout the beginning of the 1950s. In 1950, 750 children attended such courses, while in 1953 only 473 were enrolled.[40]

Affiliation with the Consistoire also dropped after the war. In March 1945, the Consistoire de Paris sent out 3,600 letters to former members asking that they pay their current and past dues (for the first several years after the war, the Consistoire was desperately underfunded and had trouble finding the money to maintain its various projects). By June the organization had received only six hundred responses. The silence could certainly be explained by the disruption of the war; most Jews were not yet in a position to pay dues to a voluntary organization as they were only first re-gaining their economic foothold. Moreover, the war's dislocation had left the Consistoire with incorrect addresses for many former members. Nevertheless, French Jews, even those who had been affiliated with the Consistoire prior to the war, were clearly in no hurry to re-connect with the institutions representing French Judaism, much less to seek solace for their losses in organized religion.[41]

Moreover, while membership numbers steadily increased, they did not reach pre-war levels. If in 1932 the Consistoire de Paris' membership rosters listed over seven thousand families, in January 1947, only 2,632 families were once again affiliated. While evidence suggested that some families were attending religious services without paying membership dues, numbers were still under the five thousand that Consistoire officials believed should be listed on their rosters.[42] By December 1948, the Consistoire reported 588 new members bringing the total to 3,339.[43] Nevertheless, in 1950, the president complained after a poor turn-out for Consistoire elections: "We can estimate [approximately] 20,000 Jewish families in Paris and in the department; [Yet] we do not have four thousand registered in the Association and we do not have seven hundred who demonstrate any interest in us during elections; this is truly a failure!"[44]

Such numbers, however troubling to Consistoire officials, may in fact indicate that the *Consistoire* was in crisis rather than Judaism as a whole. As noted above, affiliation with the Consistoire was already dwindling prior to World War II. While some of the post-war disaffiliation may have been caused by fear that active participation in Jewish institutions could prove dangerous, most was probably caused by the continued impact of the secular state on new generations of Jews. A consideration of the religious practices of immigrant Jews in France provides further evidence for this hypothesis. If, following World War II, fear served as the primary motive driving Jews from Judaism, then immigrant Jews should have numbered among those most likely to disaffiliate. As previously noted, those who had migrated to France in the 1920s and 1930s were singled out more readily for persecution during the Vichy years, deported in larger numbers than their native co-religionists, and suffered greater communal upheaval in terms of losses to their religious, political, and social institutions. As in the interwar years, however, immigrant Jewish religious institutions continued to flourish after World War II as those who survived returned to their homes and as new immigrants made their way to France. Both Orthodox and Hassidic congregations were represented in Paris "with yeshivas in the suburbs and in the provinces, with chapels scattered here and there, and even with the picturesque exterior representative of the Jewish middle Ages."[45] In addition, interest in traditional Judaism encouraged those unaffiliated with the Consistoire to form the Conseil représentatif du Judaïsme traditionaliste de France [CRJTF] in 1952, the objective of which was to protect the interests of Orthodox Jews and to promote and safeguard institutions necessary to traditional Jewish life.[46] CRJTF members criticized the Consistoire for its use of an organ in services as well as for other aesthetic reforms such as the shortening of services and the removal of the *piyyutim* (liturgical synagogue poetry) except on the most important holidays; such practices had become widespread during the mid-nineteenth century as reformers pushed for outward changes to the service as a means of accommodating themselves to the practices of the surrounding society.[47] Those affiliated with CRJTF, in contrast, attempted to maintain a Judaism that "made no concessions encouraged by the conditions of modern life."[48] Admittedly, the efforts of these more traditional Jews did not succeed in encouraging those who had already stopped practicing to begin again. Nevertheless, Jewish religious life, particularly in certain regions such as Alsace Lorraine, continued to flourish as immigrant Jews returned or migrated to those area.[49]

Among the native-born French Jewish population, observance was certainly much weaker.[50] Yet even if changing *how* they identified with Judaism, it is far from clear that French Jews were abandoning their ancestral heritage. Rather, the nature of their identification with Jewish life was shifting in response to the challenges of the twentieth century. Great changes in Jewish identification had already taken place in the first third of the century due to the interactions of native and immigrant Jews. As part and parcel of a larger immigration wave, Eastern European Jewish immigrants had more than doubled the native population in the first decades of the century. Their impact, however, was more than demographic; the new arrivals were poorer, more traditional, more politically active, and more distinctively "Jewish"—in dress, language, and customs—than the native population. Their arrival challenged the homogenous, upper middle class, and generally republican French Jewish population as the immigrants introduced their own religious and cultural institutions as well as their militantly leftist political activities, bringing a century-long consensus on the nature of Jewish identity in France into question. Conflicts dominated the interactions between natives and immigrants as the former attempted to protect their position in their own society against what they saw as the "foreignness" of the latter. Nevertheless some individuals, particularly from among the intellectual elite and the youth population, began tentatively to explore new understandings of their ethno-religious heritage. Thus, the arrival of the immigrant population slowly expanded notions of Jewishness in France and began transforming the make-up and self-conceptions of that population.[51]

Such changes were increasingly apparent after World War II. One American Jewish official, Harry Rosen, sent to France by the Joint Distribution Committee to help build a united fundraising organ in France, recognized this shift when he arrived in 1948. Expecting to find a devastated Jewish population unwilling and uninterested in maintaining any link with its ancestral heritage, Rosen found to his surprise that his assumptions were unfounded. After meeting with a wide variety of individuals, including native and immigrant Jews from a variety of class backgrounds, he concluded that the disaffiliated French Jewish population was *not*, in fact, alienated:

> [T]here *is* [in France] identification by a substantial number of Jews with things Jewish, with Jewish hopes and aspirations. ... I am not suggesting that French Jewry has suddenly become extremely Jewish-con-

scious or nationalist. I am suggesting, however, that Hitler has left his mark. I am suggesting further that the birth of *Medinat Israel* has captured the imagination and fired the hearts of the vast majority of Jews in France. I am suggesting that given something with which to identify, the greatest number of Jews here will identify.[52]

Whatever the accuracy of Rosen's observations, his conclusions served to fuel the formation of the Fonds social juif unifié [FSJU], a united fund modeled on American Jewish conceptions of communal fundraising. The FSJU, in turn, devoted itself to rebuilding Jewish communal life. By directing its resources to the establishment of numerous Jewish community centers around France (again modeled on those of the Jewish communities of the United States), this new institution provided the population with a number of new arenas in which to express their Jewishness.[53]

The details of the FSJU's development is an important subject in its own right and cannot be addressed here. It is important to note, however, that by placing emphasis on *cultural* connections to "Jewishness" rather than highlighting religious expression as the sole means of identification, the FSJU re-enforced a shift to secular definitions of Jewish participation. Earlier in the century, immigrant Jews had begun this process by importing broader definitions of Jewish identification with them in their move westward. The plurality of their religious, political, and ethnic expressions brought options to the homogenous French Jewish population previously considered only by a handful of intellectuals.[54] World War II served to solidify these changes. In its aftermath, as immigrant Jews became more integrated into the population and with the legacy of the war behind them, French Jews began exploring new modes of expressing their Jewishness. Indeed, the "spiritual crisis" in the decade following World War II may, in fact, have been a crisis of the Consistoire, a nineteenth-century institution struggling to find a place for itself in the new, more pluralistic twentieth-century French Jewish map.

2.

Like Jews in France who had survived the upheaval and persecutions of World War II, those Armenians who migrated to France after the genocide of World War I faced the difficult task of rebuilding after several years of persecution. For them, however, the upheaval was compounded by their dislocation from their ancestral lands.[55] As noted above, this dislocation disrupted established patriarchal, familial, and economic norms. To mediate this great rupture with the past and to ease their transition into their new society, the refugees quickly sought to re-establish traditional forms of familial and communal organization.[56] One key institution linking them with the world they had left behind was the Armenian Apostolic Church. Indeed, Armenian communal life in France, as throughout the diaspora, was centered around the church.[57] While serving primarily as a house of worship, it also provided a variety of social services to all members of the community, quickly becoming the one institution in which almost all members of the population eventually participated. In establishing the church as an important center of communal life, the refugees sought more than a maintenance of their religious beliefs and traditions; rather in recreating a familiar religious/communal framework, they imported organizational structures from their past into their new, unfamiliar environment.[58]

In the Ottoman Empire, where religious affiliation had been the primary factor determining the individual's relationship to the state, the function of the Armenian Apostolic Church had been much more than religious. From the fourth century C.E., when the Armenian King Tiridates was converted to Christianity by the evangelist Gregory (making Armenia the first "nation" to adopt Christianity as its state religion), a sacred culture had been born linking the history of the people with that of their religion.[59] Then in the fifteenth century, when Armenians came under Ottoman rule, the sultans gave the Armenian Patriarchate in Constantinople unprecedented political, economic, and social power to oversee the administrative affairs of the empire's Armenian population. As a result, the Constantinople Patriarchate soon evolved into a powerful body that ran Armenian affairs in the empire, including its political and administrative life (running schools and hospitals, representing Armenians to the national leaders, etc.) and its religious life (running monasteries and churches, overseeing marriages, etc.). If, by the nineteenth century, this power was being questioned by a new generation of Western-educated Armenian intellectuals who challenged the clergy for its corruption and its alliance with national authorities (although some priests actively encouraged new reforms), the overwhelming majority remained committed to familiar religious practices and maintained a strong link with the church. Another small minority responded to the call of Catholic and Protestant missionaries (the latter primarily from the United States) and left the national church to create their own religious institutions.[60]

By the end of the nineteenth century, then, three separate Armenian religious denominations administered the population's affairs in the empire, all of which were represented in the refugee population that migrated to France. As in the Ottoman Empire, the Apostolic Church was by far the most influential, attracting the greatest number of adherents and serving as the most important center of communal life (although Armenian Catholics and Protestants also established their own churches and communal organizations).[61] Unsurprisingly, the church's structure reflected that of the Armenian Patriarchate in Constantinople, which had administered the population through a network of political and religious assemblies (made up of clerical and lay members). Broadly speaking, Armenian organizational life in France was created along similar lines. Church and communal administration were, thus, linked through regional assemblies and councils, the *azkain miut'iun*, which brought lay and religious leaders together in a broad communal organization presided over by a high-ranking religious leader. The role of these unions was to control and supervise the affairs of the church and the community and to take care of the refugees' religious needs.[62] Complementing the national assemblies were the *tachagan khourhourt*, or parish councils, which gathered together Armenians from the same city (and/or parish) to implement the policies of the national councils throughout the local communities.[63]

Most of the refugees' religious life gravitated around the Apostolic Church on the rue Jean Goujon in Paris. Involved in all areas of communal life, the church created afternoon schools for children in local communities, built parishes in all areas of the country where Armenians has settled in large numbers, and held holiday parties for children. In addition, a variety of social services and organizations either operated from the church or used it as a base, including the Armenian Red Cross; a medical dispensary; a women's league; a veterans' organization; etc.[64] In Marseille, for example, the Association de bienfaisance des dames arméniennes de Marseille operated out of the church, providing financial and medical care to indigents, widows, orphans, and the infirm.[65] In addition, the church provided a meeting space where non-religious groups could come together.

If, however, the church adopted the role and structure of the Constantinople Patriarchate, its impact was considerably reduced in the French context where division of church and state was so strong. Most importantly, the church did not provide the same legally sanctioned administrative function it had in the past. Like the synagogue (and its official administrative structure in France, the Consistoire), which was recognized solely as a *religious* institution within the Third Republic, the Armenian church had no legal power to organize communal life. While maintaining some responsibilities linked to the arrival of the refugees, including taking care of certain formalities regarding the issuing of identity cards, small financial loans, and marriage and birth certificates, adherence to and participation in church activities remained purely voluntary.[66] Thus, it wielded much less control over the population than it had under Ottoman rule.

This is not to say that the church did not play an important role in communal organization. Aside from its various religious and social services, it provided the community with an arena in which those with differing political and regional affiliations could come together. For example, Armenian communists, notoriously atheistic, would often participate in major religious celebrations such as Armenian Christmas (January 6) and Easter.[67] The church, thus, served as a identifiable site of Armenian affiliation and identification, even for those who did not accept or share in its religious doctrine. Nevertheless, its new context limited the degree to which it could use that influence. Let us consider the question of schools: in the Ottoman Empire, the Patriarchate had been the primary force behind the education of Armenians, fostering (and creating) a sense of nationhood/peoplehood throughout the population. While that influence had diminished slightly in the nineteenth century when a European-educated intelligentsia began encouraging secular education for the Armenian public, the church still maintained its central role. In France, however, the church was relegated to a secondary position, its schools only reaching children one or two afternoons a week after they had already participated in the national educational system. As a result, its impact was necessarily limited.

Moreover, the French context, which had transformed the church from a legal to a voluntary organization, also encouraged a wide range of other organizations to develop simply by providing space in which they could do so. As a result, the church had to compete with political and compatriotic organizations that formed their own schools and educational agendas and communal life became increasingly diversified. Although political parties had already begun exerting a significant influence over communal life prior to the genocide, their impact had been limited by their semi-legal status and their subordinate role to the church. In France, however, political and religious organizations were essentially the same— voluntary associations in which the immigrant population participated at their own will. The French setting, which facilitated a variety of poles of ethnic identification without privileging one over the other, thus encouraged the development of alternative centers of

Armenian leadership. In one instance, for example, when the church and the pro-Communist organization, the Haistani Oknoutian Gomidé [HOG], were fighting over who would provide aid to unemployed Armenian workers, the French police intervened, forcing the two to work together.[68] In this case, the government treated the church as one among numerous sources of communal leadership rather than as the sole voice directing Armenian affairs.[69] In this setting, it should not be surprising that numerous quarrels broke out over who spoke for the community, who represented it to the authorities, etc.[70] The church, while an important organizational body, did not automatically win these fights, creating a space in which other organizations and associations could take root.

Among the institutions/associations to develop in this open setting were a wide variety of compatriotic unions. These associations, unlike the church and political parties that were institutionally rooted in the Ottoman Empire, were an outgrowth of the new dispersion, providing Armenian refugees with a non-religious organizational structure through which to express communal identities. Like French Jews who continued to move away from religious definitions of "Jewishness" throughout the twentieth century by joining secular Jewish social and political organizations, Armenians could adopt a secular connection to their ancestral past without abandoning it completely by affiliating with these compatriotic organizations. This new identification allowed them to mediate the rupture with the past while helping them integrate into their new society.[71]

As we have already seen, the new refugees did not constitute one homogenous entity. While the large majority came from the Eastern provinces of the Ottoman Empire, others arrived from Russia, Transcaucasia, and Constantinople. Although their host society labeled them all "Armenian," these regional differences were not insignificant to the refugees themselves, many of whom began forming associational networks with others from similar regions. Thus, those who had fled Russia under the Bolsheviks came together in one group and those from Constantinople formed another.[72] Most, however, were survivors from small cities or villages in the Ottoman Empire, seeking connections to one another in their new land. Armenians from Arabkir, thus, formed one group; those from Yerznga another; those from Ghantaroz another, etc.[73] Even those living in an Armenian refugee camp in Marseille, a homogenous unit in the eyes of the surrounding population, broke into sub-groups.[74]

Much like the *landsmanshaftn* that sprang up among the Eastern European Jewish immigrant population in France during the interwar years and that served as their organizational core, these

Armenian compatriotic organizations provided emotional and material assistance to their members.[75] One association of Armenians
from Tchepni (Sivas), for example, founded in the Parisian suburb
Issy-les-Moulineaux in 1930, provided financial aid to its members, developed solidarity among those from Tchepni, instituted
language courses, and aided the new refugees with their administrative problems.[76] Another group from Sivas helped its members
to establish, educate, and care for themselves; located and reunited
their dispersed families; and helped them find work.[77] Because of
their small size and limited resources, however, most of these groups
tended to have narrower goals that focused on providing aid to
orphans, unemployed workers, the elderly, and the infirm. The
Union of Armenians from Marash (in Marseille), for example, only
had sixty voting members, while in Valence more than half the
compatriotic unions had fewer than twenty.[78] In addition, because
these groups were generally comprised of day laborers, tailors,
shoemakers, and other artisans, as well as some small merchants
who could only provide a monthly membership fee of two or three
francs, they had extremely small budgets which limited their activities.[79] Nevertheless, by providing financial aid to others more
unfortunate than themselves, they helped one another integrate into
the new country.[80] Indeed, like the *landsmanshaftn*, which allowed
Jews who collectively identified with a particular foreign origin to
ease into their new environment, the Armenian compatriotic organizations also relied on regional ties to facilitate the transition to
the new country by bringing together those from a particular
region, suburb, quarter, or even street in France. All the members of
the administrative leadership of the compatriotic union from
Tomarza, for example, came from one small area of Saint-Antoine,[81]
and in many cases the associational headquarters was based in the
president's home with several members of the administrative board
living at the same address.[82] Thus, in addition to providing basic
financial assistance to members, the compatriotic associations created links on the new land among those dispersed by the Genocide
and provided them with a substitution for the physical link to the
land that they had lost.[83]

Clearly, then, the compatriotic associations played a role
greater than that of mutual aid. Uprooted from their homes and
thrown into a new, urban environment with Armenians from other
places and different traditions (and in some cases, even different
dialects), those from the same region sought to make connections
with one another and to recreate a sense of familiarity in the unfamiliar setting.[84] Having lost their own territory, they nevertheless

grouped by territory, forming enduring allegiances that, in some cases, transcended the "common" Armenian title with which they had been labeled.[85] In theory, the organizations were to transcend all divisions in the population. Therefore, they were generally inclusive, permitting membership to all regardless of sex or age (although, at times, only those over fifteen could join, and women, in some instances, were not allowed to vote). Some even went so far as to forbid political and religious debates at meetings hoping to keep a unified front among their small memberships.[86] Yet, once again, the French context that allowed for a multiplicity of groups prevailed, and when politics or religious differences interfered, the Armenian population simply broke into smaller groupings. Such was clearly the case in Marseille when two compatriotic associations from the same village opened within a few months of each other, both based in a similar region of Marseille, and both proclaiming similar goals.[87] Like all associational groups, then, the compatriotic organizations were voluntary. As such, they provided a link to the past while still being shaped by the present.

Thus, as in the case of French Jewry, the post-World War I Armenian population in France slowly began moving away from religious institutions as the primary organizing force of communal life. While not abandoning the church altogether, Armenian refugees sought other avenues for expressing their identities within the new secular environment in which they found themselves. These new associations, whether compatriotic or political, reflected their members' position as stateless refugees and genocide survivors as well as their position as an ethnic minority within a larger nation state.

3.

This paper began by asking what impact, if any, the genocides of World War I and II had on the religious practices of Jewish and Armenian survivors. Did the physical and ideological attacks against these two groups encourage survivors to flee Judaism and Christianity respectively? Was there a link between genocide and the decline of religious practices among survivors?

As the comparison has shown, France's strong secular and assimilatory political culture was far more influential in shaping survivors' religious practices than fear of future persecutions or shame of religious affiliation.[88] Certainly the dislocation of Armenian survivors caused by the genocide of World War I played a role in distancing them from Christianity in the sense that as they

moved, they left behind the more theocratic world in which they
had lived. That said, the persecutions themselves did not scare survivors from the church. To the contrary, for the first generation of
Armenian survivors in France, the church remained the most
important communal institution. Similarly, the "crisis" of French
Judaism did not arise as a specific response to the World War II persecutions. Rather, a pattern of religious disaffiliation had begun
long before the Nazi rise to power in Europe.

Yet if the comparison confirms the power of France's strong
secular heritage in shaping its immigrant and religious minorities, it
nevertheless counters claims that the genocides led escapees to abandon their communities out of fear. To the contrary, in both cases, if
religious affiliation declined, institutional life diversified and in some
cases flourished as survivors reconsidered their position in state and
society in light of the genocides of World War I and II.

Notes

1. Robert Sommer, "Où va le Judaïsme français?" *L'Amandier fleuri* 1,1 (oct. nov.
    1949), p.9, cited in Roger Berg, "La Pratique du Judaïsme en France," *Yod,* 21
    (1985), p. 83.
2. Pierre Lowell, "Les Foyards," *Évidences*, 27 (September-October, 1952), p. 36.
3. Works on Jewish persecution in Vichy France abound. For an excellent
    overview, see: Michael Marrus and Robert Paxton, *Vichy France and the Jews*
    (New York, 1983). Also see: Asher Cohen, *Persécutions et sauvetages: Juifs et
    Français sous l'occupation et sous Vichy* (Paris, 1993); André Kaspi, *Les Juifs
    pendant l'Occupation* (Paris, 1991); Serge Klarsfield, *Vichy-Auschwitz: Le
    Role de Vichy dans la solution finale de la question juive en France* (Paris,
    1983); Donna F. Ryan, *The Holocaust and the Jews of Marseille: The Enforce-
    ment of Antisemitic Policies in Vichy France* (Urbana and Chicago, 1996);
    Richard H. Weisberg, *Vichy Law and the Holocaust in France* (New York,
    1996); and Susan Zuccotti, *The Holocaust, the French, and the Jews* (New
    York, 1993). For Jewish responses to the persecution, see: Jacques Adler, *The
    Jews of Paris and the Final Solution: Communal Response and Internal Con-
    flicts, 1940-44* (Oxford, 1985); Richard Cohen, *The Burden of Conscience:
    French Jewish Leadership during the Holocaust* (Bloomington, 1987); Lucien
    Lazare, *La Résistance juive en France* (Paris, 1987); and Adam Rayski, *Les
    Choix des Juifs sous Vichy: Entre soumission et résistance* (Paris, 1992).
4. Jacqueline Mesnil-Amar, *Ceux qui ne dormaient pas: 1944-46, Fragments de
    journal* (Paris, 1957), p. 119.
5. Some Armenians converted and survived, but this was part and parcel of the
    systematic attempt to remove all traces of them from the population both

through murder and through state programs to assimilate women and children forcibly into Islamic households. Ara Sarafian, The Absorption of Armenian Women and Children into Muslim Households as a Structural Component of the Armenian Genocide," chapter 9 in this volume. For the best discussions of the Genocide, see: Vahakn N. Dadrian, "The Naim Andonian Documents on the World War I Destruction of the Armenians: The Anatomy of a Genocide," *International Journal of Middle East Studies* 18 (August 1986), pp. 311-60; Vahakn N. Dadrian, "Genocide as a Problem of National and International Law: The World War I Armenian Case and Its Contemporary Legal Ramifications, *Yale Journal of International Law* (Summer 1989); Richard Hovannisian, ed., *The Armenian Genocide in Perspective* (New Brunswick, 1986); Richard Hovannisian, ed., *History, Politics, Ethics* (New York, 1992); Robert Melson, *Revolution and Genocide: On the Origins of the Armenian Genocide and the Holocaust* (Chicago, 1992). Regarding desecration of religious sites, see: Dickran Kouymjian, "The Destruction of Armenian Historical Monuments as a Continuation of the Turkish Policy of Genocide," in *A Crime of Silence: The Armenian Genocide—The Permanent People's Tribunal*, ed. Gerard Libaridian (Cambridge, Mass, 1985): 173-183.

6. J.-Ch. Bonnet, *Les Pouvoirs publics français et l'immigration dans l'entre-deux-guerres* (Lyon, 1976); Gary S. Cross, *Immigrant Workers in Industrial France* (Philadelphia, 1983); Yves Lequin, ed., *Histoire des étrangers et de l'immigration en France* (Paris, 1992); Georges Mauco, *Les Étrangers en France: Leur Role dans l'activité économique* (Paris, 1932); Emile Temime, ed., *Histoire des migrations à Marseille*, 4 vols. (Aix-en-Provence, 1989).

7. Martine Hovanessian, *Le Lien communautaire: Trois générations d'Arméniens* (Paris, 1992); Hovanessian, *Les Arméniens et leurs territoires* (Paris, 1995).

8. For a discussion of the "comparative method" across time and space, see: William Sewell, "Marc Bloch and the Logic of Comparative History," *History and Theory* 1 (1967), pp. 208-218.

9. Minutes, 7 April 1948, AA27, Consistoire de Paris.

10. "Demandes de changements de nom," *Bulletin d'information* , May 1945, p. 3, French Jewish Communities, 13/ 2-2, Jewish Theological Seminary (JTS).

11. "Note sur les demandes de changement de nom (d'après le J.O. depuis le 1er Janvier 1945)," in Législation et demandes de changements de noms, Consistoire de Paris.

12. "Rapport sur les changements de noms," Gaston Hildenfinger, June 1947, Législation et demandes de changements de noms, Consistoire de Paris.

13. Although such fears continued, according to Annette Wieviorka, *Déportation et génocide: Entre la mémoire et l'oubli* (Paris, 1992), pp. 352-354, some consistorial leaders—and particularly Georges Wormser—saw encouraging signs as early as the late 1940s suggesting that French Judaism might recover from what he began referring to as a "religious eclipse" rather than a religious crisis.

14. *European Jewry Ten Years After the War: An Account of the Development and Present Status of the Decimated Jewish Communities of Europe* (New York, 1956), p. 199. In 1952, the *American Jewish Yearbook* also reported on soaring intermarriage rates in the provinces, "where small communities are rapidly dwindling." *American Jewish Yearbook*, Vol. 53, p. 281.

15. Report on Jewish community in France, Georges Wormser, Consultative Conference of the AIU, AJC, and AJA, June 1955, Anglo-Jewish Association papers, AJ37/6/6/6/6, Parkes Library.

16. Arnold Mandel, "French Jewry in a Time of Decision: Vestigal Remnant or Living Continuity?" *Commentary* 18, 6 (December 1954), p. 539.

17. Mandel, "French Jewry at a Time of Decision," p. 542.
18. Paul Levy, *Les Noms des israélites de France. Histoire et dictionnaire* (Paris, 1960), cited in Wieviorka, *Déportation et génocide*, p. 365.
19. Jean-Jacques Bernard, for example, a well-known native French Jewish writer (and son of the even better known French dramatist Tristan Bernard) who had been interned in Compiègne from December 1941 to February 1942, became a public proponent of radical assimilation. Already in the mid-1930s, Bernard was insisting that integration was the only plausible response to the Jewish Question. After his internment, however, he rapidly converted to Catholicism, documenting his decision in a memoir as well as in several controversial articles. Jean-Jacques Bernard, *Le Camp de la mort lente: Compiègne 1941–1942* (Paris, 1944). For a discussion of the resulting controversy, see Maud Mandel, *In the Aftermath of Genocide: Armenians and Jews in Twentieth Century France* (Dissertation for university of Michigan, Department of History, 1998), pp. 290-295. For a discussion of the worries regarding conversion, see Wieviorka, *Déportation et génocide*, pp. 361-7.
20. A particularly poignant case of this is detailed in Saul Friedländer, *Quant vient le souvenir ...* (Paris, 1978).
21. André Kaspi, "L'Affaire des enfants Finaly," *L'Histoire*, 76 (March 1985), pp. 40-53. Rabi, *L'Affaire Finaly* (Marseille, 1953). For a detailed first person account of the affair, see: Moise Keller, *L'Affaire Finaly telle que je l'ai vécue* (Paris, 1960).
22. File 367, American Joint Distribution Committee (AJDC), cited in Isabelle Goldsztejn, "Le Role de l'American Joint dans la reconstruction de la communauté," *Archives juives: Revue d'histoire des Juifs de France* 28,1 (1er semestre, 1995), p. 29. Wieviorka also shows that converted children were few and far-between.
23. Report, Office for France Activities, May 1948 through September 1948, file 310, AJDC.
24. European Executive Council, Welfare Department Report Number 3, June 1949, file 310 AJDC.
25. *Visages d'enfants,* Publication de la WIZO, February 1945, French Jewish Communities, 13/2-2, JTS.
26. Information regarding Jewish children/orphans in the first three years after the war is documented in Wieviorka, *Déportation et génocide*, pp. 369-90.
27. "Le Problème des enfants de déportés et la question des conversions," *Bulletin d'information*, May 1945, p. 2, French Jewish Communities, 13/ 2-2, JTS.
28. Approximately 11,600 Jewish children from France were killed during the war; another 72,400 (under 18) survived. Most of them, approximately 62,000, stayed with their parents or were placed directly by them into an institution or non-Jewish family. Another 8,000 to 10,000 children were saved by Jewish organizations either by smuggling them out of the country or, more often, by placing them in non-Jewish families. See Lazare, *La Résistance juive en France.*
29. D. Gluckberg, OPEJ, to Chief Rabbi Brodie, 7 August 1950, papers of the Chief Rabbinate, E1196, Greater London Records Office (GLRO).
30. *Mémorial en souvenir de nos rabins et ministres officiants victimes de la barbarie nazie* (Paris: Consistoire central, 1946).
31. Minutes, 8 May 1946, AA26, Consistoire de Paris.
32. Report to Assises du Judaïsme (unsigned), no date (summer 1951), Assises du Judaïsme français, 1950 and 1951, Consistoire de Paris.

33. *European Jewry Ten Years After the War*, p. 204. The report noted bleakly, "There is not a single rabbi for a distance of 250 miles between Paris and Bordeaux and the same distance between Bordeaux and Toulouse."

34. I have borrowed this phrase from Rabbi André Zaouie of the Union libérale israélite. "Rapport sur quelques principes d'instruction et d'éducation religieuses," Assises du Judaïsme français, 1950 and 1951, Consistoire de Paris.

35. Report, Assises du Judaïsme français, 1950 and 1951, Consistoire de Paris.

36. Historians of religion in France have recently argued that the de-Christianization of France was not, in fact, a linear process, and that Catholicism in particular has undergone periods when religious sentiment was more intense. In particular, they note the mid-1930s to mid-1960s as several decades when renewed interest in Catholicism took hold followed by a period of religious crisis (after the various upheavals of the late 1960s). See: Gérard Cholvy, Yves-Marie Hilaire, et. al, *Histoire religieuse de la France contemporaine*, vol. 3 (Paris, 1988) and Gérard Cholvy, *La Religion en France de la fin du XVIIIe à nos jours* (Paris, 1991). While Judaism and Catholicism may have followed different paths in the twentieth century (for French Jews a period of renewed interest in Judaism came in the late 1960s and 1970s, after the arrival of North African Jewish immigrants just when Catholicism was entering a period of "crisis"), it is still true that both have felt the impact of the secular state, which—with the exception of the Vichy years—has militantly enforced a separation of public life and private religious practices. For statistics on religious practices in twentieth century France, see: Fernand Boulard, Gérard Cholvy, and Yves-Marie Hilaire, eds., *Matériaux pour l'histoire religieuse du peuple français, XIXe-XXe*, 3 vols. (Paris, 1982-92).

37. Paula Hyman, *From Dreyfus to Vichy: The Remaking of French Jewry, 1906-1939* (New York, 1979), p. 30.

38. Wieviorka, *Déportation et génocide*, 353, compiles some figures on Jewish marriages, benai-mitzvah, and confirmations from different figures in the consistorial archives. Also see: Berg, "La Pratique du Judaïsme en France," *passim*.

39. Of these, only 108 were endogamous: 26 of which were between "French" Jews (native born), 135 between Eastern European immigrants and 47 between North African Jews. A similar percentage breakdown existed for 1953. Simon Schwarzfuchs, "Un Aspect démographique de la communauté parisienne," *Journal des communautés*, 22 January 1954, p. 3, concluded that the most faithful base of the community was the Eastern European Jewish immigrants followed by those from North Africa. The French Jewish population, he concluded, was persevering in its disaffection from Judaism.

40. Edgard Spira (treasurer du Consistoire de Paris), *Journal des communautés*, 24 June 1960, reported to the general meeting of the Consistoire de Paris that from 1950 to 1954 the number of students in Talmud Torah never exceeded 750 and hit a low in 1953 of 473. In 1955 the number jumped to 1265 and by 1959 had reached 2400. According to Berg, "La Pratique du judaïsme en France," 95, this jump in numbers was evidence of the progress that Consistoire officials and other members of the French Jewish elite had made since 1945 in encouraging the rebirth of Jewish faith since World War II. Berg, however, ignores the impact of North African Jews, which he claimed did not have an effect until 1960. In fact, North African Jews were already coming in large numbers by the mid-1950s. The dramatic jump in numbers attending Talmud Torah are indication that these new arrivals had started to swell the ranks of those few native French Jews attending such classes.

41. Minutes, 7 March and 6 June 1945, AA26, Consistoire de Paris.
42. Minutes, 23 April 1947, AA26, Consistoire de Paris. Also see, Roger Berg, "La Communauté juive de Paris en 1957," *Bi-tefutsot ha-golah (Dispersion et Unité)* 1 (March 1960), p. 343.
43. Minutes, 7 December 1948, AA27, Consistoire de Paris.
44. Minutes, 4 January 1950, AA28, Consistoire de Paris.
45. *European Jewry Ten Years After the War*, 203; File Yeshivoth A-Z, AJDC.
46. Note d'information du CRIF, 10 March 1952, Anglo-Jewish Association papers, AJ95/1/31, Parkes Library.
47. Phyllis Cohen Albert, *The Modernization of French Jewry: Consistory and Community in the Nineteenth Century* (Hanover, 1977), pp. 50-5.
48. Berg, "La Communauté juive de Paris," 345.
49. Note d'information du CRIF, 10 March 1952, Anglo-Jewish Association papers, AJ95/1/31, Parkes Library.
50. That said, attendance continued to remain high at high holiday services with synagogues full to capacity. In 1947, for example, estimates of attendance at *Kol Nidre* services in Paris reached fifteen thousand. While it is true that in certain synagogues these numbers were made up of Egyptian and North African Jewish refugees newly arrived in France, it is also true that a certain percentage of the French Jewish population had not abandoned their ancestral religion. Minutes, 2 October 1946, AA26, Consistoire de Paris; Minutes, 8 October 1947, AA27, Consistoire de Paris.
51. Hyman, *From Dreyfus to Vichy*. Also see: Nancy Green, *The Pletzl of Paris: Jewish Immigrant Workers in the Belle Epoque* (New York, 1986) and David H. Weinberg, *A Community on Trial: The Jews of Paris in the 1930s* (Chicago, 1977).
52. Harry M. Rosen to Joseph J. Schwartz, "United Fund-Raising for French Jewish Community," 30 June 1948, file 357, AJDC.
53. Mandel, *In the Aftermath of Genocide*, chap. 7.
54. Nadia Malinovich, "'Orientalism' and the Construction of Jewish Identity in France, 1915-1932" (paper presented at the annual meeting of the Association for Jewish Studies, Boston, MA., 21-23 December 1997).
55. In this sense, their situation more closely resembled Holocaust survivors from Eastern Europe who migrated to France in the years after the hostilities had ended.
56. Hovanessian, *Le Lien communautaire, passim.*
57. The role of the church as a central element in the maintenance of an "Armenian identity" in the diaspora has been traced in most scholarly studies of twentieth century Armenian communities. See, for example, Anny Bakalian, *Armenian-Americans: From Being to Feeling Armenian* (New Brunswick, 1993), chap. 2 and Susan Paul Pattie, *Faith in History: Armenians Rebuilding Community* (Washington and London, 1997), chap. 13. For a theoretical discussion of the link between the church and the diaspora, see: Khachig Tölölyan, "The Role of the Armenian Apostolic Church in the Diaspora," *Armenian Review* 41, 1-161(Spring 1988), pp. 55-68.
58. Hovanessian, *Le Lien communautaire*, pp. 116-22.
59. The isolation of the Armenian Church in the fifth century (over doctrinal disagreements with neighboring Christian sects) intensified the link between church and people since it prevented their potential merging with other Christian groups. "Affirmation de l'Arménie chrétienne," in *Histoire des Arméniens*, ed. Gerard Dedeyan (Toulouse, 1982), pp. 141-184.

60. Christopher Walker, *Armenia: The Survival of a Nation*, rev. 2nd ed. (New York, 1980), pp. 125-6.

61. In particular, Protestants represented a significant minority and the Protestant church also provided a variety of communal services including Armenian language courses to all children whatever their religious denomination. In addition, many Apostolics attended local Protestant churches when they had no local alternative. Hovanessian, *Le Lien communautaire,* 118-20. See also: René Leonian, ed., *Les Arméniens de France sont-ils intégrés ou assimilés* (Issyles-Moulineaux, 1986).

62. Commissaire spécial de Lyon to Directeur du Cabinet du Minister de l'Intérieur, 15 September 1928, F/7/13436, Archives Nationale (AN).

63. S. Andesian and M. Hovanessian, "L'Arménien: Langue rescappée d'un génocide," in *Vingt-cinq communautés linguistiques de la France*, vol. 2, ed. Genevieve Vermès (Paris, 1988), pp. 66-7.

64. *Le Guide des étrangers* (Paris, 1937), pp. 5-24.

65. Statutes, Association de bienfaisance des dames arméniennes de Marseille, 7 October 1931, #4170, 4M698, Bouches-du-Rhône.

66. Commissaire spécial (Lyon) to Préfet du Rhône, 20 November 1928, f/7/13436, AN.

67. Hovanessian, *Le Lien communautaire*, pp. 121-2.

68. Ministre de l'Intérieur to Ministre de Travail, 24 February 1927, f/7/13436, AN.

69. Hovanessian, *Le Lien communautaire,* pp. 131-2.

70. Such conflicts broke out *within* institutions as well. In one instance, for example, a conflict over the Armenian church's voting procedure was taken to the French courts. Commissaire spécial (Lyon) to Préfet du Rhône, 20 November 1928, f/7/13436, AN.

71. An overview of such organizations in Marseille can be found in: Marie-Françoise Attard-Maraninchi and Emile Temime, *Le Cosmopolitisme de l'entre-deux-guerres (1919-1945),* vol. 3 of *Histoire des migrations à Marseille*, pp. 103-5.

72. "Nouvelles," *Le Foyer,* 1 January 1929; Statutes, Union arménienne de Constantinople, 21 October 1931, #4177, 4M693, Bouches-du-Rhône. It is worth noting that many of the these groups declared themselves to local authorities only upon needing a bank account or after requiring some other official notarization. Thus, they may have existed for several years before "appearing" in the archives. The Union compatriotique de la ville de Zara Sivas, for example, declared itself to the government in 1929 but it was formed in 1924. Statutes, Union compatriotique de la ville de Zara Sivas, 9 July 1929, #3645, 4M761, Bouches-du-Rhône.

73. Statutes, L'Union d'Arabkir, 7 March 1935, #6716,4M694, Bouches-du-Rhône; Statutes, "Union compatriotique de Erzenga, 13 May 1939, #7139, 4M761, Bouches-du-Rhône; Statutes, Union des compatriotes arméniens de Ghantaroz, 31 August 1927, #3270, same carton.

74. For example, in 1924 residents from Bithynie formed their own compatriotic union and their entire governing board was from the camp. Statutes, Union compatriotique des arméniens de Bithynie à Marseille, 26 January 1925, #2746, 4M761, Bouches-du-Rhône.

75. In Paris, for example, there were seventy-eight *landsmanshaftn* proper and eighty-three other Jewish mutual-aid societies in the 1930s. These organizations offered communal welfare to their members by providing them with free loans and medical benefits as well as by organizing social gatherings and by

intervening on behalf of illegal immigrants in dealings with French police and immigration authorities. Jonathan Boyarin, *Polish Jews in Paris: The Ethnography of Memory* (Bloomington, 1991), pp. 17-20.

76. A.S. de l'Association des Arméniens originaires de Tchépni (Sivas), 14 January 1930, f/7/13436, AN.

77. Statuts, Union 'Senekerimain' des Arméniens de Sivas à Marseille, 20 August 1924, #9503, 4M693, Bouches-du-Rhône.

78. "Badger," *Har'ach'*, 22 April 1935.

79. Statutes, Union de Bienfaisance du Arménienne de Marache, 11 May 1928, #3433, 4M698, Bouches-du-Rhône.

80. Five compatriotic unions in Marseille, for example, worked together to open evening courses to teach the refugees Armenian, French, math, history and geography. Here again we see the compatriotic unions working to integrate the newcomers while keeping them connected to that from which they had come. "Cours de soir," *Le Foyer*, 15 April 1929.

81. Statutes, Union compatriotique de Tomarza et ses environs, 8 February 1933, #4578, 4M761, Bouches-du-Rhône.

82. The treasurer and the president of the Papert compatriotic union lived at the same address as did the president and treasurer of the Tchkhan compatriotic union. Statutes, Union compatriotique de Babert, 11 May 1939, # 7138, 4M761, Bouches-du-Rhône; Statutes, Union compatriotique de Tchkhan (de l'Everek), 17 December 1930, #3956, same carton.

83. Not all mutual-aid/compatriotic organizations were based on a link to a particular physical territory. Some, such as the Association de l'entre'aide arménienne created in May 1933, were life insurance organizations that provided financial aid to the beneficiaries of its members upon their death. A.S. Association de l'entre'aide arménienne qui sollicite l'autorisation de fonctionner comme société de secours mutuels, July 1933, f/7/13436, AN.

84. Hovanessian, *Le Lien communautaire*, 63-4.

85. In some cases, the refugees actually sought to *recreate* this physical link to their lost territory by transforming their associations into "reconstruction" organizations as soon as the membership had become financially established in France. In 1935, for example, members from the Yenihan (Sivas) compatriotic union changed their organization's statutes; subsequently the bulk of their resources were directed to rebuilding their destroyed village rather than toward mutual aid. A compatriotic union of Armenians from Ak-Chéhir followed suit in 1936. Statutes, Union de reconstruction compatriotique de Yeni-Han de Sivas, 19 November 1935, #3424, 4M 761, Bouches-du-Rhône; Statutes, Union compatriotique des Arméniens d'Ak-Chéhir, 4 September 1929 and 3 June 1936, #3683, same carton. These new villages were not to stand where they had once stood, which was a political impossibility, nor—interestingly— were they to be built in France. Rather, they were to be constructed in the newly established Soviet Armenian republic as a home for those refugees who had yet to find a stable living environment. Armenians from Tcharsandjak, thus, worked first and foremost to provide moral and financial aid to their compatriots in France and to teach them the French language and laws. Their long term goal, however, was to "rebuild" Tcharsandjak in Soviet Armenia. Statutes, Union compatriotique de Tcharsandjak, 22 August 1929, #3674, 4M761, Bouches-du-Rhône.

86. Two examples are: Statutes, Société de bienfaisance des Arméniens de la ville d'Ankara, 10 février 1932, #4170, 4M698, Bouches-du-Rhône; Statutes, Union des compatriotes arméniens d'Amassia, 10 June 1927, # 3219, 4M761.

87. Statutes, Association compatriotique de Palou, 8 September 1928, in #3497, 4M761, Bouches-du-Rhone; Statutes, Union de Bienfaissance de Palou, Okou, et Tepe, 12 December 1928, #3541, 4M698, Bouches du Rhône. Also see, Maraninchi and Temime, *Le Cosmopolitisme de l'entre-deux-guerres*, p. 104.

88. Rogers Brubaker, *Citizenship and Nationhood in France and Germany* (Cambridge, Mass., 1992); Gérard Noiriel, *The French Melting Pot: Immigration, Citizenship, and National Identity*, trans. Geoffroy de Laforcade (Minneapolis, 1996).

– Chapter 15 –

ORTHODOX JEWISH THOUGHT IN THE WAKE OF THE HOLOCAUST
Tamim Pa'alo of 1947[*]

Gershon Greenberg

For Rose Fackenheim z"l and for Emil Fackenheim,
in belated gratitude

The reflective Orthodox Jewish religious response to the Holocaust began with the rise of Hitler and continued through the war.[1] The research of Yitzhak Herman, Pinhas Pelli, Mendel Piekaz, Nehemiah Polen, Pessah Schindler, Eliezer Schweid, Ephraim Shmueli, and the present writer has shed light on the literature through 1945. Research into the religious thought of Orthodox Jews in the immediate aftermath, the era of *she'erit hapeleitah* (surviving remnant), has also begun. The materials have been identified, and the work of Simhah Elberg (Shanghai) and Ya'akov Moshe Harlap (Jerusalem) has been studied.[2] Here I introduce Hayim Yisrael Tsimerman's *Tamim Pa'alo.*

Tsimerman's work was one of three religious treatises about the catastrophe published in Palestine in 1947. The others were "Le'et Dodim" ("Moment of Love") by Harlap (1883-1951), a Kabbalist who succeeded Rav Avraham Yitzhak Kook (1865-1935) as the head of the Merkaz Harav Yeshiva, and "Hamasoret shel Sin'at Yisrael" ("The Tradition of Hating Israel") by Yehudah Leib Gerst (1906-1963), a Lodz-born educator of the Agudat Israel movement who arrived in Palestine in May 1947 from Bergen-Belsen.[3] Harlap recognized the Holocaust as a transformative event on the level of the Sinai revelation and fell silent before it. In silence, it was possible for him to grasp revealed divine wisdom—for which the writings of Eliyahu ben Shlomo Zalman, Gaon of Vilna (1720-1797) and Rav Kook served as channels.

Harlap concluded that the Holocaust belonged to an already-unfolding process of redemption that involved the inevitable catharsis of evil. The catharsis took the form of an assault by a metaphysical power of negativity, the *Sitra ahra* (realm of otherness), against the sanctified nation of Israel. Because Israel's holiness coincided with metaphysical reality, the assault was self-destructive. Indeed, the antagonism was going to set off the eruption of the redemptive realm of Torah and sacred life. History, having been consumed by the *Sitra ahra* and having excluded Israel, would be left destroyed in redemption's wake. For Harlap, the ontic-level conflict between *Sitra ahra*-destructiveness and the holiness of Israel persisting beneath the outer cataclysm corresponded to the advent of the Messiah, son of Joseph (*Sukkah* 52a); the eruption of pure light in which the conflict terminated corresponded to the advent of the Messiah, son of David.[4]

Gerst, by contrast, approached the Holocaust historically. He identified the moment of the Sinai revelation as a creation point in human culture, when divine morality was established and idolatry and unrestrained inclination were absolutely rejected. But Sinai morality also catalyzed opposition. Once Israel's existence established de facto denial of anti-Torah and *Sitra ahra*, the nations of the world struck out in attack. Gerst detailed the historical transmission of the hateful assault upon Israel, from Apion of Alexandria in the first century through German philosophy in the nineteenth and on to Hitler. The Nazis were absolutely committed to destroying Sinai morality once and for all, and given the unassailability of God, Israel became the target. In recounting his personal experiences during the catastrophe (Lodz ghetto, Auschwitz, Kaufering, Landshut, Dachau, Bergen Belsen), Gerst presented evidence that divine morality survived in Israel through defiant, concrete expressions of Torah belief and practice.[5]

Sefer Tamim Pa'alo: She'elot U'tshuvot Bidvar Ha'hashmadah Ha'ayumah shel Shishah Milyon Ha'yehudim, Hashem Yinkom Damam (The Book "His Work is Perfect" [Deuteronomy 32:4]: *Questions and Answers Concerning the Terrible Destruction of Six Million Jews, May God Avenge Their Blood)* of summer 1947 had little in common with Gerst's work, but much in common with

Harlap's. While Gerst attributed the calamity to forces outside Israel, Tsimerman focused exclusively on Israel's own role. Nor did Tsimerman speak in terms of Israel's Torah-moral activity during the catastrophe, or her resistance to, and ultimate victory over, the idolatry and anti-morality of Nazism and its supporters. For him, Israel's condition during the Holocaust was set by God and involved no active initiative on her part. And while Gerst interpreted the hatred for Israel in historical terms, Tsimerman insisted that knowledge about Israel had to do with her relationship to God, which was a-historical. Harlap and Tsimerman shared the position that human understanding of the catastrophe, which related to empirical and historical reality, should concede to revealed wisdom. Namely, that apocalyptic redemption was already in place and that the catastrophe belonged to that reality. But while Harlap identified the catastrophe as the work of cosmic-like evil forces outside Israel which went wild because redemption was imminent and that meant their end, Tsimerman was not concerned with outer forces. While for Harlap, collective Israel was pure and essentially sinless, Tsimerman was concerned with sinful collective Israel at the threshold of redemption. Indeed, Tsimerman took the radical position that the pious of Israel themselves were indirectly responsible for the Holocaust because they failed to stop Israel's trespassers, and directly responsible because they failed to restore the Land of Israel. In this regard, Tsimerman departed not only from Harlap, but from most other religious thinkers in the Land of Israel both during and immediately after the war.[6]

Hayim Israel Tsimerman

Tsimerman (1901-1967?) was born in Kosov, Poland, and educated there in a traditional *heder*. He left for Sokolov-Podliask to study at the newly-established Beit Yisrael Yeshiva of Yitzhak Selig Morgenshtern ("Admor of Sokolov," 1866-1939). The two became very close. Morgenshtern was concerned about Tsimerman's going to Warsaw to study without his knowledge, and had the father arrange for Tsimerman to return to get his approval for the course of study. Before Tsimerman married he sought his teacher's consent. Beit Yisrael Yeshiva students studied twelve hours daily (except for the Sabbath). In addition to classical studies in Torah exegesis and Talmudic texts—and, presumably, major Kabbalistic works—there were classes in German, Yiddish, and arithmetic. Beyond the twelve-hour regimen, some students participated voluntarily in the study group *(kibbutz),* which took place daily from 7 p.m. to 2 a.m.[7] The Admor of Sokolov's Judaism included strains of Hasidism and love for Zion *(hibat tsiyon).* He was descended from the founder of the Kotsk school of Hasidism, Menahem Mendl (1787-1859)—his father Hayim Israel ("Admor of Pilov," 1840-1905), who coincidentally taught Tsimerman's father Ya'akov, was the great grandson.[8] Tsimerman cited Menahem Mendl in *Tamim Pa'alo,* as well as the work of the founder of the Kotsk-associated school of Ger, Yitzhak Meir Rotenberg ("Ha'rim," 1789-1866), and Rotenberg's grandson Yehudah Aryeh Leib Alter ("Sephat Emet," 1847-1905). As if to close the circle the Admor of Sokolov, who died in Otvotsk a few weeks after it was bombed in the fall of 1939 and his son was murdered, was buried next to Ha'rim's eldest son Avraham Mordekhai. As to *hibat tsiyon:* the Admor of Pilov was a member of the Odessa branch of the Hoveve Tsiyon (Lovers of Zion) movement, and labored to establish settlements—especially by Hasidim—in Palestine. His commitment to the Land was such that he thought better of simple Jews who actually settled there, than of perfect *tsadikim* (pious ones) whose sole concern was to carry out the divine precepts.[9] The Admor of Sokolov campaigned to acquire land for agricultural development. In 1923/24 he joined a delegation to the Land of Israel, led by the "Sephat Emet's" eldest son, Mordekhai Alter (1866-1948), for the purposes of establishing Agudat Israel interests.[10] After he returned to Poland, he founded synagogues on Rehov Rashi and Rehov Ahad Ha'am in Tel Aviv for his Hasidim in the Land.[11]

By the mid-1920s, Tsimerman was attending the Warsaw branch of the Musar (moralistic) movement's Novagrudok school—founded by Yosef Yozel Hurwitz (1850-1920)—that had recently been established by Hurwitz's disciple, David Budnik. Budnik, who would be killed in Latvia in the summer of 1941, was both teacher and personal protector. He advised Tsimerman about how to escape the army, arranged for his recovery after he was hospitalized for malnutrition, and helped him get through the medical exam required to leave Warsaw for Palestine.[12] By the late 1920s Tsimerman arrived in Palestine. He served as rabbi of the two Sokolover-Kotsk synagogues established by the Admor of Sokolov. In the late thirties he was appointed a professional scholar at the new Kollel Ateret Yosef (Hurwitz), or institute for rabbinic study, in Tel Aviv. The *kollel* was established by Shmuel Idelzak (1862-1947), with the support of Tel Aviv Chief Rabbi Moshe Avigdor Amiel. Idelzak represented continuity with the Musar teaching of Tsimerman's Warsaw mentor Budnik. Trained at Musar yeshivas in Tels and Slobodka in Lithuania, Idelzak arrived in Palestine in 1922. In the twenties he and Hillel Vitkind established the Beit Yosef (Hurwitz) Novaroduk Yeshiva in Tel Aviv—which Vitkind then headed.[13]

In the year after *Tamim Pa'alo*, Tsimerman published *Da'at Hayim*, commentaries on the 16th-century legal codification *Shulhan Arukh: Orah Hayim* and *Yore Deah*. The work received an approbation from Isser Yehudah Unterman (Chief Rabbi of Tel Aviv). In 1957 Tsimerman published a volume of assorted Talmudic commentaries and interpretations of weekly Torah readings entitled *Penei Hayim*, with approbations from Unterman and Yitzhak Eyzik Halevi Herzog (Chief Rabbi of the Land of Israel), Berish Vaydenfeld (Head of Kokhav MiYa'akov Yeshivah, Jerusalem), Yosef Tsevi Halevi (Head of the Beit Din, Tel Aviv) and Alter Ya'akov Meir Brizman (Head of the Beit Din, Lodz). In the 1960s he published a study of Kashrut laws entitled *Peri Yisrael*, with approbations by Yitzhak Nissim (Chief Sephardic Rabbi of the Land of Israel), Vaydenfeld, Unterman, Meshullam Rateh (member of the Chief Rabbinate of the Land of Israel), Pinhas Epstein (Head of the Beit Din, Jerusalem), Reuven Katz (Chief Rabbi of Petah Tikvah), Shmuel Halevi Vazner (Head of Zikhron Meir Yeshivah in Benei Berak), Yehezkel Sarna (Head of Keneset Israel-Slobodka Yeshivah in Jerusalem), Avraham Rozing (Head of the Beit Din in Ramat Gan) and Yehiel Mikhal Faynshtayn (Head of Beit Yehudah Yeshivah).[14]

Sefer Tamim Pa'alo

Tsimerman stated explicitly his motivations for writing the forty-eight-page scholarly treatise. Two years after the catastrophe, the questioning persisted. Six million Jews were killed in every possible way in Europe and elsewhere, dying in sanctification of God's name. This left a painful quandary, penetrating into the heart's inner depth, distressing all Jews from the insignificant to the important, from leftists to rightists, from free-thinker to believer, from evil to righteous, from ignorant to pious. All, without exception, ultimately had this one question: "Why did God do this to His nation?" (p. 4). Was God not merciful? Assuming that He did it out of wisdom and righteousness,

> how could He not have been merciful (*rihem*) to the six million Jews? On men and women, old, young, babies, and infants nursing at the breast—[people] who did not sin? They were killed by such torture and pain that the ear cannot bear to hear about it—and when it did the heart cried deeply. Does it not say "The Lord is righteous in all His

ways" [Psalms 145:17]; that "I am the Eternal before a man sins, the same after a man sins [and repents, a God merciful and gracious (*El rahum vehanun*)]" [*Rosh Ha'shanah* 17b]?

Indeed, it could not in fact be assumed that He was righteous. The pious were killed. How could the righteous God let this happen? He would not have destroyed Sodom if Abraham had found just ten righteous people therein. Did not Warsaw, Lodz, Bialystock, Lublin and other great cities in Poland and elsewhere have ten righteous ones?

Tsimerman felt compelled to respond. But the response would be confined to certain Jews. He explained:

> My principal intention is not to compose [a treatise] for scholars and righteous ones with awe before God, constantly engaged in the study of God's Torah. They already know what I have to say, and they can search the Talmud and find explanations for and answers to the questions by themselves. Instead [this treatise] is directed to people who are so engaged in trade and labor that they have no time to immerse themselves in the sea of Talmud or probe deeply to resolve the questions. My intention is to gather the data from the Talmud and other sources into a single treatise. It would serve as a remedy. Should one or two people read it, it would be like going to a doctor who places medicine in the mouth of a sick person and alleviates the suffering. (p. 2)

The historian of Jewish thought Eliezer Schweid of Jerusalem has recently analyzed the context in which Orthodox Jewish thinkers wrote during the catastrophe. Recoiling from the unbearable historical reality, they drew from the vital spirit of Jewish tradition to offer sustenance and consolation to their respective communities. They were aware of the nature of consoling truth, of how the vital energy of tradition, justifying God and restoring wounded faith, could carry the Jew over the great void which had opened. Their act of writing down their thoughts represented a commitment to objective fixedness. It identified the thinker's stance, and made him accountable for it before God, students, and even himself. Going beyond oral expression of secret thoughts, the act of writing made the thinker responsible for the truth as he comprehended it. Once written down, the words assumed the power of objective truth which lay between the readers (present and future) and author.[15]

Schweid's insights apply to Tsimerman. As Tsimerman himself stated, he was drawing from the vital Jewish tradition to alleviate the suffering of his community. By committing his reflections to writing, he implied that he was in such harmony with the deep religious consciousness which carried him through the catastrophe, that he could share it with his community and be responsible for it forever. Did the treatise succeed in consoling his audience? This is not yet known. Tsimerman described how a certain Abraham Myerson from America bought all the copies and distributed them to anyone he knew. The copy held by the National Library in Jerusalem used for this study was donated by Tsimerman himself.[16] In 1957 Tsimerman described some responses. He recalled that he sent *Tamim Pa'alo* to Avraham Karelitz ("Hazon Ish"), the supreme authority on Jewish law (*halakhah*) and leading religious personality of the Agudat Israel world of the emerging Jewish state. Karelitz told him that "It is correct and true, that you already have explained (*teratstah*) the Holy One Blessed be He." Karelitz placed the text on his desk for several weeks, and his visitors read from it. Mordekhai Shalom Yosef Friedman of Psemishl told Tsimerman that he took the book with him when he traveled, and Chief Rabbi of Israel Unterman told him that the rabbinical world responded positively to it. The author concluded:

> Most of all, I am happy and satisfied that with the book, with God's help, I merited having a free-thinking Jew become a thorough *ba'al teshuvah* (one who returns to Judaism). The person spoke with Rabbi Alter Ya'akov Meir Brizman about his difficulties concerning the conduct of the world's creator with His people Israel during the days of the Shoah. Brizman gave him my book, and he read it. The person turned from his free-thinking position back to holy *da'at Torah* (exclusive Torah knowledge) and declared, "This is the book which enlightened me and removed the confusion which was increasing relentlessly in my thinking."[17]

Divine Wisdom

Tsimerman did not respond directly to the quandary about God's mercy and righteousness. That, he believed, was not the remedy. Instead, he took a different direction and drew from the tradition to rein in the question, and to establish a line between human and divine wisdom. He dwelled on the fact that the highest stage of knowing for the pious Jew was self-critical. Conscious of the boundary to human knowledge, he yielded to divine wisdom.

What did the tradition offer? In *Tractate Berakhot* 32b the Sages pointed to God's omniscience vis-à-vis man's limited measures of knowing. In response to Israel's concern that God had forgotten her, He pointed out how He created twelve constellations in the firmament, for each constellation thirty hosts, for each host thirty legions, for each legion thirty cohorts, for each cohort thirty maniples, for each maniple thirty camps, and for each camp 65,000 myriads of stars. All of this, He created for Israel's sake. How, then, could Israel say that God had forgotten her? The Midrash expressed the difference, by describing how God's creation of the world was planned in terms of the most minute detail: "Man's face, though only the size of a span, contains many fountains, yet they do not mingle with one another. ... All this serves to teach that in all places the Holy One, blessed be He, carries on His purpose, and that He has not created a single thing in vain" (*Bamidbar Rabbah* 18:22). The theme was expressed in philosophical terms by Maimonides, when he wrote that no common ground existed between God's wisdom, which was infinite, and man's wisdom, which was finite (*Hilkhot Yesodei Hatorah* 2; 4 *Halakhah* 2).

Tsimerman illustrated the point with anecdotes from his Hasidic and Musar legacy. A certain *hasid* of Menahem Mendl of Kotsk suffered the death of a daughter and turned to him for solace. Menahem Mendl directed the *hasid* to a particular page of Gemarah, then its Tosafot commentary, then the further commentaries of Ha'rosh (1250-1327) and Ha'ran (1310-1375). Finally, he understood that God, as creator of the world and its administrator (*gabbai*) from the beginning, knew why He decreed or did something. The believer understood that he should contain his quandary, and yield to the reality that all events, including a daughter's death, were products of God's wisdom and judgment. Once the limit to his understanding was accepted, his sorrow would yield to consolation. Tsimerman drew his last example of God's comprehensive, trans-human knowledge from a Musar discussion (*sihah*) by Budnik in Warsaw. At a particular synagogue in another large city, Budnik related, the *gabbai* was accustomed to calling congregants up for *aliyot* (Torah blessings) according to the section (south, east, west) of the synagogue they sat in. A guest once protested, saying that people should be called up serially, according to the seat they held in the respective rows. The *gabbai* retorted:

> You think you know everything? Even Moses was made "a little lower than the angels" [Psalms 8:6]. [Look], I have been *gabbai* here for forty years. I know everyone personally. I know when I'm supposed to offer an *aliyah* and when not. Some will be offered weekly, others once a year. I know who should be called for the first, second, third, and last [blessings]. Don't give me any advice! Whatever you may know, I already know. Besides, it's none of your business! (pp. 14-15)

Thus, Tsimerman declined to respond directly to his congregants' dilemma about how the merciful and righteous God could have allowed the Holocaust to happen—it was presumed that all historical events were under God. Instead, he directed the questioning to the rabbinic tradition of Israel, which was drawn from revealed sources, and showed how the questions should not have arisen in the first place. The Jew could not presume to evaluate God's mercy or righteousness according to human criteria. Rather he should yield to God's wisdom and judgment. Quandaries about why God acted as He did with the nation of Israel during the Holocaust, about the apparent absence of mercy for the innocent, or about His apparent turn away from the righteous Jews of Poland, must all recede. Man's knowledge was finite, God's was infinite, and human questions had no relevance to, or power over, God's judgments. Moreover, since God was involved in everything, all one could do was accept the realities as He determined them. And how could this console? Directed away from the quandary, the congregant would no longer be plagued by it. Instead, he would become immersed in tradition and the reality of God's presence demonstrated by this tradition. Hadn't the Sages pointed out, that sooner or later the family of an executed member had to accept the court verdict? (*Sanhedrin* 46a). If so, surely Israel had to accept God's judgment as expressed in the catastrophe.

But Tsimerman's congregants, he reported in *Tamim Pa'alo*, protested: How could questions about God's conduct be objectionable, when the greats of Scripture themselves asked questions? To this he responded, that while it was true that Moses, Joshua, and Pinhas all disputed with God (Exodus 5:22, Joshua 7:7, Psalms 106:30), they also all suffered some form of repudiation (*Midrash Shemot Rabbah* 5:23, *Sanhedrin* 82b, *Sanhedrin* 44a). When Job protested, he provoked a great tempest (*Baba Batra* 16a).

At this point, the congregant should have found solace on an existential level. He transcended individual pain to share in the larger reality of tradition and the overwhelming, omniscient presence of God. He was released from his painful questioning, and the question and the answer now belonged within the divine.

Revealed Redemption and Catastrophe

Tsimerman proceeded to explicate the content of divine omniscience, which corresponded to reality itself. The content revolved around redemption.

Again drawing from the tradition, from the Sages, and then through the conduit of the Gaon of Vilna, Tsimerman spoke of the process of redemption as being already underway. At its inception, it was mediated by history where catastrophe and redemption implied one another. Ultimately, the combined darkness and light would yield to pure light. The Sages had made the point centuries earlier. When Rabbi Akiva entered the Temple ruins on Mount Scopus and saw a fox emerging from the grounds of the Holy of Holies, he did not weep as did the others along with him. He was merry. Now that the threatening prophecy of Uriah had been fulfilled ("Therefore shall Zion be ploughed as a field," Micah 3:12), it was certain that Zechariah's hopeful prophecy would also be fulfilled ("Thus saith the Lord of Hosts, There shall yet old men and old women sit in the broad places of Jerusalem," Zechariah 8:4). The two prophecies were interconnected ("And I will take to Me faithful witnesses to record, Uriah the priest and Zechariah the son of Jeberechiah," Isaiah 8:2) (*Makkot* 24b). Surely, Tsimerman observed, the era of mediation would yield to one of total, transhistorical redemption: Israel's tribulations, by their very presence, implied that they would be succeeded by pure salvation. According to the Sage R. Huna, as quoted in the Talmud of Jerusalem,

> For that entire day Abraham saw how the ram would get caught in one tree, and free itself and go forth; then it got caught in a bush, and freed itself and went forth. Said to him the Holy One, blessed be He, "Abraham, this is how your children in the future will be caught by their sins and trapped by the kingdoms, from Babylonia to Media, from Media to Greece, from Greece to Edom." He said to Him, "Lord of the ages! Is that how it will be forever?" He said to him, "in the end they will be redeemed by the horn of this ram." *J. Ta'anit* 2:5.

The factuality of terrible sufferings meant that prophetic promises would also be fulfilled; the sufferings were, indeed, the birth pangs of the messiah (*hevle mashiah*). God and Israel mourned for a limited period only (*Sanhedrin* 97a), and surely He would put an end to the darkness. In fact, the messiah would appear quickly and bring eternal redemption.

Tsimerman was able to point to visible evidence of redemption. Having grasped higher wisdom, he was able to refer back to empirical history. Evoking the legacy of restoring the Land and building agricultural settlements which he inherited from the Admor of Pilov and the Admor of Sokolov, he cited the Sages' view that there was no more manifest sign of redemption (*kets megule*) than the fulfillment of Ezekiel's prophecy (Ezekiel 36:8) that the mountains of Israel would shoot forth their branches and yield fruit for Israel (*Sanhedrin* 98b). With God's help, he wrote, Jews have now merited

settlement in the Land. There were already cities, villages, settlements, forests, fields, and vineyards. On the mountains and plains
there were trees with fruit. One could actually see, how God had
brought Israel to the point of redemption, to the point where Uriah's
prophecy yielded to Ezekiel's (Makkot 24b). The sign of redemption
was now manifest (kets megule). The growth of the settlement in the
Land (yishuv) implied complete, authentic redemption.[18]

Revealed Sin and Teshuvah

The combined darkness and light of hevlei mashiah, which preluded
complete redemption; or, in other words, the onset of redemption
which included the catastrophic passage out of history, provided the
explanation for Israel's conduct in the decades before the war.

According to Sanhedrin 98a, the messiah would not come until
Israel was either totally worthy (kulo zakai) or totally culpable
(kulo hayav). Maharsha (1555-1631) interpreted this to mean that
Israel would either perform penitent return (teshuvah) voluntarily
and thereby become pure enough to welcome the messiah; or Israel
would fail to perform teshuvah voluntarily. In that case the teshuvah would be imposed upon Israel in the form of suffering, and the
suffering would constitute the teshuvah. Tsimerman cited Da'at
Kedoshim (1797) of Raphael ben Yekutiel Süsskind Kohen, on the
Maharshah. The teshuvah, he explained, would be done either out
of love or fear. If out of love, redemption would be accelerated. It
would take place in the month of Nissan, in which Passover fell,
when God's will and compassion (rahamim) were active. If out of
fear, redemption would take longer. It would occur in the month of
Tishrei, in which Yom Kippur and the Ten Days of Repentance fell,
when God's judgment was active. Further, citing Rambam (Hilkhot
Teshuvah 7 Halakhah 5), the people of Israel would in either case
do teshuvah at the end of exile and then be immediately redeemed.
God would help in the process, for He was merciful and would not
forsake them (Deuteronomy 4:30). Since man's trespasses resulted
from his own mind and will, so his teshuvah also had to be of his
own mind and will. Accordingly, God's help would consist of not
allowing the trespasses to prevent teshuvah.[19]

The author of Tamim Pa'alo looked to the Vilna Gaon to discover the absolute truth about which of the alternatives would prevail. According to the Gaon, kulo hayav would surely prevail. Israel
would fail to do teshuvah voluntarily and so have to do it involun-
tarily by suffering (Bi'ur Le'tikkunei Ha'zohar 126a).[20] Tsimerman

expanded upon the point. Once redemption's onset was underway, God would wait for a limited amount of time for Israel to do *teshuvah* voluntarily, with, so to speak, His hand behind His back. But Israel would not, and so God would set Israel straight by bringing *teshuvah* to her by installing a king as cruel as Haman (*Sanhedrin* 97b). Thus, in the apocalyptic reality unveiled by divine wisdom, redemption implied catastrophe and catastrophe implied sin; in other words, the world went from non-*teshuvah* (i.e., sin) to suffering to authentic redemption.

But while non-*teshuvah* (equivalent to sin) was an essential truth and reality from on high, did Tsimerman also believe that the particular form of sin in the messianic era was set from above? In one respect, yes. He cited the description of the transmigration of souls offered by the Safed mystic Hayim Vital (1542-1620), the disciple of Yitzhak Luria. In *Sefer Hezyonot (Book of Visions)*, Vital had stated that Adam's soul was divided into three souls of the patriarchs, they into the twelve souls of the tribes, and they eventually into the six hundred thousand souls of Israel. The six hundred thousand souls, each identifiable with a spark disseminated by Moses at Sinai, transmigrated *(gilgul)*.[21] In *Sha'ar Hakavanot (Book of Intentions)*, which Tsimerman cited, Vital offered specifics. The six hundred thousand souls either remained pure or were purified by immediate punishment and transgenerational punishment. The trespassing souls of Noah's generation were purified immediately by physical obliteration. They were then channeled into Noah and his family, which served as a crucible of purified souls. By the time of the Tower-of-Babel generation, the souls corresponded, as before, to the actual population. They sinned once again, and this time the purification came through division into numerous ("seventy") national entities (Deuteronomy 32:9). By the time Israel entered the Land, the six hundred thousand had regrouped and were channeled into her as a nation. But once again there was sin. Vital cited the idolatry in the era of the Judges (Judges 2:10-11) and the stoning of Zechariah, the son of Jehoiada the priest, who had accused the people of forsaking God (II Chronicles 24:20). The murder of Zechariah was a multiple sin. The people simultaneously killed a priest, a prophet, a judge, shed innocent blood, profaned God's name, defiled the Temple court, and violated the Sabbath and Day of Atonement. Zechariah's blood could not stop seething over it all. In an attempt to stop the seething, Nebuzaradan slew the men of the Sanhedrin, maidens, school children, and eighty thousand priestly novitiates, and mingled their blood with Zechariah's. But he did not succeed, until he exclaimed: "Zechariah, Zechariah!

All the choicest of them have I destroyed. Is it your pleasure that I exterminate them all?" (*Midrash Eykhah Rabbah*: Proem). Then Zechariah's blood became calm. For such multiple sin to be cleansed, the sinful souls were sent into a process of transmigration and then channeled back to history to be obliterated with the destruction of the Second Temple.

As he switched from the rabbinic myth of redemption to the observable agricultural success of the Land, Tsimerman now switched from revelation to demography. According to the Mizrahi periodical organ *Hatsofe* (edited in Tel Aviv by Meir Bar Ilan), an explosion in the hundred years before the war almost quadrupled the Jewish population. What could this be, other than the re-entry of sinful souls into history? Without specifying the sins' origin, Tsimerman concluded that the Holocaust was their final purification. That is, the sins involved in the non-*teshuvah* before the Holocaust were not committed generations earlier.[22] In any event, the author was certain that

> All the unnatural and cruel deaths were according to measure and balance. There is nothing accidental here, God forbid. Everything is according to a righteous and precise accounting. And all is for the good of the sinner, in order to clear away his sin. "The work of the Rock is perfect. ... His ways are just and right with exception" (Deuteronomy 32:3, Psalms 92:15).

In other respects, however, Tsimerman did not believe that the particular form of sin of the messianic era was set from above. As if setting aside his reining in of questions about divine righteousness and mercy in order to grasp God's wisdom and the realities it defined and bore, at this juncture Tsimerman spoke of autonomous human action. The advent of sin in general belonged to a higher reality, and every sin was definable by traditional criteria. But the initiative for particular sins belonged to man—impious and pious alike. Tsimerman was apparently untroubled by the contradiction: these sins were committed by the pre-war generation, while according to the *gilgul* scheme, the same sins came from earlier generations.

The Sages specified that when it came to setting off a calamity, direct trespass was required (*Baba Kamma* 60a). This occurred, Tsimerman believed, when the younger prewar generation distanced itself from its elders' commitment to God and Torah learning. Everything Jewish became alien. Tsimerman recalled later on how most of his peers at the *heder* simply left Jewish culture once they graduated. The phenomenon reminded him of the saying: of each thousand *heder* students, only one emerged to study Scripture; of each thousand students of Scripture, only one emerged to study Talmud; of each thousand to study Talmud, only one emerged to teach.[23]

Such abandonment of Judaism, even by only one portion of Israel, was enough to set off the massive suffering of the Holocaust. Whatever the origin of the calamity, according to the Sages, the first victims were the righteous (*Baba Kamma* 60a). According to Rashi, once immorality or idolatry took place, punishment broke out in chaotic fashion without distinguishing good and bad victims (Rashi to Genesis 6:13). There was also the principle of intensity, according to which punishment had to be proportional to the sin. If the sin was so intense that the perpetrators could not be punished enough for it, the punishment would overflow to other subjects. Rambam spoke of qualitative magnitude vis-à-vis simple quantity of sins. Thus, a man whose trespasses were qualitatively greater than his merits died immediately, no matter the purely numerical balance. Or, a state whose trespasses were greater than its merits was immediately lost. "Likewise with the entire world. If the trespasses are greater than the merits, then it is totally obliterated" (Rambam, *Hilkhot Teshuvah* 3 *Halakhot* 1-4). According to the "Book of the Generations of Adam" (Genesis 5:1), in the generation of the flood the animals and the very earth were punished along with human beings because, according to Tsimerman's interpretation, the sins were so great that the sinners alone were not a sufficient outlet for punishment.[24] The Sages provided examples where collective punishment resulted from the severe sins of individuals. Tsimerman cited the destruction of the Second Temple on account of groundless hatred (*Yoma* 9a), and the punishments set off by violating the prohibition not to return to Egypt—there were three prohibitions (Exodus 14:13, Deuteronomy 17:11, Deuteronomy 28:68) and three severe punishments, including famine and death (Isaiah 31:3, Jeremiah 42:16, Deuteronomy 28:49) (*J. Sukkah* 5:1).

But the pious of Israel were not only victims on account of the sinners. The author averred that the pious committed trespasses by themselves. According to the Sages, if a pious person could stop a member of his household from sinning but did not even try to do so, he became culpable. Thus, the citizens of Ezekiel's Jerusalem were culpable because they had the power to protest against the trespassers but did not (*Shabbat* 54b/55a). King Zedekiah was considered evil, because he failed to protest the evil of his contemporaries (*Sanhedrin* 103a). The motif was carried forward by Rambam, according to whom a pious person was guilty of trespass if he stood by and simply let an evil person do as he wanted (II Kings 24:19) (*Hilkhot Deot 6 Halakhah* 7). Finally, Tsimerman cited *Imrei Shafer al Ha'torah* (I, p. 255) by the anti-Maskil legalist Shlomo Kluger ("Maharshak," 1785-1869), according to which, excluding the tribe of Levi, all Israel was culpable for failing to stop the rabble from building the calf. He claimed that in many Orthodox and Hasidic homes in Germany, nothing was done when a member mixed with the Gentiles and emulated them. Worse, some justified assimilation as a source of income. In some cases the father protested, but the mother "would wrap her apron around the son protectively, lest the father's pinky even touch him" because she liked his becoming modern so much. Some parents even gave their children the money to go and enjoy Gentile pleasures. There were, Tsimerman said, (unnamed) religious figures who passed through Germany and saw this—and "declared that Germany had to be destroyed. And we bear witness that this was done." (p. 28). In Warsaw, newspapers were published on the Sabbath and everyone knew it. At times stores were kept open on the Sabbath. There were instances of homes in which the grandfather, father, and son, three generations together, abandoned Judaism.

Finally, there was a violation of the principle that the exile was never to be a resting place for Israel (Deuteronomy 28:65). Tsimerman, inheritor of the love for Zion of the Admor of Pilov and the Admor of Sokolov, despaired over the fact that so many pious Jews did not support the Yishuv financially. He regretted that many appeared oblivious to the fact that residence in exile was in fact a consequence of sin and should be abandoned, but instead made their diaspora homelands out to be holy lands. During the Crusades, he continued, pious Jews sacrificed everything to get to the Land. Now, when it was relatively easy to come—at least until the British White Paper—they did not. Had he the strength, Tsimerman wrote, he would compose an entire treatise just on this. But all he could do at this point was to make it clear that, in addition to the other trespasses, there was also the pious Jews' failure—he did not offer specifics—to come to the Land. The trespass was very serious: "On account of this trespass by itself, namely not ascending to the Land of Israel, the people of Israel have suffered to such a degree that they have had to endure the calamitous loss of the annihilation of a third of their number." (p. 25). In his interpretation of Exodus 14:13, Abraham ibn Ezra had explained that God let the people of Israel die in the desert because, having grown up in slavery, they were unable to rise up against the Egyptians and would be unable to fight the Canaanites to take the Land. A new generation was required. Now too, for Tsimerman, the failure to restore the Land resulted in mass death.[25]

Accordingly, the non-*teshuvah* which the Holocaust reversed consisted of two sorts of sin: inherited sin, which conformed to the heteronomous, absolutistic structure of Tsimerman's thinking, and new sin, which was initiated by impious and pious Jews independently of divine wisdom and the reality which belonged to it. This left a problem. While there was consolation in the reality of divine omniscience and in surrender of human knowledge, where was the consolation for the self-initiated sins of the congregants' parents? This issue was not addressed by Tsimerman. Instead, he continued to emphasize the absolute, trans-human basis to the apocalyptic drama.

In a striking exception to the position taken by Agudat Israel, Mizrahi, Habad, and even Slobodka-Musar thinkers, in the Yishuv and elsewhere, Tsimerman maintained that imposed *teshuvah*, i.e., suffering, and the process of redemption were set from on high and beyond all human control. While other religious thinkers focused on how Jews must take *teshuvah*-action to stop the Holocaust or the suffering which followed—whether existential (e.g., Yehezkel Sarna of Musar), communal (e.g., Yosef Yitzhak Schneersohn of Habad) or halakhic (e.g., Zalman Sorotskin of Agudat Yisrael)— Tsimerman did not.[26] Taking his key from the Vilna Gaon's *Bi'ur Le'tikkunei Ha'zohar* (p. 126a) position that the unworthy would be helpless to do anything once messianic sufferings began (Isaiah 62:23) (*Zohar Shemot* 2:7b), Tsimerman stated emphatically that the timing of the sufferings vis-à-vis redemption was set irrevocably. "At the appropriate moment [the sufferings] would depart, one way or another, whether [Israel] did *teshuvah* or did not do *teshuvah*." (p. 46). Human action was impotent when it came to changing the realities. The Sages pointed out how Judah ben Shammua was unable to change Rome's decrees against Judaism (*Rosh Hashanah* 19a), and how Shimon bar Yohai was helpless to do anything about Rome's forcing the act of intercourse with menstruant women (*Meilah* 17a/b). The Jews' attempts to liberate themselves during the eras of the Temples were useless—indeed they may have backfired and aggravated exile (*Pesahim* 118b with Maharsha). As to possibly gaining some control by knowing the timing, the Sages pointed out how Moses himself could not anticipate when liberation from Egypt would come (*Berakhot* 3b/4a). God's active presence, His *shekhinah* contained its timing within, and any estimations by Israel about the speed were inapplicable. (*Mekhilta Parshat Bo 7*).

Self-sacrifice (Mesirat nefesh)

Tsimerman's overall absolutistic response to the catastrophe and its aftermath precluded any call to action, *teshuvah* or otherwise. Instead, the "medication" he offered had to do with grasping divine wisdom and the reality it carried. But Tsimerman did call for *mesirat nefesh*, the act of self-sacrifice in which suffering was transformed into an act of faith in God. Corresponding to the epistemological journey through which pain was alleviated by accepting God's control, he enunciated the existential journey that transformed the suffering into an act of faith. Within the realm of divinely imposed *teshuvah*, suffering affirmed love for and faith in God. Without compromising the divinely controlled world, *mesirat nefesh* both reflected the metaphysical suffering existentially and provided a way actively to asssert one's piety.

The paradigm was Abraham. After waiting so long for Isaac's birth, with so much hope invested in him, anyone but an Abraham would have reacted to God's order to sacrifice his son by having heart failure. But the perfect Abraham (Yonatan ben Uzziel to Genesis 17:1) would no more question God at this juncture, than he did when he was required to pay for the very land which God had given him in order to bury Sarah (*Sanhedrin* 111a). He responded with awe for God *(yir'at hashem)*, faith and self-sacrifice *(mesirat nefesh)*. This precedent became a reality of Jewish history. Akiva entered the flames, believing that loving God with all one's soul (Deuteronomy 6:5) culminated in dying for God (*Berakhot* 61b). Hiyya bar Abba endured torture, in emulation of Abraham's *mesirat nefesh* (*Midrash Shir Hashirim Rabbah* 2:7:1). Drawing from the Musar classic *Hovot Halevavot* by Bahya ibn Pakuda (11th century), Tsimerman pointed out how the pietist responded to inexplicable suffering with intensified commitment to God. He would rise at night to declare: "My God, Thou hast made me suffer hunger, left me naked, set me in the darkness of the night. ... If Thou wert to burn me in the fire, it would only increase my love for Thee ("Sha'ar Ahavat Hashem 1"). In this tradition, in this reality imbedded in the history of Israel, the Jew was offered a way to personally enact the larger suffering which belonged to the inception of redemption.

The primacy of *mesirat nefesh* prevailed in the Novagrudok-Musar world that Tsimerman shared both in Warsaw and Tel Aviv. Hillel Vitkind, who co-founded the Beit Yosef-Novagroduk Yeshiva in Tel Aviv, wrote in 1943/1944 that the value of life in this world consisted of the opportunity it offered for piety and *mesirat nefesh* as means for a blessed life in the hereafter. The evil prospered now, but the pious sufferer prospered in the next life (Bahya, "Sha'ar Habitahon 3," *Hovot Halevavot*). The paradigm was Akiva. As he was about to be killed, he finally understood the meaning of "with all one's soul" (Deuteronomy 6:5). It meant "even if He takes thy soul"—that is, loving God through death (*Berakhot* 61b). For Vitkind, a wise man would gladly endure this-worldly sufferings for the sake of the soul's ascent upon death. Indeed, suffering was the positive vessel of spiritual existence; *mesirat nefesh* contained the eternal life of the spirit. As with Tsimerman, the suffering was dialectically related to redemption, and complete redemption would follow. In fact, the severity of the suffering would be perfectly balanced out by the redemptive world-to-come: "Make us glad according to the days wherein Thou hast afflicted us and the years wherein we have seen evil" (Psalms 90:15).[27] In 1946/1947 the Head of Beit Yosef-Novagroduk in Jerusalem, Bentsiyon Bruk, cited Abraham's silence, in response to the command to sacrifice Isaac:

> The Sages said, Give unto the Lord, O ye mighty [*benei elim*]. ... *Benei elim* [is like] *benei ilmim*, the silent. That is, those who have something to respond to God but do not. ... So Abraham, [who was thinking], "See what I had to respond to [God about the command to bind my son for sacrifice], but did not and kept silent?" (*Yalkut Shimoni*, Tehillim 709).

Silently, Abraham carried out the command. The Jews of *she'erit hapeleitah*, Bruk continued, should not pose questions to God, any more than Abraham did. God's ways were other than man's (Isaiah 55:9), His secrets were inaccessible to man. Attempts to apply secular wisdom to God only diverted man from the access to God's wisdom which Torah offered (Bahya, "Sha'ar Haperishot 2," *Hovot Halevavot*).[28]

Prayer

Were the transfer of questions into God's being, the acceptance of apocalyptic reality, and *mesirat nefesh* enough to provide the way for Tsimerman's congregants to pass over the abyss upon whose brink they stood into a vital religious future? Breaking away from his absolutistic structure and its passive means of expression, Tsimerman suddenly urged his congregants to pray. He cited the view of Ya'akov Emden (1697-1776), that while the fact of illness was determined from above, its longevity was not. Prayer could accelerate relief (Commentary to *Rosh Hashanah* 16a). Prayer was effective, because it found a path to God independent of the meta-physical, apocalyptic framework, the path of individual relation-ship to God in terms of *rahamim* (mercy).

From the Ger Hasidic tradition, Tsimerman cited Yehuda Leib Alter's distinction in *Sephat Emet* between human and divine *rahamim*. Man's was conditional and circumstantial; sometimes, as Bahya pointed out, even a function of self-interest—a matter of relieving distress over another's pitiful condition (Bahya, "Sha'ar Avodat Hashem," beginning in *Hovot Halevavot*). God's *rahamim* was an absolute, unconditional reality—applying across creation from man to cattle to the tiny bird's nest.[29] God's absolute *rahamim* was in place, ready for Israel's access, ever since Abraham followed God's command to sacrifice his son. The Talmud of Jerusalem related how Abraham might have protested and pointed out that just the day before God had promised him descendants through Isaac. How then, could He want Isaac killed? Instead, Abraham overcame his *rahamim*-impulse for his son and proceeded to carry out God's wish. He also asked God (despite the imminent sacrifice) to act on behalf of Isaac's children, should they come to a time of trouble and have no one to speak for them. (*J. Ta'anit* 2:4). Ever since Abraham, God's absolute *rahamim* was available to Israel—if Israel prayed for it. Then God would overcome His impulse for anger over sin with His *rahamim* and ease the suffering—as Abra-ham once overcame his *rahamim* to do God's will.

God's readiness to implement His *rahamim* was intensified by the fact that He sympathized, so to speak, with man's pain. Accord-ing to the Psalmist, God was present in Israel's suffering (Psalms 91:15). When she was afflicted, so was He (Isaiah 63:9). God told Moses: "Do you not realize that I am, as it were, a partner in the children of Israel's trouble?" (*Midrash Shemot Rabbah* 2:5). Even when the suffering was the result of sin, He suffered with them. Thus, when the Temple was destroyed and the people exiled, God wept so bitterly that the archangel Metatron pleaded with Him to stop, whereupon He replied: "If thou lettest Me not weep now, I wilt repair to a place which thou hast not permission to enter and will weep there" (*Midrash Eykhah Rabbah: Pesikta* 24). If this were so, how much did God co-suffer over the blood of the righteous?

> R. Meir said: When man suffers, what expression does the *shekhinah* use? "My head is too heavy for me; my arm is too heavy for me!" And if God is so grieved over the blood of the wicked that is shed, how much more so over the blood of the righteous." *Sanhedrin* 46a.[30]

As Tsimerman used the empirical evidence of the restored Land in speaking of redemption and the population figures in speaking of *gilgul*, he also spoke of events in the Yishuv as evidence of merciful response to prayer, of showing "directly or clearly that God has not abandoned His nation." He echoed the belief of thinkers across the Orthodox spectrum—including Gedaliah Bublick (Mizrahi), Ephraim Sokolover (Musar), and Moshe Prager (Agudat Israel)—that the retreat of Germany from North Africa, after coming so close to the Yishuv in summer 1942, evidenced divine intervention. He wrote how the barbaric enemy, within an arrow's range from the Land, declared that Jerusalem would be taken within a day. The Jews of the Yishuv despaired, "their souls nearly expired from the great fear of falling into the clutches of the animals of prey." The British rulers were packed and ready to abandon the Land, while Arabs danced in joy at the prospect of joining the Germans, avenging themselves against the Jews, and dividing up the spoils. "But in the fullness of His mercy *(rahamav)* He had mercy *(rihem)* for us and performed a great miracle." The enemy was decisively beaten, turned back and fled until they reached their own country. German government personnel were imprisoned. Then—Tsimerman was apparently referring to the failed 20 July 1944 plot to assassinate Hitler and the executions that followed—"In one day all ten children of Haman were hung (see Esther 9:7-10). So all enemies will be lost." (pp. 37-38).[31]

Here, Tsimerman found a place for individual, active religious faith. No matter the all-controlling apocalyptic framework, which was reflected in *mesirat nefesh*, a point still remained for prayer. *Rahamim* was absolute, it streamed through history, it was poised to respond to suffering because the divine source of *rahamim* Himself suffered. Man had but to pray to ease the suffering. And the truth to this belief could be seen with one's own eyes in the events of 1942-1944.

Conclusion

Tamim Pa'alo was an attempt to respond to the quandary and despair of the Kotsk-Sokolover Hasidim to whom Tsimerman ministered in Tel Aviv in 1947. He sought to ease the suffering by providing the vital energy of Jewish tradition to his congregants. Specifically, he set out to ease the suffering by reining in the questions, by immersion in tradition, and making room for God's wisdom and presence. What did God's wisdom offer? The truth (and truth implied reality) that redemption was underway—another source of consolation. But that redemption implied catastrophe. Upon inception, the light of redemption intermingled with the darkness of history, which intensified and manifested itself in suffering. But the very existence of suffering assured the simultaneity of relief, and the combined suffering and relief assured the onset of complete salvation.

In turn, catastrophe meant that Israel collectively failed to do *teshuvah*—a failure set from on high and unavoidable. In trying to grasp the failure, the author seemed to thrash around between higher and lower truths—between the inevitability of sin brought on by *gilgul* and the voluntary dimensions of prewar assimilation and failure by the pious to intervene as well as to practice *hibat tsiyon*. But he continued to insist that acts of *teshuvah* were irrelevant to the passage from catastrophe to redemption. In doing so, he was at odds with wartime Agudat Israel, Musar, Hasidic and Mizrahi schools of religious thinking about the Holocaust—although not uniquely so.[32]

Did this mean that Tsimerman's congregants were to passively accept the apocalyptic reality, and somewhat consoled, await the redemption? No, for he called for action in the form of *mesirat nefesh*, the existential counterpart to the metaphysical *teshuvah*-as-suffering which transformed suffering into faith. The Jew should also pray. God's *rahamim* was absolute and poised for expression, if the Jew would but seek it in prayer. Indeed, there was evidence of divine *rahamim* in the Yishuv's survival of the war.

Tsimerman's *Tamim Pa'alo* evidenced the courageous act of a communal leader to try to offer consolation from the sources of tradition. It evidenced Tsimerman's struggle, as he tried to present an absolutistic faith while lashing out at Israel's sinners on the one extreme, and responding to the existential need by speaking of *mesirat nefesh* and prayer seeped in *rahamim* on the other. The text also evidenced the author's commitment to the Land as the center of hope in the world undergoing redemption. While he resisted any probe into the timing of redemption when it came to passing out of the catastrophe and its aftermath, he was ready to verify it with the empirical evidence of the Land-in-restoration. While he resisted drawing divine *rahamim* into the scene of the European Holocaust, he found it manifest in the life of the Yishuv. The truths which brought Tsimerman inner religious harmony and which he expressed in writing to console his community were supported by the very holy earth upon which he became silent, found divine wisdom, and prayed.

Notes

*   I completed this study as a visiting scholar at the Library of Congress Office of Scholarly Programs. I am grateful for research support provided by the Institute for Holocaust Research of Bar Ilan University. The staffs of the Library of Congress Hebraica Division (directed by Michael Grunberger), the Ginzah Kiddush Hashem Archives in Benei Berak (directed by David Skulsky), and the U.S. Holocaust Memorial Museum Archives (directed by Henry Mayer) during my tenure as Associate of the USHMM Research Institute, all provided exceptional help. Discussions with Shlomo Aronson, David Assaf, Haggai Dagan, Elhanan Reiner, and especially Yosef Tsimerman, the son of Hayim Yisrael Tsimerman, provided valuable insights into the *Tamim Pa'alo* text.

1.   For an overview of wartime Jewish religious thought and the Holocaust see Gershon Greenberg, "Wartime Religious Thought and the Holocaust," in *Yale Encyclopaedia of the Holocaust*, ed. Walter Laqueur (New Haven, 2000).
2.   See Greenberg, *She'erit Hapeleitah Confronting the Holocaust: A Listing of Articles and Books Reflecting the Jewish Religious Responses to the Holocaust in its Immediate Aftermath 1944-1949* (Ramat Gan, 1994 [Yiddish and Hebrew]), and "Holiness and Catastrophe in Simhah Elberg's Religious Thought," *Tradition* 25 no. 5 (November 1991), pp. 39-64.
3.   Agudat Yisrael, founded in 1912, is a political body of Orthodox Jews committed to *Halakhah* (Jewish law).
4.   Harlap, "Le'et Dodim," *Sinai* 11 nos. 4-5/whole nos. 131-132 (December 1947/January 1948), pp. 126-138. See Greenberg, "The Holocaust Apocalypse of Ya'akov Moshe Harlap," *Jewish Studies* 40 (Jerusalem, 2000) and "Ha'gra's Apocalyptic Expectations and 1947 Religious Responses to the Holocaust: Harlap and Tsimerman" in *The Gaon of Vilnius and the Annals of Jewish Culture* (Vilnius, 1998), pp. 231-246.
5.   Gerst, "Hamasoret shel Sin'at Israel I," *Dos Yidishe Vort* 13 (24 October 1947), p. 4; "II," *She'arim* (14 September 1947), pp. 3-4; "III" (15 October 1947), p. 3. Gerst published recollections of his wartime experiences in the Agudat Yisrael periodical *Kol Israel* 25 no. 48/whole no. 1238 (12 September 1947), p. 45 through 26 no. 29/whole no. 1267 (15 April 1948), pp. 2, 4, *passim*. See Greenberg, "Yehudah Leib Gerst's Religious 'Ascent' Through the Holocaust," *Holocaust and Genocide Studies* 13 no. 1 (Spring 1999), pp. 62-89.
6.   See Greenberg, "Ontic Division and Religious Survival: Wartime Palestinian Orthodoxy and the Holocaust," *Modern Judaism* 14 (1994), pp. 21-61, and *Wartime Yishuv Confronting the Holocaust: Annotated Listing of Articles and Books Reflecting Jewish Religious Responses in the Era of Catastrophe, 1938-1948* (Ramat Gan, 1997 [Yiddish and Hebrew]).
7.   The faculty included David Lustigman, Ya'akov Lustigman, Hayim Mordekhai Branshtayn, Avraham Tsibote, Yehiel Meir Prints, Shmuel Barukh Stadzshiner, Pinhas Tsernitski, Hayim Moshe Mayzels, Shabtai Grinberg, Ya'akov Grinberg, Nahum Mordekhai Perlov (author of *Pe'er Nahum*), Shimon Valfobsky, Shaul Ze'ev Bergstayn, Hanokh Kohen, Aryeh Leib Yukht (author of *Mishnat Arye*) and Mordekhai Zalmans. Pogroms closed the yeshivah temporarily in 1920, three years after it was founded. Mordekhai Khine, "Dos Sokolover Rabbins Yeshivah" and Gad Zazlikavsky, "Ha'admor MiSokolov-Podliask" in *Sefer Hazikaron Sokolov-Podliask*, ed. M. Gelbart (Tel Aviv, 1962), pp. 29-36, 45-50.

8. On the Hasidism of Kotsk see Jakob Levinger, "Imrot Otentiot shel Harabi MiKotsk," *Tarbits* 55 (1985/86), pp. 109-135, and David Assaf, "Hasidut Polin Bameah Ha-19," in *Tsadikim Ve'anshei Ma'ase: Mehkarim Behasidut Polin*, ed. Elior, Bartal and Shmeruk (Jerusalem, 1994), pp. 366-368.

9. On the Admor of Pilov see Menahem M. Kasher, "Mispar Ketaim Misefer *Shalom Yerushalayim* Mihagaon Hakadosh Moreinu Harav Yitzhak MiPilov zts"l: Devarim Niflaim Beinyan Shivat Tsiyon," in *Hatekufah Hagedolah* (Jerusalem, 1971/72), pp. 178-193 and Pinhas Zelig Gliksman, "Admor Rabi Yisrael z'l MiKotsk Ve'*Shalom Yerushalayim*," in *Tif'eret Adam* (Lodz, 1923/24), pp. 98-102. On the Admor of Sokolov see Shmuel Rothstein, "Ha'admor MiSokolov zts"l," *She'arim* 23 (October 1947), p. 3; Meir Halahmi, "Ha'admor Rabi Yitzhak Selig Morgenshtern zts"l MiSokolov," in *Toldot Hahasidut Be'eretz Yisrael Miha'aliyah Hahasidit Harishonah*, II (Jerusalem, 1996/97), pp. 218-224; Aharon Sorsky, "Ha'admor MiSokolov Rabi Yitzhak Selig Morgenshtern zts"l," *Hamodiah* 39 no. 10922 (23 October 1987), pp. 8, 14; 39 no. 10934 (6 November 1987), p. 8; and 39 no. 10940 (13 November 1987), pp. 10, 14; and Yitzhak Levin, "Harav R. Yitzhak Zelig Morgenshtern-Admor MiSokolov," in *Ele Ezkerah: Osef Toldot Kidushei 5700-5705*, I, ed. Yitzhak Levin (New York, 1955/56), pp. 283-295.

10. The intent of the delegation, which included Tsevi Hirsh Levin of Berlin and Moshe Prager of Warsaw, was also to mediate differences between Yosef Hayim Sonnenfeld (1849-1932) and Avraham Yitzhak Hakohen Kook.

11. Tsimerman, "Hosafah Ishit," in *Penei Hayim I: Bo Ketsat Hidushim, Sugyot Vehe'arot al Shas, hen Behalakhah vehen Beaggadah. II: Ma'amarim Veiny- anim Shonim al Parshiyot Hashavuah ve'al Inyanei Moadot* (Tel Aviv, 1957/58), pp. 231-239. Aharon Sorsky, "Mitoldot Hamehaber" in *She'erit Yitzhak: Seridim shel Derushim Vehidushim asher Notru Lipeleitah Le'ahar Hashoah Venilketu Misefarim Shonim, Kitvei-Et Toraniyim Ukevatsim mimah Shekatvu Hahasidim Mishemo Umipi Hashemuah, Umiguf Ketav-yad Kodsho. Me'et Yitzhak Zelig Morgenshtern ... Sokolov-Kotsk ben ... Hayim Yisrael ... MiPilov-Kotsk, nekhed ... David ... MiKotsk*, ed. Mendel Meir Morgenshtern (Tel Aviv, 1988/89), pp. 111-130.

12. Budnik, "Sulam Ha'adam" and "Temimut Ve'armimut" in *Hayei Hamusar: Ma'amarim Upitgamim Miraboteinu Hakhmei Hamusar* (Benei Berak, 1963/64 [Ostrova: October 1935-1937]), pp. 57-60, 105-141; "Mesirat Nefesh" in *Hayei Hamusar*, 2 (Benei Berak, 1963/64), pp. 238-242; "Leyom Hazikaron Mipetirat Admor ... Y. Y. Hurwitz," and "Derekh Liteshuvah Bamidot Vedeot," in *Or Hamusar: Mukdash Leinyanei Hayir'ah Vehamusar Ve'avodat Harabim*, II (Benei Berak, 1964/65 [Poland]), pp. 26-33, 132-140, 209-217; "Arba'ah Pithei Hokhmah," and "Habehirah Habilti Gevulit," in *Or Hamusar*, II (Benei Berak, 1964/65 [Poland]), pp. 77-84, 101-102, 206-209. On Budnik see Yosef Levi, "Harav R. David Budnik-Dvinsk" in *Ele Ezkerah*, VI, pp. 163-168, and Hayim Yosef Zaytshik, "R. David Budnik—Rosh Yeshi- vat Beit Yosef BeDvinsk," in *Hameorot Hagedolim: Kavei-Or Veteiurim Mid- ioknam shel Haishim Hamusari'im Yotsrei Tenuat Hamusar Hayehem Upe'alotehem* (Jerusalem, 1966/67), pp. 386-390. On the Novagrudok school see Greenberg, "A Musar Response to the Holocaust: Yehezkel Sarna's *Liteshuvah Velitekumah* of 1944," *Jewish Thought and Philosophy* 7 no. 1 (1997), pp. 101-138. Tsimerman, "Hosafah Ishit."

13. Shmuel Idelzak, "Hadibur Vehamahshavah," in *Or Hamusar*, II, p. 236; "Beinyan Holakhah shelo Baregel," in *Yarkhon Keneset Yisrael: Mukdash*

Letorah Umusar 2 nos. 4-11 (December 1938-January 1939), pp. 11-14; "He'arah Bedivrei Harashbah," *Sefer Keneset Yisrael: Mukdash Letorah Umusar* nos. 9- 11/whole no. 40 (June-July 1942), p. 8; "Devarim Ahadim," in *Sefer Divrei Shmuel: Hidushim Ubeurim al HaRambam* (Tel Aviv, 1940/41), pp. i-viii. On Idelzak see Z. Sh., "Harav Hagaon R. Shmuel Idelzak zts"l," *Hayesod* 15 no. 537 (23 May 1947), p. 5; editor, "Darko Ha'ahronah shel Harav Idelzak z"l," *Hatsofe* 10 no. 2828 (21 April 1947), p. 4; and Tsimerman, "Hosafah Ishit" and *Tamim Pa'alo*, cover and end.

14. Tsimerman, *Da'at Hayim: Al Inyanei Orah Hayim VeYore Deah* (Tel Aviv, 1948); *Penei Hayim*, I and II; *Peri Yisrael*, I: *Mavo Lehalakhot Treifut Hareiah*, and II: *Hidushim Vehe'arot al Shas* (Tel Aviv, 1964/65).

15. Eliezer Schweid, *Bein Hurban Liyeshuah: Teguvot shel Hagut Hareidit Lashoah Bizemanah* (Tel Aviv, 1994), pp. 220-222. See also Greenberg, "Consoling Truth: Eliezer Schweid's *Bein Hurban Liyeshuah*: A Review Essay," *Modern Judaism* 17 (1997), pp. 297-311.

16. Tsimerman, "Lezekher Olam," in *Penei Hayim*, p. 31.

17. Tsimerman, "Divrei Shevah Mipi Hageonim Hagedolim al Sifri Hakodem *Tamim Pa'alo* asher Yatsah Laor Bishenat 5707," in *Penei Hayim*, p. 28.

18. Yosef Tsimerman showed me the manuscript of his father's "Yom Moledet," which enunciates his reaction to the creation of the state. Because of its critical stance, he told me, he was hesitant to have it published.

19. Raphael ben Yekutiel Süsskind Kohen, *Da'at Kedoshim* (Vilna: Katsinelinboygin Printing, 1878/79 [1797]), pp. 80-86.

20. Elijah ben Solomon, "Biur ... Tikkunei Hazohar" in *Tikkunei HaZohar im Tikkunim MiZohar Hadash Mihatanna Ha'elki Rabi Shimon bar Yohai: Im Biur Ha'gra MiEliyahu MiVilna. Ve'al Hakdamat Hatikunim Metsuraf Gam Biur Beno Avraham* (Vilna, 1867), p. 126a.

21. Hayim Vital, *Jewish Mystical Autobiographies: Book of Visions and Book of Secrets*, trans. with introduction by Morris Faierstein (New York, 1999), Part 4, nos. 37, 41.

22. Hayim Vital, "Sha'ar Hakavanot: Sha'ar Shishi" in *Sha'ar Hakavanot*, I (Eretz Israel: Kitvei Rabeinu Ha'ari z"l, 1961/1962), p. 1. See Gershom Scholem, "*Gilgul*: The Transmigration of Souls," in *On the Mystical Shape of the Godhead* (New York, 1991), pp. 197-250. I could not find the report in *Hatsofe*. Tsimerman cited the issue of 10 January 1947.

23. Tsimerman, "Hosafah Ishit."

24. It is unclear how Tsimerman derived this point from the Genesis 5ff. text, the Talmudic material (*Sanhedrin* 107b), or the *Hilkhot Teshuvah* he cited.

25. In America, Aharon Petshenik of Mizrahi levelled a similar attack. Citing Avraham ibn Ezra's commentary to Exodus 14:13 that "the camp of 600,000 people of Israel were so afraid of the [Egyptian] pursuers that they would not go to war against them," he explained that the ancient Israelites, having internalized their lowly social, economic, and military status, naturally relied more on prayer than battle when Amalek attacked. The generation had to die out and a new one, devoid of that self-destructive mentality, had to emerge for Israel to be eligible to enter the Land. For the last forty years (Mizrahi was established in 1902), Petshenik continued, Jews had resisted return. The Holocaust removed the resistant generation and enabled the birth of a generation capable of restoring the Land. Petshenik, "Der Mizrahi oyf Shaydveg," *Der Mizrahi Veg* 8 no. 3 (November 1943), pp. 7, 13; and "Golus un Geulah," *Der Mizrahi Veg* 8 no. 6 (March 1944), pp. 5, 13. See Gershon Greenberg, "Wartime Amer-

        ican Orthodoxy and the Holocaust: Mizrahi and Agudat Israel Religious
        Responses," *Mikha'el* 15 (2000), pp. 59-94.

26.   See Greenberg, "A Musar Response to the Holocaust"; "Redemption After
        Holocaust According to Mahaneh-Israel Lubavitch 1940-1945," *Modern
        Judaism* 12 (February 1992), pp. 61-84; and "Ontic Division and Religious
        Survival." Schweid, "An Ethical-Theological Response to the Holocaust as it
        Was Evolving: The Teachings of Rabbi Eliahu Eliezer Dessler," *Henoch* 17
        (1995), pp. 171-196.

27.   Vitkind, *Musar Hatorah*, I (Jerusalem, 1943/44), pp. 130-139.

28.   Bruk, "Devarim Ahadim" in *Hegyonei Musar: He'arot Vehe'arot, Hegeshim
        Vehitbonenut Betorateinu Hakodesh Uma'amarei Hazal*, I (New York,
        1946/47), pp. 7-8.
              There is a notable similarity to the 1947/48 view of *Hibat Tsiyon* writer
        Bentsiyon Firer (1914- 1988) expressed in the Ulm, Germany, DP camp. For
        him, the only positive way Israel could have responded to Sinai-generated
        hatred of Israel (*Shabbat* 89a, *Ein Ya'akov* commentary) was through *mesirat
        nefesh*. It became part of Israel's very being beginning with Abraham's *akeidah*
        (sacrifice) and culminated with the Holocaust—which by its extremity implied
        relief in the form of redemption (see statement by Rabbi Akiva, *Makkot* 24b).
        Firer identified the Land of Israel as the channel from one to the other. Unlike
        Tsimerman, Firer considered the Warsaw ghetto revolt a form of *mesirat
        nefesh*, an active parallel to the passive form of the *akeidah*. See, e.g., Firer,
        "Farvos azoy aynzaytik!" *Dos Yidishe Vort* 2 no. 14 (12 December 1947), p.
        3; "She'al avikhah veyagedekhah," *Netsah Israel* 1 (May 1948), p. 5; "Erev
        Pesah 5703—Erev Pesah 5708: Tsum finften Yortag fun varshaven Geto Oyf-
        shtand," *Di Yidishe Shtime* 2 (23 April 1958), p. 6.

29.   Yehudah Arye Leib Alter MiGur, in *Sephat Emet*, V (New York, 1952/53), p.
        47-48, paragraph 655. In discussing his father's view of prayer in *Tamim
        Pa'alo*, Yosef Tsimerman referred me to a passage in the *Sephat Emet* which
        connected omnipotence with *rahamim* and stressed that *rahamim* was evoked
        by praise alone:

              Truly, the level of prayer depends upon the intention and not on whether a
              specific request is fulfilled. Even when someone needs something, he has to
              forget about it and just praise God. There may be a response to the need—
              but that was because the need got him to praise God. ... What is prayer
              about? Whatever happens to man is because of God's judgment, and man
              should reflect upon the greatness, power, and omnipotence of God. While
              man cannot conceptualize it, God could judge man for punishment but His
              will could reverse it. But man can conceptualize the omnipotence. Moses, for
              example, knew that he would not get to the Land of Israel, but prayed any-
              way. As the Sages said, "Even if a sharp sword rests on a man's neck, he
              should not desist from prayer, as it says 'Though He slay me, yet will I trust
              in Him' [Job 13:15]. [*Berakhot* 10a/b]. With faith, man believes that noth-
              ing is too hard for God. God's greatness is accompanied by meekness. Thus,
              by giving priority to praising God, His *rahamim* may be awakened. *Sephat
              Emet*, V, pp. 17- 18, paragraph 633.

30.   The theme of God's weeping was the touchstone in Yehezkel Sarna (Slobodka),
        *Liteshuvah Velitekuma: Devarim Shene'emru Bekinus Lemisped Uteshuvah
        Shehitkayem Ba'ir B'yeshivat Hevron Keneset Yisrael Bayom 18 Kislev 5705*
        (Jerusalem, 1945). See also Yitzhak Stollman (Slobodka-Novaroduk), "Bemis-
        tarim tivkhe nafshi" in *Minhat Yitzhak*, III (St. Louis, 1958), p. 15. On Stoll-

man, see Greenberg, "Der Holocaust und die Juden Amerikas: Die Konzepte der Misrahi während des zweiten Weltkrieges," in *Das Leben leise wieder lernen: Jüdisches und christliches Selbstverständnis nach der Schoah* (Stuttgart, 1997). The central role of *rahamim* in the Slobodka school of Musar is described in Greenberg, "A Musar Response to the Holocaust."

31. I have been unable to verify the events cited by Tsimerman. On the Yishuv's reaction to the German threat from North Africa, see Haviv Kena'an, *Matayim Yemei Haradah: Eretz Yisrael Mul Tsevah Romel* (Tel Aviv, 1973/74), and "Hayishuv Hayehudi Be'eretz Yisrael Biyemei Milhemet Haolam Hasheniyah," *Masuah: Kovets Shenati Letoda'at Hashoah Vehagevurah* 4 (April 1976), pp. 151-152. See also *Nokhakh Iyum Hapelishah Hagermanit Le'eretz Yisrael Bishenot 1940-1942*, ed. Uri Breuer (Ef'al, 1981); and Yehuda Bauer, "The Danger of German Invasion (1942)," in *From Diplomacy to Resistance: A History of Jewish Palestine, 1939-1945* (Philadelphia, 1970), pp. 168-223. See also Moshe Prager, *Megilat Hashoah: Kinah al Hurban Beit Yisrael Be'eiropah* (B'nei B'rak, 1968), pp. 8-8a; Gedaliah Bublick, "Referat iber der politisher Lage in Tsiyonizim," *Der Mizrahi Veg* 7 no. 5 (March-April 1943), pp. 2-3; and Ephraim Sokolover, "Rosh Hashanah 5703 Yom Sheini [13 September 1942]," in *Penei Ephraim: Derashot Leyamim Noraim Ulemoadim* (Tel Aviv, 1965/66), p. 25.

32. The motif that once the catastrophe started there was little one could do appeared elsewhere. See for example Elhanan Wasserman, *Ma'amar Ikveta Dimeshiha Vema'amar al Ha'emunah: A Belaykhtung fun der yetstiger Tekufah* (New York, 1938/39), pp. 6-7, 23-24, 27. See Greenberg, "Foundations for Orthodox Jewish Theological Response to the Holocaust, 1936-1939" in *Burning Memory: Times of Testing and Reckoning*, ed. Alice Eckardt (London, 1993), pp. 71- 94. At the Passover *seder* of 1940 in prison Bugidki, Siberia, Shlomo Diamant-Yahalomi (Mizrahi), who came to Palestine in fall 1947, recited: "We were slaves in Poland, Lithuania, Romania, and did not want to leave. ... Why do we eat this *maror*? Because we did not want to leave our 'sweet' life; afraid that we might have to taste a little *maror* for the Land of Israel." Then in Bergen-Belsen, summer 1947, he wrote that because the Jews failed to heed the call to Zion when they should have, the return now would be mournful (*Midrash Ekhah Rabbah. Proem* 11). For once the catastrophe began, nothing could be done to stop it. Yitzhak Berglass and Shlomo Diamant-Yahalomi, *Sefer Strizov Vehasevivah* (Tel Aviv, 1990), p. 186; and Diamant, "Darkei Tsiyon Aveilot," *Di Yidishe Shtime* 1 (25 July 1947), p. 31.

– Chapter 16 –

JEWISH-AMERICAN ARTISTS AND THE HOLOCAUST
The Responses of Two Generations

Matthew Baigell

I want to compare the responses of two generations of Jewish-American artists to the Holocaust, the generation that came to maturity in the 1940s and 1950s with the current generation of artists. The earlier generation did not confront the Holocaust directly in its art. That is, artists, whether they preferred realistic or abstracted styles, did not paint or sculpt scenes descriptive of particular events or episodes based on documentary photographs or on imaginative recreations of scenes of forced marches and executions, or of ghetto and camp life. Instead, figurative artists tended to find surrogate subject matter in biblical stories or stereotypical images of Jewish elders. Abstract artists, who will be discussed below, found their subject matter in ancient and primitive myths as well as human biology.

Seymour Lipton, for example, sculpted biblical and patriarchal figures in the early 1940s. His "Let My People Go" of 1942 is a bust of a bearded man who wears a prayer shawl around his head which swoops down around his shoulders to become powerful forearms and hands. It is an image of defiance deflected onto a stereotypical figure.

But even these kinds of images disappeared from his oeuvre as the numbers of murdered Jews became known in this country. By

1945, Lipton began to explore different kinds of subject matter based on pre-Columbian ritual death sculpture, images of the biblical figure Moloch who ate his offspring, as well as other images suggestive of death and violence. Lipton's work sprouted spikes which looked as if they might impale the unwary, and once smooth contours developed jagged edges. Textures roughened to heighten emotional responses. These qualities, according to Lipton, "became important in terms of hidden destructive forces below the surface of man. ... Thorns, bones (ancient and modern), sharp tensions, tusks, teeth, and harsh forms develop and grow together in varying images as new beings of sculptural existence evoking images and moods of the primordial insides of men." He went on to say that "the drive was toward finding sculptural structures that stemmed from the deep animal makeup of man's being. ... The ferocity in these works relates to the biologic reality in men. ... They are tragic statements on the condition of man."[1]

His desire to make a timeless statement rather than one with particular narrative intent devolved from several factors. First, within the art world, a hostile reaction had arisen by the middle 1940s to the propagandistic art of the previous decade. His works, suggesting violence, had a better chance of escaping damnation as topical propaganda than obvious, realistic works. Second, within the world of left-wing politics, there might still have been a Stalinist carry-over to play down the suffering of particular groups, such as the Jews, and to emphasize instead the suffering of victims everywhere. This would also have been part of the policies of various groups in this country such as the Office of War Information, which consciously repressed information about Jewish suffering, and the motion picture industry, which did not confront the Holocaust directly until the late 1950s. Third, within the Jewish-American community, acknowledgement of persistent antisemitism inhibited artists from pursuing identifiable Jewish themes and encouraged their desire to assimilate into mainstream culture as well as to counteract the potential loss of patrons who would not purchase works with Holocaust themes.

No doubt, these same factors influenced Adolph Gottlieb and Mark Rothko, who in June, 1943, sent their now famous and often cited letter to Edward Alden Jewell, an art critic of *The New York Times*, asserting that "only that subject matter is valid which is tragic and timeless," certainly an appropriate choice of subject matter for Jewish artists at that time.[2]

Rather than create works directly related to the Holocaust, they found, especially in Frederick Nietzsche's *The Birth of Tragedy*, a way to universalize their concerns and their content. Rothko, particularly, like Nietzsche, found in Greek tragedy a way to confront death and mortality, and it is in part for this reason that he and Gottlieb professed in their letter "a spiritual kinship with primitive and archaic art." As Nietzsche had suggested, after humans began to realize their terror of death, "art [Greek tragedy] appears as a saving sorceress, expert at healing. She alone knows how to turn these nauseous thoughts about the horror or absurdity of existence into notions with which one can live."[3]

So Rothko found subject matter in Greek tragedy. *The Omen of the Eagle* of 1942, for example, refers to events in Aeschylus' *Oresteia*, the story of the House of Atreus. The painting includes the heads of two eagles, associated with Agamemnon and Menelaus, the warrior brothers. But eagles are also the national emblems of Germany and the United States. So the painting suggested some sort of warfare, perhaps fratricidal warfare, without referring to a specific war or specific event.

Like Seymour Lipton, Rothko found warfare and murder to be qualities inherent in humans, biological facts turned into social actions. As Rothko said during a radio broadcast in 1943,

> If our titles [both his and Gottlieb's] recall the known myths of antiquity, we have used them … because they are eternal symbols upon which we must fall back to express basic psychological ideas. Those who think that the world today is more gentle and graceful than the primeval and predatory passions from which these myths spring, are either not aware of reality or do not wish to see it in art.

Gottlieb responded more transparently to the events taking place in Europe.

> That these demonic and brutal images fascinate us today, is not because they are exotic. … If we profess a kinship to the art of primitive men, it is because the feelings they expressed have a particular pertinence today. In times of violence, personal predilections for niceties of color and form seem irrelevant. All primitive expression reveals the constant awareness of powerful forces, the immediate presence of terror and fear, a recognition and acceptance of the brutality of the natural world. … That these feelings are being experienced by many people throughout the world today is an unfortunate fact.[4]

Veiled allusions to the Holocaust, evident in these remarks, are also to be found in the stripe paintings of Barnett Newman, begun in 1948. In these, a single stripe, or perhaps two or three, extend from the top of a canvas to the bottom, set against a mono-colored field. Newman himself said that the stripes were based on the ideas of Rabbi Isaac Luria, the sixteenth-century Kabbalist. According to Gershom Scholem, Rabbi Luria explained that the world was created when God contracted into himself in order to create the primordial space for the world. Then God sent out a ray of light which set "the cosmic process in motion."[5] Newman's single stripe down the length of a canvas represented that first ray of light. About that stripe, Newman is reported to have said that he acted as if he were God in creating something out of nothing.[6]

What prompted Newman to confuse himself with the deity? In the same year that he created the first stripe paintings, 1948, Newman wrote that "instead of making cathedrals out of Christ, man, or 'life,' we are making [them] out of ourselves, out of our feelings."[7] This extraordinary assertion of self-willed strength came at a time when the West was still barely coming to terms with the Holocaust and about the same time that the State of Israel was founded. Newman's stripes, then, can be understood as an act of resistance to Jewish genocide and as an act of celebration of the birth and renewal of the Jewish state during a period of Jewish trauma and national revival. The stripes become Newman's personal and solitary gesture, a raw assertion of self against society and a God that perhaps did not merit his full respect. It is an affirmation of individual strength and spirit in a world he wanted metaphorically to recreate. At the same time, these works, although rooted in Jewish mysticism, also escaped their parochial roots in Jewish-American history to become universalizing gestures intended for the larger world community. Newman could be both Jewish and mainstream at the same time.

No other artist at that time or in succeeding decades made such an heroic gesture, part defiance, part affirmation, of himself as an artist and as a Jew. Surprisingly, Newman's insights were ignored in the Jewish community, and the Kaballah was soon forgotten as a source of imagery for Jewish-American artists until the 1970s—as far as I know. In addition, Holocaust imagery largely vanished until the 1970s. Since then, dozens upon dozens of artists have turned to Holocaust imagery, no longer embarrassed to identify as Jews, as Jewish-American artists, or to feel as vulnerable as the previous generation concerning the murder of so many of their co-religionists. This is not to say that the current generation of artists is more religious than the previous one, but that they evidently find in Jewish culture a sense of personal identification and strength that is reflected in their art. Finally, these artists, more often than not figurative artists rather than abstractionists, do use documentary photographs as source material and do imaginatively recreate images of ghetto and camp life. A surprising number have invoked directly the Kabbalistic notion of *tikkun olam* in their work and thought.

In Kabbalistic literature, the concept of *tikkun olam* marks the final stages of the creation of the universe and assigns the role of responsibility to people. According to the Lurianic Kabbalah, during creation itself, cosmic disturbances occurred. One interpretation holds that a certain amount of divine light was caught and placed in special vessels. But the light was so strong that the vessels burst and the light poured out. Evil elements mixed with divines ones. As a result, as Gershom Scholem has stated, "The restoration of the ideal order, which forms the original aim of creation, is also the secret purpose of existence. Salvation means actually nothing but the restitution, re-interpretation of the original whole, or *tikkun*." In effect, people are responsible for restoring the harmony and perfection of the world by recapturing the spilled divine light though good deeds and religious observance.[8]

For several contemporary artists, *tikkun olam* has become a secular obligation but with mystical overtones that they are only too happy to assume. Rather than explore notions of retribution or violence, or dwell on the brutality of human nature, as earlier artists, they feel that their art should become part of a healing process in the world and that as Jews they want to put behind them the rancor of the past. The differences might simply be generational, but they might also be gender influenced. I have corresponded with about eighty artists who have used Holocaust imagery in their work, and of that number the great majority who invoke the concept of *tikkun olam* are women whose imagery and attitudes tend to be less warlike and aggressive than those of male artists.

Ruth Weisberg, for example, has said of the etchings in her *The Shtetl Book* of 1971 and of other work she completed in the following decade,

> What I do feel very strongly is that my desire to make art, to create meaning, and to be generative is a conscious commitment I make to being affirmative in the face of the knowledge of great systematic cruelty and inhumanity. To remember and to affirm have for me a specifically Jewish sense of renewal. It is the part I can play in the repair of the world—*Tikkun Olam.*[9]

Edith Altman, who experienced Nazi brutality in her native Germany before leaving that country in 1939, offers the clearest visual statement of the mystical aspects of *tikkun olam*, particularly in a performance piece she created in 1986 entitled "When We Are

Born, We Are Given a Golden Tent, and All of Life Is the Folding and Unfolding of the Tent." The tent, made of canvas and painted a golden color, contains silhouetted figures of herself and her father who was interned for a short time in Buchenwald and was deeply scarred by the experience. She has carried the tent to various cities in this country and in Europe, and has sat with Germans, Poles, Jews, and Americans in order to speak about "the pain of the past that we shared." Like a shaman who wants to heal herself and others, Altman hopes to draw into the tent God's presence for direction, healing, and for transforming the shared pain. As she has indicated, "as I fold and unfold my tent, I hear my great-grandfather telling my father, who then told me, that the work of the Kabbalist is to repair himself or herself and to work toward the repair of the world—to bring it back into balance.

Part of Altman's search for *tikkun olam* is, as she said, "trying to face a personal dark as well as the darkness felt by other people." As a result of her own study of Kabbalah, Altman believes that "everybody has a function. I see mine as healing. The idea of *Tikkun*—which means repair—is part of Kabbalist thinking."[10]

Renata Stein, who was also born abroad, acknowledges the importance of Kabbalah. She has said "the Kabbalists have been saying that we have to create a world if our world has been destroyed." To express both destruction and re-creation, she uses found objects and fragments—"joining together broken pieces of rather humble origin into new configurations—and thus a new reality—is an act of *tikkun olam*, of mending the world and our broken spirits." And by using Kabbalistic imagery, she hopes her art will light in others sparks of inspiration and hope.[11]

For many artists with whom I have corresponded, the concept of *tikkun olam* shades off into a particularly Jewish sense of social responsibility. Altman, Stein, and others, no doubt, would agree with Hannelore Baron who witnessed Kristallnacht in 1938, when Baron said that "as an exhibiting artist [her most important pieces are probably her very small collages evocative of gates, fences and closed doors] it is my duty to make a statement for peace. ... I feel I must speak out on behalf of other victims to protect their fate, and carry with me the memory of those who succumbed." And Alice Lok Cahanna, a survivor of three concentration camps, feels that "we who survived were charged by those who did not come back to tell their story, to tell what happened. It is a silent oath we took. ... My work [largely abstracted shapes realized in broad washes of color] cannot end with the Holocaust, but with the image of freedom and hope, with survival of the human spirit."[12]

Perhaps the one contemporary work which best summarizes the varying mystical qualities several artists give to their Holocaust images is Edith Altman's "Reclaiming the Symbol/The Act of Memory," created over a four-year period beginning in 1988. She wants nothing less than to reclaim the swastika from the Nazis and to restore it to its initial meanings as a symbol of revival and prosperity. As it appears in her multi-room installation, the gold swastika is nine feet tall and is restored to its pre-Nazi configuration. Its color refers to the Kabbalistic tradition in which gold represents base matter that has been spiritually transformed. On the floor, the reflection is that of the black Nazi swastika, the impure swastika, its form a mirror image of the original. On the walls and floor are several different forms with varying kinds of Kabbalistic references.

In addressing the symbol she witnessed all too forcefully as a child in Europe, she confronted her own memories, not as a fearful child, but as a healthy adult. "By taking the swastika apart, by deconstructing its meanings and disempowering it, I hoped to change its fearful energy. In a spiritual and mystical kind of sense, I am exorcising the evil memory of the swastika, in hopes of healing our fear. My art is a healing ritual."[13] *Tikkun olam*, indeed!

Although the artists I have discussed here do not account for all positions and attitudes assumed either in the immediate post-war period or in the present, their work suggests that the Holocaust itself is not their subject, but rather a place from which to begin contemplation of the human condition. Earlier, some artists sought explication by evoking man's biological nature or by subsuming the Holocaust within Greek myth, as if the Holocaust itself were not a grand enough theme to explore. Contemporary artists, no longer interested in explanations, and understanding that the Holocaust is and will always remain incomprehensible, see their task as restorative and forgiving, one involved in re-establishing civility in the world. At the same time, these recent artists insist on remaining witnesses to the Holocaust, using its imagery, and addressing it directly in their statements. They view themselves as responding as Jews, as responding to a social and religious ethic they are pleased to call Jewish, but with the same intention as the earlier artists of getting beyond the parochial, the ethnically bound, in order to engage in the larger discourses about human actions and interactions.

Notes

1. Albert Elsen, *Seymour Lipton* (New York: Harry Abrams, 1974), 27-28; Seymour Lipton, "Some Notes on My Sculpture," *Magazine of Art,* 40 (Oct. 1947): 47; Harris Rosenstein, "Lipton's Code," *Art News* 76 (March 1971): 47.
2. For the complete text, see John W. McCoubrey, ed., *American Art, 1700-1960: Sources and Documents* (Englewood Cliffs, NJ: Prentice-Hall, 1965), 210-212.
3. Frederick Nietzsche, *The Birth of Tragedy and The Case of Wagner,* trans. Walter Kaufman (New York: Vintage Books, 1967), 60.
4. A transcript of the radio broadcast, which took place on October 13, 1943, is in Laurence Alloway and Mary Davis McNaughton, *Adolph Gottlieb: A Retrospective* (New York: The Arts Publisher, Inc., 1981), 170-171.
5. Gershom Scholem, *Major Trends in Jewish Mysticism* (New York: Schocken, 1946), 260-276; Thomas Hess, *Barnett Newman* (New York: The Museum of Modern Art, 1971), 56, 71, 52-61, and 83; and Matthew Baigell, "Barnett Newman's Stripe Paintings and Kabbalah: A Jewish Take," *American Art* 8 (Spring 1994): 33-43.
6. Hess, *Newman,* 56.
7. Barnett Newman, "The Sublime Is Now," (1948) in John O'Neill, ed., *Barnett Newman: Selected Writings and Interviews* (Berkeley: University of California Press, 1990), 170.
8. Scholem, *Major Trends,* 268.
9. Letter to author, April 2, 1994.
10. David McCracken, "Spertus Exhibit, A Different Look at Traditions," *Chicago Tribune,* May 6, 1988, sec. 7, p. 47; Sue Taylor, "Memory Is Woven into Altman's Work," *Chicago Sun Times,* May 7, 1987 (clipping); Christopher English, *Edith Altman* (Chicago: N.A.M.E. Gallery, 1987), unpag.; Mary Jane Jacob, "The Artist in Society," *Kunst Arbeit* (Chicago: State of Illinois Art Gallery, 1992), 4; Joseph S. Mella, *Edith Altman: Photography, Text, Object* (Rockford, Ill.: Rockford Art Museum, 1989), unpag.; and Gilbert Jimenez, "Altman Tries to Provoke Thought," *Chicago Sun Times,* May 6, 1988, p. 27.
11. Statement in "Never Again," exhibition catalogue, Cathedral of St. John the Divine, New York City , 1995, unpag.
12. For Baron, Statement in the [Los Angeles] *Reader* 10 (Nov. 20, 1987. For Cahana, see Barbara Rose, *From Ashes to the Rainbow: The Art of Alice Lok Cahana* (Los Angeles: Hebrew Union College Skirball Museum, 1986), 34, 39.
13. *Kunst Arbeit,* 2-6; statement in "Reclaiming the Symbol/The Art of Memory."

Chapter 17

THE JOURNEY TO POLAND

Michal Govrin

In late October 1975, when I was in my early twenties and completing my doctorate in Paris, I went to Poland. An almost impossible journey then for a young woman, alone, with an Israeli passport, at a time when there were no diplomatic relations between the Eastern Bloc and Israel. (It was only because of a French-Jewish friend, who turned me into a "Representative of France" at the International Theater Festival in Wroclaw [Breslau], that I received a special visa for a week.)

The night before the trip, when everything was ready, I called my parents in Tel Aviv and told them. I asked my shocked mother for the exact address of her family home in Kraków. Only later that winter, when I visited Israel, did I understand what profound emotion took hold of my mother's few surviving friends and relatives from Kraków when they heard of the trip.

A week later I returned to Paris. For twenty-four hours, I closed myself in my student apartment in the Latin Quarter, far from the Parisian street scenes, and feverishly wrote to my parents. A letter of more than twenty pages. First thoughts, a summary, the rapid notes taken on the trip. Even the words groped for another language, for a different level of discourse.

That year, as every year, a commemoration for the Jewish community of Kraków was held in the auditorium of my high school in Tel Aviv. News of my trip and of that letter reached the members of the community, and they wanted to read it aloud at that commemoration. I agreed, and after it was commandeered from the family circle, I submitted it for publication to the literary supplement of the newspaper, *Davar*, with the title, "Letter from Regions of Delusion."[1] Aside from some peripheral changes of style, that text appears here.

* * *

Travelling to Poland in '75 was not part of the social phenomenon it is today. The group definition of "second generation Holocaust survivors" hadn't yet been coined. You had to find everything by yourself. How to plan the trip and how to feel, how to talk about it. The letter to my parents began a long process of formulation. Even the choice of parents as the addressees of an intimate discourse was not the norm then.

Today, that trip seems like a geological rift that changed my emotional and intellectual landscape, and placed its seal on my writing. Yet, the "journey to Poland" didn't begin in '75, but in early childhood, in Tel Aviv in the 1950s. Distant shocks preceded the rift.

The "journey to Poland" began in that journey "to there"—the journey every child makes to the regions of before he was born, to the unknown past of his parents, to the secret of his birth. My journey to Mother's world began long before I "understood" who my mother, Regina-Rina Poser-Loeb-Govrin, was, before I "knew" that she survived the "Holocaust," that she once had another husband, that I had a half-brother. But there was the other "knowledge," that knowledge of pre-knowledge and of pre-language, transmitted in the thousand languages that connect a child and his parents without words. A knowledge that lay like a dark cloud on the horizon. Terrifying and seductive.

For years the journey proceeded on a double track. One outside the home and one inside it. And there was an almost complete separation between the two. As if everything that was said outside had nothing to do with Mother. Outside, incomprehensible, violent stories about the "Holocaust" were forced upon the little girl's consciousness. In school assemblies, in lessons for Holocaust Memorial Day, and later on in lessons of "Annals of the Jewish People," which were taught separately from "history" classes, and described events that happened in "another, Jewish time and place," where Talmudists and small town Jews strolled among the goats and railroad cars of the ghetto. Even the Eichmann Trial, on the radio in school and at home, was an event you had to listen to, but had no real relation to Mother. (And even if things were said about it then at home, I succeeded in repressing them from consciousness.)

At home, there were bright stories about Kraków, the boulevards, the Hebrew high school, the cook, the maids, about skiing and
summer holidays in the mountains, in Zakopane, and sometimes on
Friday evening, Mother and I would dance a "Krakowiak" on the
big rug in the living room. And there was Mother's compulsive
forced-labor house-cleaning, and her periods of rage and despair
when I didn't straighten up my room (what I called "prophecies of
rage" with self-defensive cunning), there was the everlasting, frightened struggle to make me eat, and there was the disconnected silence
that enveloped her when she didn't get out of bed on Yom Kippur.
And there was the photo album "from there" at the bottom of
Mother's lingerie drawer, with unfamiliar images, and also pictures
of a boy, Marek. And stories about him, joyful, a baby in a cradle on
the balcony, a beautiful child on the boulevard. And a tender memory of the goggle-moggle with sugar he loved so much (and only
years later did I understand the terrifying circumstances of that). And
there were the weekly get-togethers at Aunt Tonka's house (who was
never introduced as the widow of Mother's older brother who was
murdered), get-togethers so different from the humorous, confident
gatherings of Father's family (members of the Third Aliyah and the
leadership of the Yishuv and the State). At night, in Aunt Tonka's
modest apartment, I was the only little girl—"a blond, she looks like
a *shiksa*"—in the middle of the Polish conversation of "friends from
there," who looked to me like impoverished patricians, because
almost all of them had once been mayors and had papers to prove it,
"[M]aryan papers."[2] And every year there were also the visits of
Schindler, when you could go all dressed up with Mother's cousin to
greet him at the Dan Hotel. And once, when Mother and I were coming back from "the city" on bus number 22, Mother stopped next to
the driver and blurted a short sentence at him for no reason. The driver, a gray-haired man in a jacket, was silent and turned his head
away. "He was a ka-po," she said when we got off, pronouncing the
pair of incomprehensible syllables gravely. All that was part of the
cloud that darkened the horizon, yes, but had nothing to do with
what was mentioned at school or on the radio.

Poland and Kraków weren't "real" places either, no more than
King Solomon's Temple, for instance. I remember how stunned I
was when I went with Mother to the film, "King Matthew the First,"
based on the children's story by Janusz Korczak which I had read
in Hebrew. In the film, the children spoke Polish! And it didn't
sound like the language of the friends at Aunt Tonka's house. "Nice
Polish," Mother explained; "of Poles." Poles? They apparently do
exist somewhere.

* * *

Yet, a few events did form a first bridge between outside and inside. One day, in a used book store in south Tel Aviv, Mother bought an album of black and white photos of Kraków. "Because the photos are beautiful," she emphasized; "they have artistic value." And indeed, the sights of the Renaissance city in the four seasons flowed before my eyes. A beautiful, tranquil city, full of greenery and towers. Jews? No, there were no Jews in that album, maybe only a few alleys "on the way to Kazimierz."

At the age of ten, my parents sent me for private lessons in English, because "it's important to know languages." And thus I came to Mrs. Spiro, a gentle woman from London, married to Doctor Spiro, Mother's classmate from the Hebrew high school in Kraków. One day, when the lesson was over, Mrs. Spiro accompanied me to the edge of the yard of their house on King Solomon Street. I recall the sidewalk with big paving stones as she talked with me. Maybe I had complained before about Mother's strict demands, or maybe she started talking on her own,

"Of course, you know what your mother went through, she was in the Holocaust. You have to understand her, the tensions she has sometimes," she said to me directly.

That was an earthquake. A double one. The understanding that Mother was in "the Holocaust," that awful thing they talk about in school assemblies, with "the six million." And that I, a ten-year-old girl, had to or even could "understand Mother." That is, to leave the symbiosis of mother and daughter constituting one expanded body, to cut myself off from my child's view, and see Mother as a separate person, with her own fate and reasons for moods that didn't depend only on me, or on my certain guilt. I remember how, at that moment, facing the spotted paving stones, I understood both those things all at once. Like a blinding blow.

Then came high school in Tel Aviv. Since both the principal and the assistant principal were graduates of the Hebrew High School in Kraków, their former classmates in that high school, including my mother, sent their children to study there. At that school, influenced by the principal and his assistant principal, both of them historians, there was an intense awareness of the Jewish past and life in the Diaspora—a rare dimension in the Zionist-Israeli landscape of Diaspora denial—and Gideon Hausner, the prosecutor in the Eichmann Trial, initiated a "club to immortalize the Jewish community of Kraków." A group of students met with members of the Kraków community, who taught them the history of the city and the Jewish community before the destruction. The club also heard testimony from the Holocaust, with a special (exclusive?) emphasis on the activities of the Jewish underground. The women's revolt in the Gestapo prison, led by Justina, was also dramatized and performed for the community members on the annual memorial day. ("Holocaust celebrations" as the memorials were called by members of the drama club.)

I was a member of the "club to immortalize," and I also played a Polish cook in the performance of the history of the uprising. But in fact, a partition still remained between me and the others, a zone of silence so dense that, to this day, I don't know which of the childen of the Kraków community members were children of Holocaust survivors and not of parents who immigrated to Palestine before the war. If there were any, no bond was formed between us. We didn't talk about it. We remained isolated, caged in the sealed biographies of our parents.

There were other bridges here, almost subterranean ones, which, as far as I recall, were not formulated explicitly. The bond with the literature teacher, the poet, Itamar Yaoz-Kest, who survived as a child with his mother in Bergen-Belsen. In high school, there were only his influence on my literary development and a sense of closeness, a sort of secret look between "others." (Only later did I read the poems of "The Double Root" about his childhood "there," and his story describing, as he put it, a little girl who looked like me, the daughter of survivors.) And there was the love affair with the boy in my class, whose delicate smile on his drooping lower lip looked like the "different" smile of the literature teacher. His father, the lawyer, submitted reparations claims to Germany in those days—close enough to the seductive-dangerous realm. My complicated relations with that boy paralleled the shock of discovery of Kafka; and along with the tempest of feelings of fifteen-year-olds, that forbidden, denied, inflamed relation also had a pungent mixture of eros and sadism, a tenderness and an attraction to death, and above all, metaphysical dimensions that pierced the abyss of dark feelings which somehow was also part of "there."

In my childhood, when Mother was an omnipotent entity within the house, I couldn't "understand" her. Later, when she became the authority to rebel against, the enzyme necessary to cut the fruit off from the branch erected a dam of alienation and enmity between us; I couldn't identify with her, with her humanity. There had to be a real separation. I had to live by myself. To go through the trials alone. To listen slowly to what was concealed.[3]

*   *   *

Then came the move to Europe, to Paris. To study for the doctorate and to write literature intensively. I went to the Paris of culture, of Rilke, of Proust, of Edith Piaf. But in '72, soon after I arrived, the film, "The Sorrow and the Pity" by Marcel Ophuls, was released. When the screening ended in the cinema on the Champs-Élysées, I emerged into a different Paris, into a place where that mythical war had gone on. I "understood" that here, on Rue de Rivoli, beneath my garret room, German tanks had passed (ever since then they began to inhabit my dreams), I "understood" that the description of the French as a nation of bold underground fighters and rescuers of Jews—a notion I had grown up with in the years of the military pact between Israel and DeGaulle's France—was very far from reality. The clear, comforting borders between good and evil were shattered for me, and so were the simple moral judgments mobilized for ideologies. Here, far from a post-Six-Day-War Israel secure in her power, far from the official versions of Holocaust and heroism, a different time was in the streets, a time not completely cut off from the war years. Here, for the first time I experienced the sense of the other. As a Jew, as an Israeli. Wary of revealing my identity at the university that served as a center of Fatah activities, trembling in the Métro once as I read the Israeli newspaper, *Ma'ariv*, until someone called it to my attention: "Mademoiselle, somebody spat on your jacket."

Distance also allowed a different discourse with my parents, especially with Mother. In the weekly letters, without the daily tension of life at home, a new bond was opened, between people who were close, who were beginning to speak more openly with one another. Even my clothes in the European winter, in the "retro" style, began to look like the clothes in Mother's old pictures from Poland, like her hairdo in the photo next to the jeep from Hanover, when she served after the war as a commander in Aliyah B, the *Brikha*, camouflaged in an UNRRA uniform. Poland, Hanover, suddenly turned into places that were much closer, more present than the little state on the shores of the Mediterranean.

On the first Holocaust Memorial Day in Paris, I decided to stay in my apartment all day and to cut myself off from the street that lived by its own dates (for example, Armistice Day of World War I, the "Great War" that took place at the same time of the year). I spent the day reading works on the sources of Nazism, on the roots of antisemitism, on the German nationalism of Wagner (rehearsals of whose opera, "Parsifal," I had attended at the Paris Opera).

That summer, on a tour of Europe, an accident forced me to stay unexpectedly in Munich for three weeks. And then the blank

spot that filled the heart of the European map for me—Germany—
the blank, untouchable spot, that sucked up all the evil, also fell.
Here, next to the beer hall of "the Nazi buds," where some Israelis
had taken me, in what was obviously a sick gesture, there was also
an opera, where Mozart was performed, and there were wonderful
museums, and parks.

The forced stay in Germany and the Yom Kippur War the following autumn, which I spent in Paris facing the brightly lit
Champs-Élysées while my dear ones were in mortal danger, proved
to me that there is no refuge in the soothing distinctions between
"then" and "now," between "there" and "here." And I also understood that there is no racial difference, imprinted at birth between
"them" and "us," nor can we hide behind the fences of the Chosen
People. And that, in every person, the murderer and the victim
potentially exist, blended into one another, constantly demanding
separation, every single day, with full awareness. I understood that
I could no longer hide behind the collective, ready-made definitions
of memory. That there would be no choice but to embark on the
journey that is obstinate, lonely, and full of contradictions.

Germany, France, Europe. What is in that culture, in its roots,
mixed with the gold of the Baroque and the flickering brasses of
symphonies; what is in the squares, in the churches, in the ideologies that allowed what happened? Prepared it? Didn't prevent it?
What inflamed the hatred? What repressed it under pious words of
morality? What fostered it in the heart of religious belief? What
prepared it in the tales of God that man told himself to justify the
outbursts of his evil instincts under the disguise of *Imitatio Dei*?

And what still exists right before my eyes? Keeps on happening?

How to shift the borders between good and evil with a thin
scalpel under a microscope?

How to distinguish anew, here and now? All the time?

And what is the terrorizing persuasive force of tales and of
their metamorphoses into theologies, ideologies? How to struggle
with forgetting, with denial, without whitewashing, but also without reiterating the same stories, without inflaming the same evil
instincts? How to tell responsibly?

Jarring questions that filled me, that nourished my research, my
theatrical productions, my literary writing, but did not yet touch
Mother's hidden place.

*   *   *

I spent the summer of '75 between Princeton and New York, col-
lecting material for my doctorate, reading the works of Rebbi Nah-

man of Bratzlav in the old library of the Jewish Theological Seminary, and in the evenings, swallowing the plethora of fringe theater, jazz and transvestite clubs, and the international bohemian life of Manhattan. And thus I met that young violinist from Kraków who had fled Poland, and was working as a cabdriver. A handsome young man from Kraków. Kraków? A place where people live?! The summer romance was a way to confront the profound seduction of the depths of the past stamped in me, as well as the depths of my femininity.

One day that summer, my aunt, Mother's sister-in-law, came to my apartment in midtown Manhattan. I knew her vaguely from a visit she had made to Israel years before, and after the death of Aunt Tonka in Tel Aviv, my aunt from Queens, the widow of Mother's second brother, who perished in the camps, was her last living close relative. She had survived Auschwitz and her young son was hidden by a Christian woman. After the war, my aunt and her son immigrated to New York.

That day, on the balcony on the thirtieth floor, facing the roofs of midtown Manhattan, my aunt spoke in broken English only about "then" and "there," as if here and now didn't exist, as if we had never left there. She and the Polish pop music at night melted the last wall of resistance. Now I had no excuse not to translate my preoccupation with the subject into action, no excuse not to go to Poland.

*   *   *

In late October, after the administrative alibi was concocted in Paris, I left. Ready. And not ready at all.

I was not ready for what I would find or for what I wouldn't find. I was not ready for the fear. The fear of returning to the strange hotel room at night, the primal fear that I would starve to death, which impelled me to eat nonstop, completely violating the rules of Kashrut which I had observed ever since I came to Paris to study, eating with the dispensation "allowed during an emergency," that I granted myself (insolently?). Not ready for the fear that rushed me in a panic straight from the visit to Auschwitz-Birkenau to meetings with Polish artists and bohemian parties. I was especially not ready for the complexity of my responses, for their force. For what was revealed to me in "the living laboratory" I had poured by myself. The contradictory burst of fascination and revulsion, alienation and belonging, shame and vengeance, of helplessness, of complete denial. ...

When I returned, the letter to my parents was a first attempt to look at what was revealed, to talk. The restrained language of the letter reflects the difficulty in going beyond the taboo, hoping they would understand through the silence. That different, new discourse with my parents accompanied us throughout the years until their death. A discourse of closeness, of belonging, of acceptance, beyond the generational differences.

The sense of belonging —along with my parents—to the "other, Jewish story" revealed in the depths of the journey, only intensified in the following years, as the doors to the centers of European culture opened to me, as I devoted myself to writing. But at the same time, the understanding that it is impossible to go on telling as if nothing had happened also grew. Understanding that, after Auschwitz, there are no more stories that don't betray, there are no more innocent stories.

*   *   *

And what about Mother's shrouded "story"? Details continued to join together in fragments. For years, here and there, she mentioned events, some in conversations with me, some in conversations with others that I chanced upon. I listened when she spoke, and she spoke little. Never did I "interview" her, never did I ask. I respected her way of speaking, as well as her way of being silent. Even after I returned from Auschwitz, I didn't think she had to report or that I had to (or could) "know." I learned from her the lesson of the story in silence.

*   *   *

I heard the first fragment of a chronological description from my mother under extraordinary circumstances. In the autumn of 1977, she was summoned to give testimony in a German court in Hanover. I accompanied my parents to the trial, sitting with Father in the gallery and seeing Mother, with her special erect posture, surrounded by the black robes of the attorneys. In her fluent German, she described the Plaszów camp, where Jews from the Kraków Ghetto were removed, she pointed authoritatively at the maps. Her voice trembled only a moment when she came to the description of the *Kinderheim*, the children's home in Plaszów, where children were taken from their parents. In a few words, she dealt with the *Aktsia*, told how all the inmates of the camp were taken out to the square while an orchestra played lullabies, to see how the SS loaded the children onto the trucks that took them to the gas chambers. She was asked what was the name of her son, and how old was he at the time of the *Aktsia*. She replied with an effort, "Marek. Eight years old." The prosecutor asked for a momentary recess, and then the questions resumed. (That prosecutor accompanied us when we left, apologizing in shame for the accused, the deputy of Amon Goeth, the commander of Plaszów, who was absent from the courtroom, "for medical reasons". ...)

A few years later, Mother tried to dramatize the story of the revolt of the women in Kraków at the vocational high school where she taught, wanting to bring the subject close to her women students. She worked with Father on the script, and developed original ideas of staging designed to increase audience participation. But, during the rehearsals, she developed such a serious a skin disease, clearly as a rejection, that the doctor advised her to stop the production.

The presence of the Holocaust receded completely in her last months, as she struggled with the fatal cancer that was discovered in her. Death was too close to think about its old dread—at any rate, that was my feeling as I stood at her side, admiring her yearning for life, the audacity, the amazing black humor, which restored the dimensions of human absurdity even in the most difficult situations. The day before she lost consciousness, she spoke a lot, in a stupor, in Polish. What did she say? What was she still living there? I couldn't go with her. I remained alone, at her bedside. Then, as I was massaging her feet, those feet that had marched in the death march through frozen Europe, I was struck with the simple knowledge that it was to Mother's struggle, there, that I owed my birth.

* * *

I heard Mother's "story" only after her death—death that always turns a loved one into a "story" with a beginning and an end. During the *shiva*, Rivka Horowitz came to Jerusalem from Bnei-Brak. A woman with bold blue eyes, whom I knew only by name. She was one of nine women, all of them graduates of Beit Yakov, the ultra-orthodox school for girls in Kraków, whom my mother joined in the ghetto, despite differences of education and ideology. The ten women, the "*Minyan*," supported one another in the ghetto, during the years in the Plaszów camp, in Auschwitz-Birkenau, throughout the death march, and in the final weeks in Bergen-Belsen. For three years, they hadn't abandoned one another, together they fought exhaustion, disease, had lived through the selections, until all of them survived. "There was strength in them. Moral strength," Mother explained when she and Father, both of them members of the liberal secular Mapai, assiduously attended the celebrations of the friends in Bnei Brak. At the *shiva*, I heard from Rivka Horowitz for the first time about that period. She spoke for a few hours—out of a responsibility to tell me—and left. And after that, until she died, we didn't meet again. Later on, when I was almost finished writing *The Name, HaShem* (and after Mother's death, it seemed to me that, more than ever, the novel spoke of a "there" that was lost forever), came the first information about the family property in Kraków. Apartment houses, a button factory. ... Property? There? "In the regions of delusion?" And then, the name that had been common at home, Schindler, which suddenly became a book and then a film, and turned into a general legacy: the story of the rescue of Mother's cousin and his wife and Mother's refusal to join the list of workers in the enamel factory in order to stay with Marek.

And then, one evening, the telephone rings in Jerusalem, and on the other end of the line, in English with a thick Polish accent, another member of that "*Minyan*" introduces herself, Pearl Benisch, who published a book, *To Vanquish the Dragon*, with the full story of the group (from the author's religious perspective).[4] A copy arrived on Friday. On the Sabbath eve, I sat with my two little daughters in the living room and picked up the book. I leafed through it distractedly, until I came to the description of the destruction of the *Kinderheim*. And then I fled to the other room so the children wouldn't see me, and there I burst into sobs I didn't know were hidden inside me. A weeping that arose from there. Mine? Hers?

Until dawn that Sabbath, I read for the first time the story of Mother, in chronological order, dated, revealing the few facts I knew situated in their context. Even the description of the goggle-moggle with sugar that she had secretly made for Marek in the sewing workshop, where the women from Plaszów worked, smuggling the treat to the child when she came back. And how one day the Jewish supervisor discovered her stealing the egg and threatened to turn her in. And how she stood before him then in mortal danger, and accused him in front of all the workers of the sewing shop of being a traitor to his people. I read how in the *Aktsia* of the destruction of the children's home, against the horrifying background of lullabies, Mother burst into the square toward the SS men who were pushing the weeping children onto the trucks. She shouted to them to take her with the child. And how her friends, the women of the "*Minyan*," held her with all their might, pulled her back. I read about the sisterhood between the women in the group, about the pride, the unbelievable humor, how with astonishing freedom, they maintained their humanity in the *Lagers* of Auschwitz-Birkenau. They and many other women and men were described in their humanity facing the crematoria. How they succeeded in putting on make-up to get through the selections, how they sneaked the weak women out of the line of the condemned, how they secretly lit candles at Hanukah and held a Passover Seder, and how, after the death march from Auschwitz to Bergen-Belsen, they still managed to laugh together when they got the wrong-size prison uniforms. I read, frozen stiff, how, in Bergen-Belsen, Mother dared to be insolent to the female SS officer with the pride she still had left, surviving the public whipping, which few survived, without shouting, "so as not to give the SS the pleasure." Between the pages, the figure of Mother returned to me, cheering the women in Auschwitz with stories of her visit to the Land of Israel, singing them songs of the homeland on their muddy beds where they fell exhausted with typhus and teeming with lice, in Bergen-Belsen. Suddenly I understood one of the few stories Mother had told me about the camps, how she would sing to herself Tshernikhovski's poem: "You may laugh, laugh at the dreams, I the dreamer am telling you, I believe in Man, and in his spirit, his powerful spirit," emphasizing with her off-key voice the words: "I believe in Man, and in his spirit, his powerful spirit. ..."

*   *   *

Mother's "story." Discovering it in the heart of the journey to what was stamped inside me. Discovering it now in the middle of life, when I myself am a mother, and older than she—the young woman and mother who was there.

"Mother's story," or maybe only milestones around what remains hidden.

Letter from the Regions of Delusion

November 2, 1975, Paris

My dears,
Back home—what a relief!
A week in Poland is like a year, like years, like a moment. Ever since the visa was approved, a week before the trip, I felt as if I were facing an operation. I was waiting for something to stop me, for an iron curtain to block the way. And even in the dark, when the bus took us from the plane to the airport in Warsaw, I still didn't believe that the distance between me and Poland would be swallowed up just like that, in a few steps.

Your letter, which reached me just before the trip, was a lifeline in moments when the dizziness intensified; in moments when there was only a definite absence of my imaginary picture of those places, when instead, there were only the long lines in gray raincoats; in moments of awful loneliness, when there was no one to shout at; in moments when I didn't believe I could finally get on the train and leave that madness behind.

*   *   *

How to tell, and wasn't there any chronology? How to live that over again?

Wroclaw. A dreary city and a theater festival. I was ejected into the darkness in the heart of an empty field. That's how it began. Night in the hotel. An enormous radio, and voices from Russian, Polish, Czech, and Hungarian stations. Stifling heat from the furnace, the chamber-maid, a blond Gentile woman, fills the bathtub for me. In the soap box and in the closet are roaches. A strife-torn night in dreams and a gray-ish morning. The outside was stopped by the curtains. Crowds of people with rubbed out faces. A few old cars. Awful cold. Fog.

How to leave the room and go into that reality? How to be a "tourist" in it?

*   *   *

Wroclaw. In the display windows rows of laundry soap in coarse packages. Cooperative restaurants smelling of cabbage and sweat. In the festival offices full ashtrays, organizers with sleepless faces. And then a writers' café, in Kosciuszko Square, and it was as if I had come to a kind of Jerusalem before I was born, from the thir-ties, a Jerusalem I lived from books. With that blend of provincial-ism and culture. Waitresses dressed in black with starched aprons, newspapers in wooden frames, cigarette smoke, grave discussions about art, literature, politics, metaphysics. The soft tones of a lan-guage that is so familiar, so close. The intonations, the gestures, the excited seriousness.

An international festival—a few days of devotion to joy, before the regime returns its everyday gray.

And I, a stranger at the celebration. Only an "alibi" for another mission, which no one in fact has assigned to me. Yes, a few addresses for it's impossible-not-to-accept-with-a-letter-to-take before setting out. Backs of houses, yards, covered with trash and rubble. Staircase supported by boards. Number seven/two, apart-ment nine A. Two old people in the doorway. A kitchen black with soot. Examining me, the letter, with a scared look.

Sneaking back to the ongoing celebration. Just so they won't find out. It's only because of sloppiness that they haven't yet arrested me.

*   *   *

And then, early one misty morning, wrapped in a coat, at the railroad station. Among hundreds of people in a line. Buying a ticket to Kraków with black market Zlotys ... to the regions of my real trip.

Getting off the train, and simply walking into the light-flooded square, among ancient buildings, whose carved façades are sparkling in the sun. Walking among the other people on the boulevard with the autumn chestnut trees, on "Planty," Mother's route to the tennis courts. Leaves struggle on my shoes. Entering the "Rynek" Square resounding around itself. The Renaissance arches, the Sukiennice market in the middle like an island in the heart of a lagoon of light, the breeze rising from the Virgin Mary Church ... all those names, with a soft R, as I ("wonderful child!": the only two words I understood in the foreign language), would accompany Mother to the nightly suppers on an aunt's balcony, with a smell of down comforters and the saltiness of the sea air on hot Tel Aviv nights, when friends from "there" would gather. All those names, when the conversation would climb in the foreign tremolo, and in the café downstairs, in the yard of the building, the cards would be shuffled on tables. The places frozen in slides on the wall of the high school, in commemorations held with a sudden frenzy. Places that were stopped in the thirties, with an amazed look of some Jew who came on the camera by mistake. ... The warm-cool air caresses the fur of my coat, my face, moves the parasols over the flower vendors' booths.

The road rises to a high hill overlooking the city and the Vistula River. Above, the Wawel Castle covered in ivy burning with autumn leaves. And here, on the slope, along the banks of the Vistula, the way to Paulinska Street, Mother's street.

The three o'clock twilight lingers and softens. Mothers with babies in buggies at the river. (Mothers and babies? Still? Here?) Paulinska Street. On the secret side of the street the wall of a convent, and behind it fruit trees. Someone passes by on the corner. A woman in a heavy coat and old boots. Number eight. The staircase floored with blue tiles. A list of tenants in fountain pen. First floor on the left—a strange name. The door is locked. On the first floor a balcony. Closed glass doors, covered with lace curtains. To throw a stone at them mischievously, a schoolbag on the back and stockings stretched up to the knee? As I walked there, dressed carefully by Mother, among the children giggling at my different clothes. To sit down at a steaming lunch, close to the breath of forefathers I never saw? Only crumbs of medicines and old lipsticks in the drawers of the aunt who died. That silence. The quiet of houses. Take a picture? A picture of air? Quiet. Across the street, in the convent garden, a bell rings. Children pour out of the gates of the school, climb on the fences, chew on apples.

Spotted façades and the street spins. Not far from there, Kazimierz, the Jewish quarter. The soot of trams on the doorsills of the houses. In the windows of the reform synagogue, the "Temple," spiderwebs, and in the yard, a tangle of weeds. In the alley of one of the houses is a blurred sign in Yiddish, "Prayer House." The big synagogue is empty and whitewashed. Turned into a museum. Only a guard passes by like a shadow along the walls, and two fragments of tiles from back then are embedded in the entrance.

It's late now. I wander along the track to the cemetery. Here at least I am sent by permission, to an address that does exist, to the graves of the family. The gate is closed. There is no one to ask. Everything is closed.

* * *

An evening full of mist. Suddenly the trams are hurrying. The voices of the flower vendors in the Rynek are swallowed up in the fog. To go to the reserved hotel? In Kraków? Like going to a hotel in Tel Aviv instead of returning home. The desk clerk scurries up to help: "Yes, of course, Madam, here's the bus schedule to Auschwitz. From the town of Oswiecim, you have to go on foot a bit."

On the table at the entrance are old newspapers. Two elderly lady tourists are interested in a jazz festival that may not take place.

And there, at the foot of the stairs, on the way to the room, the movement that had swept me up ever since early morning stops. No, just not to return alone to the gigantic radio in the strange room! I buttoned the coat and went out in pursuit of a dubious rumor that was given to me. Slawskowska Street. Maybe. ...

* * *

And indeed, in the dark, in Yiddish, among the artisans' signs, a small address: "Mordechai Gvirtig Culture Club." A door at the edge of a yard. A doorman sits at the entrance. And in the depths, in the gloom, a few frozen figures are playing cards, gazing vacantly behind the wooden frames of newspapers. "Israel!" the doorman sits up straight, leads me with sudden importance to the "board" room. Five wrinkled faces rise up to me: "Israel!" They sit me down in the middle, following my efforts in a mixture of basic German, a few words in Yiddish, and gestures. They nod at length in deep wonder at every word, assault one another in noisy arguments. Finally, they answer together, in a strange chorus: "Ha! Yes, Poser's daughter! Poser and Abeles," they nod: "Buttons, buttons!"

"Yes, buttons," I affirm; "a button factory." "The Hebrew high school," I continue. "Yes, the high school. Now a Polish technical school." The Christian cook serves me a sandwich with a lot of bread and a cup of tea. They dismiss her with the superiority of a bygone age, and urge me: "Eat, eat." For a moment, they go back to their business. The "chairman" is dictating a petition to the "secretary" about the cultural situation. To whom? On behalf of whom? Still? Like those stencilled pages in cellars and photographs of pale-faced choirs that were presented every Holocaust Memorial Day in the glass cabinets of the school. I attempt to explain, they will certainly understand that it's impossible to get on the bus and simply ask the driver in a foreign language to tell me where you get off for Auschwitz. They certainly have their own ways of getting there. And indeed, it turns out that tomorrow, a "delegation of rabbis from America" is about to come, and they will go in a special bus. When will they arrive? When will they go? Where are they now? Impossible to know. Got to wait.

I wanted to sneak away from them now, back to the big square. To go into an anonymous café with drunkards. To be swallowed up there. But they hang onto me, wrapped up in their coats, accompany me to the hotel. Argue with outbursts of rancor, finally declare that the "secretary" will come to "guide me" tomorrow morning. They all press around, shake my hand. Downtrodden faces. So small. In threadbare coats.

In the room the suitcase was waiting, with a few things. Make up, passport. Will have to go on and move it. Impossible to hide in the suffocation under the blanket.

* * *

The next morning, before I had time to ponder the other world in my dreams, the "secretary" was already here, dragging me with a soft-limbed domination. Turning me around in dark streets, getting on and off trams, talking incessantly in the incomprehensible language, as if to herself. And I plod behind her, bending down to her, making an effort.

In Kazimierz, on the bench across from the synagogue, the doorman of the "Mordechai Gvirtig Culture Club" and two old men are already waiting for me. It's not clear if they're beggars or rabbis. They came to welcome the "American delegation." The doorman waving as he approaches, "Yes, yes!" One of the old men hurries me, opens the gates of the ancient synagogue of Rabbi Moshe Isserlish. For a minute, a separate hush. The figures that follow in my wake remained beyond the fence. A small building whose heavy walls are leaning, and a white courtyard. Inside the synagogue, there is still a warmth among the wooden benches, around the Ark of the Covenant. On the tables are old prayer books. Black letters. And in the small enclosure crows land on the ancient tombstones sunk in mist. For a moment the past seemed to continue with all its softness, without any obstacle, in that distant murmur, up to the morning covered with mist, to me.

And the doorman is already rushing me hysterically, he arranged with the gatekeeper of the "Miodowa" cemetery to be there, to open the gate. Hurry, hurry, got to get back in time for the "delegation of rabbis!" And thus, in single file, the doorman limping, the muscular Christian gatekeeper on his heels, and I behind them, we march between long rows of sunken, shattered gravestones, covered with mold. Names, names. I recite to them the names I've managed to dredge up from my memory, "Poser, Mendel, Groner." Tombstones in long rows whose edges vanish in mist and piles of fallen leaves. Many strange names. Don't find. A Christian woman with legs swathed in bandages rinses the graves with boiling water, raises her head wrapped in a turban to us: "Yes, Groner, saw it once ... maybe there." I still hold on, persist in reading the names, seeking under piles of leaves. But the limping doorman and the gatekeeper behind him are already hurrying out. We didn't find. No maps. No books. No witnesses. Mission impossible. Only a delusion of a mission. And time is limited.

Meanwhile on the bench the number of idlers and "rabbis" waiting for the "American delegation" has grown. According to the doorman, they are already in Kraków and will arrive very soon. Maybe you can find out in the hotel when they'll arrive? No, impossible to know. I break away from the doorman, tell him I'll come back in a little while, he should beg the rabbis of the delegation to wait, and I hurry to Wawel Castle, for the visit that was arranged. On the streets people in gray coats, buses, trams. You can even eat an apple. The body goes on functioning over the abyss between the worlds. And when I come back from the royal palace, from the halls with waxed floors whose walls are covered with embroidered tapestries of feast and forest, devoured by torments of betrayal , I run down the slope carpeted with fallen leaves, back to Kazimierz, to my Jews. From the end of the street, the doorman stumbles toward me. He drops his hands in a gesture of dismissal: "Well, the American delegation ... a call came that they didn't leave America. Well, the fog, they didn't leave America."

Empty. No one there. Even the idlers who were waiting on the bench had gone home.

Entrusted with the last mission, the doorman rushes me into the community organization offices. Second floor, a smell of boiled potatoes, a few old people with tin plates and spoons. Even the bright light filtering from the shutters doesn't bring the scene in the room any closer. Around an enormous table sit the activists of the "congregation," their chins leaning on their hands, and their crutches leaning on the chairs. A few old portraits on the walls. At the head of the table, Mr. Jacobovitch, an irascible Jew, head of the community organization. The mutual curiosity died out after a few sentences, and after I was given the travel arrangements, I slipped out impolitely. I also fled from the kosher meal of mashed potatoes on a tin plate and the ritual washing of the hands in a stained sink, to Sukiennice Square, to the light, to the fancy café with red velvet chairs and torte powdered like the cheeks of the Polish women. Here you can shout aloud that maybe everything is a delusion, that maybe there never were Jews here.

And it was as if a shout burst out of me in the evening, at the performance of "The Night of November Ninth," by Wyspianski, directed by Swinarski. Mythic characters singing against a background of a burning horizon. The tricolored flag of the revolution waves over the stage, and the audience is galvanized. A moment of naked yearning for freedom is revealed, of metaphysical emotion, a moment of a personal world despite the constant oppression. Something so familiar, so close in temperament, in gestures. Such belonging. Belonging?

* * *

An old car. The shaved nape of the driver's neck stuck in a cap. Poplar trees, autumn fields. I am in the back seat, huddled in my coat. On the way to Auschwitz.

And perhaps you should be silent about that trip. Not talk about the yellow flowers, the gravel in the sun, the chatter of the Polish cleaning women who laughingly point out to me that my trousers are unstitched. My trousers? On what side of the barricade?

How to write you about the heavy marching in an attempt to grasp something through the remnants of constructions—as from archaeological digs of thirty, not two thousand years ago. To understand the chasm separating sanity and madness with barbed-wire fences. The house beyond the fence, half a mile away, was always there, with the same smoke in the chimney and the same geranium pots behind the curtains. And here?

How to write about the dark steps with a group of Polish high school students on them. The wall of liquidations between two blocs. A barred window. A few fallen leaves scattered on the sill. Expressionless walls in the gas chambers, the iron doors of the ovens. Polish sky. Between the chambers, in the corridors, photographs and numbers. Printed columns of names. And the silence of another morning, now. As when I held my breath, a girl of six or seven, in the schoolyard for a whole minute, through the whole siren, so that I'd be dizzy when I intoned the words, six million.

How to write you about the forced march through the tremendous extents of Birkenau Camp. About the dampness still standing in the abandoned blocs, between those three-tiered wooden bunks, and the straw sacks on the dirt floor. How to imagine Mother within that silent madness. Mother. A shaved head at nights of hallucinations, nights among packed bodies. How to put Mother into one of the gigantic photos placed along the railroad track. How to force myself to imagine her in this emptiness?

Polish earth. Small autumn flowers. The driver waits. Dozes in the sun in the car.

And maybe all the questions are not right. For it's impossible to understand. Not even at the end of the journey to this stage set. Impossible to understand without the fear of death that catches the breath, without the palpable threat on the flesh. Impossible to grasp death from all the hundreds of photos. Maybe only the heaps of empty shoes are still hovering between life and death. There I finally recited the "Kaddish." "Kaddish" over heaps of shoes.

And maybe all the questions start only after the shoes also crumble. Beyond the crazy stage set of death, which will always remain incomprehensible. And maybe all the questions begin only with the silent emptinesses of now. How to go on living in a world that has turned into the enemy. With the fear stamped in the blood. With the constant paranoia. "Arbeit macht frei." How to live within the world and outside it. In the flow of its life and in the flow of other life and eternity. How to go on nevertheless believing in man, how to take the beloved head in the arms.

*   *   *

In the afternoon light, trivial thoughts pass through the head. Impossible to pretend suffering, that would be hypocrisy. Impossible to go back to the past—clinging or accusing —that would be the triumph of the past. There is no escape from the constant questions to be asked now, impossible to flee from them to the images frozen in the photos.

*   *   *

And in Warsaw, in the Ghetto, there aren't even any ruins where the imagination can take hold for a moment. There are no stones that are emitted outside of time. Only concrete blocks built a few feet above the ground, above the ruins and the mounds of corpses that weren't even cleared away. To hold your head in your hands and shout. Life goes on. Cars in parking lots, a few poplar trees on the sidewalks. And that emptiness. Only the lip service of a memorial with the pathos of socialist realism, and a Jewish museum behind the building of the Communist party. The director of the museum and his secretary, two Jews with bowed heads, show me a building excavation out the window. "Here was the great synagogue of Warsaw." And the cleaning woman smiles like an accomplice in a crime, points at the exit to the guest book full of emotional comments. Gray cement boulevards and gigantic statues of soldiers with forged chins. Impossible to believe that there was once a different life here. Only in the nationalized "Desa" stores, are scores of Jewish objects. Hanukah lamps, synagogue Menorahs, spice boxes. Objects with price tags. No, there is nowhere to return. The whole thing is only a delusion. Deceptions of the imagination. In my head, crushed fragments of all the artistic creations resound, the assemblies, the recitations that tried to convey the other reality to me, and they only increase the distance.

The rain doesn't let up. An awful cold penetrates the clothes, makes you shiver. Warsaw—a gray horizon by day, and gray in the pale neon lights at night. The trip back seems like an illusion, like opening the camp gate and being outside. The unbearable loneliness, the unrelenting stifling.

Only the friendship of my acquaintances, Polish theater people, supported me in the hours before the departure. Figures between reality and dream. Alicia in her theatrical clothes, waving her hands like a Chekhov character. And Andrzej with ironical humor, in fragments of literary French, with the credo from Communism to the Surrealism of Witkiewicz. Fervent confessions in small apartments, when tomorrow is unknown, and only the dream is left. Like the awakening appreciation for Bruno Schulz, thirty years after he perished, like worshipping the theater, the word spoken from the stage, received with a sigh. Like the clandestine grasping of Catholicism.

Childhood memories extend between Mediterranean summers and alleys in northern cities, woven in the dreams of Polish romantic literary heroes, shrouded in the sounds of the language, and open accounts of the blood of the dead. Life in a pre-time is always present, in the double look at all the places. Always through the other place I belong to, where you don't come on journeys. A wiped-out place, condemned to delusion, where I will never be able to rest the wandering of existences.

*   *   *

With relief, I finally board the train. Sleeping cars that came from Moscow with a conductor in an undershirt and a stifling of sweat and orange peels. A twenty-four-hour trip to Paris, like a day of fasting. To another world? At midnight, the train passes the East Berlin station. Signs in Gothic script: "Welcome to the Democratic Capital." On the platform is a white line three feet from the cars. Soldiers in riding boots with German shepherds and submachine guns are standing at regular intervals. A patrol of two soldiers goes through the train. Another patrol checks between the wheels with flashlights, and another one marches on the roofs of the cars. Maybe someone has succeeded in escaping. A white line, soldiers, and a train. Only the site of madness or freedom has changed.

*   *   *

Back in Paris. The clear sky, department store advertising instead of propaganda slogans. Quiet. The silence of the room. And that drawn orbit of life where you two are so close, at hand. "Flesh of my flesh."

*   *   *

Beloved father and mother, I press you to my heart, and once again am gathered in your arms.

– Translated from the Hebrew by Barbara Harshav

Notes

1. I borrowed the expression, "Regions of Delusion" from the title of a parable attributed to the Ba'al Shem Tov, adapted by Martin Buber, *Tales of the Hasidim*, tans. Olga Marx (New York, 1947-48).

2. Translator's Note: This is an English rendition of a pun in the original, based on the sound confluence of the Hebrew *arim* [Cities] and Aryan, which leads the child to think that they all "owned cities" over "there."

3. An amazing example of the layers of memory and forgetting was revealed to me as I wrote *The Name*. The only detail I borrowed in the novel from things I had heard from Mother was a story of the heroism of a woman who succeeded in escaping from Auschwitz-Birkenau, and when she was caught and taken to the Appelplatz, she managed to commit suicide. I also borrowed the admiring tone in which Mother spoke of the event. (Only later did I discover how it had served her as a model.) I created a biographical-fictional character of a virtuoso pianist, and "invented" a name for her—Mala—immortalized in the name of the heroine, Amalia. Only years later, as I was finishing the book, I came across a written description of the event in Birkenau and discovered in a daze that the name of the woman was the same as the name I had "invented," "Mala," Mala Zimetbaum.

4. Pearl Benisch, *To Vanquish the Dragon*, (Jerusalem-New York, 1991).

AFTERTHOUGHT
Some Reflections on Genocide, Religion,
and Modernity

Ian Kershaw

The impressive papers collected in this volume present case studies dealing with a variety of links between religion and genocide in the twentieth century. They concentrate upon four of the
most notorious instances of state-sponsored mass killing in that
benighted century—the Armenian, Jewish, and Rwandan genocides
and the severe ethnic cleansing (though not culminating in outright
genocide) in Bosnia. They do not touch upon a further notorious
case of outright genocide—the Khmer Rouge slaughter in the
killing fields of Cambodia, where class, not nationality or ethnicity
was the basis of the mass murder. About half the Cambodians with
bourgeois backgrounds were wiped out—some one and a half million in all. Nor does this collection discuss the massive population
"cleansings" on purported class grounds, involving loss of life on a
huge scale, under Bolshevism and Maoism.[1]

The papers shed much light upon the ways religion has been
used—in the Cambodian case it was not a factor—to justify genocidal actions and the lack of resistance to and complicity in genocide of representatives of major religions. This invariably shocks us.
The starting presumption is that those representing transcendental
belief systems upholding the sanctity of life should unquestioningly
strive to block the actions of states aimed at destroying life—and on
a large scale. Occasionally, this did happen. The criticism of the
persecution of the Jews by the Metropolitan Stephan of Sofia was
one factor in Bulgaria's reluctance to deport its Jews.[2] But this was

untypical. More depressingly normal was the equivocation that seems encapsulated by the silence of Pope Pius XII, which is brought out in the chapters on the behavior and attitudes of churchmen in Nazi Germany, while, as the Rwandan example shows, clergy could even be directly involved in the slaughter.

Though we are shocked, we ought not to be surprised. After all, religion has been frequently an element, sometimes a key motivator, in some of the worst atrocities and massacres throughout the ages. The proselytizing religions have been the worst offenders. Islamic conquests were accompanied by terrible atrocities. But the record of Christianity is probably most dire of all religions.

The First Crusade against the Muslim "infidel," beginning in 1095, spawned pogroms and murders of Jews on the way to the Holy Land as well as massacres of Muslims. And the Albigensian Crusade that started in 1209—the attempt, authorized by the Pope, to extirpate root and branch the Cathar heresy in the south of France—was both genocidal in attempt and, for its time, in scale. Here, too, Jews were murdered, though they had nothing to do with the actual conflict.

It was in this very era—spanning the period of ecclesiastical reform with its emphasis upon papal authority, doctrinal orthodoxy, and enhancement of the Catholic Church's temporal as well as spiritual power—that the demonization of the Jews sharply gathered pace. The more Catholicism sought to codify and militantly enforce rigid orthodoxy, the more it identified, demonized, and persecuted the groups who were different, who did not belong—the "out-groups." Heretics and Jews were prime targets. The traditional hostility of Christianity and Judaism, which had indeed always been prone to fuel attacks on Jews, now developed an even more threatening dimension as the figure of the Jew became demonized. Weird and lurid images of the Jew—often linked to the ritual slaughter of Christian children, or the poisoning of wells—fed into popular prejudice. Such images were encouraged by the clergy and promoted from a high level in the hierarchy.

By the thirteenth century, then, we can say that the Catholic Church was prepared to instigate, sponsor, or legitimize militant action—on occasion with quasi-genocidal intent and character—to destroy those with other religious beliefs and was demonizing the Jews in a special way, the "out-group" associated with the most heinous of all crimes—the killing of Christ himself. With such a potential for violent discrimination and militant intolerance, underpinned by the crusading zeal of a tightly knit belief system, existing in, arguably, the most powerful institution in Europe, it can hardly be a matter of surprise that the church in a later age could find itself implicated in far more terrible and extensive forms of modern genocide.

Nor, in retrospective view, could the wars of religion accompanying the Reformation in the sixteenth century, prompting numerous massacres in the name of religion, or the intensely bloody Thirty Years War of the seventeenth century offer much hope for a principled defense of human values by the representatives of the Christian Churches at a later date. Moreover, religion in a divided Christianity was by this time becoming increasingly associated with the territorial claims of princes and monarchs and in some instances, as in England, with the legitimacy of emerging nation-states. Not only did this apply to the various strains of Protestantism, it was also, despite its universalist claims, true of Catholicism. The churches and their belief systems were becoming bound up in the interests of what would prove to be the most dynamic political force of the modern era—the nation-state. And, despite their bitter conflicts, both of the major Christian denominations shared a common, deep hostility toward Jews.

Perhaps, it might be thought, the churches could have been expected, despite this gloomy impression of involvement in medieval and early modern atrocities and massacres, to have acted differently following the Enlightenment of the eighteenth century. But for one thing, the churches were at the forefront of the forces rejecting the humanistic and liberalizing ideas of the Enlightenment. And for another, the spread of anti-Enlightenment values was made possible by the most dynamic political idea, which the Enlightenment itself spawned—that of popular sovereignty. This idea, first instrumentalized in the American and French Revolutions and subsequently becoming the indispensable premise of political systems of varying kinds and competing ideologies throughout the world, has been a defining feature of the nineteenth and twentieth centuries. It is one of the most important elements—perhaps even the most important of all—that separate these centuries from what went before, which allows us to describe them as a "modern era." It is, in other words, an important determinant of modernity, and it made ethnic cleansing and genocide far more likely to happen than ever before.

In northwestern European—Britain, France, Scandinavia, the Low Countries—as well as in Switzerland and North America, the historic development toward nation-states had produced societies divided on class lines but without serious potential for ethnic conflict. The way the state systems emerged, with a constitutional framework underpinning the dominance of an existing and largely unchallenged ruling class and a relatively homogeneous nationality (Ireland posing a partial exception to this in the British case), encouraged internal institutionalized conflict-resolution. In such conditions, liberal constitutions showed themselves capable of managing the types of conflict that class divisions produced and of adapting to pressures for change. This type of state was far from immune to involvement in ethnic cleansing actions in the territories it colonized. Settler communities were particularly likely to engage in ethnic cleansing, as the fate of the indigenous native populations in North America and Australasia testify. And along the way, the acquisition of empires and accompanying colonialism fostered burgeoning racism in the home community. But serious ethnic violence in the homeland was unlikely to be a product of such state systems.

It was different in the ethnically mixed areas of central and eastern Europe. Here, the growth of popular sovereignty brought mounting pressure on the multi-ethnic empires of the Habsburgs and Ottomans. Even where breakaway nation-states were founded, and especially following the collapse of these empires at the end of the First World War when successor states sprang up in these regions, they were invariably ethnically mixed. Control of the state, with its resources and increasingly expanding and powerful apparatus of government, became a self-evident source of conflict, which frequently split along ethnic lines. Here, the central idea of popular sovereignty shaping the nation-state, in contrast to the thinking that produced the stratified liberal states and institutionalized conflict of western Europe, was that of the organic (or integral) nation, resting on notions of national community and integration, gaining its definition from those it excluded, such as ethnic or religious minorities.[3] In such a context, ethnic cleansing was far more likely to occur, leading, in extreme instances, to full-scale genocide.

It seems certain that the scale of civilian deaths through ethnic cleansing in the twentieth century—estimates put the number between 60 and 120 million—was vastly greater than in any previous century.[4] This was not solely a product of the greater killing capacity of modern technology or the capacity for control and repression of modern bureaucracy.[5] But it does appear to be definable as a product of modernity, both in scale and in causation—something differing quantitatively and qualitatively from the massacres and atrocities of the pre-modern age. For the underlying driving force behind this ethnic cleansing (and, in some cases, genocide) is patently modern—the quest for the unitary and organic nation-state, ethnically defined.

Religion now finds its place in this modern setting—a setting increasingly of nation-states, would-be nation-states, unifying nation-states, attempts to bring about or enforce ethnic dominance within a nation-state, or attempts to break away to form a new, ethnically defined nation-state. Religion, in some instances, provides or cements the sense of identity of the ethnic group. Where competing religions coincide with competing ethnic groups in the same territory, the scope for ethnic cleansing, possibly escalating to genocide, is considerable. In the context of war, when externally directed violence in conditions of high tension can easily be channeled inwardly at minorities, often ethnically identified, the chances of genocide are greatly magnified. So it is no surprise that, measured by the proportion of the victim population murdered, three of the most extensive genocides of a genocidal century—the Armenian, Jewish, and Rwandan genocides—all occurred in the context of war. And it should be no surprise, either, that the dominant religious forces in each case sided with and identified with the most powerful secular forces in the state against the persecuted minorities.

As Ron Suny's penetrating analysis in this volume of the Armenian genocide indicates, the killing of over a million Armenians in 1915—some 50 to 70 percent of all Armenians in Turkish lands—arose in the context of the desperate attempt by young Turks to revamp the failing Ottoman Empire in new guise, by making it more Islamic and Pan-Turkic, to a backdrop of disastrous military defeat. As an unpopular ethnic minority singled out by their Orthodox Christianity, geographically standing in the way of Pan-Turkic expansion, and seen as supporting the Russian enemy and threatening to establish a separate state with aims of domination, the Armenians provided ideal scapegoats for ethnic cleansing operations that rapidly spiraled into outright genocide. Religion had been an important ingredient in singling out "the other." But the Islamic and Christian communities had traditionally lived peacefully alongside each other before ethnic tensions started to gather in the later nineteenth century. The modernity of ethnic claims over control of the state and the crisis of that state in conditions of major war had conspired to unleash the genocide. Religion had helped define the ethnic distinctions. But it was only when religion served to underpin or justify the actions of the dominant groups in the state that it became complicit in genocide.

In the Rwandan genocide of 1994, it is estimated that one million out of a population of under eight million were systematically killed within three months. Some four fifths of the minority Tutsi population were murdered in these mass killings. Timothy Longman's disturbing contribution to this collection demonstrates forcefully that the Christian Churches cannot merely be accused of acting passively or with indifference in the face of mass slaughter. Rather, what is more shocking still, members of the clergy actively participated in or even helped to organize the killings. And, unlike the Armenian genocide, religion was not used as a distinguishing mark in ethnic conflict. Both perpetrators and victims could identify with the Christian Churches. As Longman points out, killings of fellow parishioners were commonplace. What is evident is that the active complicity of the churches in the Rwandan genocide arose directly from their integration into the structures of power in the country and their keenness to support, to their own advantage, the rulers of a modern, authoritarian state system, even when it was obvious that increasingly dangerous provocations to genocide—then actual genocide—were being deployed to sustain the power of a threatened regime. What is plain in this case, too, is the modernity of the genocide, centering on modern forms of power struggle for control of the state and whipping up ethnic tension through modern propaganda methods to create, more or less artificially, an ethnic powder keg ready to be ignited. In this highly modern genocidal conflict, the churches proved eager collaborators.

The Nazi genocide against the Jews—the Holocaust, as it has generally come to be known as—is estimated to have resulted in the murder of about five and a half million Jews in Nazi-occupied Europe, around half of the number targeted in the notorious Wannsee Conference of January 1942. In practically every respect, this genocide can be regarded as a product of modernity. It was perpetrated by individuals and agencies from a country with a highly modern (for the time) bureaucracy, with modern technology, modern industry, a modern army, and modern forms of control and repression. It was legitimized by modern strains of pseudo-scientific race theories developed in the second half of the nineteenth century and by modern notions of breeding an ideal society (implying elimination of "negative," "harmful," or "dangerous" ethnic and social groups). It was carried out in modern industrialized fashion, through gas chambers in killing centers (though we should not forget that over two million victims were simply shot by execution squads). And it was premised upon the most extreme variant of the modern concept of the organic nation-state—in this case an envisaged ethnically homogeneous and "pure" German nation-state, purged of all "impure" elements, drawing its future lifeblood from an eastern European empire stratified on racial lines, exploiting a racially defined helot underclass, and completely eradicating the ethnic group regarded as the most threatening of all to this social and political utopia.

In these ways, the Holocaust fits Zygmunt Bauman's assertion that it was—though surely not solely this—"an element of social engineering, meant to bring about a social order conforming to the design of the perfect society."[6] Bauman, in fact, applies this definition to "modern genocide" in general. He adds to this his claim that the Holocaust "arose out of a genuinely rational concern, and ... was generated by bureaucracy true to its form and purpose."[7] Again, the implication, from the tenor of his overall argument, is that it is in this way that genocide can be regarded as a product of modernity. But in arguing from the specific (the Holocaust) to the general (genocide more widely regarded), it may be that Bauman is concentrating too heavily on one, admittedly vital, aspect of modernity—bureaucracy (as emphasized by Max Weber)—at the expense of others. At any rate, it is not easy to see how his definition, stressing rationality and the design of the perfect society, so readily applies to the other two cases of outright genocide under discussion in this volume—the Armenian and the Rwandan. Rather, it might be suggested that the "modernity" of the three genocides taken together can most obviously be seen in the modernity of the notion of the ethnically defined, organic nation-state, with the corresponding need to exclude, eliminate, and even exterminate the antithetical "other" or "out-group." Circumstances and relative advancement or backwardness of technology and state apparatus would then determine the means of killing and level of quasi-rationality involved.

Even taking the aim of the ethnically defined, organic nation-state as the essence of genocide's modernity, which links the three cases of genocide explored in this volume, the Nazi genocide stands out in a number of ways. These have not primarily to do with the means of killing. As I have suggested, states engaged in genocide will use whatever means are available. In Germany's case, the level of modernity of the country meant that it was possible to resort to mechanized mass slaughter. Elsewhere, more "primitive" methods of mass shooting (also of course used by the Germans) sufficed and corresponded to a relatively unplanned, opportunistic lurch into genocide.

One peculiarity is that the genocide against the Jews was not opportunistic or contingent as was the case in the Armenian and Rwandan genocides. Though much recent scholarship has succeeded in showing the gradual emergence, with many changes of plans and much improvisation, of a systematic program of extermination of the Jews, taking shape in the changing conditions of war in eastern Europe in 1941 to 1942 in bursts of escalating radicalism, a genocidal intent—meaning initially the gradual dying out of Jews in the terrible conditions of some mass reservation through starvation, hypothermia, or the ravages of forced labor—had been present for some considerable time before the "final solution" offered a direct and immediate mass killing program as a practical possibility. Genocide, in this instance, then, was intended, even if the route and method were not worked out thoroughly in advance.

Unlike the other two genocides, moreover, this was given a quasi-rational legitimization through race theory—something that had not existed before the nineteenth century. The Jews, according to such race theory, were not simply an "out-group" in the way that Armenians could be targeted by the Turks or Tutsi by the Hutu. There was not even the semblance of an objective contest for power in the state or apparent block by the "out-group" on the ambitions of the state. Rather, a modern form of demonization on alleged race grounds of Jews was then used as justification for eliminating them systematically from German society, then expanding the aim of total elimination to the whole of German-occupied Europe. Only this demonization could be used to justify the all-out onslaught after 1933 on an ethnic group (which, oddly enough, the Nazis had to use religious criteria to define) comprising only 0.76 percent of the population in 1933. Obviously, there was no objective threat from this quarter, even if—as the Nazis never ceased to hammer home—Jews were over represented in certain economic sectors or cultural spheres. But—another oddity—far from seeing the "threat" diminishing as the Jewish community in Germany declined, the demonization was massively intensified. The notion, present from the start in Hitler's rhetoric but also that of others on the extreme racist Right, that the Jews were the wire pullers of capitalism, run from the City of London and Wall Street as well as being the controllers of Bolshevism in Moscow, had been combined with the "world conspiracy" threat popularized in the forged *Protocols of the Elders of Zion* to create the image of the Jews as not just a national but an international danger that had to be eradicated. In the context of growing international tension in the later 1930s and the looming certainty of a second world war within a generation, this demonization of the Jews became, as Norman Cohn remarked many years ago, a "warrant for genocide."[8]

We come back at this point to the role of religion and of the Christian Churches in this genocide. Plainly, the church-led demonization of Jews in the pre-modern era had fed into the modern pseudo-scientific racist forms of antisemitism to produce a lethal brew. In many cases of twentieth-century ethnic cleansings, merging sometimes into genocide, the hostility towards the outsider target group had been linked, as in the Armenian and also the Rwandan cases, to real or presumed economic exploitation and advantage over the majority, "perpetrator" population. This of course also played a role in the welling hostility towards Jews in Germany. But it was in this case no more than a modern overlay on a primary, religious-based hatred of Jews, now converted into a racial demonization. Both major Christian denominations in Germany had continued in the modern era, down to the period of Nazi rule itself, to uphold and promote the religious foundations of antagonism toward the Jews. Even in conditions of the liberal democracy of the Weimar Republic, they did little or nothing to dent the widespread and growing feeling that the Jews were a harmful presence in German society.

In the case of the Protestant Church, as Robert Ericksen's paper clearly shows, it went further than this. Leading theologians, as well as other church leaders, clergy with still strong influence over opinion formation, and extensive sections of the Protestant church-going population, were prepared to uphold Nazi racial thinking on the Jews and to marry this to the age-old forms of religious discrimination. Catholic clergy, whether in the hierarchy or at the parish level, were more inclined to distance themselves from Nazi race doctrine, though the ingrained, traditional, religious-based antagonism towards Jews, alongside the church's conventional emphasis upon obedience to authority, and the keenness not to offend the Nazi masters and incite intensified attacks on the church itself offered scant hope of any principled opposition to the increasingly radical persecution of Jews under Hitler. So while the Bishop of Münster, Clemens von Galen, as Beth Griech-Polelle shows, could take a courageous public stand in 1941 against the regime on church-related issues, and even on the "euthanasia action" (which potentially affected those under his pastoral care), he had nothing to say about the attacks on Jews, whether following the notorious "Reichskristallnacht" pogrom of 1938, or at the time of their deportation in 1941.

The point could be widened. Catholic protest at interference with church observances, arrests of clergy, abolition of denominational schools, or removal of crucifixes from classrooms, was frequent. But there was no public institutional opposition at any time—despite the continuing high level of church leaders' influence over wide sections of the population—of the persecution of the

Jews. Whatever the private disquiet at the disturbing news from the East, this was not seen as a matter of direct concern for the church. For both major denominations, traditional prejudice and institutional self-interest undermined what might have been regarded as a duty implicit in the doctrinal precept of Christianity itself, the words attributed to Jesus Christ, to "love thy neighbor as thyself, for God's sake." Without the constraints the churches might have provided, it was not difficult for gross inhumanity to flourish.

In one further, perhaps unique, way, religion (of a sort), modernity, and genocide might be said to have come together in the Holocaust: for Nazism itself could be seen as containing strains of a "political religion." This, too, would set the genocide against the Jews apart from the other major genocides—Armenian, Cambodian, and Rwandan—of the twentieth century. Admittedly, the Cambodian genocide and the massive ethnic cleansings bordering on genocide that took place under Stalin and Mao were perpetrated under the aegis of a type of "crusading," exclusivist modern ideology aimed at the renewal of society along restructured class lines. But even in their self-image, these were rigidly secular ideologies.

In the case of Nazism, the pseudo-religious component was much stronger. The close relationship of church and state in Germany since the Reformation, the investiture of religious symbolism in the person of the Kaiser, and the mystical, millennarian element—evoking the legend of the sleeping Kaiser beneath the Kyffhäuser mountain awaiting the reawakening of a new Reich—built into expectations of the new unified German state after 1871 formed strands of the backdrop. But even before 1914, the "dark" side of an almost manichean imagery saw the embodiment of all that was "evil" in the figure of the Jew. The traumatic collapse of the "old" Germany in the defeat and Revolution of 1918, ushering in a fundamentally contested, pluralist state system in continuing crisis conditions, with a completely polarized society amid distinct signs of a weakening of institutional religion—certainly of the Protestant Church, where there was much talk of a "crisis of faith"—then provided the preconditions for the rise of a new type of political leader.

Before Hitler was even heard of, voices on the neo-conservative Right were calling for a new leader who would combine the qualities of statesman, warrior, and high priest—an evident evocation of quasi-religious qualities. The mass of his fanatical following increasingly depicted Hitler as a national savior or redeemer, which is certainly how he saw himself. And Hitler was adept at using quasi-religious rhetoric to good effect in couching his mass appeal. The demonization of the Jews fitted perfectly into the countervailing vision of national salvation, a utopia to be attained through stamping out the sources of "disease" in a presumed "decadent" society, eradication of the "enemies of the people" and creation of an ethnically pure "national community." The depth and extent of the crisis in German society opened the way to the radicality of the presumed solution to that crisis and the readiness to accept it.

It then took the modernity of the German state—here I would follow Bauman—to convert this pseudo-religious vision of national salvation, involving the "removal" of those who were seen as Germany's enemies, into genocidal reality. Bureaucratic data collection and organization, railway timetables, industrial production of Cyclon-B, and profit margins of modern capitalism were all part of the most systematic genocide in history—after they had harnessed their services to the demands of a chiliastic vision of nation redemption, embodied in an enthusiastically supported political leader who saw it as his "mission," again a religiously freighted word, to destroy the Jews in bringing about Germany's rebirth. In this way, the unique character of the Nazi genocide against the Jews finds part of its explanation precisely in this combination of a dynamic movement driven by the pseudo-religious vision of national redemption allied to the bureaucratic apparatus of a highly modern state system.

The genocidal twentieth century is now itself receding into history. Unfortunately, there are scant grounds for hope that the twenty-first century will see an end to genocide. But anything resembling a repetition or recurrence of the Holocaust is unlikely. Of the major genocides of the twentieth century, the Nazi genocide seems the least likely to provide the pattern for future genocide. For the reasons given above, it was historically unique, with a number of characteristics not encountered in other genocides and arising from conditions in Europe that cannot be replicated, not least since Nazi ravages so thoroughly destroyed the traditional structures of European Jewry. Though antisemitism is far from eradicated, it no longer has the lethal force that it possessed between the wars, and the demonization of the Jews no longer has any resonance, either in Christian thinking or in secular society. Of course, antagonisms toward Jews continue to play a major part in the politics of the Middle East. But this is increasingly recognizable as a conventional, if still dangerous, element of inter-state conflict—part of the fragile international political framework in that unstable part of the world. There is nothing in it that warrants comparison with the proto-genocidal climate of the 1930s in Germany.

The type of antagonism that gave rise to the Armenian and Rwandan genocides—pressure for ethnic homogeneity in a nation-state with mixed and competing ethnic groups, with the ultimate aim of creating an "organic" nation—is more likely to lead to further genocidal horror. As the 1990s showed, international intervention was probably responsible for preventing the ethnic cleansing in Bosnia and Kosovo from escalating into full-scale genocide. Religion and nationalism were closely intertwined in the tragic events there, which were driven by demands of ethnic homogeneity and have resulted in the promotion of precisely that in the regions of former Yugoslavia afflicted by the state-sponsored ethnic tension. In the ex-colonial territories of Africa, repetitions of the Rwandan catastrophe seem to be waiting to happen. Whether what is often euphemistically labeled "the international community" will have the unity and strength of the will to prevent it remains to be seen.

Depressingly, too, when such ethnic cleansing stretching into genocide does happen, there will almost certainly be little prospect of looking to the Christian Churches, even if they are not actively involved in it as they were in Rwanda, to put a brake on it.

Notes

1. Michael Mann, "The Dark Side of Democracy: the Modern Tradition of Ethnic and Political Cleansing," *New Left Review*, 235 (May/June, 1999), 18-45, here 39, calls this "classicide."
2. Leo Kuper, *Genocide*, Harmondsworth, 1981, 129-30.
3. This draws, as do many of the accompanying ideas, on two excellent analyses by Michael Mann, "The Dark Side of Democracy" (see note 1) and "Explaining Murderous Ethnic Cleansing: the Macro-Level" (as yet unpublished). I am extremely grateful to Professor Mann for the insights that these papers provided, deepened by discussions of some of the issues with him.
4. Mann, "Explaining Murderous Ethnic Cleansing," 2.
5. The latter is stressed notably by Zygmunt Bauman, *Modernity and the Holocaust*, London, 1989.
6. Bauman, 91.
7. Bauman, 17.
8. Norman Cohn, *Warrant for Genocide: the Myth of the Jewish World-Conspiracy and the Protocols of the Elders of Zion*, New York, 1967.

CONTRIBUTORS

Yair Auron is Senior Lecturer at the Open University and the Kibbutzim College of Education in Israel. He earned his Ph.D. at the Sorbonne in Paris and is the author (in Hebrew) of *Jewish-Israeli Identity, Sensitivity to World Suffering: Genocide in the Twentieth Century,* and *We Are All German Jews,* (also published in French as *Les Juifs d'Extreme Gauch en Mai 68,* (1998). Auron's book, *The Banality of Indifference: Zionism and the Armenian Genocide,* appeared in Hebrew in 1995 and the English edition was published in 2000. He is currently preparing a curriculum about genocide for the Open University in Israel.

Matthew Baigell is Professor of Art History at Rutgers University. He has written and edited sixteen books on American, Jewish, and Russian art, including *Jewish American Artists and the Holocaust,* (1997), *Complex Identities: Jewish Consciousness and Modern Art,* (2001), and with Renee Baigell, *Peeling Potatoes, Painting Pictures: Women's Art in Russia, Estonia, and Latvia in the 1990s* (2001).

Omer Bartov is the John P. Birkelund Professor of European History at Brown University. He has written widely on Nazi Germany, interwar France, and the holocaust. His books include *The Eastern Front 1941- 45: German Troops and the Barbarisation of Warfare* (1985), *Hitler's Army: Soldiers, Nazis, and War in the Third Reich,* (1991), *Murder in Our Midst: The holocaust, Industrial Killing, and Representation* (1996), *Mirrors of Destruction: War, Genocide, and Modern Identity* (2000), and the edited volume, *The Holocaust: Origins, Implementation, Aftermath* (2000).

Doris Bergen is Associate Professor of History at the University of Notre Dame in Indiana. She is the author of *Twisted Cross: The German Christian Movement in the Third Reich,* (1996) and of numerous essays and articles on religion, gender, and ethnicity in Europe during the Nazi era. She has been a fellow of the Center for Advanced Holocaust Studies at the United States Holocaust Memorial Museum; the German Marshall Fund of the United States; and the Alexander Humboldt Foundation.

Charles de Lespinay is Researcher at the Center for Law and Culture (Paris-X, Sorbonne University), and at the Center for Rights, Cultures and Languages (CNRS, Paris). Author of a thesis in legal anthropology, "Territoires et droits en Afrique noire," he has published numerous articles, including "Culture, droit et reglement de conflits dans la region des Grands Lacs," in *Rwanda. Un Genocide du xxe Siecle,* ed. Verdier, Decaux and Chretien (1995). De Lespinay was co-organizer of the conference, "The Reconstitution of the Legal State in Africa of the Great Lakes: The Politico-Ethnic Crisis in Burundi and in the Region of the Great Lakes," December, 1997, whose papers will soon be published.

Robert P. Ericksen is Associate Professor of History at Pacific Lutheran University. He is the author of *Theologians Under Hitler: Gerhard Kittel, Paul Althaus and Emanuel Hirsch,* (1985), winner of a 1987 Merit of Distinction from the International Center for Holocaust Studies, Anti-Defamation League of B'nai B'rith, and co-editor (with Susannah Heschel) of *Betrayal: German Churches and the Holocaust,* (1999). Ericksen has been the recipient of research fellowships from the Alexander von Humboldt Foundation, the National Endowment for the Humanities, and the American Council of Learned Societies.

Michal Govrin is an Israeli writer, poet, and theater director. She teaches at the School of Visual Theater in Jerusalem, and is a visiting Writer in Residence at Rutgers University. Her critical and personal essays on the theater, the Holocaust, and contemporary Jewish theology have appeared in magazines and anthologies in several languages. Govrin's most recent novel, *The Name,* which was published also in English translation, received the Kugel Literary Prize in Israel. Other books include *Hold on to the Sun, Stories and Legends,* and the poetry volumes, *That very Hour, Words' Bodies,* and *That Night's Seder.* Laureate of the Prime Minister Prize for writers, Govrin has directed, adapted, and translated several acclaimed theatrical productions. Since the early 1970s, she has been active in the international trend of Experimental Jewish Theater, and has produced a number of plays in France and Israel.

Gershon Greenberg is Professor of Religion at American University in Washington, D.C., and was visiting professor at Hebrew, Bar Ilan, Tel Aviv and Haifa universities, as well as at the Free University of Berlin. He is currently researching Jewish religious practice in the camps and ghettos at the International Institute for Holocaust Research at Yad Vashem. The recipient of a Skirball Fellowship in Hebrew Studies at Oxford and a Fulbright Teaching Fellowship for Lithuania, Greenberg has published thirty articles and book chapters about wartime Jewish religious thinkers and movements in reaction to the catastrophe as well as a three-volume annotated bibliography of Jewish religious literature and the Holocaust through the war.

Beth Griech-Polelle received her Ph.D. from Rutgers University in May, 1999. She is currently Assistant Professor of Modern European History at Bowling Green State University. Her article, "Image of a Churchman-Resister: Bishop von Galen, the Euthanasia Project and the Summer 1941 Sermons," is forthcoming in the January 2001 issue of the *Journal of Contemporary History*. Griech-Polelle is currently preparing her dissertation for publication.

Susannah Heschel is Eli Black Associate Professor of Jewish Studies at Dartmouth College. She is the author of *Abraham Geiger and the Jewish Jesus* (1998), as well as numerous articles on Christian-Jewish relations, modern Jewish thought, and feminist theology. She is currently writing a monograph on the Aryan Jesus in Protestant thought during the Third Reich.

Ian Kershaw is Chair of Modern History at the University of Sheffield and a Fellow of the British Academy. He received the Cross of Merit of the Federal Republic of Germany for services to German history in 1994. He was a consultant of the BAFTA-winning BBC-TV series "The Nazis: A Warning from History" and of BBC2's "War of the Century." Among his many publications are, *Hitler, 1889-1936: Hubris,* (1998), *Hitler. 1936-2000: Nemesis,* (2000), and *Weimar: Why Did German Democracy Fail?,* (1990).

Timothy Longman is Associate Professor of Political Science and Africana Studies at Vassar College. He also works as a consultant for Human Rights Watch on Rwanda, Burundi, and Congo. His book, *Commanded by the Devil: Christianity and Genocide in Rwanda,* is forthcoming.

Phyllis Mack is Professor of History at Rutgers University. She is the author of several books and articles in the history of religion, including *Visionary Women: Ecstatic Prophecy in Seventeenth-Century England* (1992), winner of the Berkshire Prize in History. She was Project Director of the Rutgers Center for Historical Analysis and co-organizer of the conference on Genocide and Religion at the Holocaust Museum in Washington, D.C., (1998).

Maud Mandel is the Dorot Visiting Assistant Professor in Modern Jewish History at Brown University. She completed her doctoral work at the University of Michigan in 1998 and is currently revising her manuscript, "In the Aftermath of Genocide: Armenians and Jews in Twentieth-Century France." Her published works include "Genocide and Nationalism: The Changing Nature of Jewish Politics in post-World War II France," in *The Emergence of Modern Jewish Politics,* ed. Zvi Gitelman (forthcoming).

Ara Sarafian is a Ph.D. candidate in history at the University of Michigan. He is Editor of Gomidas Institute Books and co-Editor of *Armenian Forum: A Journal of Contemporary Affairs.* His most recent articles include, "The Ottoman Archives Debate and the Armenian Genocide," *Armenian Forum: A Journal of Contemporary Affairs,* (1999), "Reexamen du debat sur les archives ottomanes,'" *L'Actualite du genocide des Armeniens,* (1999), and "A Documentary Report: 'The Disaster of Mardin During the Persecution of the Christians, Especially the Armenians in 1915,'", *Haigazian Armenological Revue,* (1998).

Michael Sells is Emily Judson Baugh and John Marshall Gest Professor of Comparative Religions at Haverford College. He is the author of seven books, including *The Bridge Betrayed: Religion and Genocide in Bosnia,* (1996). He is also the founder of the Community of Bosnia, a non-profit organization dedicated to supporting a multireligious and democratic Bosnia-Herzegovina.

Jessica Sheetz received her Ph.D. from the University of Minnesota. She is currently completing a book on Margit Slachta and the Holocaust in Hungary.

Ronald Grigor Suny is Professor of Political Science at the University of Chicago, formerly the Alex Manoogian Professor of Modern Armenian History at the University of Michigan. He is the author of *The Baku Commune, 1917-1918: Class and Nationality in the*

Russian Revolution (1972), *The Making of the Georgian Nation,* (1988, 1994), *Looking Toward Ararat: Armenia in Modern History* (1993), *The Revenge of the Past: Nationalism, Revolution, and the Collapse of the Soviet Union* (1993), and *The Soviet Experiment: Russia, the USSR, and the Successor Sates* (1998). He has also edited several books in Russian history.

Gabor Vermes is Associate Professor of History at Rutgers University. He is a native of Budapest and left Hungary after the 1956 Revolution. His book, *Istvan Tisza, The Liberal Vision and Conservative Statecraft of a Magyar Nationalist,* was published in English in 1985, and in Hungarian in 1994.

Katharina von Kellenbach is Associate Professor of Religious Studies at St. Mary's College of Maryland, a public honors college. She has published in the areas of religion, feminist theology, Jewish-Christian relations, and Holocaust studies. Her publications include, *Anti-Judaism in Feminist Religious Writings* (1994), and biographical articles on the first ordained female rabbi, Regina Jonas of Berlin (1902-44). She is co-editor of *Zwischen-Raume: Deutsche Feministische Theologinnen im Ausland,* (2000). She is currently a research fellow of Alexander von Humboldt Stuflung in Berlin.

INDEX

War and Genocide

General Editor: **Omer Bartov,** *John P. Birkelund*
Distinguished Professor of History at Brown University

Volume 1

THE MASSACRE IN HISTORY

Edited by **Mark Levene** and **Penny Roberts**

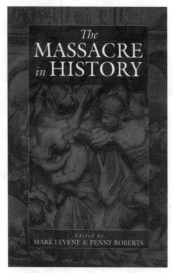

Chronologically and geographically broad in scope, this book provides in-depth analysis of particular massacres and themes associated with them from the 11th century to the present. Specific attention is paid to 15th century Christian-Jewish relations in Spain, the St. Batholemew's Day massacre, England and Ireland in the civil war era, the 19th century Caucasus, the rape of Nanking in 1937 and the Second World War origins of the Serb-Croat conflict.

The book explores the subject of massacre from a variety of perspectives—its relationship to politics, culture, religion and society, its connection to ethnic cleansing and genocide, and its role in gender terms and in relations to the extermination of animals. The historians provide evidence to suggest that the 'massacre' is often central to the course of human development and societal change.

1999. 320 pages, 6 half-tones, maps
ISBN 1-57181-943-7 Hardback **$69.95/£47.00**
ISBN 1-57181-935-5 Paperback **$25.00/£16.50**

www.berghahnbooks.com

War and Genocide

General Editor: **Omer Bartov,** *John P. Birkelund*
Distinguished Professor of History at Brown University

Volume 2

NATIONAL SOCIALIST EXTERMINATION POLICIES

Contemporary European Perspectives

Edited by **Ulrich Herbert**

Moving beyond the well-established problems and public discussions of the Holocaust, this collection of essays leaves behind the increasingly agitated arguments of the last years and substantially broadens, and in many areas revises, our knowledge of the Holocaust. Unlike previous studies, which have focused on whether the Holocaust could best be understood as the "fulfilment of a world view or as a process of "cumulative radicalisation," these articles provide an overview of how situational elements and gradual processes of radicalisation were variously combined with ever-changing objectives and fundamental ideological convictions.

Contents: Policy of Extermination – Jewish Resettlement – The Killing of the Jews in the Incorporated Eastern Territory – Anti-Jewish Policy and the Extermination of the Jewish in the District of Galicia, 1941-1942 – The German Military Administration in Paris and the Deportation of the French Jews – The Extermination of the Jews in Serbia – The National-Socialist "Solution to the Gypsy Problem" – German Economic Interests: Policy of Occupation and the Killing of the Jews in White Russia, 1941-1943

1999. 288 pages
ISBN 1-57181-750-6 Hardback **$69.95/£47.00**
ISBN 1-57181-751-4 Paperback **$19.95/£13.95**

www.berghahnbooks.com

Volume 3

WAR OF EXTERMINATION

The German Military in World War II

Edited by **Hannes Heer** and **Klaus Naumann**

Translations from the German by **Roy Shelton**
With a Foreword by **Volker R. Berghahn**

This volume contains the most important contributions by distinguished historians who have thoroughly demolished this Wehrmacht myth. The picture that emerges from this collection is a depressing one and raises many questions about why "ordinary men" got involved as perpetrators and bystanders in an unprecedented program of extermination of "racially inferior" men, women, and children in Eastern Europe and the Soviet Union during the Second World War.

2000. 400 pages, 3 maps, 12 ills., index
ISBN 1-57181-232-6 Hardback **$59.95/£40.00**

War and Genocide

General Editor: **Omer Bartov**, *John P. Birkelund
Distinguished Professor of History at Brown University*

Volume 5

HITLER'S WAR IN THE EAST, 1941–1945

A Critical Assessment

Rolf-Dieter Müller and **Gerd R. Ueberschär**

Translated from the German by **Bruce Little**
With a Foreword by **Gerhard Weinberg**

New in Paperback—Revised and Updated

This volume provides a guide to the extensive literature on the war in the East, including largely unknown Soviet writings on the subject. Indispensable for military historians, but also for all scholars who approach this crucial period in world history from a socio-economic or cultural perspective.

"... One of the best jobs of integrating Russian, German, American and British writing on the subject most students wishing to write a paper would find everything they need in the way of bibliographical materials by referring to this book."
—Slavic Review

"This serious study is a must for all interested in the history of World War Two." **—British East-West Review**

Winter 2001/02, 415 pages, bibliog.

ISBN 1-57181-293-8 Paperback **$25.00/£17.00**
ISBN 1-57181-068-4 Hardback **$69.95/£45.00**

www.berghahnbooks.com